Ashes and Dawn

Love, Loss and Survival in the Shadow of War

Raymond B. Williams

Praise for Ashes and Dawn

"*Ashes and Dawn* is a masterful and deeply moving work—an unforgettable story of endurance, love, and the will to survive against impossible odds. Raymond Williams brings to life the legacy of his father with both tenderness and grit. Written with emotional clarity and historical depth, this book reminds us that courage often lives in ordinary people doing extraordinary things. It's not just a son's tribute—it's a universal story of resilience, hope, and the strength that carries families through the darkest times into a new dawn." — **Dr. Marshall Goldsmith is the Tinkers50#1 Executive Coach and New York Times bestselling author of** *The Earned Life, Triggers,* **and** *What Got You Here Won't Get You There.*

"Raymond Williams has written something rare: a true story that reads like fiction. *Ashes and Dawn* is ultimately a story about transformation, not just survival. Williams beautifully demonstrates that compassion, resilience, and human connection aren't luxuries but survival necessities. Throughout the book, we see Bryn's unwavering commitment to protect his family, paired with his wife Alicia's fierce refusal to die. What makes this especially powerful is watching a man who acts with morality and integrity even while serving an empire that controls and brutalizes conquered peoples. It's a reminder that our choices matter, even in circumstances that seem to strip away all agency.

The book shows exactly what sustains people when everything else is stripped away. Not grand gestures or superhuman strength, but small acts of dignity, the stubborn grip on hope, the decision to care for each other when caring seems pointless. Williams illustrates how love, purpose, and human connection become survival tools in the most literal sense.

What makes this book resonate is the author's voice. He writes with emotional honesty but never tips into sentimentality. He honors his parents' courage while acknowledging their very human fears and struggles. That authenticity makes the story more powerful, not less. You're not reading about saints or symbols, but about ordinary people facing impossible circumstances and finding ways to keep going, not because they're heroes in the traditional sense, but because they refuse to give up. At its core, this is a book about love as a practical force. Not the romantic kind that makes life beautiful, but the kind that literally keeps you alive. That message, supported by this remarkable true story, can offer comfort and inspiration to anyone facing their own seemingly impossible circumstances. It's a universal story that reminds us of what truly sustains human beings: love, purpose, dignity, and hope. It gets my five-star recommendation." — **Emma Seppälä, Ph.D., faculty director of the Yale School of Management's Women's Leadership Program, and the Science Director of Stanford University's Center for Compassion and Altruism Research and Education. She is the author of two best-sellers,** *The Happiness Track* **and** *Sovereign.*

"Through the lens of historical fiction, Raymond Williams tells the true story of his Welsh-born father from childhood in the coal mines to service in the British Army in Egypt to him and his family being held by the Japanese in Hong Kong in WWII. The drama is real. We read about the experience of the power of resilience and courage in the face of overwhelming odds. Gripping and inspiring." — **John Baldoni, piano-playing author, poet, internationally recognized executive coach, keynote speaker, known for his expertise in leadership development and management coaching, and author of sixteen books. In 2025, Global Gurus ranked John a Top 10 global leadership expert, a list he has been on since 2007.**

"While *Ashes and Dawn* is rooted in history, what Raymond Williams captures here goes much deeper. This is about what keeps people going through the hardest times: love, purpose, dignity, and hope. It's a deeply personal look at resilience that will resonate with anyone who's faced real struggle and asked themselves how to carry on." — **Goodreads.**

"*Ashes and Dawn* is a powerful story of endurance, devotion, and the will to survive. From the coal mines of Wales to the deserts of Egypt and the prison camps of wartime Hong Kong, Bryn Williams' journey is one of pain and perseverance. With his wife Alicia, whose unwavering love sustains him through the darkest moments of war, he faces poverty, betrayal, and the brutality of captivity. Based on true events, this heartfelt story highlights the quiet heroism of ordinary men and women and the unbreakable human spirit that persists even amid the ruins of war." — **Tony Banham, author of** *We Shall Suffer There: Hong Kong's Defenders Imprisoned, 1942-45,* **and** *Not the Slightest Change: The Defence of Hong Kong, 1941.*

Copyright © Raymond B. Williams

All rights reserved.

ISBN:

Aurelias Publishing, Vancouver, B.C.

No part of this book may be reproduced or transmitted in any form or by any means, electronic or mechanical, including photocopying, recording, or by any information storage and retrieval system, without the prior written permission of the author and the publisher.

Dedication

For my father, Bryn Williams,
who rose from the ashes to find the light of dawn,
and whose spirit lights every page of this story.

Acknowledgments

My deepest gratitude goes to my wife, Diane Williams, my muse and guiding spirit, and editor, whose unwavering belief in me gave this book life.

To my sons, Travis, Rhett, and Bryn, thank you for your love, encouragement, and support along this journey. This story carries a part of each of you.

My gratitude goes out to my friend, Stephanie Frank who reviewed the manuscript and provided insightful feedback.

My appreciation is also extended to Dr. Marshall Goldsmith and Emma Seppälä, Ph.D., for their support and testimonials.

Preface

I never planned to write this book. For years, the story of my father, Bryn Williams, lived in fragments: a few photographs, some handwritten notes, and the memories my mother and sister shared when they felt strong enough to revisit those dark days. But as I grew older, I realized that fragments weren't enough. Not for my children, not for those who might find something meaningful in what my parents endured, and certainly not for the man who kept his family alive against impossible odds.

I was born in Stanley Internment Camp in July 1945. My mother, Alicia, was desperately ill with diphtheria when she went into labor. The doctors told my father there was a good chance we would both die. By every measure of probability and medical reality, we should have. But my mother refused to surrender, and my father refused to let go. Somehow, against all logic, we both survived.

I am Raymond Williams, the baby in this story. I have no memory of those first weeks of my life, no recollection of the candlelight vigils or the prayers that filled the camp while my mother fought for her life and mine. What I do have is a profound awareness that I exist only because of extraordinary will, fierce love, and a community that refused to let hope die.

This book honors my father first. He was not a perfect man, but he was a remarkable one. From working in a coal mine in Wales in his childhood, to serving in the British Army in Egypt during the aftermath of the Arab Uprising, he developed amazing strength, courage, resilience and integrity. Later in Hong Kong in the British health service, he served the population's health needs, in almost unsurmountable conditions. And finally, he kept his family alive through three and a half years of captivity by the Japanese in WWII. He planted gardens in soil that shouldn't have grown anything. He faced down men who would have taken food from his children. He negotiated with captors, stood up to brutality, and never once stopped believing he and his family would be liberated one day. That kind of strength doesn't come from physical power alone. It comes from somewhere deeper, some reserve of spirit that most of us never have.

This book also honors my mother, whose quiet courage matched my father's determination. She survived a pregnancy that should have killed her. She brought me into the world when death seemed the more likely outcome. She held our family together in ways that only became clear to me as an adult, when I understood how much strength it takes simply to keep going when everything around you is falling apart.

I wrote this for my children, so they would know where they came from. I wrote it for my wife, my sons, and close friends who encouraged me to tell the story. And I wrote it for anyone who might read these pages and find something that speaks to them. Maybe it's a reminder that ordinary people can do extraordinary things. Maybe it's evidence that love really does have power, even in the worst circumstances. Maybe it's simply a good story about survival, resilience, and the refusal to give up.

Whatever you take from these pages, know that it comes from a place of deep gratitude. I am here because my parents fought for life when it would have been easier to surrender. Their story is my story. And now, I hope, it could be part of yours.

Raymond B. Williams

Vancouver, Canada, 2025

Table of Contents

Acknowledgments ix
Preface xi
Chapter 1: The Spark in the Dark 17
Chapter 2: Breaking Chains 21
Chapter 3: The Angel's Shelter 25
Chapter 4: No Looking Back 33
Chapter 5: From Salt to Sand 41
Chapter 6: Everything Tastes of Ashes 49
Chapter 7: Conscience Over Command 57
Chapter 8: Invisible Enemies 63
Chapter 9: Mountain Meets Water 71
Chapter 10: Foreign Ghosts 77
Chapter 11: City of Darkness 83
Chapter 12: The Price of Truth 93
Chapter 13: The Healer's Path 111
Chapter 14: Between Worlds 129
Chapter 15: The Heart's Compass 137
Chapter 16: Ashes and Pearls 145
Chapter 17: Permission to Love 153
Chapter 18: Building a Home 161
Chapter 19: The Last Goodbye 167
Chapter 20: The Gathering Storm 175
Chapter 21: The Burden of Duty 189
Chapter 22: Refugees and Resolve 195
Chapter 23: New Life, Old Wounds 207
Chapter 24: The Empress of Asia 215
Chapter 25: Deception and Escape 223

Chapter 26: Sanctuary 235
Chapter 27: Homecoming 245
Chapter 28: Fortress of Paper 255
Chapter 29: Silent Night, Violent Night 261
Chapter 30: Safe Harbor 275
Chapter 31: The Weight of Silence 279
Chapter 32: The Roundup 285
Chapter 33: Searching the Ruins 293
Chapter 34: Hell's Antechamber 305
Chapter 35: Against All Odds 311
Chapter 36: The Work of Survival 319
Chapter 37: Negotiating with Shadows 327
Chapter 38: Bread, Rice and Resolve 331
Chapter 39: The Price of Integrity 337
Chapter 40: Thirty-Three 345
Chapter 41: The Long Wait 353
Chapter 42: The Fight 363
Chapter 43: The Miracle 371
Chapter 44: Liberation 379
Chapter 45: Reunion 395
Chapter 46: Dawn Breaking 411
Afterword 425
About the Author 427

Chapter 1

The Spark in the Dark

"In the darkness of the mine, a man finds what he's truly made of."

Anonymous Welsh Miner

Rhondda Valley, Wales, October 1923

Bryn's fingers clenched the wooden door handle tightly as footsteps echoed down the tunnel. Heavy boots. Two sets. His stomach twisted more than his grip, which was coal mine strong for a fourteen-year-old.

Boots thumped along the mine floor, one heavy, one slow behind. Two boys approached him, clearly in a hostile mood. Richard Price, swaggering as always, led the way. Behind him, Glyn Davies trudged silently, stocky and loyal.

Richard Price had been waiting for this moment since the morning shift started. Word spread through the tunnels that Bryn's father owed money to the company store again, making the Williams family fair game. Behind Richard, his friend Glyn understood only one thing clearly: Richard's approval was more valuable than any pit boy's dignity.

"Well, well. Look what the rat's got himself," Richard barked, his voice carrying the authority of someone whose father was a deputy overman.

Richard's lamp bobbed closer, casting flickering shadows on tunnel walls that shimmered with condensation. The sight of Bryn Williams, small and alone with his pitiful meal, filled Richard with familiar satisfaction. Here was someone smaller, weaker, and more afraid, someone whose family's debt made him vulnerable.

Bryn kept his eyes on the bundle in his lap, a small onion wrapped in yesterday's Western Mail. Five hundred feet underground, halfway through another ten-hour shift. Only the onion mattered. Only getting through another day.

"Didn't know vermin got dinner breaks," Richard continued, his Welsh accent sharp as broken slate.

Ashes and Dawn

The ancient tunnels seemed to hold their breath. Coal dust drifted in spirals through the amber glow of safety lamps, settling on everything like black snow. Somewhere deeper in the maze of passages, pit ponies snorted and stamped. Down the mineshaft, pickaxes struck the coal seam in their eternal rhythm, a sound that had echoed here since Bryn's grandfather was a boy.

"It's my dinner," Bryn replied, his voice steadier than he felt.

"It's my dinner,"Richard mimicked in a high, mocking voice. "Listen to him talk, Glyn. Like he's something special. Like his *tad* (dad) didn't owe twelve pounds to the store."

Bryn bit into the onion's papery skin, savoring the bitter juice that flooded his mouth. Each piece was rationed like his uncle's war stories from the Great War. Precious, life-sustaining, never enough.

Bryn's mind flashed to old Morgan Thomas, who'd taught him to box behind the mine's slag heap. "Fighting's not about winning, *bach* (boy). It's about making sure the other bastard hurts more than you do."

In one swift motion, Richard snatched the onion from Bryn's fingers.

"Give it back!" The words roared from Bryn's throat, raw and desperate.

Richard dangled the onion just out of reach, his laughter echoing off damp stone walls. "What's the matter, rat? Hungry?" He tossed it to Glyn, who caught it with a meaty paw and a gap-toothed grin.

Something sparked inside Bryn. Every empty morning, every ache in his spine from crouching at the ventilation door, every time he'd felt small, poor, and powerless, all of it condensed into a single, blazing point of fury. Bryn threw himself at Richard. They collided with the tunnel wall, coal dust bursting around them. Bryn's fists struck with mechanical accuracy: solar plexus, floating rib, the soft spot below the ear where balance resides.

"Get him off!" Richard's swagger dissolved into panic. The natural order had flipped, and he found himself on the wrong side of violence for the first time.

Glyn lumbered forward, but Bryn spun and drove his knuckles into the bigger youth's throat. The impact echoed like a pick striking bedrock. Glyn dropped the onion, gasping.

Blood streamed from Bryn's busted lip down his coal-dusted chin. He stood between them, chest heaving, eyes blazing with something that pierced the mine's endless darkness. He wasn't afraid anymore.

Richard scrambled to his feet, backing away. "Not worth my time," he muttered, but something in Bryn's eyes warned him the old rules no longer applied.

Chapter 1: The Spark in the Dark

Bryn picked up his onion, now dirty and streaked with blood. He wrapped it carefully in the newspaper.

The foreman's whistle pierced the air with three sharp blasts. Time to resume work.

"You're awfully quiet today, *bach*," a familiar voice called.

Old Morgan Thomas shuffled past, his safety lamp casting flickering shadows. Decades underground had carved trenches into his face deeper than mine shafts, but his bright blue eyes still held life. Morgan had watched boys transform into men down here, had seen the exact moment when some stopped accepting their fate and began choosing their future. "What happened?" Morgan asked, studying Bryn's bloodied lip and the new set to his shoulders.

"Just thinking," Bryn replied.

"Dangerous habit, that." Morgan's weathered hand touched Bryn's shoulder. "Thinking leads to wanting. Wanting leads to changing. And changing..." He gestured around the tunnel. "Changing means leaving all this behind."

Bryn met the old man's gaze. "What if I stay here? I've been here two years already. What will happen to me?"

Morgan was quiet for a long moment. "Look at me, son. Thirty-three years I've been coming down here. My lungs are as black as the coal I've cut, my back's permanently bent, and I'll die coughing blood into a rag." His voice dropped to a whisper. "I had dreams once. Wanted to see London, maybe even America. But I told myself there'd be time later. There's never time later."

"My father says I've got to keep working in the mine," Bryn said sadly.

"Your father's trapped, just like me," Bryn, "just like every man down here who didn't have the guts to climb back up that shaft and never came back."

The weight of Morgan's words settled on Bryn like coal dust, but instead of feeling heavy, they felt like possibility. Tonight, he would tell his father. No more mine. No more darkness. He would find a way to school, to books, to a world beyond these tunnels. His father's rage would be terrible, weeks of cold fury, threats to throw him out, reminders of family duty and the money they needed. But Bryn knew he could survive his father's anger. He couldn't survive thirty years underground. The decision hardened like coal under pressure, transforming from soft hope into something unbreakable.

"The hardest coal to crack is the one you're most afraid to strike," Morgan whispered, seeing Bryn's eyes gaze toward the end of the shaft.

Tonight, Bryn would strike.

Chapter 2

Breaking Chains

"Every chain has a weak link, and every cage has a door."

Thomas Reid, Scottish philosopher

The shift whistle's shriek echoed across the valley as Bryn climbed the final slope toward home in Mayhill, his boots heavy with coal dust and the weight of his decision. Three days had passed since the fight with Richard Price, three days of working in silence while his resolve hardened like cooling iron.

The terraced stone houses stood in neat rows against the sharp Welsh wind, their soot-stained walls broken only by faded curtains glimpsed through small windows.

Bryn paused at his family's door, hand on the worn brass handle. Inside, he could hear his father's voice raised in complaint about something, probably the mine owners again, or the government, or the weather. Always something beyond Gwilym Williams' control, never anything within it.

The cottage's main room seemed smaller every time Bryn entered. Low-beamed ceiling, flagstone floor worn smooth by generations of Williams' feet, and the constant smell of coal smoke that no amount of scrubbing could remove. His mother, Katherine, sat hunched in her corner chair, but tonight something felt different. Her hands were steady as she mended a torn shirt, and her eyes, usually clouded with gin, held an unsettling clarity.

At the scarred oak table, his father Gwilym bent over the week's accounts, pencil stub working slowly across figures that never seemed to add up right. A half-empty bottle sat beside the ledger, not his first of the evening.

Ten-year-old Evan crouched by the fireplace, carefully whittling a piece of driftwood with their grandfather's old knife. Nine-year-old Mary sat protectively beside seven-year-old Bernice, their heads bent together over a piece of paper. Bernice was drawing something with a stub of charcoal, her tongue poking out in concentration.

"*Hwyr eto*" (Late again), Gwilym said without looking up.

"Stayed to speak with Henderson," Bryn replied, setting down his tea tin and washing bowl. "The Deputy Overman."

This brought Gwilym's head up. "Henderson? What did you talk to him about?"

Bryn felt the folded sketches in his jacket pocket, images of landscapes beyond these valleys, ships in distant harbors, faces of people he'd never met but hoped someday to understand. "*Mae'r galon yn gwybod ei ffordd*" (The heart knows its way), his grandfather had always said.

"I told him I won't be coming back to the mine," Bryn replied, his voice on the edge of cracking.

The words dropped into the cottage's close air like stones into still water. Evan's whittling blade stopped mid-stroke. Mary's arm tightened protectively around Bernice. Katherine's mending fell still in her lap.

"What?" Gwilym bellowed.

"I'm not going back," Bryn said, his voice steadier than he felt. "No more crawling through tunnels in the dark. I want to go to school, maybe study art in Pontypridd."

The silence stretched like a held breath. Then Gwilym slowly rose, his chair scraping against the stone, and for just a moment—so brief Bryn almost missed it—something flickered across his father's face. Not softness, but something raw. Recognition, maybe. Regret, maybe.

"Art?" The word came out like something poisonous. "Art studies? What fool put that notion in your head?"

"I've been drawing since I was small, *tad*.' You know that. I'm good at it. Maybe I could..."

"Good at it?" Gwilym's laugh was harsh. "You think being good at something puts food on the table? You think dreams pay for coal?"

Katherine spoke softly from her corner. "He draws like your father did, Gwilym. Remember?"

The silence that followed was charged with old pain. Gwilym's hand tightened on the bottle. "My father drew pictures of places he'd never see," Gwilym said, his voice rough with anger. "Died with his lungs full of coal dust and his head full of foolishness."

"Maybe," Bryn said carefully, "but at least he tried."

Gwilym's blow came fast and hard, knocking Bryn sideways, but he stayed on his feet, never breaking eye contact with his father.

Chapter 2: Breaking Chains

"*Diawl bach!*" (Little devil) Gwilym's face blazed red. "Think you're better than us? That mine feeds this family!"

"Feeds us?" Bryn touched his burning cheek, tasting copper. "Look at Mary and Bernice. Skin and bones because you pour half your wagers down your throat at the Lamb and Flag."

Bryn's sisters pressed further into the shadows, but their eyes held something dangerous to Gwilym: hope for an escape.

Gwilym stood toe-to-toe with Bryn. "You'll go back tomorrow, or you'll never darken this door again!"

Katherine rose from her chair with surprising steadiness. "Gwilym, enough."

"You'll stay out of this, woman!" Gwilym snapped.

Bryn felt the weight of four generations pressing down on him. Williams' men, who had never questioned their place or looked up from the coal face long enough to see the sky, seemed trapped by history. But his grandfather's voice grew louder in his mind. "*Mae'r dyfodol i'r rhai sy'n barod i'w gipio.*"

"No, I won't," Bryn said defiantly.

Gwilym moved to the door and threw it wide, as the October wind rushed in. "Out then! Don't come back unless it's to work proper in the mine where you belong."

Bryn walked to the room he shared with his brother Evan. His sisters sat frozen in their chairs, afraid of what might follow.

Katherine had moved to an old tin box on the mantelpiece. "I've been saving this for you," she said to Bryn, withdrawing something wrapped in cloth. She handed him a small leather journal, its pages yellowed but intact. "Your grandfather's. Full of his drawings, his plans, and all the places he wanted to see. Take it with you, cariad." She automatically accepted Gwilym's edict would stand, and Bryn would not back down.

Gwilym's face went darker. "Katherine, you fool woman, you can't..."

"I can, and I will." She faced her husband's fury without flinching.

Bernice suddenly sprang up from her spot on the floor, clutching her charcoal drawing. "Bryn! Before you go!" She pushed the paper toward him, a surprisingly good sketch of a bird in flight. "I drew you a robin. Mama says they always find their way home."

Evan had returned to his whittling, working frantically. "For your pictures." He handed Bryn two art pencils.

As Bryn gathered his few belongings, he could hear his father muttering about ungrateful sons and foolish dreams, but the words held more bitterness than true conviction.

When Bryn returned with his canvas bag, Katherine pressed a bundle of food into his hands. Her voice stayed steady, but tears ran down her cheeks. "*Dos at Modryb* Eileen" (Go to Aunt Eileen). "*Mae hi'n dy garu di*" (She loves you). "Write to us when you can. Even if... even… if we can't answer."

Mary stepped forward, clutching something in her small fist. "This is all I have," she said, opening her hand to show three pennies. "For when you're hungry."

Gwilym stood silhouetted in the doorway, his face hard as stone. "If you're going, go," he said roughly. "And don't come snivelling back when the world chews you up and spits you out."

Bryn walked toward the door, then stopped beside his father, oddly feeling compassion for him. "I'm sorry it has to be this way, *tad.*"

For a fleeting moment, Gwilym's hand slightly lifted, as if he might touch his son's shoulder. His mouth parted, and a hint of something flickered across his face, almost like regret. A remnant of a man he could have been. The anger seemed to crack for just an instant. Then Gwilym's face hardened again, the moment lost. His hand fell to his side and curled into a fist. "Go on then," he said, his voice rough with renewed bitterness. "Get out of my sight before I throw you out."

Bryn looked once more at his family, the pain deep in his soul.

Gwilym slammed the door behind him hard enough to shake soot from the chimney and retreated to his bottle on the table.

Bryn stood alone on the muddy path, clutching gifts that held pieces of his family's hearts. Behind him, weak light leaked from cottage windows. Through the glass, he could see his father's silhouette, bottle raised to his lips, and his mother moving to comfort the younger children.

The September night brushed against Bryn's face as he stepped onto cobblestone streets slick with moisture.

He lifted his canvas sack and started walking. The road to Aunt Eileen's house in Sketty was far from Mayhill, and he used the hours to replay the past moments in his mind. His boots echoed against the cobblestones, keeping rhythm with his grandfather's words: "*Mae'r dyfodol i'r rhai sy'n barod i'w gipio.*"

He was no longer just a miner's son but someone new, forged in the breaking of chains.

Chapter 3

The Angel's Shelter

"Kindness is a language that the deaf can hear and the blind can see."

Mark Twain

Night enveloped Bryn like a mourning cloth as he walked the final mile toward Aunt Eileen's cottage in Sketty. His feet throbbed from the long journey down from the Rhondda Valley, nearly twenty-five miles of walking and catching rides whenever he could. The cottage sat at the end of the lane like a lighthouse, windows spilling light across flagstone paths worn smooth by decades of careful maintenance.

His cheek still burned from his father's hand. The ache in his heart burned deeper. Taking a breath that tasted of lavender and possibility, he knocked.

The door swung open before the echo faded. Light spilled onto the step like the morning breaking, and Aunt Eileen Davies stood framed in the doorway, her gray-streaked hair escaping from a loose bun. She took everything in at once: the purple bruise spreading on his cheek, the exhaustion etched into his young face, and how he clutched his bag like armor against the world.

"Bryn!" She reached out, pulling him inside with hands that smelled of carbolic soap and freshly baked bread. Her left hand, the one missing two fingers from a mill accident, trembled slightly as it always did when she was upset. "What's happened to you, *bach*?"

His voice cracked like pond ice. "I walked most of the way from Porth. Caught a ride on a coal wagon for the last bit. I told *Tad* (Dad) I wasn't going back to the mine. He hit me and told me to get out and not come back."

Something dangerous flickered in Eileen's eyes, steel beneath silk, the kind of Welsh steel that had stopped Roman legions cold. She spoke quietly, but her words carried the weight of a chapel judgment. "You were right to stand up to him, Bryn. Right as rain. And you'll stay with me now."

The cottage interior welcomed him like his *Mam-gu's* (grandmother's) arms had before the consumption took her. A coal fire crackled in the blackened grate, its light dancing across whitewashed walls where carefully hung prints were aligned with carpenter's measurements. Constable's landscapes. Turner's seascapes. A daguerreotype of Great Uncle Emrys in his Boer War uniform, moustache waxed to perfection.

Eileen led him to the kitchen table, its scrubbed pine surface bearing honest scars from daily use. She put out thick slices of *bara brith* (fruit bread), a pat of golden butter in a China dish decorated with bluebells, and a steaming cup of tea that smelled like comfort itself.

"Eat, *cariad* (love).” You look half-starved, and there's no point in talking on an empty stomach." She poured Bryn a cup of tea. "Tell me everything." Her voice carried the gentle authority of women who'd raised children through the Great Strike of '26.

The story spilled from him like water through a burst dam. His father's rage, his mother's tears, his siblings' modest gifts, and the door slammed shut with finality.

"I couldn't stay, Auntie. Not in the mine. It's not just the darkness. It's watching men in the die little by little, seeing how it kills their spirit before it takes their body. I won't die like that."

She nodded, tears shining in her eyes like stained glass windows in the morning light. "*Ti ddim wedi dy eni i'r tywyllwch*" (You weren't born for the darkness). I've watched you since you were small, Bryn. Seeing how you'd stop to sketch a robin or a rose while other boys threw stones at cats. You have the gift. A way of seeing beauty that this world needs more than it needs another pair of hands down the pit.”

"I want to study art properly," he said, the words tumbling out even faster now. "Go to the Technical College in Swansea, maybe even the Cardiff School of Art someday. But tad would never..." his throat constricting.

“Then we'll find another way," Eileen interrupted, reaching across to grasp his hand with surprising strength. Her palm was warm as fresh bread, calloused from decades of honest labor. "Whatever it takes, *bach*. You're not fighting this battle alone anymore.”

He looked up, hardly daring to believe. "You mean it?"

“With all my heart. I've got my pension from the mill, but it's not much. Twelve shillings a week. You'll have to find some part-time work if you want to go to school, but we'll manage together," she smiled, and in that moment, Bryn glimpsed what true family could be: not blood obligation but chosen love. "You're special, Bryn Williams. I've known it since you were a wee one, and it's high time

Chapter 3: The Angel's Shelter

you had the chance to prove it to yourself."

"I can find work, maybe the docks in Swansea…" Bryn replied.

"Not the docks. They kill you like the mine. Mrs. Patterson's bakery is looking for someone to do deliveries because her boy left, and you could take evening classes at the Technical College. We'll make it work together."

"I'll do anything to be able to stay with you, Auntie," Bryn replied gratefully. "What should I do about…about visiting home? Seeing Mam and the little ones?"

Eileen's face grew sad. "Oh, *cariad*. It's not like walking down the lane, is it? Twenty-five miles to Porth and then up the valley. That's a day's wages just for the train fare, if you can afford it. And your father has made his feelings clear. But you could write to them."

The distance suddenly felt like an ocean between him and his family.

They sat in peaceful silence, the weight of possibility settling around them like evening mist. The mantel clock, a wedding gift from her late husband's mother, measured the seconds with gentle precision. Finally, Eileen spoke again, her tone as thoughtful as a church deacon contemplating Scripture. "There's something else to think about when you turn eighteen. The Services."

The suggestion caught Bryn off guard. "The Army?"

She nodded, warming to her theme. "It's not an easy path, mind you. But it offers what you need most: a way out of Wales, a chance to see the world beyond these valleys. Many young men find their calling in foreign places. India, Singapore, Hong Kong. Places where a man with artistic talent and a smart mind might find opportunities that don't exist in Swansea docks."

"I'd never thought of that," he admitted softly.

"You've got four years to decide," Eileen assured him, rising to clear the dishes with practiced efficiency. "But whatever path you choose, Bryn, know this. You've got a home here. And someone who loves and believes in you completely."

As she moved around the kitchen, humming an old Welsh hymn softly, Bryn felt something he hadn't experienced since childhood: the steady feeling of unconditional love. The coal fire settled into the grate with a contented sigh, and in the distance, a church bell rang out the hour.

Bryn found purpose in his daily care routines, which had shifted from obligation to devotion. Each morning, he would light the fire with kindling and yesterday's *Western Mail*, a ritual as comforting as prayer. Each evening, he fixed whatever needed repair: loose floorboards with wood salvaged from Vivian's Mill, torn curtains with thread saved from Eileen's days as a seamstress, and broken crockery with careful application of flour paste. And for the first time in his life, he went to school.

The fireplace became the centerpiece of their shared world, witnessing many evenings of peaceful silence interrupted only by contented sighs. Eileen would darn socks or work on her endless supply of church embroidery, while Bryn sketched by lamplight or got lost in whatever book his teacher had lent him. What began as gratitude grew into something deeper, a love that filled the emptiness left in his heart by his mother's emotional absence. Eileen never tried to replace his mother but gave him the love and acceptance that come with devoted motherhood.

December 1923

The first winter was harder than he had imagined. Bryn's earnings from the bakery barely covered his keep, and Eileen's careful budgeting couldn't stretch to cover both food and his school fees. Some evenings they shared a single egg between them, thinned into soup with yesterday's bread.

Maybe I should go back," Bryn said on a particularly cold night, watching Eileen darn his only good shirt by candlelight to save lamp oil. "At least in the mine, I could send money home to help Mam and my brother and sisters."

"And what good would that do them if you're dead in five years with black lung?" she replied, but he could see the strain around her eyes. "We'll manage."

It was then that Bryn discovered she'd been selling her few pieces of jewelry, one by one. First her mother's brooch, then her wedding ring's matching bracelet. When he confronted her, she simply said, "What good are pretty things if they can't help the people we love?"

That night, Bryn wrote his first letter home, knowing it would take days to reach them and cost precious pennies to post.

"Dear Evan,

I hope you are well and still carving. I am staying with Aunt Eileen in Sketty near Swansea and going to school in the evenings. It is very far from home. Please tell Mary and Bernise I think of them every day. How is Mam? Is tad still angry?

Your brother, Bryn."

The letter came back unopened, his father's handwriting scrawled across it: "Return to sender."

Mr. Clements, Bryn's art teacher, was a thin man with paint permanently under his fingernails and opinions as sharp as his pencils. "Williams," he said one evening, examining Bryn's latest sketch. "This is competent work, but competent isn't enough. Where's the passion? Where's the risk?"

Bryn had been drawing safe subjects: still lifes and careful copies of master works. But Clements pushed him toward something more personal.

"Draw what matters to you," the teacher insisted. "Draw your truth."

That night, Bryn sketched his family from memory. David whittling by the fire. Mary protecting Bernice. His mother was in her chair, but as she used to be, before the gin. When he showed the sketches to Clements, the older man nodded slowly. "Now you're beginning to understand what art can do."

"I wish I could show them to my family," Bryn said quietly. "But they're so far away, and my father..."

"Sometimes art has to be its own reward," Clements replied. "At least for now."

Summer 1925

They received news that there had been an accident at the mine. Cave-in on the lower level. Three men trapped, including Richard Price. They got two out alive, but Richard didn't make it.

The news came through the Swansea papers, delayed by days. Bryn read it over breakfast, his hands shaking. "I should go," he said. "Pay my respects. See if my family..."

Eileen gently took the paper from his hands. "With what money, *cariad*? The train fare alone would cost us two weeks' grocery money. And your father made it clear..."

"But Richard is dead. Maybe that would change things," Bryn said.

Eileen shook her head. "Maybe. But maybe it would just cause more pain for everyone."

That evening, Bryn wrote another letter, knowing the chances of it reaching Evan were slim: *"Evan, I heard about Richard Price. I'm sorry. Are you all safe? I wish I could be there."*

This letter, like the others, came back unopened.

Autumn 1926

A miracle happened. Mrs. Patterson at the bakery mentioned that her nephew, who worked on the Cardiff to Swansea rail line, had seen a boy matching Evan's description at Porth station. The boy had been asking about mail delivery to

Swansea.

Three days later, a small package arrived with no return address. Inside was a carved wooden robin and a brief note:

"Bryn, Mam is very sick. The gin and something in her chest. Mary asks for you every day. Can't write more. Tad would thrash me. The robin is from Bernice. She remembers your promise. – E."

Bryn held the carved bird in his hands, tears streaming down his face. "I have to go," he told Eileen. "I have to see them."

"How?" she asked gently. "We've got three shillings to last the week. The train fare would cost us twice that."

"I'll walk," he said.

Eileen shook her head. "It's twenty-five miles, *cariad*. And winter's coming. And even if you make it, what then? Your father throws you out again, and you've lost your job here?"

They argued for a while, but in the end, practicality won. Instead, Bryn wrote a careful letter:

"Evan: Hide this from Tad. Tell Mam I love her and miss her. Tell Bernice to keep drawing birds. Tell Mary to be strong. I would come if I could, but it's too far and tad made his feelings clear. Someday, when I can, I'll find a way. – B."

Spring 1927

Mr. Griffiths, the literature teacher, was reading the newspaper during their evening break when he looked up sharply. "Williams, where did you say your family lived?"

"Rhondda Valley, sir. Mayhill. Why?"

Griffiths folded the paper carefully. "There's been another accident. Bigger this time. The whole of Becker Street row was evacuated due to subsidence."

Bryn's blood went cold. Becker Street. Where his family lived. This time, there was no question. Bryn borrowed money from Eileen's small emergency fund, took the train to Cardiff, then another to Mayhill. The journey took the better part of a day and cost them a month's careful savings. When he arrived, Becker Street was empty, houses marked with danger signs. Neighbors said the families had been relocated, but no one knew where the Williams family had gone.

"Council said they'd find them new housing," old Mrs. Jenkins told him. "But that was weeks ago. Haven't seen hide nor hair of them since."

Chapter 3: The Angel's Shelter

Bryn searched for two days, walking from temporary shelter to temporary shelter, spending their last pennies on food and a night in a workingman's lodging house. But his family had vanished as completely as if the earth had swallowed them. "It's like they've disappeared," he told Eileen when he returned, defeated and penniless.

"Maybe it's better this way," she said gently, though her own eyes were red with worry about their finances. "Maybe now they'll have a fresh start somewhere safer. And maybe your father will have learned that family matters more than pride."

But Bryn couldn't shake the feeling that he'd lost them forever. The distance that had once seemed protective now felt like an unbridgeable chasm.

As Bryn's eighteenth birthday approached, he poured four years of learning and love into an oil painting that would express what words couldn't. For weeks, he secretly watched Eileen, observing how the afternoon light danced in her silver hair as she tended her beloved garden, and how serenity rested on her face as she worked among the late roses.

The canvas took up his evenings and weekends. Mr. Clements had given him access to the school's oil paints, a treasured gift that Bryn valued deeply. Every brushstroke was intentional, and each color was mixed with the care of an alchemist seeking gold. When he gave it to her on her birthday evening, the cottage seemed to hold its breath. Eileen's hands flew to her mouth, and tears started to roll down her cheeks before she could say anything.

"Oh, son," she whispered through tears that caught the firelight like diamonds. "You couldn't have given me a finer gift than your presence in my life. This will hang above the fireplace where I can see it always."

The word "son" hung unspoken between them yet rang true in Bryn's heart. Her embrace held years of unspoken understanding: shared meals and quiet evenings, nightmares soothed, and small victories celebrated like festivals. In this painting, Bryn had captured not just Eileen's likeness but the transformation she had wrought in his life: from a broken boy to a young man with purpose.

The night before he was set to report to the recruitment office in Swansea, Bryn and Eileen sat by their fire one last time. The oil painting now hung above the mantel, catching the light just as he'd hoped. "The cottage will feel empty without you," she admitted one evening, her fingers gentle on his arm. "But Swansea has too many shadows for you, *cariad*. Sometimes we need to step into the light to see our way clearly."

"I'm not running away like I did from home," he said, though he wasn't sure if he was reassuring her or himself.

"I know, *cariad*." She reached over and took his hand, her palm warm and steady. "You're running toward something. That's brave. And it's time."

Chapter 4

No Looking Back

"Every journey of a thousand miles begins with burning the map home."

Regimental saying, South Wales Borderers

The walk to Swansea station felt like a pilgrimage through memory. Each step from Aunt Eileen's house in Sketty echoed with fragments: the corner where she had taught him to ride her late husband's bicycle, the wall where Bryn had kissed Mary Evans behind the baker's shop, the bench where he'd sit for hours sketching the sunset as it painted the bay gold and crimson.

At the station, the Great Western Railway train to Brecon waited like an iron beast, steam hissing between its wheels with mechanical impatience. The platform buzzed with travelers: businessmen with newspapers, farmers heading to market, and scattered young men with the same determined look Bryn recognized in himself.

He climbed on the train, and found a window seat, watching the familiar landscape fade away as the train departed the station. The rolling hills of South Wales blurred into a patchwork of green and gray, marked by the stark geometries of coal tips and mine heads that had shaped his childhood.

Across the aisle, an older man in a worn tweed jacket studied Bryn with knowing eyes. "Off to join up, then?" he asked in the soft accent of the Rhondda Valley.

"Yes, sir. South Wales Borderers," Bryn replied.

The man nodded approvingly. "Good regiment. Lost my eldest at the Somme." He said it without bitterness, as if discussing the weather. "They're brave lads. They'll make a man of you if you let them."

Bryn nodded and smiled.

Brecon's South Wales Borderers Barracks pulsed with the nervous energy. Young men from all over Wales had gathered at this large group of Victorian brick buildings, each with their own reasons for joining up. The recruitment office was busy as clerks processed applications with mechanical efficiency. Lord Kitchener's stern visage loomed from a wall poster, his pointing finger offering both admonition and challenge: "Your Country Needs You."

Captain Davies presided over the recruitment process with the calm authority of a man who had evaluated hundreds of young souls and found them either lacking or promising. He leaned back in his chair, studying Bryn across a desk marked by years of nervous fidgeting and desperate pleas. Steel-blue eyes that had seen action in the Boer War measured Bryn in seconds. "So, Williams," Davies said, glancing at the application before him. "Tell me why you want to join the Army."

I want to serve, sir," Bryn kept his Welsh accent steady and controlled.

"And the South Wales Borderers specifically?"

"Yes, sir. Good regiment. Brave men." Bryn's expression barely changed. "The kind who stand their ground when others run."

"Indeed they are," Davies said, making notes on the application. "You'll need to pass a medical, of course. But you've got the look of a man who can take orders and give them when necessary."

Davies stamped the papers with military precision. and the Empire's relentless hunger for soldiers. After his medical, Bryn returned to Davies. "Your application is approved, Williams. Transport to Infantry Battle School at Dering Lines departs in two hours. You'll join other recruits there for basic training."

April 1928.

The quartermaster's stores handed over his new identity piece by piece. Sergeant Major Thompson, a seasoned veteran with scars from campaigns in Afghanistan and South Africa, supervised the process with the efficiency of someone who had spent twenty-seven years transforming civilians into soldiers. "Right then, lads," Thompson barked to the assembled recruits. "Everything you're about to receive belongs to His Majesty's Army. Lose it, damage it, or sell it, and you'll answer to me. And trust me, you don't want that conversation. You're all numbers now. Learn yours. It'll follow you to your grave."

Bryn was assigned to Third Platoon, B Company, along with twenty-nine other recruits. The barracks became his new world: a narrow cot with a thin mattress, a grey blanket that smelled of carbolic soap and previous occupants, and a small wooden locker for the few possessions that mattered.

The bunk to his left was claimed by Tom Jones, a pale, slight young man with clerk's hands and nervous energy that manifested in constant finger-drumming.

Chapter 4: No Looking Back

"Cardiff," Tom said by way of introduction, his accent thick with valley vowels. "Worked at the coal board offices until they made cuts. You?"

"Rhondda originally. Been staying with my aunt in Sketty." Bryn didn't mention the mine, or his father, or the door that had slammed shut behind him. "Been attending a Technical College."

"Technical College?" The voice came from the bunk across the aisle. Its owner was a young man with the lean, wiry build of someone who'd done hard physical labor since childhood. "Owen Lewis. Rhondda Valley, same as you. Been down the pit since I was eleven."

"Why'd you leave?" Tom asked.

Owen's smile held no humor. "Cave-in last winter. Saw three good men buried under a million tons of rock because the company wouldn't spend money on proper supports."

That first week passed in a blur of shouted commands, endless drill, and the systematic breaking down of civilian habits. Sergeant Morgan, a lean Scotsman with Aberdeen vowels and absolutely no patience for weakness, supervised their transformation with the dedication of a craftsman shaping raw steel. "You're not individuals anymore," Morgan announced on their third day, as they stood swaying with exhaustion after two hours of rifle drill. "You're soldiers in His Majesty's Army. Act like it. Think like it. Or find your way home to your mothers."

Weapons training started that week. The Lee-Enfield rifle felt heavier than Bryn expected, its weight serving as a constant reminder of its deadly purpose. Sergeant Williams (no relation, as he reminded everyone daily) demonstrated proper handling with the bored efficiency of a man who had taught this lesson to hundreds of young soldiers.

Bryn learned to strip the rifle blindfolded, to clean it in the dark, to love it like a brother and fear it like death itself. Around him, other recruits underwent the same ritual transformation: Tom's soft clerk hands grew calluses from rifle practice, Owen's mining experience served him well in the systematic care required for military equipment.

The letters from Aunt Eileen arrived every Tuesday, filled with updates about her garden and the neighbors, carefully avoiding mention of how quiet the cottage felt without his presence. She wrote about Mr. Clements asking about him and changes in Sketty, along with the seasonal progress of her cherished roses. *"You are in my prayers every morning and night,"* she wrote in her careful script. *"Remember who you are, cariad. Remember that you are loved."*

Bryn wrote back every Sunday, describing his training in careful terms that wouldn't worry her, sketching the barracks and his fellow soldiers, sharing the small victories and friendships that were growing in the crucible of shared hardship.

May 1928

Six weeks into training, they faced their first real test. Dawn arrived not with the gentle ringing of chapel bells, but with the loud clatter of rifle bolts and hobnailed boots on stone. The barracks erupted into controlled chaos as thirty young men prepared for what Sergeant Morgan had ominously described as "character building."

"Right then, you beauties," Morgan's Aberdeen growl cut through the morning mist like a blade through silk. Behind him, the Brecon Beacons loomed like sleeping giants, their peaks swallowed in clouds that promised weather tough enough to make strong men weep. "Pen y Fan," he continued, stabbing a scarred finger toward the highest peak. "Eight hundred and eighty-six meters of Welsh granite that's broken better men than you sorry specimens. Four hours to reach the summit, traverse to Corn Du, and return. Full kit. Anyone who falls behind gets left for the ravens."

"Jesus, Mary, and Joseph," Tom whispered, his voice barely audible. "That's not a hill. That's a bloody mountain."

The Bedford trucks sat in the courtyard like mechanical beetles, their olive canvas covers rolled up to reveal smooth wooden benches worn by countless recruits who had made this same journey into the Welsh hills. The smell of diesel and damp canvas mixed with the mountain air that carried hints of rain. During the truck ride up the winding mountain roads, Bryn found himself studying his companions more closely than ever before. Tom's nervous energy had evolved into something more focused over the past weeks. The soft clerk's hands were now calloused, and there was a steadiness in his pale blue eyes that hadn't been there during those first terrifying days of training.

Owen sat quietly, conserving energy with the wisdom of someone who'd learned efficiency in the mines. At nineteen, he carried himself with the lean strength of someone who'd been hauling coal for years, but six weeks of military training had added something new: the confidence that came from mastering unfamiliar skills.

When they dismounted from the transport trucks, Pen y Fan loomed above them like a stone leviathan, its slopes vanishing into low clouds that clung to the mountainside like smoke from a chapel chimney. Dew-slick grass concealed ankle-breaking scree beneath its innocent surface, waiting to catch the unwary.

"Form up!" Corporal Jenkins's East London bark cut through the mountain air. The man had learned his trade in the streets of Whitechapel before the Army gave him purpose and three stripes on his sleeve. "Three ranks! Section leaders set pace! Fall behind and answer to me!"

Chapter 4: No Looking Back

Bryn quickly found his rhythm, muscle memory from years underground helping him conserve strength, read the ground, and trust his feet to find purchase on uncertain surfaces. But Tom was already struggling, his breathing ragged and labored. "Easy," Bryn murmured, reaching over to adjust his friend's pack straps. "You're fighting the weight. Let it settle. Work with it, not against it."

The formation stretched like taffy as weaker recruits fell behind. Morgan moved among them like a predator, noting who struggled and who adapted, storing away information that would influence future assignments. Halfway up, they encountered their first casualty. Perkins from Merthyr slumped against a boulder like a discarded marionette, his face pale as pit slag, chest heaving with the desperate gasps of a man whose lungs had never learned to handle thin mountain air.

Morgan appeared beside him like mountain mist turned human, his face unreadable. The sergeant had seen this moment hundreds of times: the instant when a man's body betrayed his will, when determination clashed against physical limits. "On your feet, soldier!" Morgan barked, though his tone carried more disappointment than anger. "The enemy won't wait while you catch your breath!"

Three-quarters up the mountain's face, Tom's legs buckled without warning. He stumbled forward, only Bryn's quick reflexes preventing a tumble down the slope. Without thinking, Bryn grabbed Tom's webbing, taking some of his weight. Around them, other recruits kept climbing, some offering words of encouragement, others too focused on their own pain to notice the weak. Owen stepped up beside them, silently taking Tom's other arm.

The summit emerged from the mist like a revelation, wind whipping at their faces with the wild joy of weather that refused human control. For a moment, clouds parted to reveal Wales stretched below them like a worn patchwork quilt, fields separated by stone walls that had stood since before the Romans arrived.

Tom collapsed onto a rock, tears mixing with rain on his face. "I won't... won't forget this, Bryn...Owen."

Sergeant Morgan stood on the highest point, observing recruits gather with the patience of a man who knew that mountains taught lessons no drill instructor could. His scarred face revealed nothing, but his eyes lingered on Bryn, Owen, and Tom a moment longer than the others. "Half done," Morgan announced to the assembled group, his voice carrying clearly despite the wind. "Corn Du next, then down. The mountain's tested you going up. Now it'll test your sense coming down. Move out!"

The descent proved more dangerous than the climb. Loose scree threatened to send them tumbling down slopes as steep as chapel roofs, while tired legs fought to keep balance on slick surfaces of rain and crushed stone. But they made it.

Together. Stumbling into the valley with minutes to spare, thirty young men were transformed by their encounter with Welsh granite and their own limitations.

That evening in the barracks, as they tended blisters and aching muscles, something had changed among the three friends. The mountain had forged bonds that mere proximity could never create.

"Funny thing," Tom said, carefully bandaging a blister on his heel. "Six weeks ago, I couldn't march two miles without falling over. Today I climbed a bloody mountain."

Bryn lay on his bunk, staring at the ceiling and thinking about the day. He'd left the Rhondda Valley to escape the darkness of the mines, but today had shown him something unexpected: the darkness wasn't in the place, it was in accepting limitations. On Pen y Fan, he'd discovered he was stronger than he'd known.

"Owen," Bryn said quietly. "What do you think they're preparing us for?"

The pit worker was quiet for a long moment. "Word is we're headed overseas. Egypt, maybe. India. Somewhere the Empire needs soldiers who can handle hard conditions."

"Egypt," Tom repeated, wonder and worry mingling in his voice. "Can you imagine? Pyramids and sand and..."

"Heat and flies and people who don't want us there," Owen finished pragmatically. "But orders are orders, and we'll do our duty."

Bryn thought about Aunt Eileen's latest letter, which had mentioned news reports about unrest in Egypt, about British soldiers maintaining order in a land that seemed increasingly unwilling to accept their presence. *"Be careful, cariad,"* she'd written. *"The world is changing, and not always for the better. Come home safe to me."*

Outside, Welsh rain drummed its eternal rhythm against the barracks windows, the same sound that had accompanied his childhood. But now it felt like a farewell song, the last voice of home before they ventured into places where rain might be a precious memory. Sleep came eventually, bringing dreams of coal dust and mountain mist, his mother's lullabies sung in Welsh while rain drummed against cottage windows. But now the dreams carried new elements: the weight of a rifle, the bonds of brotherhood forged in hardship, and the uncertain promise of distant lands where boys became men and men discovered what they were truly made of.

The next morning, thick fog covered the training ground like an unshakable blanket. Twenty recruits formed a rough circle around Corporal Jenkins, all showing bruises and tired eyes from three weeks of rough training with the British Army. Jenkins stood in the center, feet shoulder-width apart, with a face that revealed nothing. Sergeant Morgan watched from behind the group, smoking his

Chapter 4: No Looking Back

pipe and examining each man as if deciding their futures.

Something was different today. You could feel it in the air, that sense that whatever was coming would matter. A small, wiry soldier stood next to Jenkins, and just having him there changed everything. The man moved like he knew exactly what his body could do, and that curved knife on his belt had every recruit staring.

"Right then, lads" Jenkins called out in that East London voice they all knew by now. "Today we're learning close quarters work with proper steel. Not just your bayonets, but real blade work." He nodded toward the other soldier. "This is Lance Corporal Prakash Gurung from the Second Gurkha Rifles. He's going to show you how it's done."

The Gurkha stepped forward with movements that looked effortless. His dark eyes swept over the recruits, taking note of who stood straight and who was already backing up, who met his gaze and who found somewhere else to look.

"For those who don't know," Sergeant Morgan said, and there was something like respect in his voice, "Gurkha soldiers are some of the best fighters in the world. Nothing scares an enemy quite like hearing '*Ayo Gurkhali*' (the Gurkhas are coming) in the dark."

Gurung drew his kukri in one smooth motion that made half the recruits flinch. The curved blade caught what little sunlight there was; it was sharp enough that you could tell this man took care of his weapons. "This knife belonged to my father, and his father before him," Gurung said. His English was clear, just touched with an accent. "We learn to use these before we learn to read." His serious expression suddenly broke into a grin that completely changed his face. "Today I show you why the British Army says it's better to die than meet a Gurkha in the dark."

What happened next was like watching a master at work. Gurung moved like water, but water that could kill you. The kukri became part of his arm, showing slashes, thrusts, and that devastating upward cut that made the curved blade so dangerous. Jenkins joined in to demonstrate defense, and the two of them moved together like they'd done this a thousand times. Professional killers showing their craft at half speed so the recruits could actually see what they were doing.

"Now," Gurung said, and his smile turned sharp, "we show you real speed."

Bryn could barely follow what came next. The kukri turned into a silver blur, cutting through the air with sounds that promised death. Jenkins dodged each attack by inches, his own movements proof of reflexes earned in trenches where being slow meant being dead. Nobody said a word.

"You," Gurung said suddenly, pointing straight at Bryn. "Valley boy. You've been watching. Show me what you learned."

Bryn stepped up and took the wooden practice knife, trying not to let his hands shake too much. He'd been paying attention, noting how Gurung used tricks and misdirection instead of just trying to overpower his opponent. They circled each other slowly, Bryn keeping his blade low and ready while Gurung waited with the patience of someone who knew that rushing usually got you killed.

When the attack came, it was beautiful and deadly. A fake high that pulled Bryn's guard up, then the real strike came low. But working in the mines had taught him to read the small signs that came before cave-ins, and he managed to get his blade in the way, mostly. They kept going for several minutes, Gurung picking up the pace while calling out corrections and encouragement. By the end, Bryn was battered and breathing hard, but he'd lasted longer than any of the others.

"The Williams boy learns fast," Gurung told Morgan afterward. "He has good instincts. Patient."

The posting assignments came the following week, and everyone had been waiting for them with equal parts excitement and dread. Dawn was just breaking when the barracks exploded into chaos. Word traveled through the ranks like fire. Bryn and Tom rushed to the company board outside the orderly room to see where their names had ended up. "There!" Tom pointed with a shaking finger. "South Wales Borderers section." They found their names together on the typed list: "Williams, B. South Wales Borderers: Overseas Deployment. "Egypt! Egypt!" Tom's voice cracked.

The excitement wore off fast when Major Thompkins briefed them that afternoon. The officer was a Great War and Boer War veteran with grey hair and steady eyes that had seen too much. He spoke to the assembled recruits with the kind of professional calm that came from experience.

"Gentlemen," Thompkins began, his Welsh accent carrying authority earned the hard way, "since the Egyptian Revolution in 1919, we've been dealing with increasing resistance from nationalist groups. The situation is volatile and requires constant attention. Your job will be maintaining order, protecting British interests, and guarding key infrastructure. The Suez Canal, government buildings, railway lines. All essential to keeping the Empire running."

That night, lying in his bunk while rain tapped against the windows in that steady Welsh rhythm, Bryn found himself wrestling with doubts he hadn't expected. This wasn't the clear-cut heroism he'd imagined when he walked away from his father's house. Instead of facing enemy soldiers on a battlefield, defending home and country, they'd be controlling civilians and enforcing British rule over people who saw them as invaders.

Chapter 5

From Salt to Sand

"The sea takes what it wants. Best you make peace with that before you board."

Old Harry from the docks, before the Titanic sailed

Morning mist clung to Southampton's Victoria Dock like coal smoke trapped in a valley, but saltier. HMS Dunera loomed before them, five hundred thirty feet of gray steel that used to carry passengers comfortably but now hauled soldiers toward whatever waited for them. The ship looked exhausted. War had stripped away any of her former elegance, turning passenger decks into troop quarters and dining rooms into mess halls. She was still seaworthy, but just barely. Like everything else Britain was using in this war, she could get the job done, but she wouldn't do it gracefully.

Bryn watched other ships load at the nearby docks. The same scene played out in Liverpool, Glasgow, and Portsmouth. Convoys heading east with their cargo of young men toward places most of them couldn't find on a map. Egypt. Palestine. India. The empire was calling in its debts, and the payment came in Welsh boys, Yorkshire lads, and Scottish farmers' sons.

B Company! Form up! Boarding in ten minutes!" The warrant officer's voice cut through the dock noise like a saw through timber. Around Bryn, the other soldiers shouldered their gear and started moving toward the gangway. Welsh boys mixed with Londoners and country lads from Devon. The army had a way of blending everyone together until you couldn't tell where anyone was from anymore.

The gangway was steep and narrow, with their boots clanging on metal steps that had been worn smooth by thousands of men who had made this journey before them. Behind them, Southampton stretched out gray and familiar. Ahead, the ship's corridors promised weeks of discomfort and seasickness.

"Welcome to your new home," a ship's officer announced without much enthusiasm. "D Deck, Frame 58, Mess 23. Follow the red lines painted on the bulkheads. Stow your kit. Departure at fourteen hundred hours."

Ashes and Dawn

Below decks, the conversion from passenger liner to troop transport was obvious and brutal. Where rich passengers had once enjoyed spacious cabins, soldiers now slept stacked three high in bunks that barely had room to turn over. The only privacy came from hanging a blanket, and even that was considered luxury.

Bryn found his bunk and tossed his kit bag onto the thin mattress. Through the porthole, he saw the dock where families were gathered to wave goodbye—mothers, wives, and sweethearts holding handkerchiefs like white flags. Nobody was there for him.

The ship's horn sounded the departure. One long note that seemed to carry all the sorrow of England with it. The Dunera pulled away from the dock, and Britain began to shrink behind them.

The first days at sea were miserable. Atlantic waves as tall as Welsh hills rocked the ship like a toy, and most of the lads spent their time hanging over the rails, feeding fish with whatever they managed to keep down from breakfast. The ship creaked and groaned like an old mine shaft settling, and the smell of sickness, diesel fuel, and too many bodies crammed together made everything worse.

Bryn found Tom on the deck one morning, gripping the rail and staring at the horizon as if he was trying to steady himself. "Scuttlebutt says we'll be fighting Arabs," Tom said. "Don't know much about them except they're not like us."

The desert war already had its own mythology. Stories spread through field hospitals and supply depots, via letters home and conversations in officers' messes. Sand got into everything. The heat could be deadly. An enemy that knew the terrain and used it as a weapon. But behind these stories, few acknowledged a hard truth: this was where the empire's fate would be decided, among the dunes and rocky outcrops of North Africa.

History would judge them, these young men sailing toward war. But survivors wrote history, and survival often depended on choices made in moments of fear and chaos. The philosophers and politicians who sent them here would never have to explain to a mother why her son hesitated when he should have fired, or why mercy in one moment led to slaughter in the next.

Calm evenings brought simple pleasures. Card games in the mess, stories over strong tea, and the gentle roll of the ship beneath them like being rocked to sleep. For a few hours at a time, they could almost forget where they were headed. The cards fell, and the ship sailed on. Two Welsh boys were becoming something else as they traveled through the Mediterranean night toward whatever awaited them in Egypt.

Chapter 5: From Salt to Sand

City of a Thousand Minarets

Alexandria rose out of the morning heat like something from the Bible, all white stone and impossibly tall towers reaching toward a sky that hurt to look at. HMS Dunera groaned against the dock after twelve days at sea, and Bryn had never been so glad to see solid ground.

This wasn't the endless desert Bryn imagined. Buildings rose white as chapel walls, bleached by the sun that had baked this land since before Moses walked through it. Palm trees swayed in the breeze that carried scents both familiar and strange. Coffee, spices, and car exhaust, but beneath it all, something older that made his skin crawl and his heart race at the same time.

"*Duw!*" (God) Tom whispered, his Cardiff accent thick with wonder. "Look at the size of it."

They marched through Alexandria's streets in formation, their boots echoing beneath ceilings painted with scenes from some empire's glory days. The railway station was all marble and crystal chandeliers, as if someone had built a palace and then decided to run trains through it. Sergeant Morgan walked alongside them, his eyes taking in everything with the careful attention of a man who'd seen enough of the empire to recognize the warning signs.

The train to Cairo was third class, naturally. Wooden benches, smoothed by countless passengers who had taken this trip before, lined the car. Through windows that hadn't been properly cleaned since Kitchener's era, the Nile Delta stretched out green and surreal, as if someone had forgotten to finish turning it into desert.

At every stop, vendors crowded around the carriages like they'd just discovered that British soldiers had money that spent as well as anyone else's. Boys sold oranges through the windows, calling out in Arabic, their voices mingling with the sound of wheels on tracks. Men carried brass trays of tea, and the air filled with smells of honey and mint and spices that didn't have names in Welsh.

The countryside changed as they traveled south. Green fields gave way to brown earth and scattered settlements that seemed to grow out of the landscape itself. Bryn watched farmers working their fields with wooden plows that Moses might have recognized, following rhythms established when Britain was still just tribes fighting over sheep.

Cairo announced itself long before they reached the station: smoke, dust, and the sound of a thousand voices calling in languages older than conquest. The train squealed into Bab El-Hadid station like a beast finally reaching water after a long journey through hostile territory. The platform erupted into chaos that somehow made sense. Military personnel in crisp whites moved through crowds of locals in robes and modern suits, children darting between legs like quicksilver, vendors hawking everything from brass trinkets to what looked like live chickens.

Bedford trucks waited to carry them through streets that twisted like sheep paths in the Welsh hills, shaped by centuries of feet and wheels and hooves instead of any kind of planning. Bryn held the side rail as they bounced over cobblestones worn smooth by time, watching a city that had been ancient when London was still a Roman camp.

The British barracks at Abbassia sat in the heat like something dropped from a great height and landed badly. British efficiency was imposed on Egyptian land with all the cultural sensitivity of miners stripping a hillside. Functional, profitable, and completely indifferent to what had been there before. The parade grounds baked under the sun, turning the sand into furnaces. Training fields stretched between buildings that looked exactly like every other British base, as if the War Office had decided that familiarity was more important than adapting to local conditions.

As their truck passed the headquarters building, Bryn saw a small figure in RAF uniform walking alongside army officers, his face weathered by the desert sun that had bleached him like old bone. Even from a distance, there was something about the way he moved that set him apart.

"That's him," a soldier's voice called out from the back of the truck, "T.E. Lawrence, Lawrence of Arabia. He's the man who promised the Arabs freedom. I saw his picture in the Times."

"Many people said we betrayed the Arabs and took their freedom away," someone else in the truck called out.

Critical of the British Empire? Bryn thought. He was surprised to hear it said out loud.

Their quarters were standard army issue. Narrow cots, thin mattresses, wooden lockers that smelled of disinfectant and previous occupants. But through the windows, Cairo's ancient skyline reminded them constantly that they were guests in a land that had been welcoming unwelcome visitors since before memory began.

Over the following weeks, as they settled into the routines of occupation duty, Bryn learned what empire really meant. It wasn't the noble mission the recruiting posters promised, bringing civilization to grateful natives. Instead, they found themselves managing ordinary people trying to live normal lives under a system that saw them as resources to be exploited rather than human beings to be respected. In his mind, Bryn came to a realization: "They don't need civilizing. They need us to leave them alone." But the politicians in London and the officers at headquarters had different ideas, and those ideas didn't consider what the Egyptians might want for themselves. The change came slowly, like water wearing

Chapter 5: From Salt to Sand

away stone. Each small act of imperial arrogance: officers dismissing local knowledge, property destroyed without compensation, and traditions treated as obstacles to British efficiency, chipped away at the certainties Bryn carried from Wales to Egypt.

Master Sergeant Evans called them together, his Valley accent cutting through the morning air. "Right, you lot. Listen up. Cairo's heating up. Not just scattered protests anymore. The resistance is getting organized."

Evans spread out a map on the table, showing streets with names Bryn couldn't pronounce. "We're initiating enhanced patrols. Four-man teams. Six-hour rotations. Intelligence says the independence movement is gaining strength. We need to see trouble coming before it starts."

The afternoon heat hit like walking into a furnace. First patrol. Bryn and Tom, along with Corporal Thomas and Private Smith, headed into the city. Four Welsh boys walking the streets older than Wales itself. Islamic Cairo unfolded around them like something from a fever dream. Narrow alleys wound deeper than mine shafts. Wooden screens cast shadows on stones worn smooth by centuries of feet. The air was thick with incense and cooking smells, and the tightly packed lives of too many people in too small a space.

The Khan el-Khalili market hit them with scents that seemed almost tangible. Cardamom, roasted lamb, donkey dung, and sewage. Life squeezed into spaces too tiny to contain it all. A mosque appeared, its minaret reaching toward the sky like a prayer made of stone. The call to prayer began, its voice drifting across the city like wind through chapel bells. Everything paused. An elderly merchant waved them over after prayer, his white robe as bright as a Sunday chapel shirt. "Welcome, welcome! Finest cotton for soldiers!"

They moved into a wider street lined with cafes where men played backgammon and smoked apple tobacco. University students passed by, girls in bright hijabs that caught sunlight like stained glass windows. Then someone dropped a metal pot. The clatter echoed off the walls, and four British rifles swung up to a ready position before their owners' brains caught up.

False alarm. But the soldiers were wound tighter now.

They approached a fruit stand where oranges were stacked high like coal heaps. Voices cut through the market noise, speaking Arabic words that sounded like accusations. "*Al-Ingleez! Ifranj!*" The words meant English foreigners, and they weren't spoken in a friendly way. A boy stepped forward, maybe fifteen years old, wearing a simple robe. His face was twisted with something Bryn recognized from the mines. He picked up an orange, his arm cocked back to throw it.

"Hold your positions," Corporal Thomas said calmly.

Ashes and Dawn

The orange hit Tom square in the chest, juice spreading across his khaki uniform like blood. Tom's face went white with shock and fear and something that looked like panic.

Out of the corner of his eye, Bryn could see Tom move his rifle into a firing position. "Hold Tom!" Bryn shouted, lunging toward his friend.

Too late. Tom's rifle cracked like thunder underground. The young Egyptian crumpled, red blooming across white cloth like poppies in a Welsh field. Time moved swiftly. The market erupted into chaos. Stalls toppled, pottery shattered, and people screamed in languages that all sounded the same. The crowd pushed forward, faces twisted with shock, grief, and rage.

"Close order!" Corporal Thomas barked, grabbing Tom's shoulder. The color had drained from Tom's face like water from a broken bucket.

Some of the crowd surged forward toward the patrol. Being closest to the crowd, Bryn raised his rifle horizontally like a barrier. "*Zar* (back)!" "Please, back!"

The crowd closed in from all sides. The alley became a trap, like a narrow coal seam, walls pressing closer. Private Smith stumbled, a rock having struck his head. Blood on his forehead shimmered like coal dust on pale skin. Corporal Thomas fired warning shots into the air. The sound reflected off the stone walls, amplifying everything.

"Stay with me," Bryn yelled at Tom, shaking him by the shoulders.

They fought their way out, using rifle butts to push rather than strike, trying to clear a path without adding more bodies to the count. The cavalry arrived—horses and steel, soldiers firing shots into the air. The crowd scattered, leaving only debris on the cobblestones. The dead boy's body was gone by the time they retreated, leaving nothing but dark stains on the ancient stones.

The patrol returned to base in silence, accompanied by the horse soldiers. Corporal Thomas supported Private Smith, who was still woozy from the rock that hit his head. That evening, the barracks were quiet except for prayer calls echoing across Cairo. Tom sat on his bunk, still in his stained uniform, staring at his trembling hands like autumn leaves. Bryn sat beside him on the narrow canvas.

"I killed him, Bryn." Tom's voice was broken. "Over an orange. Just a bloody orange."

Listen to me, Tom Jones," Bryn said, gripping his shoulder. "You're not a murderer. You were scared. Fear makes us do things we'd never choose in our right minds."

The next morning brought consequences and commendations. Sergeant Evans praised Bryn's restraint and Corporal Thomas's leadership. Tom was

Chapter 5: From Salt to Sand

ordered to receive additional training and was suspended from patrol duty for a month. No mention was made of compensation for the family of the boy who was killed. And no apology. The incident would be filed away, a minor note in the endless paperwork of the empire. One Egyptian dead, one British soldier injured and one traumatized, but order was maintained. Somewhere in the darkness, a family mourned their son. In the barracks, a Welsh soldier struggled with the weight of what he'd done. The empire's machinery ground on, leaving marks on everyone it touched.

Every empire has produced men like Tom: ordinary boys who become tools of control and then bear the weight of what control demands. The Romans understood this, the Spanish learned it, and now the British are discovering it again. Empire didn't just corrupt those it ruled; it also corrupted its leaders, one frightened boy at a time.

Chapter 6

Everything Tastes of Ashes

"Cairo doesn't seduce you slowly. It grabs you by the throat and shows you what you never knew you wanted."

Master Sergeant Evans

Bryn had been in Egypt for four years when he was promoted to Corporal. His rise to NCO happened faster than usual because Sergeant Evans pushed it through, thanks to Bryn demonstrating superior leadership qualities. What this meant was he could speak Arabic to the Egyptian workers without sounding like he was ordering his hunting dogs around. The new rank came with better quarters, access to the NCO mess where crystal glasses replaced tin cups, and meals served on porcelain plates decorated with regimental crests. Although he didn't bunk with the other recruits like his friend Tom Jones, he still met up with Tom for social activities during their time off.

It was an off-duty evening. The air was thick with the scent of cardamom and charcoal-grilled lamb as Bryn and Tom strolled down Sharia Muhammad Ali. Civil servants in crisp white *gallabiyahs* hurried past, while barefoot children chased hoops made from discarded wire between the legs of donkeys loaded with cotton bales.

Cairo's nightlife stretched out before them like a fever dream. In Ezbekiyya district, theaters and cabarets towered three stories high in some spots, music pouring out of doorways like wine from a tipped bottle. French chanteuses, Syrian comedians, and belly dancers who could make a bishop question his vows all performed within blocks of each other, immersed in champagne and hashish smoke. Wagh El-Birket, the main entertainment district in Cairo, was always lively. Casino Badia drew crowds ranging from British generals and Armenian merchants to Egyptian effendis (important people) in European suits, pretending they weren't watching the French women dance.

The Café Bosphore sat between a traditional *ahwa* (coffee house) with its wooden chairs and backgammon boards, and a European-style bistro with checkered tablecloths. The building seemed unsure which world it belonged to. A crimson awning stretched over windows framed in brass that caught the gaslight like captured stars. The doorman, a Nubian man whose *fez* (headdress) was embroidered with silver thread, nodded to them with practiced assessment.

They found a table near the elevated stage just as a Greek singer finished her warbling tribute to lost love in three languages. Tom ordered arak (anise-flavored drink), which arrived in glasses so clear they seemed to hold light itself.

Bryn was raising the glass to his lips when she appeared. And everything stopped for him.

She stepped through curtains of glass beads that chimed softly, wearing a gown that shifted from midnight blue to silver as the lights caught it. Her hair was styled in finger waves that framed her face, while kohl-lined eyes seemed to hold ancient secrets.

"Yasmine Delacroix," Tom whispered, having cornered the waiter for information. "Father was a French diplomat who fell for an Alexandrian singer. Studied at the Conservatoire in Paris."

Bryn didn't hear Tom say her name. She was mesmerizing. It wasn't just her beauty, although she was stunning. Auburn hair that caught the stage lights, brown eyes that seemed to hold entire conversations, and skin like warm alabaster. No, something else drew his attention: intelligence flickering behind those eyes, subtle defiance in how she carried herself. She refused to be merely decorative.

Her voice filled the room as she started to sing. A French chanson that somehow included Arabic quarter tones, creating something entirely new yet hauntingly familiar. The melody wrapped around conversations and pulled them into silence. Bryn leaned forward, captivated not just by her beauty but by how she commanded the space between cultures. When she finished her set with an Edith Piaf number that made tough colonial officers dab their eyes with handkerchiefs, her gaze swept the room and landed on Bryn. The look lasted maybe three seconds but felt like forever. Something unspoken yet understood, like two people realizing they shared the same dream.

Tom stood up. "Think I'll head to the bar. Might be there a while." He melted into the crowd just as Yasmine approached, balancing a delicate coffee cup.

"Your friend is very tactful," she said, standing behind Tom's chair with fluid grace. Her English was perfect but carried a French accent. "Most British soldiers I meet are not so... subtle."

Bryn stood to pull out her chair properly, as Aunt Eileen had taught him. "Most British soldiers you meet weren't Welsh coal miners."

That earned genuine laughter. Not stage amusement, but something authentic that changed her entire face. "Ah, so that's it. I saw something different in your

Chapter 6: Everything Tastes of Ashes

eyes. Tell me, Monsieur...?"

"Corporal Williams. Bryn Williams."

She sipped her coffee, leaving lipstick on the porcelain rim. "Tell me, Corporal Bryn Williams, how does a Welsh miner end up in Cairo? And please, make it a story worth hearing, not a military report."

That started their first evening together, which turned into many more. Two months of weekly meetings became a sacred ritual. They uncovered hidden corners of the city together: ancient mosque courtyards where stone had been smoothed by centuries of faithful hands, secluded gardens where peacocks wandered among date palms, quiet cafés where afternoon light streamed through stained glass. Their physical expressions remained cautious, restrained by cultural boundaries that governed both their worlds. Fingers intertwined in markets, stolen kisses in shadowed doorways, embraces that lingered just enough to memorize heartbeats.

Yasmine described Paris with longing that made her voice tremble. Electric lights along the Seine, music that filled the night air with promises of freedom. But something always remained unspoken in her stories, shadows flickering behind her eyes when she mentioned specific dates or places.

"Sometimes I feel like I've traded one cage for another," Bryn admitted one afternoon as they sat by a fountain in the gardens. The spray caught late sunlight, creating brief rainbows.

"What do you mean?" Her fingers intertwined with his, natural as breathing.

"The army saved me from the mines, but now..." He gestured around them. "I see what we do here. How we treat people. It's not so different from how the English treated us back home."

Yasmine was quiet for a long moment. "Do you know what happened to my friend Hassan last week?"

Bryn shook his head.

"He was beaten by soldiers for peacefully protesting. They broke two of his ribs." Her voice was steady, but her grip on his hand tightened. "He's sixteen years old, Bryn. Younger than you were when you left Wales."

The words hit him harder than any accusation. "I'm sorry."

"I know you are." She turned to face him fully. "That's what makes this so difficult. You're not like the others. You understand what it means to be under someone else's boot." They sat in silence as the fountain played and the afternoon light shifted through the palm fronds overhead. "My grandmother used to read palms," Yasmine said eventually, tracing the curved line across Bryn's palm with touches as light as butterfly wings. "She'd say the heart line tells everything about love. Yours is deep and clear. She'd say you love with your whole soul."

Bryn brought her knuckles to his lips, tasting salt on her skin. "What does your heart line say?"

"That I'm afraid." Her eyes met his, pupils wide in the dusk. "Afraid of how much I feel for you."

He drew her closer, one hand at the back of her neck where tiny hairs escaped her careful styling. When he kissed her, she melted into him, fingers clutching his shirt as if he might disappear. Around them, the evening call to prayer echoed from distant minarets. When they parted, both breathless, Bryn rested his forehead against hers. "I'm falling in love with you, Yasmine."

She closed her eyes, a single tear sliding down her cheek. "And I with you, my Welsh coal miner." Her hands cupped his face. "But love is never simple in Cairo," she added ominously.

Love and duty pulled him in opposite directions now. The woman Bryn loved saw his uniform as a symbol of oppression. The army that had saved him from the mines demanded loyalty to an empire he was beginning to question. Somewhere between those truths, Bryn realized that a man could love his country while hating what it did to others. Walking back to the barracks one night after another evening in the gardens, with Yasmine's words echoing in his mind, Bryn noticed unusual activity around the British Consulate. Extra guards, late-burning lights, and the nervous energy that comes before either very good news or very bad violence all signaled that something was coming. He could feel it like pressure before a storm.

"Yasmine is everything I ever dreamed of, Tom," Bryn admitted. They sat in the barracks courtyard where oak trees somehow survived in Egyptian soil, their British roots struggling in foreign ground. Late afternoon sunlight filtered through the leaves, casting dappled patterns on the institutional green benches that matched every British base from Gibraltar to Hong Kong. "When she sings, time stops. The way her eyes light up when she laughs, how deeply she cares about everyone around her." Bryn's hands fidgeted with loose threads on his trousers. "I'm completely in love with her."

"I could tell you were taken when you first saw her," Tom said softly. "What are you going to do?"

Bryn took a deep breath. "I'm going to ask her to marry me. I've checked the regulations for NCOs. Sergeant Evans said my application should go through without problems."

Tom whistled low. "That's a big step, my friend. You sure?"

"Never been more certain about anything." Bryn's voice grew stronger. "When my enlistment's up in two years, I'm leaving the Army. I'll tell her I'll move to Paris

Chapter 6: Everything Tastes of Ashes

with her."

"When will you ask her?" Tom queried.

"Tonight." His hand unconsciously patted the small velvet box in his pocket. "After her performance. I haven't seen her for a week."

Tom pulled Bryn into a fierce embrace. "You deserve to be happy. You both do."

Bryn arrived at Café Bosphore just as the evening crowd was filling the space. The café had become a reflection of Cairo's colonial complexity: Egyptian waiters pouring French wine for British officers while Lebanese musicians played for audiences ranging from Armenian merchants to European expats. He made his way to his usual table with its perfect view of the small stage where Yasmine had sung songs that bridged worlds. Tonight felt different somehow, charged with both possibility and dread. In the corner, the café owner, Karim Bishara, sat at his usual table, coffee cooling untouched before him. Their eyes briefly met across the room. Bishara's lip curled slightly. He'd never approved of the British soldier's attention to his star performer.

House lights dimmed and Bryn's breath caught in anticipation. But when the spotlight hit the stage, it wasn't Yasmine's slender figure stepping through the curtain. Instead, the Greek singer appeared, her voice pleasant but missing the smoky richness that had first captivated him when he first saw her.

"*Where is she?*" he thought.

He waited through one song, then another, his unease growing with each passing minute. When the third song started, he couldn't sit still any longer. He walked over to Bishara's table. "Where is Yasmine tonight?" Bryn asked, struggling to keep his voice steady.

Bishara examined his fingernails with practiced indifference, deliberately taking his time before looking up.

Bryn switched to Arabic, words clipped and precise. "*Ayna Yasmeen hadhihi al-layla?*" (Where is Yasmine tonight?

"She's gone." Bishara waved his hand dismissively, as if shooing away a fly. "Back to Paris. You're a fool if you thought she'd stay."

He had to suppress the rising anger inside him as he clenched his fists. "If you're lying..." He dashed out of the café and reached her apartment building within minutes, running up the stairs two at a time. The building was typical of Cairo's newer European quarter: cream-colored stone with wrought-iron balconies that tried to look Parisian but somehow remained stubbornly Egyptian.

"Yasmine!" His fist pounded against her door, the sound echoing off walls covered in English countryside wallpaper. "Yasmine, please!"

A door creaked open behind him. Mrs. Hadad, Yasmine's elderly neighbor, peered out with eyes that had seen too much sorrow to be surprised by more. "She asked me to give this to the soldier who would come looking for her." The old woman extended a cream-colored envelope, Bryn's name written across it in Yasmine's elegant handwriting.

Bryn stared at the letter in his hands as if it might bite him. The paper felt impossibly heavy. "When?" he managed.

"This morning. Early train to Alexandria, then the ship to Marseille." Mrs. Hadad's voice was gentle. "She cried when she gave me the letter."

Bryn clenched the letter in his hand and stumbled his way back to the base, the pain heavy in his heart.

"I thought you'd be with Yasmine tonight," Tom said when Bryn appeared at their usual bench in the gardens. "What's happened?"

The words came out in a rush, the story spilling from him like water from a broken dam. "She's gone to Paris. Just... gone. Left this morning."

Tom's face fell. "Gone? But I thought you two..."

Bryn pulled out the envelope, still sealed. His hands trembled slightly. "She left this. I can't... Tom, would you stay while I read it?"

"Of course," Tom nodded.

Under the gentle glow of garden lanterns, Bryn broke the seal and unfolded the letter.

"My dearest Bryn,

By the time you read this, I will be on my way to Paris. Please don't try to follow me. Some doors, once closed, should remain so.

These past months have been like a beautiful dream, but dreams must end. My father is ill and my family needs me. But that's not the whole truth, and you deserve better than half-truths. I have not been honest with you.

I've watched love growing in your eyes. I knew where this path was leading, and I let myself walk it too long. But I am not free to love you as you deserve. There is someone in Paris, an arrangement made years ago by my family. I thought I could escape it by coming here, but some promises cannot be broken without destroying something far more precious.

Please forgive me for not telling you sooner. I was selfish, wanting to hold onto our time together. Your kindness, your passion, your fierce intelligence made me forget, for a while, what waited for me back home. I have hurt you deeply, and I will always regret it.

Chapter 6: Everything Tastes of Ashes

Remember me as I was singing Piaf under the stars that first night. Remember me smiling. Remember me free.

I do love you. I wish you could find a woman who can love you as you deserve.

Yasmine."

Bryn read the letter twice before the words fully sank in. When they did, he felt something break inside his chest. "An arrangement," he said finally, his voice hollow. "Made years ago. She was engaged the whole time."

Tom reached out and gripped his shoulder. "Bryn, I'm so sorry."

The velvet box in Bryn's pocket felt like it weighed a thousand pounds. He pulled it out and stared at it—this small thing that carried such enormous hope just hours earlier. "I was going to ask her tonight." His voice cracked. "Had it all planned out. After her last song, I was going to get down on one knee right there in the café." He opened the box. The ring caught the lantern light, a small white gold and ruby ring that had cost him three months' pay. It looked so foolish now, so naive. "What kind of fool am I, Tom? Thinking a woman like that could love someone like me?"

"Don't blame yourself Bryn." Tom's voice was fierce. "Don't you dare think that. What you two had was real. I saw it, everyone saw it. She did love you."

"But not enough."

They sat in silence as the night deepened around them. Somewhere in the distance, music drifted from the cafés and cabarets, the sound of Cairo continuing its ancient rhythms while Bryn's world collapsed.

Bryn closed the ring box with a sharp snap.

Above them, stars appeared one by one in the darkening sky, the same lights that had witnessed countless lovers' partings in this ancient city. Somewhere in the distance, a muezzin's call echoed through streets where empires had risen and fallen, where hearts had been broken and mended and broken again. Bryn sat on the bench that had become their refuge, the letter crumpled in one fist and the ring box in the other. Around them, Cairo settled into its nighttime rhythms, the eternal dance of a city that had seen everything and remembered it all.

In the ensuing weeks, Egyptian resistance to British occupation would grow bolder. The empire would tighten its grip, and Bryn would have to choose which side of history he wanted to stand on.

But tonight, he was just a man whose heart had been shattered by a woman who loved him but wasn't free to choose him.

Tonight, everything tasted of ashes.

Chapter 7

Conscience Over Command

"A man's conscience is like coal dust in his lungs. Once it settles there, it never leaves."

Lewsyn yr Heliwr (Lewsyn the Hunter,) after the Merthyr Rising, in Merthyr Tydfil, Wales, 1831

The evening sun cast long shadows across Master Sergeant Evans' office as Bryn entered, his boots scuffing the worn wooden floor that had been polished by countless soldiers' feet over the years. The familiar scent of pipe tobacco lingered in the air like prayers in an empty chapel.

"Have a seat, Bryn," Evans said, gesturing toward the chair opposite his desk. The sergeant's weathered face maintained its usual stern expression, but something else lingered there. Perhaps concern, maybe calculation.

"You've been different since Yasmine left," Evans said, the words falling into the room like stones into still water.

"My commitment to my duties hasn't changed, Sergeant," he replied, forcing his voice to stay steady.

"I know your duty hasn't suffered," Evans continued, shuffling through papers on his desk. "But a man can't patrol the same streets that hold his ghosts forever. Sometimes, a change of scenery is what's needed."

Evans pulled out a folder decorated with several stamps, including one in red ink that read "CONFIDENTIAL." "There's a vacancy in the Special Operations Unit, or SOU, though most simply call it the Cairo Unit. They're looking for men with your particular skill set."

"My particular skill set? Bryn queried.

"Physical attributes, courage, composure under fire, and intelligence," Evans continued.

Bryn felt his stomach tighten like a rope under tension. He had heard whispers about the SOU in the barracks, conversations that would cease whenever officers approached. It operated in the shadows, handling aspects of the British occupation that left no official records and didn't create heroes' graves.

The situation here is complicated," Evans continued, his tone growing more serious. "The streets you patrol are a powder keg waiting for a spark. Just last week, we lost three men in that bombing near the market. Some call themselves freedom fighters, claiming they're defending their homeland. They attack military installations, sabotage railways, and target civilians who collaborate with British authority. We call them terrorists."

"And the SOU's role, Sergeant?" Bryn asked.

"Maintaining order by any means necessary," Evans replied. "The regular army is limited by bureaucracy and public scrutiny. Questions asked in the House of Commons, reporters filing dispatches, rules of engagement written by men who've never heard a bullet whistle past their ears. The SOU operates in the shadows."

"Torture and assassination?" The words felt like ash in Bryn's mouth, dry as desert sand. "How do we justify that, sir? What sets us apart from the terrorists?"

Evans sighed, the sound carrying years of compromises and moral adjustments. "This isn't about ideals, Bryn. It's about control. The Empire wasn't built solely on noble intentions." Evans leaned back in his chair, studying Bryn with the keen eye of a man who had spent decades reading other men's hearts. "You're struggling with this, aren't you? More than just the SOU offer."

"I've been reading T.E. Lawrence's *Seven Pillars of Wisdom*," Bryn said carefully, choosing his words carefully. "His account of the promises made to the Arabs during the Great War... the promises we broke." He met Evans's eyes directly, soldier to soldier. "Aren't we just continuing the same pattern of betrayal?"

"Ah, Lawrence." Evans' expression softened slightly. "A romantic figure, no doubt. Yet he was an idealist who failed to understand that empires aren't built on pure intentions." He paused, reaching for his pipe. "But your question goes deeper than Lawrence. You're questioning our whole reason for being here." Evans struck a match, the flame illuminating his weathered features. "Let me tell you something, lad. I've been wrestling with these same questions for thirty years. Every order I've given, every mission I've completed, every young soldier I've sent into harm's way." He puffed the pipe to life. "You want to know what kept me sane?"

Bryn nodded, sensing they had crossed some invisible threshold in their relationship.

Evans stood up and moved to his bookshelf, pulling out a worn leather-bound book. "Marcus Aurelius. Meditations. Written by a Roman emperor who spent his life fighting wars he didn't necessarily want to fight, governing people who didn't necessarily want to be governed." He opened the book and read aloud: "You have

Chapter 7: Conscience Over Command

power over your mind—not outside events. Realize this, and you will find strength." Evans looked up. "The Stoics understood something we often forget. We can't control our circumstances, Bryn. We can only control how we respond to them."

"But surely we have some control over our circumstances, sir? I chose to enlist," Bryn replied.

"Did you?" Evans' voice was gentle but probing. "A Welsh miner's son with few other options? Facing poverty and a dying industry? Your choices were controlled by forces larger than yourself, just as mine have been, just as every man's are." He moved around the desk, settling into the chair beside Bryn rather than behind his desk. "The question isn't whether our circumstances are just or unjust. The question is: given these circumstances, how do we live with honor?"

This was a side of Evans that Bryn had never seen. Not just the career sergeant, but a man who had grappled with the same moral conflicts that now tormented him.

"I've done things in service to the Empire that I'm not proud of," Evans continued, his voice dropping to barely above a whisper. "Things that haunt me in the quiet hours before dawn. But I've also done things I am proud of. Protected good men from bad orders. Taught young soldiers like yourself to think for themselves. Protected civilians from disaster and death. Tried to temper the Empire's worst impulses with whatever decency I could muster."

"But doesn't that make us complicit, Sergeant? Doesn't that make us part of the machine?" Bryn asked.

Evans smiled grimly. "Marcus Aurelius asked himself the same question. He concluded that we are all part of something larger than ourselves, whether we like it or not. The question is whether we choose to be a force for good within that system, or whether we abandon it entirely to those with fewer scruples."

"Is that why you're offering me the SOU position? To be a force for good within it?"

"I'm offering you choices, Bryn. That's all any of us can do for another man." Evans went back to the book and grabbed another one from the shelf. "'Every new beginning comes from some other beginning's end.' That's not Marcus Aurelius; that's from a Latin poet, but the Stoics would appreciate the sentiment."

Bryn felt something shifting inside him, like tectonic plates grinding toward a new configuration. "What if I said no to the SOU? What if I said no to all of it?"

Evans' eyes narrowed. "You mean quit the service completely?"

"When my enlistment ends, yes." Bryn anticipated a negative response from

Evans but didn't get one.

"That's not a small decision, lad. The Army's been your life since you were barely old enough to shave." Evans studied him carefully. "But I sense you've been thinking about this for some time."

"It's been a big part of my life," Bryn acknowledged. "But maybe it's time for a different kind of living. I'm finding it harder to reconcile with my conscience. Not just the SOU; all of it."

Evans nodded slowly. "I understand. More than you know." He was quiet for a long moment, working his pipe. "But let me ask you something. If you leave military service, what then? Return to the valleys? Work the mines again?"

"I don't know."

"Well, think about this. The Empire would not like to lose a man of your talents. It offers programs for veterans. Training for civilian roles. Sanitary Inspector, for example. Work that truly impacts people's lives." Evans looked directly at Bryn. "The kind of work that might suit an intelligent young man with a strong moral compass."

Sanitary Inspector," Bryn thought. "*Not glamorous, but honest work. Work that helps instead of hurts.*" But then another thought hit him, sharp as a blade. "Sergeant, wouldn't that still be serving the Empire? Just in a different role?" he asked.

Evans' eyebrows rose slightly. "A fair question. One that I wondered if you'd ask."

"I mean, if my moral objection is to imperial rule itself, to the very idea of one people governing another without their consent, then how is civilian service any different from military service?" Bryn asked.

"How do you see it, Bryn?" Evans asked.

"Disease doesn't recognize political boundaries," Bryn said slowly, working through his thoughts. "A child dying of typhoid is a child dying of typhoid, whether under British rule, Egyptian rule, or no rule at all. Public health serves humanity first, politics second."

"And yet," Evans pressed gently, "effective sanitation requires enforcement of regulations. It requires the authority of the state, even if that state is an occupying power. Are you comfortable wielding that authority?"

Bryn was quiet for several minutes, wrestling with the contradiction. Evans waited patiently, seemingly content to let him work through the ethical maze. "I suppose," Bryn said finally, "the difference is in the intent. Military force exists primarily to maintain control, to impose one group's will on another. Public health work exists primarily to preserve life, to prevent suffering. Even if it requires some

Chapter 7: Conscience Over Command

measure of authority, the goal is fundamentally different."

"And you can live with that distinction?" Evans asked.

"I think so. At least, I can live with it more easily than I can with the alternatives," Bryn replied.

Evans smiled, the first genuine smile Bryn had seen from him in this conversation. "Marcus Aurelius again: 'Very little is needed to make a happy life; it is all within yourself, in your way of thinking.' You've found a way of thinking about this work that aligns with your conscience. That's no small thing."

They sat in peaceful silence for several minutes, the office growing darker as the sun set over Cairo. Finally, Evans spoke again. "You know, Bryn, I've watched dozens of young men pass through this office over the years. Most of them see only two paths: complete acceptance of the system or complete rejection of it. You're one of the few who's found a third way."

"What's that, Sergeant?" Bryn asked.

"Principled engagement. Working within the system to serve something greater than the system itself," Evans said as he rose and moved to the window, gazing out at the city. "It's not a perfect solution. There are no perfect solutions. But it's honest work that addresses real human needs, and it preserves your integrity while putting your skills to good use.

"You really think I should do it?" Bryn queried.

Evans turned back to him. "I think you should do what you can live with, lad. What you can wake up to each morning without feeling sick to your stomach." His voice grew softer. "I've spent thirty years finding ways to serve something larger than myself while maintaining some measure of personal honor. It's not always been easy, but it's been possible."

"And the SOU offer?"

"I'll withdraw your name. There are other men better suited to that kind of work. Men who don't ask the questions you ask, who don't wrestle with the contradictions you wrestle with." Evans' expression grew serious. "That's not a criticism, Bryn. The Empire needs men like you more than it needs more men like them."

Something was happening between them, Bryn realized. Some barriers were dissolving, some distances were closing. For the first time, he felt like he was talking not to his commanding officer, but to a man who genuinely cared about his welfare. "Why are you telling me all this, Sergeant?"

Evans was silent for a long moment. "Because, lad, in another life, in a different world, I would have been proud to call you my son."

The words hung in the air between them, heavy with meaning and emotion that had been building for years. Bryn felt something crack open in his chest, a warmth spreading through him that had nothing to do with the Egyptian heat. "And I would have been proud to call you my father, sir," he replied, his voice thick with emotion he hadn't expected.

Evans nodded, his own eyes bright. "Then we understand each other."

They talked for another hour as darkness settled over Cairo, covering topics from Stoic philosophy to practical concerns about civilian training. The conversation now felt different, more like a father guiding a son than a sergeant briefing a subordinate. When it was time to leave, Evans handed him the copy of *Meditations*. "My father gave me this when I was commissioned. I'd like you to have it."

"Sergeant, I can't..."

"He told me to pass it on when I found someone who would understand it properly." Evans opened the book, showing an inscription in his neat handwriting: "To Bryn. Remember that the highest good lies not in the orders you follow, but in the way you choose to follow them."

Without thinking, Bryn stepped forward and embraced the man who had been more than just his commanding officer. He had been a teacher, a guide, and now, a father he never had. Evans returned the embrace without hesitation, two men from different generations united by understanding that went beyond rank and regulation.

"*Mae'n ddrwg gen i dy fod ti'n mynd*" (I'm sorry you're leaving), Evans said softly.

"*Diolch am bopeth, Tad*" (Thank you for everything, Father), Bryn replied, the word "father" coming naturally.

The silence that followed was perfect in its completeness, a moment beyond words that contained all the understanding and respect that had grown between them over the years.

"Now, on your way, son," Evans said finally, his voice gruff with emotion. "We'll talk more about this tomorrow."

Bryn held the treasured book close to his chest, feeling its weight like a compass guiding him toward whatever lay ahead. Outside, the evening call to prayer drifted on the breeze, and he realized that, for the first time since Yasmine's departure, he felt truly at peace with his path. Above him, the same stars that had watched pharaohs, Caesars, and countless other empires rise and fall now observed one Welsh ex-soldier take his first steps toward whatever comes after Empire, carrying the weight of conscience, the gift of philosophical wisdom, and the understanding that some treasures can only be gained through loss.

Chapter 8

Invisible Enemies

"Disease is like gas in the mines, isn't it? Invisible, silent, lethal if you don't know the signs."

Major Hugh Blackwood

The pre-dawn call to reveille echoed across Abbassia military base as Bryn Williams rolled out of his narrow bed in the civilian quarters, the sound piercing dreams where Welsh valleys and Egyptian minarets intertwined like pit ponies and pyramids sharing the same unlikely stable.

His small room had become a sanctuary over the months since he left active service. A metal-frame bed that creaked like mine timbers under shifting earth, a simple wooden desk scarred by many previous occupants who had carved initials and dates into its surface like miners marking tunnel walls, and a ceiling fan that fought Egypt's relentless heat with the grim determination of Welsh miners facing cave-ins. The walls remained bare, except for Evans's gift: *Marcus Aurelius* was propped against the window, where morning light could illuminate whatever wisdom the old Roman had left for modern Welshmen trying to make sense of the contradictions of the Empire.

The walk to Abbassia Military Hospital took him past the parade grounds where new recruits stumbled through morning drills, their movements as awkward as his had been not too long ago. But watching them now, he felt the distance that had grown between his old life and whatever this new one was becoming.

At the hospital, Captain James Thornton's handshake was firm and professional, his uniform crisp despite the early hour. "Welcome, Mr. Williams. We've been expecting you."

The other five men training as sanitary inspectors were already gathered in the sterile classroom, each carrying stories told in accent and bearing. Derek Thompson, a former railway clerk from Manchester, whose careful notes suggested years of handling bureaucratic details. Shamus O'Brien, an Irishman who had worked the Dublin docks and understood how disease spread through crowded, unwashed places. Amrit Singh, a Sikh from Punjab whose military bearing spoke of frontier service, his turban spotless despite the heat. Edward Davies, another Welshman from the Rhondda, whose handshake bore the familiar calluses of underground work. And Brendan Peterson, a Yorkshireman whose quiet manner hid sharp intelligence that revealed itself in the questions he asked.

Captain Thornton outlined their plan with military precision: sanitation and hygiene, public health law, housing regulations, infectious disease control, and medical response in extreme environments. The words sounded impressive enough, but Bryn wondered how much of it would actually be useful when facing real people with real problems.

The morning lectures at Abbassia covered the fundamentals: water systems, sewage management, building codes that existed more on paper than in practice. Thornton was thorough and competent, but Bryn could see how the other men's attention wandered when the Captain read directly from regulations that seemed designed for London rather than Cairo.

Everything changed that first afternoon at Kasr El Aini Medical School when Major Dr. Hugh Blackwood demonstrated his water safety testing technique. The Major was built like a Highland boulder, barrel-chested with prematurely silver hair and laugh lines around eyes that had seen too much of the Empire's underbelly to stay innocent but somehow kept their humor intact. Blackwood moved through the laboratory with casual expertise, his hands steady as he prepared slides and adjusted equipment. But it was his voice that caught attention, a Scottish brogue warming his words like peat fires in Highland cottages, carrying authority that came from experience rather than rank. "The enemy is invisible," he said, focusing his microscope with practiced movements. "Cholera vibrio, typhoid bacillus, dysentery parasites. They disregard borders and defy regulations. They simply kill, efficiently."

After the demonstration, as the other trainees filed out, discussing what they'd seen, Blackwood's gaze settled on Bryn with curious assessment. "You're not from a medical background, are you, Williams?" The question carried no judgment, just genuine interest.

"No, sir. From Swansea. coal mining, " Bryn replied.

Blackwood nodded thoughtfully. "You watch things differently from the others. They're looking for a theory to memorize. You're looking for practical application."

The observation was accurate enough to be unsettling. Bryn had noticed himself doing exactly that: mentally translating everything into terms he understood, seeing water systems like mine drainage and disease transmission like gas seepage.

"Nevertheless," Blackwood continued, "you've got a keen eye and ask

Chapter 8: Invisible Enemies

questions that matter. Join me for tea tomorrow afternoon, lad. I want to hear about your experience in the mines."

The next afternoon, Bryn navigated the maze of corridors at Kasr El Aini Medical Center, searching for Blackwood's office. The medical school seemed different from the military hospital: older, more organic in its growth, with wings and additions that appeared to have sprouted based on need rather than plan.

Blackwood's office, when he finally found it, reflected the complexity of its occupant. Medical texts and journals crowded shelves alongside books on history, philosophy, and engineering. Maps covered one wall, showing disease outbreaks across the Empire, marked with colored pins, much like military campaigns fought against invisible enemies. The desk was a chaotic mess. Reports, correspondence, and laboratory results were arranged in piles that made sense only to their creator.

"Sit down, Williams," Blackwood said, gesturing toward a worn leather armchair in the corner, its stuffing compressed from years of supporting worried bodies. "Tell me about the mining. What did you learn about keeping men alive in dangerous places?"

The question was more complex than it appeared. Bryn settled into the chair, accepting the cup of tea Blackwood offered, and tried to find words for knowledge that had always been more feeling than thought.

"You watch for signs," Bryn said carefully, stirring his tea while memories of pit ponies and canary cages flickered through his mind like lamp flames in darkness. "Gas in the air; you can smell it sometimes, or see how it makes the flame burn differently. Sounds that don't belong, like timber creaking where it shouldn't, water running where there's supposed to be none. But mostly you learn to trust the men around you, because they're all that stands between you and the dark."

Blackwood leaned forward, his attention complete. "And when the signs appeared? When you knew there was danger?"

"You warned everyone you could. You didn't wait for orders from the surface, because by then it might be too late." Bryn paused, remembering the faces of men who hadn't made it out. "Sometimes you had to choose between following company rules and keeping people alive. We usually choose the men."

"Disease is like gas in the mines, isn't it?" Blackwood said with the understanding of someone who had fought his own battles against death. "Invisible, silent, lethal if you don't know the signs."

That first conversation stretched through the afternoon and into early evening. Blackwood shared stories of fighting cholera in Indian slums where death moved faster than gossip and proved just as deadly, and of bureaucrats who debated procedures in offices while bodies piled up in the streets below. He spoke of the frustration of watching preventable diseases kill people whose only crime was poverty, and the small victories that came from understanding how illness traveled through communities like poison through a water supply.

When Bryn finally left the office, the sun was setting over Cairo, painting the medical school's corridors in shades of amber and shadow. He walked back to Abbassia with his head full of new ideas and the strange feeling that he'd found something he hadn't known he was looking for.

The training program settled into a routine over the following weeks. Mornings at Abbassia with Captain Thornton covering regulations and procedures, and afternoons with Major Blackwood at Kasr El Aini, focused on the practical applications that made the regulations important. Bryn found he had a talent for the technical drawings needed in their reports. Years of sketching had taught him to see spatial relationships clearly and to capture complex systems with simple lines that could be understood by people who had never seen the reality they depicted.

"These technical drawings of yours are excellent," Blackwood remarked one afternoon, examining Bryn's notebook filled with water system diagrams and housing sketches. "We need more people who can communicate complex ideas clearly. Too many of our reports get buried in jargon that helps no one and heals nothing."

The other trainees began to form their own connections with the material and with each other. O'Brien and Davies shared a love of practical jokes that helped ease tension during challenging lectures. Singh's military background proved very helpful when they studied procedures for medical response in emergencies. Peterson's quiet observations often pinpointed the core of issues that others tried to complicate unnecessarily. Thompson's bureaucratic experience assisted them in navigating the administrative requirements that would shape their future work.

But it was with Blackwood that Bryn felt most at ease, during those afternoon conversations that stretched long past the official end of training. The Major had a gift for listening without judgment, asking questions that opened doors rather than closing them.

"Tell me about Wales," Blackwood said one evening as they sat in his office watching Cairo's eternal dust dance in shafts of golden light. "What was it like growing up in the valley?"

The question reopened memories Bryn hadn't explored in months. He found himself describing the unique quality of light that came through Welsh rain, how sound traveled differently in mountain air, and the sense of community that arose from knowing everyone's business and having them know yours. He talked about poverty, hunger, and his estrangement from his family.

Chapter 8: Invisible Enemies

"It sounds like a place that shapes the people who come from it," Blackwood observed.

"Aye, it does that. For better and worse." Bryn paused, considering. "But I couldn't stay there. I was not wanted. The best part of my life was living with my Aunt Eileen after leaving home at fourteen."

Blackwood nodded with the understanding of someone who had made his own difficult choices about where to belong. "Sometimes we have to leave home to figure out what home actually means."

"The Stoics would say we carry home with us: that it's not a place but a way of being," Bryn said. "Maybe leaving Wales wasn't running away. Maybe it was running toward something I couldn't see from the valley."

Blackwood smiled a broad grin and nodded. Nothing needed to be said.

The first real test of their training came in the fourth week, when reports of typhoid reached Kasr El Aini from a crowded neighborhood near the Citadel. Captain Thornton assigned the investigation to Blackwood, who surprised everyone by requesting that the trainee inspectors accompany him. "This is what the work actually looks like," he told them as they loaded equipment into a borrowed military truck. "Not lectures or examinations, but people getting sick and dying while we try to figure out why."

The neighborhood they entered was a maze of narrow alleys and overcrowded tenements, built layer after layer over generations without planning or oversight. The first thing they noticed was the smell—cooking fires, human waste, garbage, and beneath it all, the sickly-sweet odor indicating disease had taken hold.

Blackwood guided them to a house where three children from the same family had become sick within a week. The mother, a young woman who couldn't have been more than twenty-five but appeared older, watched them approach with the wary suspicion that experience had taught her. "We're here to help," Blackwood said in Arabic, his pronunciation careful but clear. The woman's expression softened slightly, although she kept her distance.

"He speaks their language," Bryn mused. *"Actually speaks to them, not at them."*

What followed was a careful dance of investigation and diplomacy. Blackwood examined the family's water source, a shared pump serving six buildings, showing signs of contamination from a nearby privy. He traced the paths the sick children had taken through the neighborhood, identifying other families who might be at risk. He asked about food preparation, about where clothes were washed, about a dozen seemingly unrelated details that slowly built a picture of how disease had entered and spread through this small community.

Throughout it all, he treated the residents not as obstacles to overcome but as partners in solving a puzzle that threatened everyone. He listened to the grandmother who believed the illness was caused by evil winds, then gently explained how understanding the true source could protect other children. He collaborated with the local *imam* to arrange proper disinfection procedures that wouldn't conflict with religious requirements. He took notes in both Arabic and English, making sure that local authorities could follow up on his recommendations.

Bryn found himself thinking of Yasmine, of what she'd said about British certainty and Egyptian wisdom. Watching Blackwood work, he saw a different possibility. Not the certainty of conquest, but the humility of collaboration.

The investigation took most of the day. By evening, they had identified the contamination source, arranged for temporary alternative water supplies, and begun the contact tracing that would prevent further spread. It was careful, methodical work that reminded Bryn of the patience needed to map dangerous mine conditions, one careful step at a time, always watching for signs that might reveal hidden threats.

That night, riding back to Abbassia in the truck's bed under stars that seemed impossibly bright after the day's intensity, one of the other trainees, Singh, voiced what they were all thinking. "That wasn't what I expected."

"What did you expect?" asked Blackwood asked.

"More... authority, I suppose. More giving orders and having them obeyed," Singh replied.

Thompson nodded agreement. "In Manchester, sanitary inspectors were like police. People feared them."

"Fear doesn't cure disease," Blackwood observed quietly. "It just drives it underground."

Bryn realized that Blackwood had been teaching them something more valuable than procedures or regulations. He had been showing them how to see people as allies in their own health rather than as problems to be solved or obstacles to overcome.

Master Sergeant Evans kept his fatherly interest despite Bryn's civilian status, scheduling regular Friday afternoon meetings that became as essential as chapel services back home. His office in the base administration building felt like a refuge from the complexity of medical school, with its familiar military order and Evans's reassuring presence.

Bryn! Get in here and tell me what you've learned this week," Evans would boom, his voice carrying the authority of decades spent shaping young men into

Chapter 8: Invisible Enemies

something better than they'd been when they arrived. Despite his gruff exterior, the Master Sergeant Evans possessed a keen interest in developing talent, particularly fellow Welshmen who understood that strength came from community rather than conquest.

Their weekly meetings had become sacred times that Bryn eagerly anticipated. Evans listened intently as Bryn shared his training progress, occasionally interrupting with sharp questions that revealed surprising knowledge of public health issues. "Had to deal with my share of outbreaks in the field," Evans explained when Bryn commented on this unexpected expertise. "Nothing teaches you the importance of proper sanitation like watching dysentery tear through your unit like fire through a dry shaft." His weathered face would turn serious during these moments, as he recalled the challenges that had tested every lesson he had learned about keeping men alive in hostile environments.

Evans also offered a perspective that balanced Blackwood's idealism with military pragmatism. When Bryn described their collaborative approach to disease investigation, Evans nodded approvingly but added cautions based on experience. "That's good work, lad, treating people like partners instead of problems. But remember, you're still wearing the King's uniform, even if you're now in civilian clothes. Some folks will trust you because of that, while others will hate you for it. Your job is to figure out which is which and act accordingly."

Between Blackwood's medical expertise and Evans's practical military experience, Bryn received an education that extended far beyond the official curriculum. He was learning not only technical skills but also the human wisdom that gave those skills their true meaning. The earnest but uncertain young man who had arrived at Abbassia was becoming more confident, capable, and aware of his role in the complex machinery of Empire and healing.

The formal training ended with a ceremony that felt more meaningful than Bryn had anticipated. Captain Thornton awarded each graduate their certification and assignment orders, while Blackwood gave individual comments that showed how closely he had observed each person's progress. "Bryn Williams," Blackwood said when it was his turn, "you've shown real talent for this work. More importantly, you've demonstrated the kind of character that makes the difference between just following procedures and truly healing communities."

That evening, Blackwood invited Bryn to his office for a private farewell that felt more meaningful than official ceremonies. The Major had prepared two gifts that seemed heavier than they looked, filled with meaning beyond their material worth. The first was a well-used copy of Sir John Simon's *English Sanitary Institutions*, its pages marked by years of use and annotated with notes in Blackwood's careful handwriting. The inscription read: "*To Bryn Williams. May you always remember that our work serves humanity first, the Empire second. Your friend and colleague, Hugh Blackwood."*

The second gift was Blackwood's own brass microscope, a veteran of many investigations across three continents; its case, smooth from handling, spoke of late-night examinations and careful dawn observations. The instrument was elegantly made, with precision optics and mechanical adjustments that showcased the finest British engineering used in medical science. "This old fellow has helped me solve more mysteries than I can count," Blackwood said, patting the microscope's case with the affection of a miner for a trusted lamp. "Now it's your turn to put it to good use."

"Sir, thank you sir, I am honored," Bryn said earnestly.

They sat in comfortable silence for a moment, the weight of transition settling between them like dust after blasting. Bryn understood that this was more than the end of training. It was the beginning of responsibility that would shape the rest of his life.

"Major," he said finally, "I want to thank you for... well, for seeing something in me that I didn't see in myself."

Blackwood smiled, the expression warming his weathered features like sunrise over familiar hills. "You had it all along, lad. I just helped you recognize it."

Chapter 9

Mountain Meets Water

"The Chinese have medical traditions that go back thousands of years. Their understanding of health and disease is connected to concepts we barely grasp: balance, harmony, and invisible energies. You'll find resistance to Western medicine, not out of ignorance but because of different knowledge."

Major Hugh Blackwood

The news that would change everything arrived on a scorching Cairo afternoon when the heat felt like a heavy weight and even the ceiling fans seemed to struggle against the stifling air. Blackwood's office felt like a furnace despite the closed windows and the pitcher of ice water that melted almost as fast as it was refilled.

"Hong Kong, sir?" Bryn stood before the Major's desk, transfer notice trembling in hands that had grown steady over months of learning to heal instead of hurt.

"I would have preferred for you to stay here in Cairo," Blackwood said, moving to the large map that dominated one wall of his office. "There's important work to be done in Egypt, and you've shown real understanding of local conditions. But there were no positions available in the Egyptian health service, and Hong Kong presents... different challenges and opportunities."

"What's Hong Kong like?" Bryn queried. Blackwood pointed to the small dot on the map that represented the colony, impossibly distant from everything Bryn had come to understand about his place in the world.

Less than a century ago, Hong Kong consisted of fishing villages and salt farms spread across islands that most maps didn't bother to name. The Tanka boat people lived on their junks, following seasonal fishing patterns that had sustained them for generations. Hakka farmers worked the rugged land, growing just enough to survive in a landscape that seemed designed to test human endurance.

Blackwood's finger traced shipping routes across the South China Sea, paths worn by centuries of trade that connected Hong Kong to networks stretching from

Singapore to Shanghai. "The Canton System kept foreign traders under tight control, limiting them to specific areas and seasons, requiring them to work through Chinese intermediaries who understood both cultures. It was orderly, profitable for all parties involved, and likely sustainable. Until the opium trade changed everything," he said.

His expression darkened with the weight of historical knowledge that carried personal implications for anyone wearing a British uniform, civilian or military. "British merchants selling Indian opium to China. Quite profitable, at least until Emperor Daoguang decided that flooding his country with drugs might not be in his people's best interests. He had over twenty thousand chests of opium destroyed at Humen in 1839. The First Opium War gave us Hong Kong Island as compensation for that destroyed opium. The Second Opium War took Kowloon Peninsula when we decided the island wasn't quite enough."

Blackwood spread photographs across his desk, images that captured a city caught between different worlds and centuries. Victorian architecture rose alongside traditional Chinese temples, their distinct approaches to the relationship between earth and sky creating a skyline that belonged to no single culture. Steamships shared Victoria Harbor with ancient junks whose designs had remained unchanged since Marco Polo's era, their coexistence representing the uneasy marriage of tradition and progress that defined colonial life.

"Look at it now," Blackwood continued, his voice carrying both pride and regret. "Victoria Harbor's one of the finest natural ports in the world, with British trading firms dominating commerce that connects China to markets they could never have imagined. We're building a modern city on five-thousand-year-old foundations, and sometimes the ground shifts in ways we don't expect."

The photographs showed European merchants in white suits conducting business alongside Chinese traders in silk robes, their negotiations happening in languages neither group fully understood but both had learned to navigate out of necessity and mutual benefit.

"And the Chinese population, sir?" Bryn asked, though he suspected he already knew the answer from Blackwood's tone.

Blackwood's pause carried the weight of problems that had no easy solutions, the kind of silence that preceded difficult truths. "That's where you come in, lad." His voice grew serious, carrying weight that had nothing to do with military rank and everything to do with human responsibility. "The city's growing faster than anyone can manage. Chinese districts are overcrowded, unsanitary by any reasonable standard, but they're home to people who've created functioning communities under impossible conditions."

He pulled out photographs of crowded tenements that seemed to defy gravity

Chapter 9: Mountain Meets Water

and common sense equally. Buildings rose five stories without obvious foundations, connected by walkways and additions that had been added as families grew and needs changed.

"These are *tong lau*, traditional Chinese tenements. Five stories, shared kitchens, communal facilities, extended families living in spaces that were never designed for so many people. That's where most of the Chinese population lives, and where disease spreads like wildfire when conditions are right."

He continued. "When a plague hit in 1894, it revealed all the flaws in our way of governance. We had rules made for English towns, sanitation standards suited for London's climate, and building codes based on European middle-class lifestyles. None of these reflected the reality of Chinese family structures, traditional building techniques, or the economic limits that forced people to make do with whatever shelter they could find."

Blackwood moved to the window, where Cairo spread below them like a lesson in the complexity of governing people who remembered what life was like before you arrived to improve it. The eternal dance of old and new, sacred and secular, traditional and progressive played out in the streets below with a vitality that no amount of regulation could fully contain or control.

"The Chinese have medical traditions that go back thousands of years," Blackwood continued, his voice carrying respect that many colonial officials would have found incomprehensible. "Their understanding of health and disease is connected to concepts we barely grasp: balance, harmony, invisible energies that flow through the body like underground rivers. You'll find resistance to Western medicine, not out of ignorance but because of different knowledge that's served them well for longer than Britain has existed."

He returned to his desk and took out a bottle of whiskey, pouring two glasses with the careful ceremony that such conversations seem to call for. The amber liquid caught Cairo's afternoon light, glowing like trapped sunshine or frozen time.

"The city's at a crossroads, lad. The British administration and wealthy merchants live high atop Victoria Peak, in mansion houses with spectacular views and good ventilation, making decisions about people they rarely see and communities they don't understand. Chinese traditions in the crowded districts below, adapting ancient wisdom to modern problems with mixed success. Steam-powered ships in the harbor sit alongside junks that were old when Marco Polo was young, their coexistence creating new possibilities neither culture expected.

Bryn accepted the whiskey, feeling its warmth spread through his chest like courage or foolishness, both of which seemed equally necessary for what lay ahead.

Blackwood said, settling into his chair with deliberate movements as a man choosing his words carefully, "Your job isn't just about sanitation. It's about finding a way forward that respects both worlds, that acknowledges the wisdom in Chinese traditions while addressing the health challenges created by modern urban density."

The whiskey was seeping into Bryn's thoughts like warmth spreading through cold stone, revealing connections he might not have noticed in the harsh light of sobriety. The parallels between colonial Hong Kong and colonial Wales were becoming impossible to ignore.

"Hong Kong's Governor is aggressively promoting modernization," Blackwood continued, "by enforcing building regulations based on London standards that don't work well in subtropical heat and monsoon rains. Meanwhile, the Chinese community follows practices that were effective for their ancestors but don't always suit the density of modern city living. Both sides are right and both sides are wrong, depending on your viewpoint.

"You'll be working with Dr. A. R. Wellington, the Chief Sanitary Inspector, who heads the sanitation branch of the colony's health service. Wellington is a good man but he tends to see the Chinese population as medical problems to be solved rather than people with their own wisdom to contribute."

Blackwood leaned forward, his expression intense with the urgency of lessons that can't be taught through lectures or textbooks. "Your strength, Bryn, is that you've learned to see people as partners instead of subjects. You've realized that the best solutions come from understanding rather than forcing, from listening rather than lecturing. That's exactly what Hong Kong needs. It needs someone who can bridge the gap between official policy and human reality."

The implications for Bryn were becoming clear, and they were both exciting and frightening. Hong Kong would challenge everything he'd learned about medicine, diplomacy, and the subtle art of helping without patronizing. "What if the Chinese ways work better than ours?" Bryn asked, the whiskey making him more daring than wisdom might recommend. "What if we're trying to fix things that aren't broken?"

Blackwood smiled, his weathered features brightening like a sunrise over familiar hills. "Now you're asking the right questions, lad. That's exactly why I recommended you for this posting." He raised his glass in a salute, the gesture carrying the weight of blessing and challenge in equal measure. "To Hong Kong, where mountain meets water, where East confronts West, and where a young Sanitary Inspector might just learn that healing has more to do with understanding than authority."

As Bryn sipped his whiskey, his mind filled with images of ancient traditions blending with Imperial ambitions: wooden junks navigating among iron steamships that belched smoke into air that had known only wind and weather;

Chapter 9: Mountain Meets Water

Chinese physicians with knowledge older than Britain itself working alongside Edinburgh-trained doctors who thought they understood the human body; colonial administrators making decisions about people whose ancestors had been solving similar problems for thousands of years.

The posting letter in his pocket felt heavy with responsibility, both frightening and necessary. Through the window, the sun was setting over Cairo, painting the sky in shades of gold and crimson that reminded him of Welsh twilight filtered through industrial smoke.

A muezzin's call drifted through the evening air, reminding him of lessons learned in this ancient city where cultures had been meeting and blending for thousands of years. He had learned to see through Yasmine's eyes, to question assumptions about civilization and progress that had once seemed as natural as breathing when he left Wales.

The microscope Blackwood had given him would help him see invisible threats to human health, but the deeper insight, the ability to see people as partners rather than problems, would prove even more valuable.

Outside, Cairo kept its eternal dance between past and future, sacred and secular, traditional and modern. Soon he would leave this city that had taught him so much about the complexity of human communities and the delicate art of bridging different worlds.

"The art of living is more like wrestling than dancing," Bryn thought. *"In Wales, I was dancing to other people's music. In Egypt, I've learned to wrestle with questions that had no easy answers. In Hong Kong, perhaps I'll find my own rhythm between the two."*

Chapter 10

Foreign Ghosts

"Watch yourself when they start treating you like a gentleman, Williams. That's when Empire's got its hooks deepest. Poor boys who taste silk pajamas will do terrible things to keep them."

Master Sergeant Evans

Salt spray stung Bryn Williams's face as HMS *Eastway* sliced through the swells beneath the gray morning light. Alexandria's white buildings had disappeared three days earlier, though the train ride from Cairo still felt fresh in his mind.

The *Eastway* was built for endurance rather than comfort, her cargo holds filled with manufactured goods while her passenger quarters housed civilians sailing toward uncertain futures. Captain McAllister remained on his bridge watching gauges. The Lascars (non-European seamen) operated the engine rooms with practiced ease, their voices calling across the deck in languages Bryn was gradually learning to understand.

In the cramped saloon reserved for civilian passengers, mahogany panelling absorbed conversations that drifted between hope and homesickness. The brass fixtures caught lamplight that swayed with the ship's movement, casting shadows that danced like memories refusing to stay buried. Bryn mostly kept to himself, reading medical texts by day, sketching and writing in his leather journal by night, and recording observations that might prove useful in whatever awaited him ahead.

Old deckhand John Henderson, whose weathered face told of decades battling waves and weather, spat tobacco juice over the rail before sharing his wisdom. "City of devils and opportunities, boy. Chinese call us gwai lo, foreign ghosts. Reckon they're not wrong, considering what we've done to earn the name."

During the voyage, he met Dr. Margaret Sinclair in the ship's small library. She looked up from her medical text, her gray eyes sharp with intelligence that reminded him of Yasmine's careful way of watching the world. "Can't sleep either?" she asked, her Scottish accent softened after years in the Empire. "The heat makes resting impossible."

"The mind keeps churning when the body can't settle." Bryn selected a volume from the shelf. "You're heading to Shanghai?"

"To study traditional medicine." She marked her place, extending her hand in greeting. "Dr. Sinclair. British Army?"

"Bryn Williams…Ex-Corporal Williams. Still feels strange wearing civilian clothes," Bryn replied amiably.

"What drew you to leave the service?" Sinclair enquired.

"I started questioning whether the uniform made me a better man or just a more effective one. Spent seven years in Egypt watching us improve people who never asked for improvement," he replied.

Dr. Sinclair nodded, her expression suggesting complicated feelings about Empire's good intentions. "Shanghai's much the same. British merchants convinced they're bringing civilization to people who invented writing while we were still painting ourselves blue."

"And you? What takes a doctor to Shanghai?" Bryn asked.

"Research. I'm studying traditional Chinese medicine and how it might complement Western practices. Her smile held edges that spoke of professional challenges faced and overcome. "My colleagues think I'm chasing folklore and superstition. But I've seen too many patients recover from treatments that shouldn't work according to our understanding."

They talked until the oil lamps flickered low. Both were leaving behind certainties to pursue work that might bridge worlds kept deliberately apart.

"Your work in Hong Kong," she said as they prepared to part. "Don't let them convince you that Western methods are always better. Sometimes the old ways last because they work, not because people are too ignorant to change."

They parted, wishing each other honest and warm goodbyes.

Singapore passed by in a haze of white colonial buildings rising from lush green jungle. Malaysian *dhows* shared harbor space with British steamers, their sails catching the wind that carried scents of nutmeg and wild plants beyond civilization's reach.

The South China Sea challenged them with harsh weather changes. Hong Kong appeared through the morning mist like something from a dream. Mountain silhouettes rose sharply from the water, with Victoria Peak dominating the skyline like a sleeping dragon. The city spread out in layers. Colonial buildings lined the lower slopes in neat rows, their white walls and red roofs as orderly as mine shafts. Below, Chinese districts sprawled in tighter clusters, with rooflines flowing like water finding its level.

Chapter 10: Foreign Ghosts

The harbor contained everything that could float. British steamers dominated the deep channels, Chinese junks operated in the shallows, and sampans hurried between larger vessels with expert agility. Sound moved across the water with impressive clarity: men shouting orders in English and Cantonese, cargo cranes creaking, women's voices echoing from the sampans where families spent entire lives on the water.

The air told stories. Salt and coal smoke formed familiar base notes. Over them floated scents that belonged to no Welsh valley: dried fish, burning spices, sweet incense, and something indefinable but utterly foreign that spoke of histories stretching back before Britain was more than warriors hiding in forests.

Captain McAllister called him to the bridge, his Scottish accent thick with concern that had nothing to do with weather patterns. His weathered hands adjusted the wheel with movements that spoke of decades fighting wind and wave. "Hong Kong's got its own kind of darkness, Williams. Beautiful as a siren's song and twice as treacherous."

"What should I expect?" Bryn asked, hoping to gain as much knowledge from everyone he could.

"Seven hundred thousand souls packed tighter than coal in a ship's bunker. Chinese districts that climb the hillsides like terraced gardens but filled with people instead of vegetables." The captain's voice carried the weight of experience earned through countless voyages to ports that held their own secrets. "The British live up on The Peak, cool air and clean views. The Chinese work down below in heat that'd melt a Scotsman's resolve."

McAllister's expression grew thoughtful, his eyes reflecting knowledge gained through watching ports change over decades of empire-building. "You'll be walking into neighborhoods where diseases move faster than gossip and politics run deeper than any mine shaft you've known. The Chinese have their ways of dealing with sickness, Williams. Ways that go back thousands of years before we arrived with our regulations and good intentions."

"Any advice for staying alive long enough to do some good?" Bryn asked.

"Listen more than you talk. Watch more than you act." The captain's Scottish accent grew thicker with emotion, hinting at personal experience behind the words. "The Chinese aren't savages needing civilization, no matter what some might tell you. They're people trying to survive in a world that's changing faster than they can understand."

Hong Kong emerged through the morning mist like something out of a dream or prophecy. First, mountain silhouettes rose from the water with improbable steepness, their peaks shrouded in clouds that looked soft as Welsh wool but likely held their own storms. Victoria Peak dominated the skyline like a sleeping dragon, its massive form both beautiful and menacing against a sky that shifted between gray and gold.

The gangplank lowered with precise mechanical movement, while dock workers moved with choreographed efficiency that revealed many repetitions. Chinese coolies carried cargo, and British officials checked manifests with the careful attention of mine inspectors reviewing safety reports. The mixture of voices formed a symphony of commerce that had its own rhythm, its own logic, and its own risks.

Bryn shouldered his kit, feeling the weight of Blackwood's microscope case against his shoulder and Evans's book pressed against his ribs where he had tucked it inside his jacket. The crowd pressed around him with energy that reminded him of pit shifts changing, hundreds of men moving with shared purpose through spaces too small to hold them all comfortably.

Above the Dragon

Waiting on shore for Bryn was Sanitation Department Inspector David Bristol, a middle-aged man with an air of authority. "Urgent reports from the Western District require my attention," he explained, sketching a quick map. "Give this to your taxi driver. Follow Queen's Road Central west, then up Garden Road. Look for the Europeans heading home to the Peak." Bristol quickly flagged down a taxi, leaving Bryn to endure the afternoon heat that pressed against him like furnace breath from deep underground.

Central on Hong Kong Island at sunset revealed its colonial machinery running at full tilt. Government workers left their offices, their faded white uniforms damp with humidity, standing out from Chinese workers who moved with practiced efficiency. Rickshaw pullers shouted in rapid Cantonese, competing like auctioneers at a mineral rights sale.

The Peak Tram station displayed Victorian details that seemed more fitting for Bath than for tropical China. Inside, wood-paneled walls echoed conversations in English, German, and Portuguese. Bryn purchased his ticket from a Chinese clerk who switched easily between Cantonese and English. The tram rose toward cool air and clear views bought with others' suffering. As Hong Kong changed beneath him, Bryn saw the social landscape shift with every foot of altitude gained.

Peak Mansions emerged from the mist like lost European grandeur. The building's Victorian architecture sharply contrasted with the surrounding foliage, its red brick and white-trimmed windows evoking Liverpool.

The Chinese doorman stood sharp in his white uniform, with brass buttons shining. "Good evening, Master. You must be Mr. Williams. Your Head Boy, Ah-

Chapter 10: Foreign Ghosts

Min, is expecting you in apartment 3B." The marble-floored lobby radiated a sense of bought luxury: potted palms, rattan furniture, and a ceiling fan lazily turning, indifferent to the heat rising from the city below.

The door to 3B opened just as Bryn reached for it. A dignified older Chinese man stood waiting, his white jacket spotless, his demeanor reflecting years of service combined with unmistakable self-respect. "Welcome to your home, Master Williams. I am Wong Chun Min, but you may call me Ah-Min. I am your Head Boy, the Hong Kong equivalent of a British personal valet."

The apartment stretched out before him with high ceilings and large windows designed to catch the evening breezes. Bryn's trunk sat in the middle of the living room, surrounded by colonial furniture: leather armchairs, a writing desk positioned to overlook the harbor, and empty bookshelves waiting for books.

Bryn watched as Ah-Min began unpacking his trunks with methodical care, arriving earlier and evaluating each piece of clothing before placing it properly. His medical books were organized by size, photographs were arranged on the mantel, and writing materials were spread across the desk in precise patterns. Watching Ah-Min move through the apartment, Bryn sensed depths beneath the surface: acceptance without resignation, service without servility, a kind of philosophical grace that turned mundane tasks into something close to meditation. Even his silence felt intentional—not the silence of submission, but of someone who had learned when words matter and when they only add clutter. There was something about Ah-Min's manner that hinted at years of study, not just of service but of life itself.

"Your housekeeper and cook, Wu Mei Lan, although you can call her Mrs. Wu, is preparing dinner," Ah-Min continued, his tone remaining formally neutral. "She has extensive experience with European families and understands Western preferences."

The kitchen was at the back of the apartment, where Bryn met a strong woman in her mid-forties moving confidently at the stove. She turned and gave a slight bow, her round face showing genuine warmth. "Good evening, Master. Dinner will be ready at eight unless you prefer a different time."

"Eight is perfect, thank you, Mrs. Wu," Bryn replied.

The apartment's western windows offered a sweeping view of Victoria Harbor. As night fell, ship lights began twinkling like scattered coins on black velvet, while Central's lights created a glittering carpet where Chinese laborers still worked by torchlight.

In the bedroom, Ah-Min arranged fresh clothes with careful precision: a crisp white shirt, pressed trousers, and a light smoking jacket. "Dinner is served, Master," Ah-Min announced at exactly eight, gesturing toward the dining room.

The table, set for one, displayed colonial etiquette: starched linen, bone China, silver cutlery reflecting light.

As Bryn took his seat, Ah-Min gracefully unfolded a napkin across his lap. "We begin with soup, Master," he announced as Mrs. Wu entered carrying a tureen. "Clear consommé of Chinese ham and winter melon, prepared in the traditional manner but suited to European tastes."

The meal proceeded with perfect coordination between his servants, their efficiency flawless but distant. No unnecessary conversation, no personal details shared.

"I understand you have worked for several European families, Mrs. Wu," Bryn ventured.

"Yes, Master. Each family has different requirements. We learn what is needed." Her answer was polite but revealed nothing personal.

As the meal ended, Ah-Min offered some English breakfast tea. "Would you prefer your tea outside on the terrace, Master? The evening air is delightful, and the harbor view is especially lovely at this hour."

On the terrace, before Bryn could light his cigarette, Ah-Min handed him a silver case. "Chief Inspector Wellington sends this with his compliments." Bryn opened the case to reveal a stack of business cards with his name and title embossed. "Is there anything else I can do for you at this time, Master?"

"No, thank you Ah-Min. I think I'll retire early. Tomorrow will need me alert," Bryn replied.

Ah-Min bowed with dignity that endured despite circumstances meant to diminish it. "I have laid out nightclothes. The silk will be more comfortable in this climate.

Later, lying in bed wearing silk pajamas, Bryn's thoughts drifted between his current luxury and memories of Welsh winters when his family went to bed hungry. The irony wasn't lost on him.

As sleep began to claim him, his thoughts drifted. Bryn realized that Britain had exported more than governance to its colonies. It had transplanted entire social structures, with rigid class divisions intensified by racial prejudice. The answer was in the silk pajamas and sterling silver, in the harbor view and the bell that called servants with a gentle ring. The Empire provided them a lifestyle they could never afford at home, made them complicit in their own rise, then watched as conscience fought comfort, and comfort usually won. The weight of that realization settled in his chest, one that would only grow heavier as he learned more about how the Empire functioned.

Chapter 11

City of Darkness

"Watch yourself when they start treating you like a gentleman, Williams. That's when Empire's got its hooks deepest. Poor boys who taste silk pajamas will do terrible things to keep them."

Sergeant Evans

The gentle chime of Bryn's alarm echoed through the bedroom right at 6:30 am. He shifted under Egyptian cotton sheets, their thousand-thread count a luxury against skin that still remembered rough Welsh wool. Outside his window, Hong Kong moved like a brewing storm before dawn, although up here on The Peak, the morning had a different feel, one of privilege and distance from the energy below.

A gentle knock at the door announced Ah-Min's arrival. "Good morning, Master," he said gently yet clearly. "Your bath is ready. Breakfast will be served in thirty minutes."

After his bath, Bryn dressed in his crisp white uniform, leaving the collar open against the rising heat. By the time he stepped into the dining area, Ah-Min had transformed the space into something straight out of a fever dream about gentility. The glass-topped dining table was set with bone china and sterling silver flatware. A freshly pressed copy of the South China Post lay folded beside his plate. "Tea Master?" Ah-Min asked, appearing with a silver pot of fresh black Ceylon tea.

"Please." Bryn watched him pour, the rich aroma rising from tea.

Mrs. Wu emerged from the kitchen with two perfectly poached eggs, their whites set just right, with yolks still luxuriously soft beneath. They sat on rustic sourdough from a French bakery in Central that delivered fresh to The Peak every morning. Bryn savored every delicious bite.

"Is everything satisfactory, sir?" Mrs. Wu inquired.

"Mrs. Wu, these are the best eggs I have ever tasted, thank you," Bryn replied. He found himself eating slowly and carefully, hyperaware that he was using silver cutlery while the woman who'd prepared his meal probably ate with chopsticks from ceramic bowls.

By 7:45 am, as he finished his tea, the mist had nearly vanished, revealing a breathtaking view of Hong Kong Island, Kowloon, and the South China Sea beyond. From this height, he could see everything but was detached from it all, precisely the position Empire intended for its servants.

At 8 am, Ah-Min announced that a Sanitary Department vehicle had arrived. "Your driver is waiting, Master. I have prepared your medical bag and papers." He paused, then added quietly, "If you are going to be outside a good part of the day, I'd suggest you take your hat. It will be hot today."

"Thank you, Ah-Min, a good suggestion. I'll just visit the lavatory and I'll be on my way," Bryn replied.

The Sanitation Department section of Hong Kong's health services division occupied a solid Victorian building on Queen's Road Central, its limestone facade proclaiming British efficiency. Inside, a Chinese receptionist directed Bryn to the second floor.

Dr. James Wellington, Chief Sanitation Inspector and head of the department, rose from behind a mahogany desk stacked with reports and maps. A man in his fifties with graying temples, he wore the colonial health service uniform with practiced authority.

"Williams! Welcome to Hong Kong." Wellington's handshake was firm, his Scottish accent carrying years of managing impossible situations. "I trust your travel from Egypt to your lodgings in Peak Mansions went well?"

"Yes, sir, the ship voyage was long but uneventful, and my lodgings are far more luxurious than I expected, including my house staff," Bryn replied.

"The colony treats its expats well, Bryn," Wellington replied. "Now, let's get you up and running quickly here. Inspector Bristol is out making his rounds, but I'll introduce you to a fellow Inspector Jason Lam after our discussion."

Wellington moved to a wall map of Hong Kong. "Right, let's get you oriented. Your territory covers Central and Western districts mainly, though you'll help elsewhere when needed. We handle restaurant inspections, tenement housing, water quality, waste removal and disease outbreaks." He tapped various sections of the map. "The challenge is we're operating where Chinese and British law often conflict, corruption runs deeper than you'd expect, and one contaminated well could kill thousands."

"What about cooperation from the population?" Bryn asked.

Wellington's expression darkened. "Mixed. Some Chinese people are genuinely helpful, others see us as foreign interference. A bigger problem is our

Chapter 11: City of Darkness

own ranks." He lowered his voice. "We've had inspectors taking bribes, overlooking violations, even warning restaurant owners before inspections. And the police force here has been riddled with corruption."

"How widespread?" Bryn asked.

"Enough that I'm careful who I trust with sensitive work." Wellington studied Bryn's face. "Your Egypt record suggests that won't be an issue with you. The work requires balance. Too aggressive, you create enemies who make your job impossible. Too lenient, people die from preventable diseases. You'll learn when to enforce regulations strictly and when to work with local customs that might seem backward but actually serve public health."

Wellington rang a small bell. "I'm assigning Inspector Lam for orientation. He knows the territory better than anyone, and has both communities' trust."

Jason Lam entered, his mixed heritage evident in features that bridged both sides. Wellington made introductions, then said, "Give him the full tour Jason, Central, Western, and the Walled City."

Jason nodded with understanding that suggested this was significant. "Of course, sir. We'll start with regulated areas, then cross to Kowloon."

"Bryn," Wellington said as they prepared to leave, "what you'll see today will either convince you this job is impossible or show you why it's necessary."

After shaking hands with Wellington, Bryn left his office and the building with Jason. They walked west along colonial streets, past maintained lawns surrounding government buildings. As they approached Queen's Road Central, the city's character began changing.

"My father worked as a comprador for Jardine's," Jason said suddenly. "One of the few Chinese permitted in European buildings. Even then, only through the side entrance."

They continued through districts where buildings gradually became less European, with colonial administrative structures giving way to Chinese businesses. The sidewalks narrowed and grew more crowded. The air shifted, becoming thicker and filled with scents of dried seafood, traditional medicine shops, and incense mixed with burning coal.

"The area we're heading to," Jason said as they walked, "isn't technically in your territory, but you'll be called to assist there. It's where the real challenges lie."

They approached the ferry harbor crossing. Across the water, the Walled City loomed like a fever dream made concrete. A chaotic jumble of buildings stacked haphazardly, defying gravity and sanity alike. Fourteen-story towers leaned dangerously, their walls meeting at impossible angles, creating nightmarish geometry that seemed to distort reality itself.

"Good God," Bryn breathed, stopping in his tracks. "That can't possibly meet any building standards."

Jason laughed, a short, sharp sound that held no humor. "Standards? There are not standards in there, Bryn. That's rather the point."

The stench reached them even from this distance: a complex miasma of cooking oil, sewage, and humanity packed too tightly together. Rotting garbage blended with acrid industrial chemicals, underlined by greasy frying food and sickly-sweet opium smoke.

"This is where British law has no teeth. Inside, it's another world, one that the Administration pretends doesn't exist because acknowledging it would require taking responsibility for it," Jason said.

"And we're expected to inspect there?" Bryn asked.

Jason nodded. "Occasionally. Though 'inspection' might be too formal a word. More like diplomatic missions. We go in, note the worst violations, make recommendations nobody follows, and leave before sunset. The key is to be seen making the effort without actually changing anything fundamental. All before sunset."

"Why sunset?" Bryn queried.

"Triads control everything after dark. During the day, they mostly leave government officials alone, bad for business otherwise. But night..." Jason shook his head. "Night belongs to them."

Bryn studied the impossible jumble of buildings. "How many people live in there?"

Jason looked up. "Best estimates? Between thirty and fifty thousand."

The Walled City grew larger and more impossible as they approached. What had seemed like architectural chaos from a distance revealed itself as something far more complex, a vertical village where every inch of space had been claimed, subdivided, and claimed again. The ingenuity of it was staggering, but so was the desperation that had made such ingenuity necessary.

"All stolen utilities," Jason explained as they drew closer. "They tap municipal water pipes, siphon electricity from the grid. Nothing metered, nothing regulated. Look there…" He pointed to a tangle of electrical wires strung between buildings like spider webs. "That's how they get power. Completely illegal, completely dangerous, completely necessary. One short circuit could burn the whole place down in minutes."

Chapter 11: City of Darkness

The smell hit him like a physical blow. Not just sewage and garbage, but the concentrated essence of too many people living in too small a space: cooking odors, unwashed bodies, medicinal herbs, incense, and something else he couldn't identify but that made his stomach turn. This morning he'd complained inwardly about Ah-Min using too much perfumed soap to clean his bathroom. Now he understood what luxury that complaint represented.

They approached one of the entrances, a narrow alley that seemed to swallow light like the opening of a mine shaft. "What exactly will be my responsibility here?" Bryn asked.

Jason stopped and turned to face him. "Your primary duties will be on Hong Kong Island and in regulated parts of Kowloon. But occasionally, we conduct wellness checks here. We focus on the most critical issues: raw sewage exposure, contaminated water sources, and disease clusters. It's about harm reduction, not solving the problem. Stay close," Jason murmured. "It's easy to get lost in here, and we don't want to wander into the wrong territory. Some areas are controlled by different Triad factions, and they don't appreciate unannounced visitors."

They moved through passages so narrow Bryn could touch both walls with outstretched arms. Above them, the buildings seemed to lean inward, creating a maze of courtyards and light wells that defied any logical plan. Pipes and electrical cables ran along the walls at eye level, dripping condensation and occasionally sparking. Children darted between their legs, laughing and shouting in Cantonese. Their clothes were patched but clean, their faces bright with the resilience of youth. One woman ran past carrying a bucket of water nearly as large as herself, navigating the treacherous footing with practiced ease.

"Water has to be carried up by hand," Jason explained, noting Bryn's attention. "No pumps, no pressure systems. Every drop climbs those stairs one bucket at a time. The woman who carried that water probably walked two miles today just fetching water for her family."

They passed a tiny restaurant, barely more than a hole in the wall with a charcoal stove and two stools. The owner, an elderly man with kind eyes, nodded respectfully as they went by. The smell of frying noodles mixed with the general miasma, and despite everything, Bryn's stomach growled.

"That man probably feeds fifty people a day," Jason said quietly. "No license, no health inspection, no official recognition. But his customers trust him, and nobody gets sick. Which raises the question: what exactly are we inspecting, and who are we really serving?"

"Disease?" Bryn asked, though he thought he already knew the answer.

"Tuberculosis, cholera, dysentery. Most cases are unreported. People treat themselves or visit unlicensed doctors inside. There's a dentist on the seventh floor of that building," Jason pointed upward, "who's been practicing for fifteen years without a license. Probably saved more teeth than the colonial dental service."

A woman emerged from a doorway carrying a basin of dirty water, which she threw directly onto the alley floor. The liquid ran down a groove worn into the pavement, joining other streams that eventually found their way to drains that may or may not have been connected to anything resembling a sewer system.

"How do residents respond to our presence?" Bryn asked.

"Mixed," Jason replied, "some welcome help, especially families with children. Others see us as an unwanted intrusion. Most are indifferent; they've learned to survive without government assistance."

"And the Triads?" Bryn asked.

Jason lowered his voice. "They watch us. Sometimes they send someone to accompany us, for our 'protection.' Really, to monitor what we're doing."

Bryn's gaze traveled upward along the ramshackle buildings. "And the other government authorities?"

Jason's face hardened. "Officially? The Walled City is a regrettable anomaly that will eventually be addressed. Unofficially? It's a convenient dumping ground. Chinese refugees, criminal elements, the desperately poor: keep them contained here, out of sight from colonial districts."

Bryn took a big breath. "And you? What's your view of all of this?"

Jason was silent for a moment. "I was born in Kowloon, not far from here. The Walled City isn't just a failure of urban planning; it's a monument to survival. These people have built their own society in the cracks between empires."

"How do you possibly manage disease control here?" Bryn asked. "I've seen rural villages with better sanitation."

"That's the impossible part of the job," Jason sighed. "We can't enforce regulations, can't seal off contaminated areas, can't properly track outbreaks. At best, we distribute medicine and information, hoping people listen and act of their own volition."

"The stagnant water alone is a breeding ground for mosquitoes," Bryn said.

"That's the least of our worries," Jason said grimly. "You know what keeps me awake at night? Plagues. Hong Kong faced outbreaks in 1894, 1901, and again in the 1920s. Thousands died. The conditions here are perfect for it. Or cholera. One contaminated water source, and we could lose half the population before we even identify the problem."

Bryn stared at the city. "So, what's the solution?"

Chapter 11: City of Darkness

Jason gave bitter laugh. "The plan, as far as I can tell, is containment. Keep any outbreaks isolated here. Protect the colonial districts at all costs. The Chinese residents are..." he hesitated, "expendable in the greater calculus."

"Don't you get discouraged?"

"Yes, often, but I'm committed to make life more liveable here, particularly for Chinese people. you know, in Chinese medicine, they believe disease comes from imbalance. Too much of one thing, not enough of another."

Jason led Bryn back to the Sanitation Department offices and introduced him to the remaining staff and his own office in silence, Jason sensing that Bryn had to process everything he saw and experienced.

When Bryn returned home that evening, the apartment's luxury felt obscene after seeing the Walled City. He stood in the doorway for a moment, taking in the electric lights that worked at the flip of a switch, the polished mahogany furniture that gleamed with regular care, the Persian carpet beneath his feet. The contrast to what he had seen was almost nauseating.

He found Ah-Min arranging fresh flowers. The older man looked up as Bryn entered, and for just a moment, his professional mask slipped enough to reveal genuine concern.

"You look troubled, sir," Ah-Min observed. "Was your first day... instructive?"

The choice of word was careful: not "good" or "successful," but "instructive," as if Ah-Min understood exactly what kind of education Bryn had received.

"Inspector Lam took me to the Walled City. He called it the City of Darkness," Bryn said. He moved to the sideboard where crystal decanters held whiskey and poured himself a measure, his hand shaking slightly.

Ah-Min paused in his flower arranging, and something flickered across his features: pain, perhaps, or recognition, before the professional expression returned. "It is... a very difficult place for many people."

"How can fifty thousand people live that way? And how am I supposed to make any difference? I'm one inspector with a bag of testing chemicals against... against human desperation itself," Bryn replied, exasperated.

Ah-Min continued arranging flowers, his movements precise but somehow tense. After a long moment, he spoke carefully. "In my... experience, Master, problems that seem impossible are often problems of... how you say... perspective."

"I'm not sure I follow," Bryn said quizzically.

Ah-Min set down the flowers and turned to face him, his expression remaining guarded but his voice carrying quiet intensity. "Perhaps... a man who sees a mountain thinks only of an obstacle. But water finds a way through the mountain. Not by fighting the mountain, but by... patience. By understanding where the mountain is weak, where it will accept change."

"I don't think I understand, Ah-Min," Bryn said.

Ah-Min sipped his tea thoughtfully before responding. "When I was a young boy, my father took me to see a mountain stream. The water crashed against rocks, sprayed into mist, and carved through stone. 'Water,' he told me, is soft, yet persistent. It does not fight the mountain; it finds its way through. Confucius teaches us that the superior man thinks of virtue; the small man thinks of comfort. In the Walled City, many think only of today's survival. But you must think of virtue, what is right, what is good, even when it seems impossible."

Bryn looked into his teacup, seeing his own reflection distorted by amber liquid. "But what practical difference can I make? The British administration doesn't seem to care about the Chinese people. The Triads control everything. The residents are just trying to survive."

"The Buddha teaches that a thousand candles can be lit from a single candle, and the life of that candle will not be shortened," Ah-Min replied with voice that carried certainty earned through years of contemplation. "You cannot save everyone at once. But each person you help, each child protected from disease, each family given clean water, each restaurant serving clean food, their light spreads to others. The rice farmer does not lament that he cannot harvest all fields at once. He tends the field before him, seed by seed, day by day."

Bryn shook his head. "And what if a plague breaks out? Or cholera? Jason says it's only a matter of time."

Ah-Min's eyes fixed on him with surprising intensity. "Then you will do what you can, with what you have, where you are. This is all any of us can do. The path of duty may be long and difficult, but it is still the path we must walk. This is what Confucius teaches us."

They drank tea in silence, the sounds of Hong Kong at night filtering through thin windows: distant boat horns, street vendors calling out their last sales, the omnipresent hum of a city that never truly slept. "Thank you, Ah-Min," he said simply.

"It is my duty to serve, Master. Will you require dinner at the usual time?" Ah-Min said abruptly, sensing Bryn needed to reflect.

"Yes, thank you," Bryn said thoughtfully.

Mrs. Wu served dinner with polite efficiency, though when she thought he wasn't looking, he caught her giving a small, approving nod at how he ate the fish:

Chapter 11: City of Darkness

properly, using chopsticks rather than demanding Western utensils. Such small gestures might mean nothing, or they might be the first steps toward the kind of trust he'd need to do any real good in this impossible place.

Later that evening, alone on his terrace overlooking the harbor lights, Bryn reflected on his first day. The Walled City represented everything wrong with colonial rule: exploitation, abandonment, and willful blindness to suffering. Meanwhile, he lived in luxury built on the same system that created the suffering. But perhaps that was exactly why he was here. Not to be another tool of oppression, but to use his position: his access, his authority, his resources, to help people in ways the system never intended. It would require the kind of careful navigation Ah-Min had warned him about, the patience of water finding its way through stone. He pulled out writing materials, knowing he could no longer postpone the letter he owed Aunt Eileen.

"18th October, 1935.

Peak Mansions, Hong Kong

Dear Auntie,

I'm writing this from a terrace overlooking Victoria Harbor, about to don my silk pajamas that cost more than you earned in a month, after dining on bone China while Chinese servants waited on me hand and foot.

You asked me to let you know which I'm becoming, broken or changed. I think I'm becoming something I didn't expect: angry. Not the helpless rage I felt in Wales watching the owners grind us down, or the frustrated solider in Cairo, having learned compassion for the people from Yasmine, but focused anger that might actually be useful.

They've given me an apartment that belongs in a London gentleman's club, complete with Chinese servants who maintain perfect professional distance. My Head Boy, Ah-Min, is clearly brilliant, but he treats me with the careful politeness you'd show a dangerous animal. Can't blame him. How many colonial officials has he served who started with good intentions and ended up as just another cog in the Empire's machine?

Today I toured something called the Walled City in Kowloon, a place where British law doesn't exist and fifty thousand people have built their own society in the cracks between empires. Children playing in sewage, families sharing spaces smaller than our old scullery, but also communities that work, trust networks that keep people alive, and wisdom about survival that goes back generations.

Here's what I realized: Sergeant Evans was right about Empire's seduction, but maybe not in the way he meant. They give you silk pajamas and harbor views to make you complicit, yes. But what if I can use their comfort against them? What if I can take their resources and redirect them toward the people they're meant to distract me from?

My colleague Jason Lam says the plan is containment. Keep disease isolated among the

Chinese so it doesn't reach colonial districts. Fifty thousand lives written off as acceptable losses. But I have inspection authority now, official stamps and seals, access to medicines and clean water. What if I used all of that not to contain problems but to actually solve them?

It would require walking a very careful line. Chief Inspector Dr. Wellington warned me that too much independence can destroy a career, and in Hong Kong, that apparently means more than just losing a job. But maybe that's exactly what this work needs: someone willing to risk their comfortable position for people who have no positions at all.

Remember your poultices that healed cuts faster than any army surgeon's stitches? You taught me that sometimes the old ways last because they work, not because people are too ignorant to change. I met people today who've created functioning communities in impossible spaces, who've built trust networks that keep families alive. Maybe my job isn't to impose British solutions on Chinese problems, but to learn their solutions and find ways to support them.

Please write back to me and tell me your thoughts. Tell me if I sound naive or if I sound like I'm finally learning out how to be useful. Sometimes a man needs his aunt to tell him when he's being an idealistic fool and when he's being the kind of fool the world needs more of.

I think about you every day and miss you dearly. I hope your health is good and you are managing well. I've enclosed twenty pounds to help you pay for whatever you need it for, and will send you something every month.

Your loving nephew,

Bryn."

He sealed the envelope, knowing it would reach Sketty weeks before he'd learned whether his hopes were naive dreams or the beginning of something that might actually matter.

Tomorrow would bring more challenges, more contradictions, more questions about how to use privilege as a tool for justice rather than just another comfortable prison. But at least now he understood the scale of what he was facing, and more importantly, the scale of what might be possible if he was clever enough, patient enough, and careful enough to navigate the dangerous waters between duty and conscience.

Chapter 12

The Price of Truth

"When you shine a light in dark corners, don't be surprised if the shadows bite back."

Old Morgan Thomas

The manila envelope felt heavier than it should, its corners already worn from Bryn's nervous handling. He sat in his cramped office on the third floor of the Sanitation Department building, watching dust motes dance in the afternoon sunlight streaming through windows streaked with Hong Kong's constant haze.

Bryn had quickly adapted to the demands of the job over seven months, and was connecting positively with the Chinese community. As was his custom, he carried his Leica camera with him on his rounds in the even he need some photographic evidence. Little did he know the photographs would reveal much more than the sanitary conditions in restaurants.

Inside the envelope in his hands were photographs and documents that could ruin a man's career, or his own. David Bristol accepting a thick envelope outside Marcello's Italian restaurant on Wellington Street. Bristol again, this time shoving cash behind Romano's Delicatessen near the Star Ferry pier. A third image showed him shaking hands with the elderly owner of Golden Dragon, the Cantonese restaurant that somehow passed every health inspection despite conditions that should have led to its immediate closure.

Bryn had spent three weeks documenting Bristol's activities, shadowing him through the maze of Sheung Wan's streets during what were supposed to be routine inspections. He watched from doorways as money exchanged hands with the practiced efficiency of men who had perfected this dance years ago. The proof was irrefutable. Yet, holding these images now, he felt not triumph but a growing unease that settled in his chest like the oppressive humidity of the colony.

The decision to approach his colleague Jason Lam first seemed logical. Jason was honest, capable, and had shown Bryn nothing but kindness since his arrival eight months earlier. If anyone would understand the need to expose Bristol's corruption, it would be Jason.

Ashes and Dawn

Jason's office was situated in a corner of the building with windows facing both north toward the harbor and west toward the Peak, where taipans and senior civil servants retreated each evening to escape the heat and noise of the city. His desk was carefully organized, with files arranged neatly, and a small jade Buddha sitting beside his official Colonial Service pen set. On the walls hung his certificates from King's College London alongside a scroll of Chinese calligraphy that Bryn had never asked him to translate.

"Got a minute?" Bryn asked, hovering in the doorway.

Jason looked up from a report he was reviewing, adjusting his wire-rimmed glasses. "For you? Always. Close the door." In his pressed white shirt and perfectly tied tie, he appeared every inch the proper colonial administrator; yet something in his demeanor always hinted at depths his official persona didn't reveal. He was born in Hong Kong to Chinese parents, educated in England, and returned to serve in a system that would never fully accept him despite his obvious skill. Maybe that explained the careful neutrality he kept, the way he observed everything while committing to nothing.

The latch clicked softly in the quiet room. Bryn sat into the worn leather chair across from Jason's desk, feeling the familiar give of cushions that had supported many colonial officers through numerous awkward conversations. He placed the envelope between them, like an offering or maybe an accusation.

"I found something. About David Bristol," Bryn said.

Jason's dark eyes carefully examined each photograph, his face remaining professionally neutral even as a fleeting emotion crossed his features, too brief to discern. He sighed deeply, the sound carrying the weight of a man who had seen too much and spoken too little for too many years. When he leaned back, his chair creaked with the familiar protest of government furniture bought in bulk and built to last decades rather than provide comfort.

The silence between them lingered, filled with the ambient sounds of the building around them: distant typewriters clicking in offices, the wheeze of old elevator machinery, footsteps echoing in corridors that felt both crowded and lonely. Outside, a street hawker called his wares in sing-song Cantonese, while nearby, a radio played American jazz, the saxophone's wail adding a note of melancholy to the tropical afternoon.

"And?" Jason's voice carried no inflection, but Bryn caught something in his stillness that felt like resignation rather than surprise.

"He's taking bribes, Jason. Cash for passing inspections that should fail. That's corruption." Bryn leaned forward, surprised by the vehemence in his own voice. The certainty that had carried him through weeks of surveillance now seemed somehow naive in the face of Jason's calm and composed demeanor.

Chapter 12: The Price of Truth

Jason rubbed his temples with his fingertips, a gesture Bryn had noticed during especially tough cases. The afternoon sunlight filtered through the venetian blinds, casting prison bar shadows across his face and emphasizing the fine lines that had appeared around his eyes during his years in service. When he spoke, his voice carried the weariness of a man who'd fought battles leaving no visible scars. "Look, Bryn. You're a good man who takes his job seriously. That's why I'm being straight with you." He pushed the photographs back across the desk with the deliberate care of someone handling evidence he'd rather not acknowledge. "This isn't news."

The words hit Bryn like cold water. He'd expected moral outrage, demands for immediate action, perhaps even gratitude for his diligence. Instead, he found himself confronting a truth that seemed to drain the strength from his convictions. If this wasn't news, then what did that say about the system he'd sworn to serve? What did it say about the men who served it?

"What do you mean?" Bryn asked incredulously.

"I mean, this is just how things work sometimes. Bristol's been here a long time. He has relationships. Important relationships."

"Relationships." Bryn thought of his own connections: his army buddy Tom Jones; Sergeant Evans from his army days; Jasmine, whose memory still occasionally ambushed him in unguarded moments; Major Blackwood, who had sparked a passion for sanitation; Auntie Eileen, who had raised him like a son; and now Ah-Min, his house servant who had become something close to a friend and advisor. All honest connections, built on mutual respect rather than mutual benefit.

But perhaps that distinction mattered less in Hong Kong than it did in Wales. Maybe survival there required different calculations, weighing integrity against influence, principle against pragmatism. The thought made him feel a little sick.

Jason leaned forward, clasping his hands on the desk. His gold signet ring, a family heirloom from his grandfather, caught the light briefly before vanishing back into shadow. "You know, I was like you once. Full of righteous indignation. Three years in, I reported Bristol myself."

Bryn straightened, feeling the leather upholstery stick to his back through his shirt. "You did? What happened?" Finally, he thought. Someone else who'd tried to do the right thing. Someone who understood the burden of carrying unwelcome truths.

"Nothing. Absolutely nothing." Jason's laugh was bitter, devoid of humor. "Except me being known as the department snitch. My cases got reassigned. Colleagues stopped talking to me. I spent six months reviewing sanitation reports for the prison at Stanley, filing forms about sewage systems for criminals and political prisoners. That's not all. For several months, I was followed by men on my rounds. I have no doubt that they were Triad."

The revelation settled over Bryn like a blanket, smothering and heavy. "So, everyone just accepts it?"

"It's not just the Sanitation Department, Bryn. My brother-in-law is on the police force, too. Same story there. Some officers accept their weekly 'tea money' from merchants who prefer understanding rather than enforcement. Others get regular donations to their benevolent societies from gambling dens and opium parlors. And some tip off the Triads about upcoming raids. Jason took off his spectacles and cleaned them meticulously. "The system has its own logic. Follow it, and you can have a comfortable career. Challenge it, and you discover just how uncomfortable that career can become."

"I thought we were supposed to be an example of integrity and honesty," Bryn stated.

Jason's expression softened slightly, and for a moment Bryn caught a glimpse of the idealistic young man he once was before Hong Kong taught him the cost of idealism. "We are, in our way. But the world isn't black and white, especially not here. Trust me, you don't want to rock this boat."

An awkward silence passed between them. Bryn stood up without a word and left Jason's office, deeply disappointed. And angry.

Two days later, Bryn found Bristol in the department's break room, a cramped space that always smelled of stale cigarettes. The older man stood alone at the small counter, carefully stirring milk into his morning tea with deliberate movements that seemed more ritual than necessity. Through the single window, Victoria Harbor shimmered in the morning light, its surface broken by the wakes of Star Ferry boats carrying office workers from Tsim Sha Tsui to Central, the graceful curve of junks with their distinctive red-brown sails, and the occasional Royal Navy vessel reminding everyone who ultimately controlled these waters.

Bristol cut an impressive figure even in the dingy break room. His gray hair was carefully pomaded and parted with military precision, his white colonial uniform pressed to parade standards despite the heat that would wilt it within hours. He carried himself with the confidence of a man who had never faced a serious challenge to his authority, whose position in the colonial hierarchy felt as permanent as the Rock of Gibraltar itself.

The confrontation Bryn had imagined for two days suddenly seemed foolish and risky. This wasn't just a corrupt cop taking small bribes from dock workers. This was a senior government official with connections all through the colonial system, someone who had survived changes in governors and political storms that ended others' careers. What made Bryn think he could take down such a person with three photos and a sense of moral outrage?

But the alternative was complicity, Bryn thought, and that path led toward the

Chapter 12: The Price of Truth

kind of man he'd sworn never to become.

"David. May I speak with you?" Bryn asked calmly.

Bristol turned, his usual smile disappearing as he took in Bryn's expression. The older man had a disconcerting talent for reading people quickly and accurately, a skill that likely served him well in balancing official duties with unofficial dealings. His pale blue eyes, unexpectedly sharp, scrutinized Bryn as a chess master evaluates an opponent's strategy.

"What can I do for you Bryn?"

Bryn closed the door, the click echoing in the small space like a gunshot. "I know about the payments. Or should I call them bribes?" Bryn took the photos out of the envelope and spread them on Bristol's desk.

Bristol's face didn't change, but something shifted behind his eyes, a recalculation of threat and opportunity. He set his teacup down with deliberate care, the porcelain making a soft sound against the scratched wooden counter. When he looked up, his smile had vanished entirely. "What are these? Where did you get them?"

"You know what they are." Bryn met his gaze, fighting the urge to look away from the older man's unsettling intensity. "You're taking envelopes full of money. From restaurant owners who somehow always pass their health inspections regardless of actual conditions."

Bristol chuckled, a sound lacking warmth that seemed to fill the tight space. "You've been here what, eight months? And you think you understand how things work?" He shook his head with what might have been real amusement. "You're still wet behind the ears, lad. You have no idea how this system functions, how it's always worked."

The patronizing tone ignited something in Bryn's chest, a flash of Welsh temper that he'd learned to control but never entirely suppress. "I understand bribery is illegal."

"Legal, illegal." Bristol waved his hand dismissively. "Bureaucratic concepts that don't account for reality. Our Chinese community has its own way of doing business, its own understanding of proper relationships. It's about *guanxi*, about face, about mutual obligation. You come in with your military rulebook and your holier-than-thou morality, slapping violations on people who've been running successful businesses since before you were born, and you think you're serving justice?" He looked out the window. "You're not serving justice, Bryn. You're destroying livelihoods and crushing spirits."

"Health code violations cause illness. That's not cultural, it's biological," Bryn replied curtly.

"Of course it is. And if I see rats running across restaurant tables or sewage backing up in kitchens, you think I'd let that slide? I nail the worst offenders without mercy." Bristol's voice carried the conviction of a man who genuinely believed his own justifications. "But there's a difference between dangerous violations and bureaucratic nonsense. The difference between protecting public health and destroying small businesses over technicalities written by men who've never worked a day in food service."

The argument had a seductive logic, Bryn realized. Bristol wasn't presenting himself as a simple criminal but as a pragmatist, a man who understood local realities better than distant lawmakers. It was probably how he'd justified his actions to himself over the years, how corruption always justified itself, through incremental compromises that eventually became indistinguishable from principle. But it was a slippery slope. "The health regulations don't make that distinction."

"Because the regulations were written by bureaucrats in London who think Hong Kong is just another Surrey suburb!" Bristol's voice rose before he caught himself, glancing toward the door. He smoothed his tie and continued more quietly. "Look around you, Bryn. Look at what we make, what this job pays. You think that's enough for a decent life? Enough to send children to the best schools, maintain the kind of respectability the service expects from its officers? You think you'll have that beautiful apartment you live in on the after your retirement?"

The appeal to economic necessity was another familiar note in corruption's symphony. Bryn had heard similar arguments from constables in Swansea who skimmed evidence room seizures, as well as from army quartermasters in Cairo who sold supplies on the black market. Need and greed were close cousins, often indistinguishable even to the men who served them.

"So that justifies taking bribes?" Bryn asked.

"It's supplemental income," Bristol interrupted, his tone growing colder. "Payment for providing a service that helps small businesses navigate an impossible regulatory maze. I keep good establishments open, protect genuine public health where it matters, and ensure that hardworking families aren't destroyed by bureaucratic zealotry. Everyone wins."

"Except the public that thinks health inspections actually mean something," Bryn replied.

Bristol's facade cracked, revealing something uglier beneath. The mask of benevolent pragmatism slipped, exposing the calculating opportunist inside. "Listen carefully, Bryn. You're messing with my livelihood, with relationships I've cultivated for fifteen years. You think you understand how business works in the Chinese community? You think they'll respect you more for your rigid honesty than they respect me for my practical accommodation?"

Chapter 12: The Price of Truth

"Is that what you call it?" Bryn asked.

"I call it survival." Bristol's voice dropped to barely above a whisper, forcing Bryn to strain to hear him over the ambient noise of the building. "And I call it understanding that there are consequences for young officers who don't learn the local customs quickly enough. Hong Kong can be a very welcoming place for those who fit in, or a dangerous one for those who don't."

Bristol's veiled threat hung in the air between them like a tangible presence. Bryn felt his heartbeat quicken, his palms growing sweaty despite the air conditioning struggling against the colony's heat. A cold knot formed in his stomach, radiating outward until his fingers tingled with adrenaline. He had faced drunken miners in Wales and assassins in Cairo, but this felt different; it was more personal and more dangerous because it offered no clear enemy to fight.

"Relax, lad." Bristol's smile returned, but it didn't reach his eyes. "I'm trying to help you understand how things work around here. You're smart, you'll figure it out eventually. Most do." He picked up his teacup and moved toward the door, pausing to pat Bryn's shoulder with mockingly paternal familiarity. "We all learn to play the game, Bryn. The only question is whether we learn before or after we've made ourselves irrelevant."

The following afternoon, Bryn sat in Dr. Wellington's office, watching Hong Kong's senior health administrator study the photographs with the methodical attention of a man accustomed to making decisions that could destroy careers or save lives.

Wellington himself was a product of that system, a Scottish physician who'd arrived in Hong Kong twenty years earlier as a young medical officer and risen through competence, political acumen, and the kind of careful neutrality that allowed him to serve successive governors without becoming too closely identified with any particular faction. His graying hair and weathered face spoke of decades spent navigating tropical diseases, colonial politics, and the endless bureaucratic battles that characterized life in the civil service. He was known as a fair man, a competent administrator, and someone who understood both the official requirements of his position and the unofficial realities that determined how those requirements were actually fulfilled.

"These are serious allegations," Wellington said finally, his Scottish accent still audible despite decades in the colony.

Bryn shook his head. "They're not allegations. They're facts. I have dates, times, and amounts. I can provide sworn statements from witnesses if necessary."

Wellington tapped his fingers on the desk, the sound crisp in the quiet office. "Thank you for bringing this to my attention, Bryn. I appreciate your integrity. It's... refreshing."

Something in his tone made Bryn pause. There was respect there, certainly, but also what sounded like regret, as if integrity was a luxury that the colony couldn't afford. "So, you'll take action?"

Wellington nodded. "Of course. I'll open an investigation immediately. These matters require discretion and proper procedure, you understand. We can't simply act on photographs without considering the broader implications." Wellington tucked the envelope into his desk drawer with the practiced efficiency of a man who'd filed many uncomfortable truths in similar drawers over the years. "In the meantime, I'd advise keeping this between us. No good can come from rumors spreading before we have all the facts."

"Thank you, Dr. Wellington. I know this isn't comfortable, but…"

"The right thing rarely is," Wellington interrupted with a smile that didn't quite reach his eyes. "Give me two weeks. I'll handle it personally."

But two weeks turned into three, then four, then five. Bristol kept his rounds with the same confident swagger, greeting colleagues warmly, conducting inspections that always seemed to lead to the outcomes that best served his private interests. When Bryn finally found the courage to ask about the investigation's progress, Wellington was always in meetings, away on official duties, or unavailable for comment.

In the sixth week, a departmental memo appeared on every desk announcing Bristol's nomination for the Colonial Service Medal, recognizing his "outstanding contribution to public health and community relations in Hong Kong." The accompanying photo showed him shaking hands with Wellington himself, both men smiling broadly for the camera as if celebrating not just an award but the triumph of a system that protected its own regardless of their crimes.

That same afternoon, Bryn found a reassignment notice in his pigeonhole, typed on official stationery with the colonial seal embossed at the top. Effective immediately, he was to be transferred to Kowloon District, with specific responsibility for the Walled City, that notorious maze of unlicensed food stalls, makeshift restaurants, opium dens, and gambling houses that operated in a legal gray area beyond effective government control. It was the most challenging, dangerous, and thankless assignment in the entire health department, a place where careers went to die, and idealistic young officers learned the cost of their principles.

The note attached was brief and unsigned: "Your attention to detail will be valuable in this high-compliance sector."

High-compliance sector. The bureaucratic euphemism would have been amusing if it weren't so clearly vindictive. The Walled City was many things, but compliant wasn't one of them. It was a place where colonial authority meant little, and survival mattered most, where the usual rules of law and order gave way to

Chapter 12: The Price of Truth

older, more fundamental codes of conduct. Sending him there wasn't just punishment; it was exile.

That evening, as rain hammered the windows of his apartment in Peak Mansions, Bryn sat amidst the remnants of his failed crusade: files documenting violations that would never be prosecuted, photographs that had proven more dangerous to their creator than their subjects, reports that would gather dust in some forgotten drawer until the tropical humidity finally destroyed them. The apartment itself was a symbol of colonial privilege at its peak: spacious rooms with soaring ceilings, designed to let in every breath of mountain air, gleaming hardwood floors cared for by Chinese servants, and furniture imported from England, arranged with the relaxed confidence of men who never questioned their right to such luxury. From his living room windows, the entire colony stretched out below like his own domain: Victoria Harbor sparkling with ships and boats, the busy maze of Central and Wan Chai, the green hills of Kowloon rising across the water, all seen from the high vantage point where Hong Kong's ruling class lived far above the heat, noise, and chaos of the city they ruled.

Ah-Min appeared in the doorway with his characteristic silent efficiency, carrying a silver tray with whisky, tea, and the evening's South China Morning Post. But tonight, something was different in his bearing. The usual composed mask had slipped slightly, revealing worry lines around his eyes that Bryn had never noticed before.

"Difficult day, Master?" Ah-Min inquired, but his voice carried an undertone that suggested he already knew the answer.

"Word travels fast in the servants' quarters, doesn't it?" Bryn said, accepting the whisky. He'd learned enough about Hong Kong's invisible networks to know that news moved through the Chinese community faster than official channels could manage.

Ah-Min hesitated, then settled into the chair across from him without being invited. It was a breach of colonial etiquette that he would never have attempted in front of other Europeans, but their relationship had evolved beyond such formalities. "Mrs. Wu's cousin works in the Government House kitchens," Ah-Min admitted. "She heard the *taipans* discussing your transfer over dinner. They seemed... pleased."

"Pleased that the troublemaker is being sent to the Walled City?" Bryn asked.

"Pleased that Inspector Bristol's arrangements will continue undisturbed." Ah-Min leaned forward, his composure cracking further. "Master, you must understand something. What you discovered about Bristol, it's not just his corruption. It's a system that reaches into every aspect of life here."

Bryn studied his companion's face, seeing fear there for the first time. "You know something about this."

"I know everything about this." Ah-Min's voice was bitter. "My first employer, Mr. Richardson from Jardine Matheson, taught me how it works. 'Ah-Min,' he would say, 'the Chinese understand business better than we give them credit for. Sometimes the most honest thing is to pay for what you really want rather than pretend the system will give it to you for free.'"

"You're talking about your former boss paying bribes?" Bryn asked.

"I'm talking about my former boss being killed for trying to stop paying them." Ah-Min stood abruptly, moving to the window with agitated steps. "1927. He decided his conscience wouldn't allow him to continue the arrangements his company had maintained for decades. Three weeks later, his car went off the road near Repulse Bay. Mechanical failure, they said."

The revelation hung between them like a physical presence. Bryn felt his understanding of Hong Kong's dangers shift from abstract to personal. "You think it wasn't an accident?"

"I think a man who could drive military vehicles through French mud in the Great War should have been able to handle a colonial road in good weather." Ah-Min turned back from the window, his eyes reflecting the harbor lights. "I also think his replacement immediately restored all the old arrangements and added several new ones for good measure."

"Why didn't you ever tell me this before?" Bryn asked, somewhat annoyed.

"Because you seemed determined to learn how to make mistakes on your own." Ah-Min's voice carried a frustration that revealed the depth of his concern. "I understand your old Morgan Thomas from the mine back home gave you some advice about standing up to bullies. It assumes the bullies fight fair. Here, they don't fight at all. They simply make you disappear or make you irrelevant."

Bryn set down his whisky, his hands suddenly unsteady. "So, what are you suggesting? That I should have kept quiet about Bristol? Let him continue stealing with impunity?"

"I'm suggesting that charging a fortress head-on is suicide." Ah-Min returned to his chair, leaning forward with an intensity Bryn had rarely seen from him. "But there are other ways to take a fortress. You can starve it. You can corrupt its defenders. You can make its position untenable through patience and strategy rather than direct assault."

"That sounds like surrender," Bryn said.

"Does it?" Ah-Min's smile was sad but knowing. "Let me tell you about my grandfather, Master. He was a merchant in Guangzhou when the British first

Chapter 12: The Price of Truth

arrived. The foreign devils, as he called them, wanted to change everything immediately. New laws, new taxes, new ways of doing business. My grandfather and his associates could have fought them openly, could have organized resistance, could have died heroically for the old ways."

"But they didn't, I'm assuming," Bryn offered.

Ah-Min nodded. "They learned English. They studied British law. They formed partnerships with European traders. Within ten years, they controlled more of the Pearl River trade than they ever had under the imperial system. Not by fighting the new reality, but by understanding it better than its creators did."

Bryn found himself leaning forward despite his skepticism. "And you think that's what I should do with Bristol?"

"I think Bristol is a small man in a large system. You've been trying to destroy the man instead of understanding the system." Ah-Min's voice grew more animated as he warmed to his theme. "But what if you became indispensable to the system? What if you made yourself so valuable to the colonial establishment that they needed your integrity more than Bristol's corruption?"

"That's what this new position Wellington offered might allow?"

"If you're clever about it." Ah-Min paused, seeming to wrestle with himself before continuing. "Master, I must tell you something else. Mrs. Wu and I, we've been... preparing."

"Preparing for what?" Bryn asked.

"For you to get yourself killed." The bluntness of it was shocking coming from Ah-Min's usually diplomatic tongue. "We have savings. We have connections. If you had pressed the Bristol matter further, if you had become genuinely dangerous to the wrong people, we were prepared to help you disappear. Leave Hong Kong, start somewhere else. Perhaps Macao."

Bryn stared at him, overwhelmed by the implication that his servants had been ready to sacrifice their own security for his safety. "You would have done that? Given up your positions, your lives here, for me?"

"You're not like the others, Master." Ah-Min's voice was quiet now, almost embarrassed by the admission. "Most Europeans see us as furniture, useful but replaceable. You see us as people. That's rare enough to be worth protecting."

They sat in silence for a moment, the rain drumming against the windows while both men grappled with the shift in their relationship. The colonial hierarchy that usually governed their interactions had dissolved entirely, replaced by something more honest and more complicated. "So, what do you suggest now?" Bryn asked finally.

"You accept Wellington's reassignment with grace. You grow your Community Health Initiative into something truly powerful. You support the Chinese community in ways that make you indispensable to them."

"What if Bristol doesn't have a weakness?"

"Everyone has a weakness, Master. Even the stone that defies the river has cracks where the water can enter." Ah-Min smiled, but it was more calculating than serene. "My grandfather used to say that the best revenge is to become so successful that your enemies must beg for your help. Perhaps it's time you learned to think like a Chinese businessman instead of a Welsh coal miner or a British soldier. Greed will be Bristol's downfall. Let him fall."

"And if that doesn't work?" Bryn asked.

Ah-Min's expression grew serious again. "Then Mrs. Wu and I will help you disappear. But let's hope it doesn't come to that."

Mrs. Wu appeared in the doorway, her motherly presence adding warmth to what had become an intense philosophical discussion. In her simple black servant's dress with white collar and cuffs, she represented the thousands of Chinese who made colonial life possible while remaining largely invisible to those they served. Her English was limited, but her understanding of household management was encyclopedic, encompassing everything from the daily rhythms of her employers' lives to the complex social networks that connected servants throughout the Peak's mansions and estates.

She bowed. "Dinner ready, Master. Fish with ginger, vegetables from market, rice. Good for thinking on difficult day."

As if she'd known exactly what kind of day he'd had and what kind of meal might provide comfort. Perhaps Ah-Min had told her, or perhaps she'd simply recognized the signs of a man grappling with problems that had no easy solutions. In any case, her timing was perfect, offering both sustenance and interruption before the philosophical intensity became overwhelming.

Over dinner, they talked of lighter things: Mrs. Wu's plans for the weekend market, where she would select ingredients with the discriminating eye of someone who'd fed families for decades; the progress of Ah-Min's nephew's studies at Queen's College, where he was learning to navigate the same complex cultural waters that his uncle had mastered; the new family that had moved into 4A, bringing with them the kind of domestic drama that made excellent servant gossip but posed no threat to anyone's existential equilibrium.

Yet underneath the pleasant conversation, Bryn felt something shifting in his understanding of his situation. Perhaps his transfer to the Walled City wasn't simply punishment but opportunity, a chance to learn about Hong Kong from the

Chapter 12: The Price of Truth

ground up, away from the careful facades of Government House and the sanitized corridors of the Secretariat. Perhaps failure, properly understood, was simply education by another name.

As the rain finally began to ease outside and the harbor lights twinkled like earthbound stars through the clearing air, Bryn realized that his discouragement was transforming into something more useful: determination informed by humility, integrity guided by wisdom rather than mere righteousness. He still didn't know exactly how to handle Bristol's corruption, but he was beginning to understand that the answer lay not in forcing things to happen, but in learning to see what was there. And be patient. The world as it is, not as he wished it were. Perhaps that was the first lesson in effective action, the foundation upon which all other strategies must be built.

Several weeks later, as autumn began to temper Hong Kong's merciless heat and the southwest monsoon gave way to drier winds from the mainland, Bryn received an unexpected summons to Wellington's office. He found the department head standing at his window, hands clasped behind his back, gazing out at Victoria Harbor with the expression of a man contemplating problems that had no easy solutions.

"Ah, Bryn. Close the door behind you." Wellington's voice carried an odd quality that Bryn hadn't heard before, a combination of weariness and regret that suggested this conversation would be different from their previous encounters. The older man's posture spoke of a burden carried too long in private and of decisions made under pressure that had seemed necessary at the time but now felt increasingly hollow. "We need to talk properly this time."

Wellington turned from the window, his weathered face showing every year of his service in the colony. The afternoon light streaming through the Venetian blinds highlighted the deep lines around his eyes and the slight tremor in his hands, suggesting either age or stress, or possibly both. When he spoke, his voice carried the weight of a man who'd spent too many years balancing principle against pragmatism and was no longer certain he'd chosen correctly.

"About Bristol. About your report. About why I've handled this entire situation so badly." He moved to his chair but didn't sit; instead, he gripped its back as if needing the support. "First, I want you to know that I have tremendous respect for your integrity, Bryn. What you did, reporting Bristol's corruption despite knowing the personal cost, was courageous. The kind of courage this colony needs more of, not less."

The admission hung in the air between them like a confession, heavy with implications that neither man was quite ready to acknowledge. Wellington's tone was different from their previous encounters, more personal and less bureaucratic, as if he'd decided that official distances were no longer worth maintaining.

"You've also done exceptional work since arriving here. Your investigations are thorough, your reports are honest, and your commitment to actually helping people rather than simply enforcing regulations is exactly what this department should represent." Wellington finally sat, his movement conveying a exhaustion that went deeper than physical fatigue. "Which makes what I have to tell you so much more difficult."

Bryn felt his carefully maintained composure begin to crack. For weeks, he'd assumed that Wellington had simply chosen institutional loyalty over justice, that his supervisor was either corrupt himself or too weak to challenge corruption in others. The possibility that Wellington's actions might have been motivated by something other than cowardice or complicity hadn't occurred to him.

Bryn waited.

Wellington reached for his pipe with the mechanical movements of a man seeking comfort in familiar ritual. "I did follow up on your report. Immediately. The day after you filed it, I personally delivered your documentation to Police Inspector Patterson at the Anti-Corruption Branch. Every photograph, every witness statement, every piece of evidence you'd so carefully assembled."

The words hit Bryn like a physical blow. *"If Wellington had followed proper procedure, if the police had received all the evidence, then why...?"* he pondered.

"They conducted what they called a 'thorough investigation,'" Wellington continued, lighting his pipe with deliberate care. "Three weeks of interviews, document reviews, surveillance reports. At the end of it all, Police Inspector Patterson informed me that they'd found insufficient evidence to proceed with charges."

"Insufficient evidence?" Bryn leaned forward in his chair, feeling anger and confusion compete for dominance. "I documented everything. Times, dates, amounts, witnesses. How could there be insufficient evidence?"

"Because someone with considerable influence intervened." Wellington's expression darkened with remembered frustration and what might have been shame. "Someone with the power to make inconvenient investigations disappear, to redefine evidence as insufficient, to transform corruption into misunderstanding."

The pieces began falling into place with sickening clarity. Bristol's confidence, his casual dismissal of Bryn's threats, his certainty that consequences would fall on his accuser rather than himself. It hadn't been bravado; it had been knowledge, the security of a man protected by forces more powerful than individual integrity or institutional justice.

"Bristol's connections run deeper in the colonial establishment than either of

Chapter 12: The Price of Truth

us imagined," Wellington continued, drawing on his pipe with movements that seemed designed to buy time for difficult truths. "Banking interests who profit from his flexible interpretations of regulations. Shipping companies whose cargo receives expedited clearance. Government officials whose own arrangements benefit from Bristol's willingness to accommodate rather than enforce." Wellington stood and walked back to the window, his silhouette outlined against the harbor light. "When Patterson told me the investigation was being closed, I started hearing rumors. Whispers in the club about young officers who needed to learn respect for local customs. Comments at official dinners about the dangers of excessive zeal in junior staff. Suggestions that some people might benefit from assignments that broadened their understanding of how the colony really functions."

"You thought they might try to intimidate me?"

"I thought they might do worse than intimidate." Wellington's voice was quiet but clear. "The Triads don't usually limit themselves to gentle persuasion when significant money is at stake, and Bristol's operation involves sums that would make violent response economically rational." He turned back to face Bryn, his expression grave. "Moving you to Kowloon, keeping you away from cases that might intersect with Bristol's interests, giving you assignments that would demonstrate the complexity of actually governing this colony, none of that was punishment, Williams. It was the only way I could keep you safe while maintaining the fiction that you'd been appropriately disciplined for making unfounded accusations."

The revelation completely recontextualized everything that had happened over the past weeks. Wellington hadn't been undermining him; he'd been protecting him. The reassignment hadn't been retribution; it had been camouflage, a way of removing Bryn from immediate danger while preserving his career for future use. "Why didn't you tell me?" Bryn asked, his voice barely above a whisper. "I thought you'd lost faith in me, that you regretted supporting my report."

Wellington returned to his desk, this time sitting heavily as if the conversation had drained him of some essential energy. "Because the fewer people who knew about the threats, the safer you'd be. And because I was ashamed." He drew on his pipe, exhaling slowly into the afternoon light. "Ashamed that I couldn't protect one of my best officers properly. Ashamed that corruption runs so deep in this colony that doing the right thing puts good men in mortal danger. Ashamed that twenty years of service had taught me to choose safety over justice without even questioning the choice."

They sat in silence for several minutes, the only sounds the distant noise of the harbor and the soft tick of the clock on Wellington's desk. Outside, the afternoon was giving way to evening, the light shifting from harsh clarity to the softer gold that made Hong Kong's skyline seem almost magical despite all the human complexity it contained.

"Where does this leave us now?" Bryn finally asked.

Wellington smiled for the first time since the conversation had begun, an expression that contained both sadness and something that might have been hope. "With work to do. Real work, the kind that might actually make a difference." He opened a folder on his desk, revealing documents bearing official seals and signatures. "Your assignment to the Walled City, while originally intended as protective camouflage, has given you insights that no desk job could have provided. You've learned how communities actually function when government authority is weak, how people organize themselves when official systems fail them."

"The Walled City has certainly been educational," Bryn agreed.

"More than educational. It's been preparatory." Wellington's voice carried a note of excitement that transformed his appearance, making him look younger and more energetic than he had in months. "The Colonial Office has approved funding for your Community Health Initiative, your joint program between the Sanitation and Health Departments with authority to implement innovative approaches to public health challenges throughout the territory. While you've unofficially initiated that, I want to formalize it. I support you in your efforts to treat Chinese residents as partners rather than subjects. Community health workers trained to understand local conditions. Medical stations that work with traditional healing practices rather than dismissing them. Emergency response protocols that build on existing social networks rather than trying to replace them."

Wellington looked up from the folder, his eyes bright with possibility. "I've recommended to my boss, and he's approved it, that you head the initiative. Full authority, substantial budget, and the backing to actually implement changes rather than just study problems. To bring some authority to it, you have been promoted to Deputy Chief Sanitary Inspector, reporting directly to me."

The offer was staggering, completely unexpected after months of feeling like a pariah within the colonial system. "After everything that's happened? After I've been transferred, marginalized, essentially exiled to the worst posting in the territory?"

"Because of everything that's happened," Wellington replied firmly. "You understand both the official requirements and the practical realities. You've proven that you can maintain your integrity while adapting your methods to local conditions. Most importantly, you've learned that effective change requires patience, strategy, and understanding rather than just righteous anger."

Bryn considered the implications. "What about Bristol? The corruption issues

Chapter 12: The Price of Truth

we originally discussed?"

Wellington's expression sobered, but his voice remained steady. "Still there. Still protected by interests more powerful than either of us can challenge directly. But this new position would allow you to work around him rather than through him, to build alternative structures that don't depend on his cooperation or his corruption."

"You're talking about long-term change rather than immediate justice."

"I'm talking about effective change rather than symbolic gestures," Wellington replied, meeting Bryn's eyes directly. "Bristol will make mistakes eventually. Men like him always do, especially when they feel secure in their protection. When that happens, we'll be ready with evidence, resources, and allies. And if the mistakes come at the expense of the Triads, he'll face a justice more certain than any we can provide. But in the meantime, we can build something better alongside the existing system, something that serves the people of Hong Kong rather than just the interests that currently control it."

The strategy was essentially what Ah-Min had suggested: understand the system, work skillfully within its constraints, create change through patience and wisdom rather than confrontation. It required swallowing his pride, accepting partial victory over total defeat, building for the future rather than demanding immediate satisfaction.

"I accept," Bryn said. "With one condition."

"Which is?"

"Full communication from now on. If there are threats, political pressures, or administrative constraints I should be aware of, I want to know about them. I can handle dangerous truths better than I can handle comfortable lies."

Wellington smiled, extending his hand across the desk. "Partners then. With complete honesty on both sides."

As they shook hands, Bryn felt something he hadn't experienced since arriving in Hong Kong: genuine optimism about his ability to make a meaningful difference in this impossible, fascinating, frustrating city. The handshake felt like the beginning of something important, a partnership that might actually change lives rather than just enforcing regulations.

Chapter 13

The Healer's Path

"The good physician treats the disease; the great physician treats the patient who has the disease."

William Osler, on the art of healing

Six weeks after his talk with Ah-Min, the heat had become alive and malevolent, pressing down on Hong Kong like the breath of a fever god. Bryn Williams stood at his apartment window in the pre-dawn dark, watching the harbor shimmer with an oily glow that seemed to trap the night's heat and reflect it back toward the city. Even at this hour, before the sun started its assault on the colony, the glass burned against his palm.

The thermometer outside his window showed thirty-two degrees. In Wales, such temperatures would be cause for celebration, a rare gift from unpredictable weather gods. Here, it was just a cool break before another day that would soar, turning the narrow streets and crowded tenements into ovens that baked human desperation into the very stones. Add the constant high humidity, and for many, it was unbearable.

His mind kept returning to the report that had arrived the previous afternoon, delivered by a breathless messenger who had climbed the Peak in the scorching heat to ensure its immediate delivery. Three deaths in Tai Ping Shan, the crowded district where Chinese laborers and their families lived packed together in conditions that challenged every principle of sanitation he had learned. Severe diarrhea, vomiting, rapid dehydration, and death within hours of symptom onset.

The symptoms clearly indicated cholera, the invisible demon that could turn a healthy neighborhood into a death zone within days. Rice-water stools, the medical term that reduces human suffering to clinical language, hide the truth that this disease killed people faster than they could receive last rites, faster than they could say goodbye to their families, and faster than most could even understand what was happening to them.

Bryn had read enough medical reports during his military service to grasp the mathematics of epidemic disease. Cholera didn't spread randomly; it followed the paths of human contact and contaminated water, spreading through crowded communities where sanitation was poor and medical care was limited. Three deaths yesterday could become thirty by the end of the week, three hundred by month's end if the outbreak wasn't contained quickly and effectively.

The irony wasn't lost on him that his first major challenge in his new role as Deputy Chief Sanitation Officer and head of the Community Health Liaison would involve exactly the kind of systematic public health crisis that David Bristol's corruption had helped create. All those falsified inspection reports, all those overlooked violations in exchange for cash payments, all those compromises with wealthy restaurant owners who knew their connections would protect them from serious consequences. The web of corruption that had seemed like an abstract moral problem was about to turn into concrete human suffering in the city's poorest neighborhoods.

When Bryn entered the Sanitary Department offices two hours later, he saw Dr. Wellington standing in front of the large wall map that dominated the main conference room, surrounded by Jason Lam and most of the department's senior staff, including David Bristol. The map depicted Hong Kong Island in precise detail, with every street and building carefully marked, but this morning it looked more like a military campaign chart than an administrative tool.

Red pins clustered in Sheung Wan district like drops of blood on white fabric, each one indicating a confirmed case or suspected death. Even as Bryn watched, Wellington jabbed another pin into Wing Lok Street, the sharp movement showing both precision and barely controlled urgency.

"Three more cases overnight," Wellington announced without turning around, his Scottish accent thickening as it always did when he was under severe stress. "Two confirmed dead, one showing advanced symptoms and not expected to survive the morning."

He turned to face the assembled staff, and Bryn could see the strain of the past twenty-four hours etched into every line of his weathered face. Wellington had been managing public health crises in various colonial postings for over twenty years, but cholera remained the one disease that could humble even the most experienced administrator. "Confirmed by Dr. Renwick at Victoria Hospital an hour ago," Wellington continued, his voice carrying the flat precision of a man reporting battlefield casualties. "We have ourselves a proper epidemic. The kind that can kill hundreds if we don't respond correctly, and thousands if we respond incorrectly."

Epidemic. The word lingered in the air like incense, heavy with implications that stretched far beyond medical terms. Bryn found himself thinking of Aunt Eileen's stories about the cholera outbreaks that had periodically swept through the Welsh mining towns during her childhood. She rarely talked about those times

Chapter 13: The Healer's Path

in detail, but when she did, her eyes would look distant and her voice would drop to barely above a whisper, as if the memories were too terrible for regular conversation.

"Bryn," Wellington said, his attention fixed on Bryn with the kind of focused intensity that made it clear this conversation would determine the trajectory of the next several weeks. "I want you and Jason in Sheung Wan within the hour. Full inspection of that Wing Lok Street tenement complex, complete assessment of sanitation conditions, and preliminary recommendations for containment measures."

Wellington paused, studying Bryn's face as if trying to gauge his readiness for what was about to happen. "Dr. Sarah Thompson from the Health Department will be joining you for the medical assessment. This is exactly the kind of integrated response that your new position was designed to coordinate, so consider it a test of everything we've discussed about community-based public health initiatives."

The weight of responsibility bore down on Bryn like a heavy burden. After weeks of feeling marginalized and ineffective in his new role, he was finally given the chance to demonstrate that collaborative approaches to public health could be more effective than traditional colonial methods. But the stakes couldn't be higher: people were already dead, more were dying, and his decisions in the next few hours could determine whether this outbreak stayed contained or spiraled out of control, overwhelming the colony's limited medical resources.

Wellington's eyes narrowed slightly as he delivered his final instruction, and Bryn caught the undertone of warning that had become characteristic of their interactions since the Bristol incident. "And Bryn? Tread very carefully down there. Those merchants on Wing Lok Street have extensive connections throughout the district, and some of them extend into government circles. The last thing we need during a health crisis is political complications arising from mishandled community relations." Wellington's eyes briefly focused on Bristol and then quickly away.

Always the same delicate dance around wealth and influence, Bryn thought, even when people were dying from diseases that could be prevented by proper sanitation and honest inspection practices. But he was beginning to see that this was simply the reality of colonial administration: every decision had political implications, and every action required considering factors that extended far beyond immediate public health concerns.

The trip from Government Hill to Sheung Wan normally took fifteen minutes by rickshaw, but the outbreak had altered the usual pace of city life in ways that made travel both more urgent and more complicated. Police cordons had been set up around the affected areas, creating bottlenecks that slowed traffic. This produced exactly the kind of visible official response that could either reassure the public or cause panic, depending on how it was handled.

Ashes and Dawn

As their rickshaw neared the affected district, Bryn detected a smell that grew stronger with each passing block. It wasn't the usual blend of cooking food, human sweat, and industrial fumes typical of Hong Kong's crowded neighborhoods. This was something more complex and unsettling: human waste, decaying organic matter, the sickly-sweet scent of illness and death, all baked together by the relentless heat into an almost solid atmosphere.

The stench hit them with full force when they finally stepped out of the rickshaw. Human waste, rotting vegetables, the unmistakable smell of decay, and beneath it all, something else that might have been fear itself, Sweat and anxiety pressed together by heat and crowding, registering as much through the skin as through the nose.

Two bodies were removed from the Wing Lok Street building this morning," Jason said, consulting the notes he'd brought from the department. "Mother and daughter, ages thirty-two and eight. The father is still inside, showing advanced symptoms. Three other families in the same building are reporting illness."

A crowd had gathered at the entrance to the narrow alley leading to the affected tenement, faces showing a mix of fear, curiosity, and resentment that Bryn was beginning to recognize as the typical colonial response to official intervention. The elderly woman who approached them moved with the careful deliberation of someone whose joints had stiffened after decades of physical labor, but her eyes were sharp, and her manner indicated she was used to speaking for her neighbors when authority figures showed up.

She spoke quickly to Jason in Cantonese, her words punctuated by gestures toward the leaning four-story building that somehow managed to house fifteen families in spaces cramped for five. The building itself seemed to sag under the weight of its human cargo, its walls stained with moisture and age, and its windows blocked by laundry lines that kept any meaningful ventilation from happening.

She says the well water has tasted off for weeks, Jason translated, his voice carrying the flat tone of someone trying to stay professional while processing disturbing news. "Bitter and cloudy. But it's their only water source for cooking, cleaning, everything."

"Tell her we'll test the water immediately," Bryn replied, though he was already beginning to suspect what they would find. "And ask her if anyone has reported this problem to the authorities before today."

Faster conversation in Cantonese, the woman's voice rising slightly as she gestured toward the building and then back toward the government offices they'd come from. Other residents gathered around to listen, their expressions suggesting this discussion was about issues that had been lingering much longer than the current outbreak.

Chapter 13: The Healer's Path

She says they've filed multiple reports over the past two months, Jason said, his translation careful and precise. "Water quality, sewage overflow, overcrowding, structural problems. She has the documentation if we want to see it."

The accusation hit Bryn like a punch to the stomach. Reports of sanitation issues had stacked up on department desks while inspectors like Bristol were busy accepting bribes and forging inspection records. Multiple warnings about conditions that could lead to this kind of outbreak were ignored or delayed, as the bureaucracy focused on more politically sensitive matters. "Tell her we're here to fix the problems now," Bryn said, though he could hear the inadequacy of his response even as he spoke the words. "Tell her we'll test everything, address the immediate health risks, and work with the community to prevent this from happening again."

The well sat in a small courtyard at the center of the tenement complex, surrounded by laundry lines heavy with damp clothes that created a humid microclimate even more oppressive than the surrounding air. Bryn peered into the depths and immediately understood why people had been complaining about water quality for weeks. Even in the dim light filtering down from above, he could see the yellowish tinge that indicated serious contamination.

Contaminated, almost certainly with sewage runoff from the inadequate waste disposal systems that characterized this part of the city. Probably breeding cholera bacteria in conditions ideal for rapid reproduction and concentration. Bryn thought grimly that this well illustrated how public health disasters occur: a mix of structural neglect, administrative indifference, and systematic corruption that created conditions where disease could thrive and spread. He covered his mouth with a mask, and gathered water samples, while trying not to breathe too deeply, sealing each container with movements that had been drilled into him during military training for handling potentially dangerous materials. The samples would need to be tested right away, but he was already confident about what the results would reveal.

"These people have nowhere else to get water, Bryn," Jason pointed out, his voice reflecting the practical concerns from three years of balancing ideal solutions and available resources. "The nearest public well is six blocks away, and most of these families don't have the time or energy to carry water that distance every day."

Then we bring clean water to them," Bryn replied, his voice more confident than he truly felt about the logistics involved. "Daily deliveries until we can establish a safe, permanent water source. I have emergency authority under the Community Health Initiative to approve any necessary expenditures."

"Wellington will need to approve anything that significant," Jason said, though his tone indicated he was starting to realize that standard administrative procedures might not suffice for this situation.

Ashes and Dawn

I'll inform him after we've started the delivery service," Bryn said, applying what he'd learned from Ah-Min about working within systems while remaining flexible enough to respond to immediate crises. "People are dying, Jason. We can handle the paperwork afterward."

Shouting erupted from inside the building before Jason could say anything, angry voices echoing in the narrow courtyard with a volume that suggested desperation rather than just disagreement. On the second floor, visible through an open doorway, a middle-aged man stood leaning against the doorframe, his face twisted with grief and rage. When he saw Bryn and Jason in their official uniforms, his expression hardened into something close to pure hatred.

The man spoke rapidly in Cantonese, his words carrying clearly across the courtyard despite the distance. Even without understanding the language, Bryn could hear the accusation in his tone, the kind of raw anger that came from watching preventable tragedy unfold while the people responsible for prevention remained safely distant from the consequences of their failures.

"He says we knew the water was bad for weeks," Jason said.

The accusation hit Bryn as if it were completely true. Reports about water quality issues had piled up on department desks, while inspectors were busy with other tasks. Bristol's corruption was just one part of a bigger system that often put political interests before public health. It also showed how the needs of Chinese residents were seen as less important than the comfort of European colonists and wealthy Chinese merchants who had ties to colonial officials.

"Tell him we're here now," Bryn said, though he could hear the ineffectiveness of his response even as he spoke. "Tell him I give my personal word that we'll address these problems immediately and work to prevent them from happening again."

Before Jason could translate, the man suddenly doubled over, retching violently onto the wooden floor of the corridor. Even from across the courtyard, Bryn could see that the vomit contained the characteristic clear fluid indicating advanced cholera symptoms. The man was infected, probably for hours or even days, and was now entering the stage of the disease where survival depended on immediate medical help.

"He needs medical attention right now," Bryn said, starting toward the building. "Where is Dr. Thompson? She should have been here by now."

"Inspection may be premature without proper medical assessment," came a crisp, authoritative voice from behind them.

Bryn turned to see a woman in a white medical coat approaching across the courtyard, carrying a black leather bag and moving with the confident stride of someone used to taking charge in crisis situations. She was younger than he'd thought, probably in her early thirties, with the kind of precise posture and direct gaze that suggested extensive training in environments where competence meant the difference between life and death.

"Dr. Sarah Thompson, Health Department," she said, extending a gloved hand toward Bryn. "You must be Deputy Chief Inspector Williams. I apologize for the delay, but I was detained at Victoria Hospital reviewing similar cases that were brought in overnight."

Her English reflected the precise diction of London medical training, but there was something in her manner that indicated more familiarity with Hong Kong's realities than most recently arrived colonial professionals had. She moved through the courtyard with the kind of spatial awareness that results from experience in crowded, chaotic settings, and her interactions with the Chinese residents seemed more natural than the careful formality typical of most official colonial encounters.

"How many similar cases?" Bryn asked, though he wasn't sure he wanted to hear the answer.

Seven confirmed, three more showing symptoms," Thompson replied, her voice carrying the flat precision of medical reporting. "All from this immediate area, all presenting with classic cholera symptomatology. We're definitely looking at a significant outbreak that could expand rapidly if we don't implement containment measures immediately."

She moved toward the building where the man was still retching, her examination bag already in her hand. "But we need to be careful about our response. Unnecessary panic can spread faster than the disease itself, and inappropriate isolation measures can actually accelerate transmission by forcing people into closer contact while they're trying to avoid official attention."

"Finally," Bryn thought. *"Someone who understood that effective medical response requires considering social and political factors, not just clinical protocols."* But as he watched Thompson approach the sick man, he noticed something that made him slightly uncomfortable: she moved with a confidence that suggested she had already decided how to handle the situation before she had a chance to assess local conditions or consult with people who understood the community dynamics.

Jason translated as Thompson spoke softly to the retching man in careful, textbook Cantonese. Her pronunciation was accurate, and her vocabulary was sufficient, but there was something slightly artificial about her interactions, as if she were using learned techniques rather than drawing on real cultural understanding. The man responded to her questions, but his manner suggested the wariness that Chinese residents typically showed toward colonial officials, even those who genuinely seemed to try to help.

Thompson drew a blood sample efficiently and started showing the rest of the man's family how to prepare oral rehydration solutions with salt and sugar using the water from a container marked "safe water." Her instructions were medically correct, and her tone was calming, but Bryn wondered whether these people would actually follow her advice when she left or if they would go back to traditional remedies that might be less effective but felt more culturally right.

"Your approach seems different from standard colonial medical protocol," Bryn observed as Thompson finished her initial assessment.

Her smile was professionally bright but hinted at defensiveness. "Standard protocol assumes that Chinese families are incapable of caring for their own sick members if they're given proper information and safe supplies. My experience suggests that assumption is both incorrect and counterproductive."

It was exactly the right answer, the kind of culturally sensitive response Bryn had been hoping to hear. But something about how she delivered it made him wonder whether her 'experience' was extensive enough to support such confident claims or if she was relying on theoretical knowledge from medical school rather than practical wisdom gained through years of working in this environment.

The rest of the morning blurred into a series of inspections, sample collections, and initial assessments that painted a more unsettling picture of widespread neglect and institutional failure. Thompson's presence did influence how they interacted with residents, but not always in ways Bryn found comforting. While he and Jason had faced open hostility from past encounters with uncaring colonial officials, she fostered polite cooperation that might have reflected real trust but could also have been the careful deference Chinese residents learned to show when dealing with any European authority figure.

Thompson's medical expertise was clearly extensive, and her recommendations were sound from a clinical perspective. However, Bryn began to notice that her solutions consistently involved interventions that required significant trust in colonial authority: isolation of sick family members, transport to European-run medical facilities, and compliance with quarantine procedures that would separate people from their support networks and sources of income.

By late afternoon, when they returned to the Sanitary Department offices, the atmosphere had shifted from urgent concern to barely contained crisis management. Wellington stood at the heart of operations like a general leading a battlefield, directing reports, resources, and personnel with the focused intensity born from years of managing colonial emergencies.

"Williams! Lam! Thompson!" Wellington called out as they entered, his voice cutting through the buzz of conversation and activity that filled the main office. "I need immediate briefings from all of you. The Governor has declared a full health

Chapter 13: The Healer's Path

emergency based on reports from Victoria Hospital, and quarantine measures are scheduled to begin at sunset."

Bryn handed over his preliminary report as he tried to process the implications of what Wellington had just announced. A full health emergency would necessitate martial law provisions, mandatory evacuations, and enforced isolation measures, effectively placing the affected communities under military control until the outbreak was contained. It was the kind of response that could be medically necessary but politically devastating, especially if it was implemented without adequate consultation with community leaders.

Wellington scanned Bryn's report with the rapid attention of someone processing multiple streams of urgent information simultaneously. "Contaminated well water, inadequate sewage disposal, overcrowded housing conditions," he muttered, checking items off a mental list. "How many families affected directly?"

"Fifteen families in the immediate building, probably fifty more in the surrounding area drawing water from the same source," Bryn replied. "And Dr. Thompson identified several additional buildings that appear to have similar contamination issues."

Wellington looked up from the report, his weathered face showing every year of his experience with colonial public health crises. "Hospital's already setting up overflow facilities. They're at capacity now and expect to see dozens more cases over the next twenty-four hours."

"Dr. Thompson and I identified several buildings in the affected area that could serve as temporary medical stations," Bryn said, drawing on ideas he'd been developing during the morning's inspections. "With her medical staff and community health workers from my initiative, we could provide early treatment locally instead of overwhelming the hospital with cases that could be managed effectively in the community."

Wellington's attention sharpened, and Bryn could see him rapidly calculating the practical and political implications of such an approach. Community-based medical treatment would be more efficient and less expensive than hospital care, but it would also represent a significant departure from established colonial procedures.

"I think it's the best way to approach this crisis," Thompson added.

"She suggested that community-based treatment would be more effective than trying to transport every suspected case to Victoria Hospital," Bryn replied, though he was beginning to realize that Thompson's suggestions had been more tentative than he'd initially understood.

"The medical logistics are certainly favorable," Thompson added, though her tone carried a note of caution that hadn't been present during their earlier conversations. "But we'd need to ensure proper oversight and maintain adequate professional standards. Community treatment can work, but only if it's properly supervised and supported."

"Approved," Wellington said without hesitation. "Set it up immediately, whatever resources you need. But I want daily reports on every case, clear protocols for when patients need to be transferred to hospital care, and absolute certainty that we're not compromising treatment standards in the interest of administrative convenience."

Wellington moved to the wall map and started adding more red pins, each one representing another confirmed case or suspected death. The pattern was growing beyond the original focus area, indicating that the outbreak was following exactly the kind of transmission patterns that public health experts most feared.

"The evacuation starts at sunset," Wellington said. "Police cordons, mandatory family relocations from affected buildings, and quarantine facilities set up at the old military barracks on Stonecutters Island. We're handling this as a full epidemic response until we have clear proof that transmission has been stopped."

The announcement hit Bryn like cold water. Mandatory evacuation meant forcing families out of their homes at gunpoint if necessary, separating people from their livelihoods and support networks, and concentrating potentially infected individuals in facilities that could actually speed up disease transmission instead of stopping it. It was the kind of heavy-handed colonial response that could turn a medical crisis into a political uprising.

"Sir," Bryn said carefully, "based on what we observed today, I think the community would respond better to voluntary cooperation than forced evacuation. These families have been trying to report problems for weeks. They want the health issues addressed, but they're afraid of losing their homes and their ability to earn income."

Wellington's expression suggested he'd heard similar arguments before and found them well-intentioned but naively impractical. "Bryn, I appreciate your concern for community relations, but cholera doesn't respond to voluntary cooperation. It responds to rigorous quarantine measures and aggressive medical intervention. We can't afford to let political considerations override public health necessities."

The evacuation started as the sun painted Victoria Harbor in shades of gold and crimson that would have been beautiful under any other circumstances. Police cordons appeared around the affected blocks with military precision, while residents emerged from their buildings carrying whatever possessions they could manage on short notice. Children cried with the particular desperation that came

Chapter 13: The Healer's Path

from not understanding why their familiar world was suddenly disappearing. Elderly people protested in voices that carried decades of experience with arbitrary official decisions. Everywhere Bryn looked, he saw the raw fear of people losing control over their own lives.

The scene painfully brought to mind military operations he had seen during his service, where civilian populations were displaced for strategic reasons that made complete sense from a command perspective but caused human suffering that would last long after the military goals were met. The medical reasoning for these evacuations was solid, but the human cost was borne by people who had no say in the decisions affecting their lives.

A group of young men had barricaded themselves inside one of the condemned shophouses, refusing to let police enter despite repeated warnings about what could happen if they didn't comply. Their shouts clearly echoed across the narrow street, angry voices demanding to know why they should trust officials who had ignored their earlier pleas for help with the same issues now being used to justify taking their homes.

"We're not leaving!" one of them shouted through a broken window, his voice filled with the desperation of having nowhere else to go. "This is our home! These are our businesses! Why should we abandon everything we have just because you failed to do your jobs properly?"

Bryn positioned himself between the protesters and the increasingly agitated police officers, who were beginning to show the kind of impatience that could easily escalate into violence. The senior constable was a man Bryn recognized from previous encounters, someone who had little patience for what he considered Chinese resistance to legitimate colonial authority.

"I understand your concerns," Bryn called out, his voice loud enough to reach the barricaded building but calm enough to avoid escalating the situation. "The disease spreading through these buildings is genuinely dangerous, and people are already dying from it. But we're not here to take your homes or destroy your community."

"Then why can't you bring doctors and medicine here instead of forcing us to leave?" another voice called back. "Why must we abandon everything we've worked for just because you finally decided to pay attention to problems we've been reporting for months?"

It was a reasonable question and one that exposed the core contradictions in the colonial response to this crisis. The same officials who had dismissed repeated complaints about sanitation issues were now demanding that residents trust them with decisions about evacuation and quarantine.

"We are bringing medical care to this area," Bryn replied, drawing on the arrangements he'd discussed with Thompson and Wellington. "Dr. Thompson and I are establishing treatment facilities right here in the neighborhood, so you can receive care without being separated from your families and your work. But the buildings where people have already died need to be cleaned and disinfected before they're safe for occupancy again."

The protesters exchanged glances, visibly surprised by this response. Most colonial emergency measures involved removing Chinese residents from areas authorities aimed to control, rather than providing services that allowed people to remain in their communities while receiving necessary care.

"You promise this?" one of the young men called out. "You promise we can return to our homes as soon as they're safe? You promise medical care will be available here, not just at the European hospital where our families can't visit us?"

"I give you my word," Bryn replied, though he was acutely aware that he was making commitments that went beyond his actual authority. "You'll be able to return as soon as the buildings are medically safe, and treatment will be available locally for anyone who needs it."

Before anyone could respond to this exchange, someone from the back of the crowd threw a brick at the police line. The projectile flew past Bryn's head, missing him by inches, before smashing against a police shield with a sound like a gunshot.

The constables charged forward immediately, batons up and shouting warnings about the consequences of attacking colonial authority. Bryn could see the situation falling into exactly the sort of violence that would make medical treatment harder and community cooperation impossible.

Stop!" Bryn stepped directly into the path of the advancing police officers, arms spread wide to block their way. "These people are afraid, not violent. They're watching neighbors die from preventable diseases because we haven't done our jobs right. Give me two minutes to de-escalate this before anyone gets hurt unnecessarily."

The senior constable hesitated, his baton still raised but his advance temporarily stopped. "Inspector Williams, these people are resisting lawful authority during a declared health emergency. We have orders to clear this area by sunset, using whatever force is necessary."

"And we'll clear the area," Bryn replied, his voice carrying the kind of calm authority he'd learned during military service for dealing with potentially explosive situations. "But we'll do it through cooperation rather than violence, which will make our medical response more effective and reduce the risk of this situation spreading to other neighborhoods."

Bryn turned back toward the barricaded building, raising his voice so everyone

Chapter 13: The Healer's Path

nearby could hear him clearly. "I know you have no reason to trust colonial officials. We've failed you repeatedly, ignored your genuine concerns, and let problems grow until they became crises. But Dr. Thompson and I are asking for the chance to show that not all colonial officials are the same."

He paused, trying to find words that would bridge the gap between official necessity and human dignity. "We can't undo the mistakes that led to this outbreak, but we can work together to prevent it from getting worse. The medical facilities we're establishing will be staffed by people from this community who understand your concerns and speak your language. The cleaning and disinfection will be done as quickly as possible, and you'll be kept informed about progress every day."

"How do we know you won't disappear once the immediate crisis passes?" one of the protesters called out, echoing concerns that reflected years of experience with promises made during emergencies and forgotten once normal operations resumed.

"Because this is my neighborhood too now," Bryn replied, surprising himself with the honesty of his response. "I live in Hong Kong, I work here, my future is tied to this community's welfare. What happens to you happens to all of us. We succeed together or we fail together."

The young men inside the building spoke among themselves in rapid Cantonese, their conversation animated but less angry than their previous exchanges. Finally, the apparent leader appeared in the doorway, his expression still suspicious but no longer openly hostile.

"You will allow us to return as soon as the buildings are safe for occupancy?" he asked.

"As soon as it's medically advisable, yes," Bryn replied.

"And medical care will be provided here, by people who understand our language and our customs?"

"Yes. Dr. Thompson is already recruiting staff from this community," Bryn said.

"And you will keep us informed about progress, not just issue orders that we're expected to follow without explanation?"

Bryn nodded. "Daily updates, and you'll be involved in decisions about how the work proceeds."

More discussion inside the building, then the leader nodded slowly. "We will cooperate, but we will be watching to make sure these promises are kept. If you disappoint us the way other officials have, there will be consequences."

"That's fair," Bryn replied, though he was acutely aware that he'd just committed himself to obligations that would require considerable diplomatic skill to fulfill.

The evacuation continued, but the mood had shifted from confrontational to cautiously cooperative. Word spread quickly through the affected area that the foreign inspector had made specific commitments about medical care and community involvement, and that this wasn't just another colonial seizure of Chinese property disguised as public health necessity. But the cooperation came with a price: Bryn now found himself personally responsible for making sure that the promises he'd made were actually kept, despite having limited control over the resources and personnel needed to fulfill them. He'd learned from Ah-Min about working skillfully within existing systems, but this situation required him to push these systems further, either to prove the effectiveness of community-based approaches or to reveal their limitations under colonial administrative realities.

Past midnight, after the immediate crisis was resolved and the evacuation finished without serious violence, Bryn finally ascended the winding road to his Peak apartment. The city stretched out below him, transformed by the health emergency, with quarantine lights glowing in windows and patrol boats moving across the harbor to stop unauthorized movement between districts.

Ah-Min was waiting with tea, as he always was during times of crisis, his calm presence offering a counterbalance to the chaos and uncertainty that had marked the day. But tonight, Bryn found himself looking at his mentor with new questions, wondering whether the philosophical wisdom that had seemed so profound during their previous talks would be enough for the practical challenges he was now facing.

"Difficult day, Master?" Ah-Min asked, though his tone suggested he already knew the answer.

"Cholera outbreak, forced evacuations, community resistance, political complications," Bryn replied, accepting the cup of tea gratefully. "And I may have promised more than I can actually deliver."

Bryn settled into his chair and tried to organize his thoughts about the day's events. "There was one encouraging development, though. Dr. Thompson appears to understand the importance of collaborating with communities rather than imposing medical solutions on them. But I'm not sure her confidence is based on real experience, and some of her suggestions might not work as well in practice as they sound in theory."

Ah-Min prepared his own tea with characteristic deliberation, and Bryn found himself observing the older man's movements more carefully than usual. There was still that quality of centeredness he'd noticed before, but tonight it seemed less like philosophical wisdom and more like the cautious composure of someone who

Chapter 13: The Healer's Path

had learned to handle complex situations by avoiding commitments that might prove impossible to meet.

"In Chinese medicine," Ah-Min said finally, "we understand that healing the body without considering the patient's social and spiritual context often results in only temporary improvement, followed by deeper illness. True healing needs relationship and trust, not just technical skill."

It was the kind of response Bryn had come to expect from Ah-Min, profound-sounding but not directly addressing the practical challenges he was facing. Tonight, for the first time, he wondered whether his mentor's wisdom was as applicable to his current situation as he had assumed.

"That's definitely what Dr. Thompson claims to believe," Bryn replied. "But I'm starting to see there's a big difference between understanding community-based medicine as a theory and actually putting it into practice during a colonial health crisis."

Ah-Min nodded slowly, his expression indicating he understood the point Bryn was making. "Perhaps the greatest challenge isn't choosing the right approach, but staying with it when systems resist because they weren't built for it."

The observation was more tangible than Ah-Min's usual philosophical musings, and it directly addressed the concern that kept Bryn awake despite his fatigue. He'd made promises today that relied on cooperation from colonial officials who might not share his dedication to community-centered solutions, and he'd committed himself to working with a medical colleague whose practical experience might not match her theoretical knowledge. "I'm worried that I've set myself up for failure," Bryn admitted. "The promises I made today about medical care and community involvement, they all depend on resources and cooperation that I can't guarantee. If I can't deliver on those commitments, it won't just be my credibility that's damaged. It will be the credibility of any future efforts at genuine cooperation between colonial authorities and Chinese communities."

Ah-Min sipped his tea thoughtfully, and when he spoke, his voice carried a note of caution that Bryn hadn't heard before in their conversations. "Master, in my experience, the most dangerous promises are those that assume others will change their nature to make our good intentions possible. Dr. Thompson may understand the theory of community-based medicine, but theory and practice often diverge when faced with the pressures of actual crisis management."

The warning was subtle but clear: Bryn might have been too quick to assume that Thompson's apparent understanding of community dynamics would lead to effective collaboration, and too optimistic about his capacity to influence colonial medical practices through personal commitment and good intentions.

"What would you suggest?" Bryn asked, though he was no longer sure he trusted his mentor's guidance as completely as he had before.

"That you prepare for the possibility that your new medical colleague's priorities may not align with yours as entirely as they seemed during today's crisis," Ah-Min replied. "And that you develop alternative approaches that do not depend solely on her cooperation or the colonial administration's willingness to support community-based solutions."

It was practical advice, but also very discouraging. Bryn had hoped that Thompson's arrival would be a chance to show that collaborative approaches to public health could succeed within colonial systems. If she turned out to be just another colonial professional who talks about community involvement but actually enacts top-down solutions, then his promises to the evacuated families would become impossible to keep.

The next morning brought another scorching day and a crisis that had worsened overnight, making yesterday's challenges seem almost simple by comparison. When Bryn arrived at the makeshift medical station he'd helped set up, he found Thompson reviewing patient charts with an expression that suggested serious complications had arisen since their last conversation.

"How are the patients responding to treatment?" he asked, though he could already sense from the atmosphere in the converted warehouse that the news wasn't going to be encouraging.

"Better than we might have expected given the delayed response to their initial symptoms," Thompson replied, her tone carefully professional. "But we're dealing with more cases than anticipated, and some of them are presenting with complications that require more intensive care than we can provide in this setting." She pointed to a part of the warehouse where several beds were separated behind makeshift screens. "Those patients need to be moved to Victoria Hospital right away, but the hospital is already full, and their transport could put them at additional risk during the trip across the city."

Bryn could see the dilemma taking shape. The community-based medical station was working better than expected for most cases, but the most serious cases required exactly the kind of intensive hospital care that the community had been trying to avoid. Moving those patients would break his promises about keeping families together, but leaving them in inadequate facilities could cost lives.

"What do you recommend?" he asked, though he suspected he wasn't going to like the answer.

"That we acknowledge the limitations of community-based care and focus on providing the best possible treatment for each individual case, even if that means compromising some of our initial commitments about keeping families together," Thompson replied.

Chapter 13: The Healer's Path

Her response was medically sound and professionally responsible, but it was also exactly the kind of decision that would undermine the trust he'd worked so hard to build with the evacuated communities. Once it became clear that the promised local medical care was sufficient only for minor cases, families would lose confidence in the entire effort and start demanding transport to European medical facilities regardless of the risks involved.

Bryn realized he was facing exactly the kind of situation that Ah-Min had warned him about: a crisis where good intentions clashed with practical limitations, and his promises were being tested against realities that might make them impossible to keep.

The real test of his community-based approach was just beginning, and he was no longer confident about how it would end. But for now, he was committed to working cooperatively with Dr. Thompson and use all the resources of the Sanitation Department until the cholera emergency was under control. He was determined to make his partnership with Thompson work and trust that he could help her see his perspective more clearly.

Chapter 14

Between Worlds

"Take risks that matter. Love deeply when love finds you, regardless of what others may think proper. I have observed that propriety often stands in the way of the very happiness it claims to preserve."

Aunt Eileen Williams

The evening air was thick with humidity as Bryn Williams adjusted his bow tie in the back seat of the rickshaw. His white dinner jacket, perfectly pressed that morning, was already starting to wilt in Hong Kong's relentless climate. The narrow streets of Wan Chai pulsed with life around them: vendors calling out in rapid Cantonese, the sweet smoke of joss sticks drifting from doorway shrines, and the distant sound of a gramophone playing American jazz from an open window above.

"You'll enjoy the Golden Phoenix," said Police Inspector Thomas Harrington, running a finger around his collar. His weathered face cracked into a grin that hinted at years of experience with Hong Kong's nightlife. "Finest dance hall in Wan Chai, if you ask me."

Both Welshmen abroad had formed a bond that went beyond professional ties. Thomas had been Bryn's unofficial guide to the colony's more complicated social customs since his arrival six months earlier. Tonight was one of their occasional outings, away from the watchful eyes of senior colonial officials who preferred their subordinates to maintain stricter propriety.

Their rickshaw weaved between motor cars and other rickshaws, past shophouses where warm yellow light spilled onto the pavement through wooden shutters. The air carried a mix of cooking oil, incense, and the salty scent of Victoria Harbor. Street vendors had set up their evening stalls, selling everything from roasted chestnuts to steaming bowls of noodles.

Thomas continued, lowering his voice as their coolie navigated around a slow-moving cart loaded with live chickens, "The Manager May Lin runs what the Chinese call a 'tight ship.' She ensures proper conduct and keeps the authorities satisfied. It's not some back-alley dive."

Bryn nodded, though he felt a familiar flutter of nervousness. His social confidence, so assured in the British army, had yet to fully adjust to Hong Kong's unique blend of East and West.

The rickshaw halted in front of a striking three-story building painted in deep red lacquer with gold trim. A curved staircase with polished brass handrails led upward from the street, and the entrance was lit by silk lanterns casting warm pools of light against the humid night. Music floated down, the unmistakable notes of a foxtrot played by what sounded like a Filipino band.

"Best part of twelve Hong Kong dollars for three dance tickets," Thomas muttered as they climbed, fishing coins from his waistcoat pocket. "Worth every penny, though."

The door opened into a completely different world. Crystal chandeliers hung from an ornate tin ceiling, casting prismatic light across a spacious dance floor of polished teak. Red silk wallpaper adorned the walls, featuring hand-painted golden phoenixes and delicate bamboo motifs. The air was cooler here, stirred by large *punka* fans operated by young Chinese men who pulled the ropes in steady rhythm.

Round tables encircled the dance floor, occupied by men in evening wear: naval officers in white tropical uniforms, merchant bankers in perfectly tailored dinner jackets, and fellow civil servants whose faces Bryn recognized from Government House receptions. The conversations were a mix of English, Portuguese, and Cantonese.

A booth near the entrance housed an elegant Chinese woman in her fifties, her iron gray hair pulled back into a sleek chignon secured with jade pins. Her black silk *qipao* seemed to absorb light, its mandarin collar fastened with small gold buttons. Her sharp eyes missed nothing as she rose to greet them.

"Ah, Inspector Harrington," she said, her English precise and unaccented. "Welcome back to the Golden Phoenix."

Thomas stepped forward with a slight bow. "Miss May Lin, may I introduce Deputy Chief Sanitary Inspector Bryn Williams."

May Lin's smile was knowing. "Any friend of Inspector Harrington's is welcome here. I trust you gentlemen will have an enjoyable evening." She gestured toward a Chinese man in a white jacket. "Ah Keung will show you to a table and arrange for dance tickets."

Thomas bought dance tickets: small, ornate cards embossed in gold with a phoenix in flight. "Two Hong Kong dollars each," Thomas explained quietly. "Consider it your welcome to Wan Chai."

Chapter 14: Between Worlds

Their table provided a perfect view of the dance floor, where couples moved in graceful synchronization to "Ain't She Sweet." The musicians, five Filipinos in white dinner jackets, played from a small, raised platform decorated with potted palms.

The dance hostesses stood along one side of the room, each wearing a numbered badge discreetly pinned to her dress. Their diversity amazed Bryn instantly. Chinese women in perfectly tailored *qipao* showcased Shanghai fashion elegance, their hair styled in finger waves. Russian émigrées wore European evening gowns that hinted at former wealth. Several Eurasian women possessed an exotic beauty that seemed to combine the finest features of both East and West.

"That's Miss Chen," Thomas whispered, nodding toward a striking woman in a crimson *qipao* embroidered with golden phoenixes. "Best dancer in the place. The blonde is Katya Petrova, Russian family that fled the Bolsheviks. The tall one by the pillar is Mary Wong. Eurasian beauty, speaks five languages."

"So many beautiful women," Bryn observed. "Are they also...?"

"Prostitutes?" Thomas shook his head firmly. "Absolutely not. May Lin is fanatical about maintaining distinctions. This is precisely what it advertises, a place where gentlemen can enjoy elegant company and dancing without compromising their social standing."

Thomas gestured toward other patrons. "See that fellow? Major Whitworth of the Royal Artillery. Books six or seven dances with Miss Chen every evening, and they discuss classical music. She's quite an expert. Charles Sutton heads Lloyd's Bank Far Eastern division. Prefers dancing with different partners to practice his languages."

A waiter appeared: a young Chinese man in a white jacket who spoke excellent English. "Good evening, gentlemen. May I bring you drinks?"

"Whiskey soda for me," Thomas said. "Bryn?"

"The same, thank you."

While waiting for their drinks, Bryn observed the interactions. Mrs. Lin occasionally intervened with subtle gestures, a meaningful look when a customer's hands wandered, a quiet word when conversations became too intimate. Her particular attention to the younger hostesses was unmistakable. "How does one actually approach them?" Bryn asked.

"Simple," Thomas replied. "Present your ticket, ask politely for the pleasure of a dance, and conduct yourself as you would with any lady. Remember that most are educated, intelligent women who have chosen this profession."

Taking a steadying breath, Bryn crossed the floor toward Miss Chen. She was even more striking up close, her crimson *qipao* tailored to perfection, her black hair styled in victory rolls. As he approached, she turned with a professional but genuinely warm smile.

"Good evening," he said, presenting his ticket. "Would you do me the honor of this dance?"

"The pleasure is mine," she replied, accepting his ticket. "I don't believe we've met. I'm Doris Chen."

"Bryn Williams. Sanitary Inspector."

Her eyebrows rose with interest. "A health inspector? How fascinating. You must see quite a lot of Hong Kong that most colonial officials miss entirely."

Her hand was cool and light as it settled in his, and when they stepped onto the floor for "The Blue Danube," Bryn was impressed by her flawless technique. Miss Chen moved with such skill that he felt transformed from a somewhat stiff civil servant into something approaching debonair.

"You dance beautifully," he said, grateful for those intensive lessons with Jasmine in Cairo.

"Thank you. I studied ballet and ballroom in Shanghai before coming to Hong Kong." Her English was precise, her voice melodious. "Tell me, Inspector Williams, how are you finding our city?"

The conversation flowed smoothly as they moved across the floor. Miss Chen proved well-informed, asking insightful questions about his work and sharing observations about recent performances at the Hong Kong Theatre. She seemed genuinely interested in his thoughts on the colony's public health challenges.

"You see the true Hong Kong," she observed during a complex series of turns. "Not merely the European quarters that most officials know."

As the waltz concluded, she stepped back with a graceful curtsy. "Thank you for the dance, Inspector Williams. I hope we'll have the opportunity again this evening."

Returning to Thomas, Bryn felt a curious mixture of exhilaration and cultural vertigo. "Quite something, isn't it?" his friend remarked. "A world within a world."

"She's remarkably intelligent," Bryn said. "I wasn't expecting such... depth."

"That's the beauty of this place," Thomas replied. "These women aren't acting out fantasies. They're fine women, providing elegant conversation and skilled dancing to men who appreciate both. Most support families, some save for business ventures, others simply enjoy the work."

Over the next hour, Bryn danced with several other hostesses. Elena Volkov,

Chapter 14: Between Worlds

a Russian émigré in sapphire blue silk, regaled him with witty observations about Hong Kong's social hierarchy while they foxtrotted. Her family had owned estates outside St. Petersburg before fleeing with nothing but their education and manners.

Miss Sarah Wong embodied different elegance: tall and graceful in a silver gown with traditional Chinese motifs. Her mixed heritage gave her exotic beauty that turned heads, and she effortlessly switched between English and Cantonese. "In Hong Kong, we must all learn to make our way among different peoples," she observed during their waltz. "Each of us finds our own place in this remarkable colony."

Between dances, their group expanded. Major Whitworth joined them, along with other civil servants and a Portuguese merchant named Silva who knew everyone and provided running commentary on the evening's social dynamics. The entire scene reflected 1930s Hong Kong's unique charm: a place where colonial society's strict boundaries could slightly loosen within carefully defined areas. The Golden Phoenix was such a place, where Eastern and Western cultures could interact on terms impossible in Government House's formal settings.

As the evening progressed, the crowd became livelier. Champagne flowed, the band's tempo increased, and Bryn found himself relaxing into the atmosphere, his nervousness replaced by genuine enjoyment. It was during a brief pause between dances that everything changed completely for Bryn. Near the far side of the room, close to the band platform, three young women stood together in animated conversation. Even from a distance, their family resemblance was obvious: the same graceful posture, the same shiny dark hair, the same elegant gestures. But it was the youngest that took Bryn's breath away.

She wore a silver gown that seemed to catch every light in the room, the fabric gracefully complementing her slender figure while maintaining perfect modesty. Her black hair was swept back into a soft chignon with loose curls framing her face, and she wore a simple diamond necklace whose understated elegance highlighted the gentle curve of her neck. When she laughed at something one of her companions whispered, her entire face lit up with genuine joy. Time seemed to slow as Bryn observed her. The music, laughter, and clinking glasses faded to a distant hum, leaving only her image etched in his mind. She moved with natural grace, her gestures effortless and genuine, her attention entirely on her companions' conversation. Something about her felt different from the other hostesses: less rehearsed, more authentic, as if she hadn't yet learned to treat every interaction as professional exchange.

"Thomas," Bryn said quietly, his voice strangely hoarse. "Who are they?"

Thomas followed his gaze and smiled knowingly. "Ah, the Valenzuela sisters. That's Mary, the eldest, in gold. Quite popular with Portuguese businessmen. The middle sister is Greta, in burgundy. And the youngest..." His grin widened. "That's Alicia, causing quite a stir since she started here."

"Alicia," Bryn repeated, tasting the name.

"Mexican parents. All three dance here to support their family. They're known for being particularly... selective about their dance partners."

As if sensing his attention, Alicia glanced across the room. For one breathless moment, her dark eyes seemed to meet his across the crowded space. The eye contact lasted only seconds, but Bryn felt something electric pass between them: recognition, perhaps, or possibility.

Without conscious decision, he began walking toward their group. His usual social confidence had returned, replaced by something deeper and more certain. As he approached, he could hear their conversation more clearly: they were discussing a recent art exhibition, their commentary revealing cultural sophistication and genuine intellectual curiosity.

Mary noticed his approach first, her expression becoming professionally welcoming. Greta followed her sister's gaze and straightened slightly. But Alicia continued speaking about the exhibition, seemingly unaware until he stood directly before them.

"Good evening," Bryn said, his voice steady despite his racing heart. He looked directly at Alicia, whose dark eyes met his with frank curiosity. "I'm Bryn Williams. Would you honor me with this dance?"

The band had begun another waltz, and couples were moving onto the floor around them. For a moment, nobody moved. Then Greta stepped forward smoothly, extending her hand with practiced grace. "I would be most pleased to," she said, positioning herself directly between Bryn and Alicia with a determined smile.

"But..." Alicia began, then stopped, stepping back slightly while maintaining eye contact with Bryn. Her expression showed surprise and perhaps disappointment, but also resigned acceptance that suggested this wasn't the first time her sister had intercepted a potential partner.

Creating a scene would be ungentlemanly and potentially harmful to all three sisters' reputations. With reluctant grace, Bryn bowed slightly to Greta and offered his arm. "Of course. It would be my pleasure."

As they moved onto the dance floor, Bryn caught one more glimpse of Alicia's face. She was watching them with an expression he couldn't quite read: part disappointment, part amusement, and something that might have been anticipation.

Chapter 14: Between Worlds

Greta proved skilled and persistent. She leaned in closely during the waltz, her perfume heavy, her comments aimed at showcasing her wit and sophistication. She discussed her family's background, her ambitions, her knowledge of Hong Kong society, all while maintaining flirtatious banter.

"I do hope we'll have many more opportunities to dance together," she said as the music concluded. "Perhaps we could move to a quieter table where we can continue our conversation over champagne?"

Bryn smiled politely as they returned to where Mary and Alicia waited. "Thank you for a most enjoyable dance, Greta. You're a lovely partner."

Greta's smile brightened with what she took as encouragement. "Would you like to join us for drinks?"

"Thank you for the kind invitation," Bryn replied carefully, "but I find myself in a dancing mood this evening." He turned to Alicia, whose dark eyes had been following the exchange with obvious interest. "I would be honored to have this next dance with you, Alicia, if you're willing."

Alicia's face lit up with genuine pleasure. "I would like that very much," she said simply, taking his offered hand.

As she led him toward the dance floor, Bryn caught a glimpse of Greta's expression. Her practiced charm had cracked slightly, revealing hurt pride and unmistakable annoyance.

The moment Bryn took Alicia in his arms, the world around them seemed to dissolve completely. The orchestra was playing "La Vie En Rose," and as they moved together, their steps synchronized with an ease that surprised them both. Her hand fit perfectly in his, her movements graceful and fluid, following his lead with intuitive understanding that felt almost supernatural. "You dance beautifully," he said softly, his voice barely audible over the music.

Her smile was radiant. "That's a lovely thing to say, though I wonder if you're not just being gallant."

"I'm Welsh," he replied with mock seriousness. "We're not known for gallantry. We're known for speaking our minds, sometimes to a fault."

Her laugh was genuine and unguarded. "Then I'm doubly complimented."

They continued dancing as the band moved from waltz to foxtrot, neither willing to break the spell that had settled over them. Between songs, they talked about Hong Kong, their different worlds, books and music and dreams. Alicia's intelligence shone through her beauty, her conversation sharp and engaging. As the song ended and they remained close together on the dance floor, both breathing slightly from the dancing and the intensity of their connection, Bryn felt something shift inside him. This evening had become far more than a casual night out in Wan Chai. Standing there with Alicia, her dark eyes reflecting the chandeliers' light, he understood that he was at a crossroads that would define everything that followed.

"Would you join me for a drink?" he asked, gesturing toward a quiet corner table away from her sisters and the main crowd. "Somewhere we can talk properly."

Alicia glanced toward Mary and Greta, then back to his face. Something in her expression suggested she felt the same magnetic pull that had drawn him across the crowded room to her.

"I would like that very much," she said softly.

Chapter 15

The Heart's Compass

"Some encounters are written in the stars, inevitable regardless of our conscious choices. The question is not whether such feelings are wise or foolish—they simply are. The question is how we choose to act upon them."

Ah-Min

At their secluded table, with glasses of champagne between them and the noise of the dance hall providing privacy, their conversation deepened. Bryn found himself sharing thoughts he'd rarely voiced aloud: his ambitions beyond colonial service, his observations about Hong Kong's complex social structure, his occasional homesickness for Welsh valleys.

"Tell me about your life before Hong Kong," she asked during a pause in the music.

Bryn discussed his childhood in the Welsh mines, his rescue by Aunt Eileen, and his service in Egypt, carefully leaving out his relationship with Jasmine. He shared his love for art and literature, along with the sound of Welsh choirs echoing through the valleys.

"You've seen more of the world than most men twice your age," Alicia observed thoughtfully.

"What about you? Your family, your dreams?" Bryn asked.

For a moment, her expression became guarded. "My father, Ramon, owned an orchard, and was of Spanish heritage. My mother, Lupe of native Mexican heritage, kept us together after my father passed away." She paused, seeming to weigh her words carefully. "We came to Hong Kong when I was sixteen because my sister, Mary had married a Chinese San Francisco businessman, who had family here in Hong Kong. . . But that's another story…well, we do what we must to survive."

There was pain in her voice that spoke of trauma and misfortune. Bryn sensed deeper currents but respected her reluctance to share more. "And your dreams?"

he pressed gently.

"To travel, to continue learning. I'd like to write someday, perhaps about this remarkable colony and all its peoples. Hong Kong is unlike anywhere else in the world, caught between the old ways and the new, between China and the Empire."

"You see much more than you let on," he observed after she made a particularly insightful comment about colonial attitudes toward local customs.

"Most gentlemen seem quite surprised when I express opinions about art or politics," she admitted with a knowing smile. "They expect pretty conversation about the weather and little more."

"Then most men are fools."

"Most gentlemen are shaped by their upbringing and station," she corrected gently. "But some choose to see beyond what they were taught to expect."

Alicia's wisdom impressed Bryn. Here was someone who understood the world's complexities despite her youth.

Hours passed like minutes. The band played set after set, couples rotated on and off the dance floor, but Bryn and Alicia remained absorbed in their conversation. Bryn was concerned that Miss Lin would interrupt their conversation and encourage Alicia to return to the dance floor, but she didn't. Bryn and Alicia discovered shared interests in literature and music, debated colonial policy with university-level intensity, and found themselves laughing at observations about the social absurdities of Hong Kong.

As the evening wound down and the crowd thinned, Bryn made a decision that surprised him with its certainty.

"Alicia," he said, leaning slightly across the table to ensure privacy. "I'd like to see you again. Not here, but somewhere we can truly talk without interruption." He paused, aware of the significance of what he was proposing. "Would you allow me to take you to dinner at the Hong Kong Club?"

Her eyes widened slightly. They both understood what such an invitation meant in Hong Kong's rigid social hierarchy. The Hong Kong Club was the preserve of the colony's elite, where Chinese residents were barely tolerated as guests, never as members. For a Mexican dance hall hostess to dine there as a colonial official's guest would be a statement impossible to misinterpret. "That's a very significant invitation," she said carefully.

"I'm certain I want to spend more time with you," he replied honestly.

Her smile, when it came, was radiant. "I would be honored to accept, but I must have my mother's approval first, and clear it with Miss Lin, my employer."

Chapter 15: The Heart's Compass

"Of course. If you need me to speak to them, I'd be pleased to do so."

As their hands touched across the table, Bryn felt a certainty he'd never experienced before. Whatever this was between them, attraction, infatuation, or something deeper, it was only beginning. "Shall I make reservations for next Saturday?" he suggested.

"Send word to me here once you've arranged things. I'll let you know if Mother and Miss Lin approve."

As the Golden Phoenix began its closing rituals and the remaining patrons prepared to leave, they rejoined Mary and Greta for the final courtesies of the evening.

Greta's displeasure was barely concealed beneath her professional smile, but Mary seemed genuinely pleased by her youngest sister's obvious happiness. "It was lovely meeting you, Inspector Williams," she said warmly. "I hope we'll see you again soon."

Outside, the night air felt heavier after the fan-cooled dance hall. Thomas, who had tactfully remained at their original table for the latter part of the evening, rejoined Bryn as they waited for rickshaws.

"Well?" Thomas asked, lighting a cigarette. "Was it worth bending your usual strict adherence to propriety?"

Bryn considered the evening: the music, the conversation, the moment when Alicia's eyes had met his across the dance floor, and most significantly, the easy intimacy of their extended conversation. "A man needs certain cultural experiences to truly understand a place," he said finally.

Thomas's laugh echoed down the quiet street. "Cultural experiences indeed. Welcome to the real Hong Kong, Bryn Williams."

As their rickshaws pulled away in different directions, Bryn settled back against the worn leather seat and watched the sleeping city pass by. The streets were quieter now, most vendors having packed up their stalls, but the night still hummed with Hong Kong's particular energy. When he reached his flat on Victoria Peak, Bryn found Ah-Min waiting as usual, despite the late hour. Although officially Ah-Min was his Best Boy and servant, he had become a trusted advisor; their evening conversations had evolved into something resembling friendship, though social conventions required them to maintain certain formal boundaries.

"Good evening, Master," Ah-Min said quietly, appearing from the kitchen with his usual silent efficiency. "I trust your evening was enjoyable?"

Bryn removed his jacket, handing it to Ah-Min along with his bow tie and collar studs. The ritual was familiar and comforting. "It was... illuminating,

Ah-Min. More so than I expected."

"The dance hall was satisfactory?"

"The Golden Phoenix exceeded all expectations." Bryn moved toward the French doors that led to his veranda, throwing them open to let the cooler night air circulate. The view of Victoria Harbor, partially obscured by low-lying clouds, reminded him of Hong Kong's unique position between worlds. "There's something I'd like to discuss with you, if you have a moment."

"Of course, Master. Shall I prepare tea? The night air suggests a storm approaching."

"Something stronger, I think. It's been an evening for... new experiences."

Ah-Min returned with a crystal tumbler of excellent Scottish whiskey and settled into the chair Bryn indicated. Over the months, these informal evening conversations had become one of Bryn's greatest pleasures in Hong Kong.

"I met someone tonight," Bryn said without preamble. "A young woman. Alicia Valenzuela. She's..." He paused, trying to find words that would convey her impact. "She's unlike anyone I've encountered in Hong Kong."

Ah-Min's expression remained carefully neutral, but Bryn caught something in his eyes that might have been concern. "A dance hall hostess?"

"Yes, but that doesn't... it's more complicated than that."

"Such things usually are," Ah-Min replied diplomatically. "If I am not intruding…may I ask about your intentions?"

"I've invited her to dinner at the Hong Kong Club."

This time Ah-Min's reaction was impossible to miss. His eyebrows rose slightly, and he set down his teacup with particular care. "That is indeed a significant step, Master. Such an invitation will attract considerable attention."

"I'm aware of the implications."

"Are you prepared for the consequences? The colonial community can be quite... unforgiving of social boundary crossings."

Bryn had been asking himself the same question since making the invitation. "I don't know," he admitted. "But I know that I want to see her again, to understand this... connection I felt tonight."

Ah-Min was quiet for several moments, his gaze focused on the harbor lights flickering through the mist. When he spoke again, his voice carried the weight of experience. "In Chinese philosophy, we speak of *ming yun*, or destiny. Some encounters are written in the stars, inevitable regardless of our conscious choices.

Chapter 15: The Heart's Compass

Others are mere coincidences, important only in the moment."

"How does one tell the difference?"

"Time reveals all truths. But there are signs for those who know how to read them. When two people meet and find themselves speaking thoughts they have never voiced aloud, when conversation flows like water finding its natural course, when the artificial boundaries of society seem suddenly... transparent." He paused. "These can be indicators of something deeper than mere attraction."

"You think I'm being foolish?"

"I think you are being human," Ah Min corrected gently. "Such feelings are not easily commanded by reason. A wise man considers what honor requires of him when his heart pulls him toward new paths."

They sat in comfortable silence, listening to the night sounds of Hong Kong: the distant horn of a late ferry, the rustle of palm fronds in the rising wind, the soft percussion of early raindrops beginning to fall.

"There's something else," Bryn said eventually. "Tonight, at the Golden Phoenix, I was struck by the artificiality of so many social boundaries we maintain here. Watching Chinese, European, Russian, and Eurasian people interact so naturally within those walls, I wondered why such interactions seem impossible everywhere else."

"Because the Golden Phoenix exists outside normal structure," Ah-Min replied. "It is what we call a 'neutral space': like tea houses where merchants of different cultures meet for business, or temples where people of various faiths come to pray. In such places, the usual rules are suspended by mutual agreement."

"But why can't more of Hong Kong be like that?"

"Because power requires order to maintain itself. When the established order is disturbed, those who benefit from it become uneasy. This is why such mixing is permitted only in certain places, under careful watch."

"Do you think such arrangements can last?"

"All things pass away in time," Ah-Min replied. "Dynasties rise and fall like the tides. What endures are the bonds between people who seek understanding despite the differences that separate them."

Bryn considered the weight of his words in silence.

The rain had intensified, creating a steady drumming against the windows and filling the air with the clean scent of tropical downpour. It was during this peaceful contemplation that Ah-Min quietly excused himself and returned with a silver tray bearing the day's delayed post. "A letter arrived this afternoon from Wales, Master.

Ashes and Dawn

The postmark indicates it has been several weeks in transit."

Bryn recognized his Aunt Eileen's careful handwriting immediately, and something in the weight of the envelope made his heart quicken with apprehension. Setting aside his whiskey, he opened the letter with careful fingers.

"My Dearest Bryn,

I hope this letter finds you thriving in your exotic posting. Your last correspondence painted such vivid pictures of Hong Kong that I felt I could almost smell the harbor air and hear the blend of languages in your bustling streets.

Thank you from the bottom of my heart for the money you have been sending me on regularly. It has made my life more comfortable and given me a chance to spoil myself with special treats.

I write with news that I fear will trouble you, though I pray you will receive it with the strength and wisdom I know you possess. Dr. Stevenson has been quite frank about my condition. The weakness in my chest has progressed beyond what the doctors can do. He estimates that I have perhaps six months, possibly less, before I must make my final journey. I have chosen to remain at home rather than in the hospital.

I don't know if I am able to see you once again before I pass, but in a way you have never left me. Do not feel like you need to rush back to see me once more. Your spirit still is here with me in my home. I am content with that and see your face often in my dreams.

I am comfortable, and Mrs. Thomas from next door checks on me daily. More importantly, I sense from your letters that you are discovering something vital about yourself in that distant colony. Some discoveries cannot be rushed or interrupted without great cost to one's soul.

Live fully while you are young, my dear son. Take risks that matter. Love deeply when love finds you, regardless of what others may think proper. I have observed that propriety often stands in the way of the very happiness it claims to preserve.

And remember that you did the right thing to leave Wales, however difficult it has been for you.

And remember that I will never leave you as long as there is a place for me in your heart, as there is for you in mine.

With all my love and prayers,

Aunt Eileen."

Bryn sat motionless for several long minutes, the letter trembling slightly in his hands. The woman who had raised him, who had sacrificed her own chances for marriage and family to ensure his education and advancement, was preparing for death with the same gentle dignity she had brought to everything in her life.

Ah-Min, who had observed the change in his master's expression, spoke softly. "Difficult news from home?"

Chapter 15: The Heart's Compass

"My Aunt Eileen. She's..." Bryn's voice caught slightly. "She's dying. Six months, perhaps less."

"I am deeply sorry, Master. She is the woman who raised you?"

"Yes. She gave up everything for me. And now, when she needs me most, I'm half a world away, falling in love with a dance hall hostess and contemplating dinner invitations that could destroy my career." The irony struck him with painful clarity.

Ah-Min was quiet for a moment, studying the rain patterns on the windows as if seeking wisdom there. "Perhaps," he said finally, "she would not see these things as contradictory."

"What do you mean?"

"A woman who sacrifices her own happiness to ensure another's future understands the value of seizing opportunities when they arise. Your meeting tonight, your feelings for Miss Valenzuela, these are not betrayals of her sacrifice. They are fulfillments of it."

Bryn read the letter again, focusing on her words about taking risks that matter and loving deeply when love finds you. "She says I shouldn't rush home immediately. That I'm discovering something vital about myself here."

"Wise woman. She understands that some lessons can only be learned in their proper season. But she also ensures you know that time is finite, that choices deferred can become choices lost."

The rain drummed steadily against the veranda roof. In its rhythm, Bryn heard echoes of the evening's waltz, of Alicia's laughter, of his aunt's gentle voice reading to him by lamplight in their small Swansea cottage.

Ah-Min reached for a familiar wooden box. "The night is still young, and the rain will continue for some time."

Bryn smiled, watching Ah-Min's practiced hands arrange the Go board between them. The black and white stones seemed to mirror Hong Kong's complexities: patterns of conflict and cooperation, territory gained and lost, simple rules creating infinite possibilities for both harmony and discord. As they began their game, Bryn found his thoughts returning to Alicia's face as she had looked at him across the crowded dance floor, intelligent, beautiful, and somehow inevitable. Whatever consequences awaited his decision to pursue this connection, he knew the Golden Phoenix had lived up to its name.

The game proceeded in comfortable silence, each man absorbed in strategy and contemplation. Outside, Hong Kong settled into its humid dreams, while inside, a young Welshman and British civil servant tried to reconcile the pull of home with the promise of something entirely new blooming in the tropical night.

As Ah-Min captured a significant group of Bryn's stones, he looked up with a slight smile. "In Go, as in life, sometimes we must sacrifice the familiar to discover new possibilities."

Bryn studied the board, seeing not just the game but the larger patterns it represented. "And sometimes," he replied, placing his next stone with careful deliberation, "those discoveries change everything we thought we knew about ourselves."

Through the clearing mist, the lights of Victoria Harbour appeared like scattered stars against dark water. Sampans and junks rode at anchor alongside great steamers that connected Hong Kong to London, Shanghai, and San Francisco. It was a view that never failed to remind Bryn of Hong Kong's unique position as a crossroads of cultures and possibilities.

Just like the crossroads he now faced himself.

Chapter 16

Ashes and Pearls

"The most dangerous secrets are the ones that masquerade as love stories, because by the time you realize the truth, you're already trapped in someone else's war."

Lupe Valenzuela

The brass nameplate at 1 Jackson Road gleamed under gaslight as the Bentley taxi pulled to the curb. The Hong Kong Club rose before them like a fortress of colonial privilege, its neoclassical columns speaking of an empire that never questioned its right to exist.

Alicia smoothed her emerald silk evening gown, the one extravagance she'd allowed herself since beginning work at the Golden Phoenix. The pearls at her throat, a gift from a generous patron who'd appreciated her conversation about Spanish poetry, felt cool against her skin.

"Are you certain they'll accept me?" she asked, though her voice carried none of the uncertainty it might have held two years ago. "Your Hong Kong Club has rather specific restrictions regarding race and ethnicity."

Bryn's jaw tightened as he helped her from the taxi, his hand lingering at her elbow longer than strictly necessary. The warmth of her skin through the silk made him acutely aware of her proximity. Her perfume, something subtle with hints of jasmine, seemed to wrap around him as she stepped close. He'd been naive to think this would be simple. "Leave that to me, Alicia."

The doorman's practiced bow slightly faltered as his eyes took in Alicia's light olive skin and dark hair. Bryn caught the hesitation and felt his temper rise. This was exactly what he'd hoped to avoid.

Inside, oil portraits of governors gazed down from mahogany walls while crystal chandeliers cast warm light across Persian rugs. The air smelled of tobacco, aged whiskey, and institutional money.

"Inspector Williams!" A thin man in a tailored tuxedo approached with measured stride. "How delightful to see you again."

"Evening, Matthews," Bryn nodded. "I would like to introduce my companion tonight, Miss Alicia Valenzuela."

Matthews' smile never wavered, but his eyes performed the same subtle calculation they'd seen at the door. "Miss... Valenzuela. From Spain, Valencia perhaps?"

"Mexico," Alicia replied truthfully, her chin lifting with hard-earned pride. "My father came from Valencia to settle in Mexico. My mother is native Mexican."

Bryn watched Matthews' face change and felt his patience evaporating. Alicia caught the shift in his posture, the way Bryn's shoulders squared and his voice took on a sharper edge. Something warm unfurled in her chest at being defended by a man who expected nothing in return.

"I'm afraid there might be complications regarding dining room access. Club policy about guests of... non-...background..." Matthews said.

"Perhaps Director Whitmore is available," Bryn said, cutting off Matthews' stammering response. His tone carried the authority of someone accustomed to getting his way in official matters.

"Yes, of course, Inspector, I'll get him right away," Matthews replied, scurrying back to the offices.

Within minutes, the Club's Director materialized, portly but with unshakeable confidence. His handshake was firm, his visual assessment of Alicia swift and calculating. "Spanish, I take it?" he asked after introductions.

"My citizenship is Mexican, having been born there. My father's family came from Valencia in Spain." While it was the truth, but not the whole truth. She wouldn't mention the modest adobe house, the desperate flight to Hong Kong, the dance hall where she now earned her living.

"Land ownership. Always the mark of respectability." Whitmore turned to Bryn with renewed interest. "Spanish patrons have always been welcome at the Club. Matthews must have misunderstood." Whitmore snapped his fingers and the maître d' appeared. "Show Inspector Williams and Miss Valenzuela to their table." Whitmore smiled genuinely. "Have an enjoyable dinner."

As they were led to the dining room, Bryn felt the familiar satisfaction of authority properly applied. He'd used his position to protect her, and it felt right. The possessive gesture of his hand at the small of her back felt right too. Conversations paused as they passed, society matrons peering over champagne glasses at the exotic beauty on the Inspector's arm.

"You're furious," Alicia murmured as they were seated overlooking the harbor.

Chapter 16: Ashes and Pearls

"Bloody right I am. And honestly, I naively thought there would not be an issue," Bryn replied.

"Welcome to my world, though usually the discrimination is more direct." She adjusted her pearl necklace. "Thank you for handling that."

The sincerity in her voice surprised him. Most women in his social circle expected such interventions as their due. Alicia seemed genuinely grateful, as if she'd grown accustomed to fighting those battles alone.

The dining room stretched before them, a cathedral of colonial excess. At nearby tables, Alicia caught fragments of familiar conversation about shipping rates and plantation profits. The same chatter that had surrounded her family at the Peninsula Hotel, back when they'd thought they were honored guests rather than unwitting pawns.

"Tell me something," Bryn said after they'd ordered wine, leaning forward slightly. The candlelight caught the amber flecks in his eyes, and Alicia found herself studying the strong line of his jaw, the way his hands moved with quiet confidence around his wine glass. "And please don't be offended... How does a woman with your grace, elegance and intelligence end up working as a dance hostess?" He watched her consider the question, noting how the flickering candlelight played across her throat above the pearls, how she tilted her head slightly when thinking.

"It's quite a story, Bryn."

"I have all evening."

She studied his face in the candlelight. "We weren't always refugees. Our orchards were just outside Hermosillo, in Sonora. My father Ramon was beloved by the community." Her voice softened with memory. "Papa had the most beautiful voice. In the evenings, neighbors would gather to hear him tell stories. Ancient Yaqui legends from my mother's people, tales of his Valencia ancestors."

Bryn found himself leaning forward, drawn by something in her tone. This wasn't the polished patter he'd expected. "What happened?"

"Papa died when I was sixteen." The words came out flat, practiced. "Mama tried to keep the orchards going, but a Yaqui woman and three girls couldn't manage it alone. We were going to lose everything. Then Mary, my sister, met and fell in love with a Chinese businessman, Kin Wah Chan from San Francisco."

Bryn felt a chill of recognition. "Not the Chan family from Victoria Peak?"

"You knew them?"

"Knew of them. Kin Wah's father controlled significant business interests in Hong Kong. But rumors circulated they weren't all legitimate." His professional instincts sharpened. "What happened?"

The familiar tightness gripped her chest. "Kin Wah offered everything. He would Mary, pay off our debts, have us move to San Francisco to live with him, and bring us to Hong Kong for the wedding." She took a sip of wine. "Mary was so excited, so in love with the idea of joining such a prestigious family."

"But you weren't convinced."

"Something felt wrong. Too much money from sources no one would explain clearly. Too many men who deferred to Kin Wah despite his youth." She met his eyes directly. "While we were staying at the Peninsula Hotel, preparing for the wedding, there was a huge explosion in the Chan home, destroying everything and everyone."

Bryn's expression shifted, pieces clicking into place. "I remember reading about that. Massive explosion on Victoria Peak, prominent Chinese family killed." His eyes sharpened. "Though I recall thinking at the time that the circumstances seemed... unusually thorough for a gas leak."

"You weren't the only one with suspicions."

The turtle soup arrived, but Bryn barely noticed. His mind was working through the implications, connecting this personal tragedy to cases that had crossed his desk. "Blue Dragons," he said quietly. "The police suspected territorial disputes over drug networks."

"The Chans weren't just wealthy merchants, Inspector. They were the Dragon Head family of the Red Phoenix Triad."

This changed everything. Bryn reached across the table, covering her hand with his, feeling the slight tremor in her fingers. Her skin was soft, warm, and he found himself tracing his thumb across her knuckles without thinking. The simple touch sent an unexpected current through him. "How did your family survive?"

Alicia looked down at their joined hands, surprised by the gentleness in his touch. Most men grabbed or grasped, but his fingers held hers with careful strength. She didn't pull away. "The Chan family had arranged for us to stay at the Peninsula Hotel while they made the marriage arrangements at their home."

"The hotel booking saved your lives," he said quietly, professional understanding replacing romantic interest for the moment. "If you'd stayed at the estate..."

She nodded. "Mrs. Chan insisted we stay at the Peninsula. I thought it was hospitality. It was protection."

"Or keeping potential witnesses at a distance."

Chapter 16: Ashes and Pearls

The main course arrived as Alicia continued her story, describing their desperate weeks at the Peninsula, the kindness of the hotel's guest relations manager, their eventual move to Sham Shui Po. "The Golden Phoenix saved us," she said simply. "Mr. Lee, the owner, runs a respectable establishment. We dance with businessmen and government officials, nothing improper. The money is enough to keep a roof over our heads and food on the table."

Bryn found himself reassessing everything he thought he knew about places like the Golden Phoenix. In Alicia's telling, it became not a den of vice but a lifeline for desperate women. "Your mother allowed this?"

"Mama is remarkable. She researched the Golden Phoenix thoroughly before letting us accept positions there. She knew we needed honest work that paid well." Alicia's voice filled with admiration. "Every night when we come home, she's waiting with tea and whatever small treat she's managed to afford. Mama has kept us safe and together when everything else fell apart."

"She sounds formidable."

"She has to be. A Yaqui woman protecting three daughters in a foreign city." Alicia's chin lifted with pride. "We've survived, and we've done it honestly. We're not the same naive Mexican girls who stepped off that ocean liner, but we're not broken either."

"And now?"

"Now I'm having dinner at the Hong Kong Club with a British Inspector who asks dangerous questions." Her smile didn't quite reach her eyes. "Quite an improvement."

"Is that what I am? An improvement?"

The question hung between them, charged with possibility. Bryn realized he genuinely cared about her answer in a way that surprised him. When she looked at him directly, her dark eyes holding his with an intensity that made his breath catch, he felt something shift between them.

"You're different. Most men want fantasy. They want the exotic Spanish dancer, the mysterious beauty with a tragic past. You seem interested in reality." Her voice had dropped lower, more intimate. "You look at me like I'm someone worth knowing, not just worth having."

"Reality is more interesting. Usually more dangerous too."

"Are you warning me or yourself?"

His smile was rueful. "Both, probably."

They lingered over coffee and brandy, the conversation having moved beyond social convention. Bryn found himself forgetting to maintain professional distance, drawn by her intelligence and the strength beneath her beauty.

The rest of the evening was occupied with lighter conversation about Mexico, about Wales and Egypt, and adapting to Hong Kong's colonial culture.

As they prepared to leave, threading through tables where conversations continued about stock business deals and weekend parties, Bryn caught their reflection in the restaurant's mirrors. They left the club arm in arm in silence but with a new powerful connection.

"Thank you," she said as they settled into the taxi. "For dinner, for defending me, for treating me like someone whose thoughts matter."

"They do matter. You matter."

The words carried more weight than he'd intended. At the Golden Phoenix, he realized, she was valued for performance. This felt different. He reached for her hand and held it gently in his. "I admire and respect you so much for the courage and resilience you have shown through your ordeal and after."

Alicia leaned over and kissed Bryn gently on the cheek. "Thank you. That means a great deal coming from you."

"Where to, Inspector?" the driver asked.

Bryn looked at her questioningly. "The Peninsula?"

"No," she said quietly. "We have a flat in Sham Shui Po now. Much more practical."

As the taxi wound through Hong Kong's narrow streets, the leather seat brought them closer together with each turn. Alicia was aware of the solid warmth of Bryn's shoulder nearly touching hers, the way his presence seemed to fill the small space. The intimacy of being enclosed together in the dim cab made every shared glance feel weighted with unspoken possibility.

"Will I see you again?" Bryn asked as the taxi slowed.

She looked at him in the dim light, this man who'd shown her glimpses of the life she might have had if things had been different. "Do you want to?"

"Yes, and many more times," he replied enthusiastically.

"Then you'll find me," she said, stepping out into the Hong Kong night. As she moved to close the taxi door, their eyes met one final time. For a moment, she hesitated, her hand on the door frame, and he thought she might say something more. Instead, she offered him a smile that promised possibilities. "I'm not hard to find, Bryn. After all, you know where I work."

Chapter 16: Ashes and Pearls

The taxi pulled away, carrying him back toward whatever official duties awaited, while she climbed the narrow stairs to the flat she shared with her mother and sisters. Bryn watched through the rear window until her silhouette disappeared into the building, then settled back against the leather seat with a sensation he'd almost forgotten existed. Want. Not just physical attraction, though God knew that was there. Something deeper that made his chest tight and his thoughts scattered. Something he'd sworn he'd never feel again after Yasmine.

He'd loved Yasmine with the desperate intensity of youth, believing their connection could survive anything. Her sudden departure from Cairo to honor an arranged marriage obligation had damaged him so completely that he'd convinced himself that kind of vulnerability was finished for him. Work became his refuge. Cases, evidence, the clean logic of investigation where answers existed if you looked hard enough. But watching Alicia navigate the club's casual racism with such grace, listening to her describe survival without self-pity, seeing the strength beneath her beauty... it stirred something he'd buried with Yasmine's memory.

This was different, though. Yasmine had been sheltered, protected by family wealth. Alicia had already walked through fire and emerged transformed but not broken. She understood survival in ways Yasmine never had to learn. The realization unsettled him. He'd spent three years telling himself that what he'd felt for Yasmine was irreplaceable, that honoring her memory meant closing off that part of himself permanently. But sitting in this taxi, still tasting wine and still feeling the warmth of Alicia's hand under his, Bryn understood that grief and love weren't the same thing.

He could mourn Yasmine and still want Alicia. He could honor the past without sacrificing the future. The dangerous part wasn't just that he wanted her. The dangerous part was that he wanted her to want him back, not as another patron seeking entertainment, but as a man worthy of the woman who'd just trusted him with her family's tragedy.

Tomorrow he would return to his files and reports, to the careful world of colonial law enforcement where everything had its proper place. But tonight, riding through Hong Kong's neon lit streets, Bryn Williams allowed himself to imagine what it might feel like to be someone's choice rather than their duty. What it might feel like to love a woman who'd already proven she could survive anything.

Chapter 17

Permission to Love

"When asking permission to upset the natural order of things, bring flowers and speak softly. The revolution can wait until after tea."

Oscar Wilde

Three Months Later

The South China Morning Post lay folded on Wellington's desk, its headline clearly visible: "JAPANESE NAVAL EXERCISES INTENSIFY IN SOUTH CHINA SEA." Bryn tried not to stare at it as sweat pooled beneath his starched collar despite the struggling ceiling fan. His promotion papers sat beside the newspaper, signed but still lingering after two weeks.

Wellington had been distracted lately, and something troubled him beyond the usual colonial bureaucracy.

"Dr. Wellington will see you now, Bryn," Alice Chen announced from behind her neat desk. Her knowing smile seemed more subdued than usual, touched with something that might have been worry. Young colonial officers requesting personal meetings weren't unusual, but these weren't normal times.

The chair creaked as Wellington lowered his fragile frame. His ruddy face displayed the constant redness from years of tropical bureaucracy, but today it bore additional strain. Dark circles shaded his eyes, and his normally immaculate desk was cluttered with papers and half-finished correspondence.

"What brings you here today, Bryn? I hope there's no trouble in your district."

Bryn's throat tightened. "No, sir. Everything runs smoothly there." He paused, gathering courage like ammunition. "I'm here about a personal matter. I'd like to announce my engagement to Alicia Valenzuela."

The words escaped in a rush. Relief flooded through him as if a dam had burst. "And I realize I need official approval."

Wellington's tired features softened, and for a moment, the weight seemed to lift from his shoulders. "Congratulations, my boy! Wonderful news." His voice carried Cambridge precision warmed by genuine affection. "When you first introduced Alicia to me, I could see she'd captured something in you. A remarkable young woman."

The sincerity in Wellington's voice loosened something tight in Bryn's chest. "Thank you. I'm happier than I thought possible."

Wellington's expression grew more layered, joy mixing with something close to concern. "The timing is... interesting." He gestured toward the newspaper. "These are complicated days, Bryn. The political situation impacts everything now, even personal matters."

"How so, sir?"

Wellington stood up and moved to the window, hands clasped behind his back. Victoria Peak rose into low-hanging clouds despite the morning sunshine. "The Colonial Office has become more... particular about marriage approvals. Security considerations, they call it. Questions about loyalty and divided allegiances."

Bryn felt his stomach tighten. "Are you saying approval might be difficult?"

"I'm saying it needs careful handling." Wellington turned back, his eyes filled with paternal concern. "You mentioned the family name is Valenzuela. She's from Mexico?"

The intersection of love and imperial politics was about to complicate everything. "Her family originates from northern Mexico, and her father's family is from Spain," Bryn said.

Wellington nodded thoughtfully. "Let me be frank about the current landscape. The situation with Japan has made everyone nervous. Questions arise about non-British connections, especially from countries with…complex international relationships." He returned to his desk and opened a folder with official seals. "Mexico maintains diplomatic relations with Germany. Trade agreements that concern London. It's not personal, you understand, but these connections matter now in ways they didn't before."

Bryn leaned forward. "Surely Alicia's family background can't be seen as a security concern?"

"In normal times, certainly not. But we're not living in normal times," Wellington's voice carried the weight of inside knowledge.

Wellington's eyebrows lifted with genuine interest. "Spanish heritage through her father? That changes everything. European ancestry, Christian background, colonial administrative traditions." He smiled warmly. "Spanish blood provides exactly the documentation we need." Wellington was genuinely pleased, not just

Chapter 17: Permission to Love

solving a problem but happy for Bryn's happiness.

"The name Valenzuela derives from Valencia, I believe," Bryn added.

"Indeed, it does. If we can establish Miss Valenzuela's Spanish lineage properly, that addresses any bureaucratic concerns." Wellington moved to his filing cabinet. "I'll need family documents, birth certificates, church records, anything establishing European heritage."

"I'll speak with Alicia's mother Lupe, about family papers."

Wellington's expression became more paternal than official. "Bryn, I want you to succeed in this. You deserve happiness. But I need you to understand the broader picture."

He leaned forward secretly. "The political situation is worsening faster than most realize. Japanese forces now control northern China. Their navy patrols these waters regularly." He pointed toward the harbor. "Hong Kong might face challenges we've never seen before."

"War was coming, and Wellington was preparing me without saying it directly," Bryn thought. "What kind of challenges?"

"The kind that make personal relationships politically sensitive. Mixed marriages, foreign connections, divided loyalties." Wellington's voice dropped. "In such circumstances, Spanish heritage becomes vital protection. But even then..."

"Even then what?" Bryn asked.

"Even then, you'll need to be very careful. Social activities noted. Travel restricted. Communications monitored." Wellington met his eyes directly. "Are you prepared for that level of scrutiny?"

Bryn felt the weight of the choice before him. "If it means marrying Alicia, yes."

Wellington smiled with genuine warmth. "Good man. Alicia's Spanish heritage provides excellent cover, and I trust your judgment completely. If you've chosen her, she must be exceptional." There's something else," Wellington continued. "Your promotion to Deputy Chief Sanitary Officer has been approved. The salary increase will support a family nicely, and the position carries sufficient status for social acceptance."

Relief and gratitude washed over Bryn. "Thank you, sir. For everything."

"Thank me by being happy, my boy. Build your life, love your wife, but stay alert to changing times."

That evening, Bryn sat at his writing desk in Peak Mansions, fountain pen poised over cream-colored paper. He began the letter, then stopped, considering his words carefully.

"My dearest Aunt Eileen,

I hope this letter finds you still managing your illness as best you can. I think about you often now."

He paused, thinking of her cottage in Wales, of the woman who had raised him when his own parents proved inadequate to the task. How could he explain the complexities of colonial life, the bureaucratic hurdles that love must navigate here? How could he not focus on the fact that she was dying?

"I have news that I believe will bring you joy. I have fallen deeply in love with a remarkable young woman named Alicia Valenzuela. She is seventeen, the daughter of a Mexican family residing here in Hong Kong. I plan to ask her to marry me if she'll have me."

The pen felt heavy in his hand as he considered how much to reveal about their circumstances.

"You would adore her, Aunt Eileen. She has your quick wit and talent for seeing through pretense. When we first met at a dance, she challenged my assumptions about colonial life with such intelligence that I found myself speechless."

That memory still made him smile. Alicia's directness had been both unsettling and captivating.

"She has Spanish heritage through her father, which helps navigate certain bureaucratic considerations here. Dr. Wellington has been wonderfully supportive, though he warns that these are complicated times for personal matters."

He set down the pen, staring out at Victoria Harbor where British warships had become increasingly visible. How much should he worry Aunt Eileen with political realities?

"More importantly, Alicia makes me want to be a better man. Not just a more successful administrator, but someone worthy of her respect and love. I find myself questioning assumptions I once took for granted, seeing this colony through her eyes. In so many ways she reminds me of you. She's direct, strong, and yet infinitely kind and compassionate."

The letter continued, but writing it forced him to confront how much his world had changed since meeting Alicia.

"Your blessing would mean everything to me. I know you would grow to love her if you met. I will be discussing the possibility of having us both visit you if I can get an official leave of absence. I'll write again to update you on my plans soon. Enclosed is some more money to help you."

All my love,

Bryn."

Chapter 17: Permission to Love

Two months later, Bryn tugged at his collar as he arrived at the Valenzuela family house in Kowloon Tong. The small velvet box in his pocket felt impossibly heavy, weighed down not just by the ring but by conversations about Spanish heritage and political documents.

The months of courtship with Alicia had gone by like it was minutes, with each dance, each dinner, and each walk around the city strengthening their bond. It was along the waterfront on the Tsim Sha Tsui Promenade, with a beautiful view of the lights of the harbor and city, that Bryn had proposed to Alicia and she had enthusiastically accepted, although she made it clear that her mother Lupe would have to give her blessing. She did so enthusiastically, joined in her joy with Alicia's sisters Mary and Greta.

Bryn recognized he would also have to share with the Valenzuela family his conversation with Dr. Wellington about their heritage to gain official approval for the marriage. He arrived at the Valenzuela home one evening to have that discussion. He was greeted with the usual warmth and Mexican open hospitality that evening. Through the open door, he could hear quiet conversation in Spanish between Alicia and her sisters, their usual laughter replaced by more serious tones. He decided he would raise the issue of formal government approval first.

Lupe Valenzuela entered carrying a Chinese tea set, her dignified bearing showing strain around the edges. "Bryn, as always, it's good to see you. But your request for this meeting sounded somewhat official, not personal."

She knew something. Wellington's inquiries about documentation had clearly reached her. "Mrs. Valenzuela, thank you for agreeing to meet with me."

"I understand there are questions about our family background. Official questions."

Shuffling from the hallway announced the presence of Mary and Greta, eavesdropping with their usual lack of subtlety.

"Girls," Lupe called without turning, "if you wish to listen, please join us properly."

Mary and Greta appeared looking somewhat sheepish. "We're not eavesdropping, Mama," Greta protested. "We're providing proper supervision."

"Actually," Bryn said, "it might be better if everyone stays. What I have to discuss affects the entire family. Questions have arisen about international connections, family backgrounds, potential divided loyalties. It's not personal, but administrative policy has become more stringent."

Lupe leaned forward. "Are you saying they might refuse approval of the marriage because we're Mexican?"

Bryn could see where Alicia got her direct manner from. "Dr. Wellington believes we can address any concerns by properly documenting your family's Spanish heritage. European ancestry, Christian background, colonial administrative traditions."

Understanding dawned in Lupe's eyes, followed by something that might have been anger. "They want proof that Alicia is sufficiently European to be acceptable."

"I wish it weren't necessary, but yes," Bryn replied.

Greta's usual cheerfulness vanished entirely. "She has to prove she's good enough?"

"She and all of you more than good enough," Bryn said firmly. "This is about imperial bureaucracy, not personal worth. But if we want approval, we need to work within the system. Mrs. Valenzuela, I hate that we need to play these games. I hate that European bloodlines and bureaucratic standards must measure your family's worth." His voice grew stronger. "But I love your daughter more than I despise the system. If proving Spanish heritage gets us approval, then we'll prove Spanish heritage."

Lupe studied him carefully. "You understand what you are asking?"

"I'm asking you to help me navigate imperial prejudice so I can marry the woman I love. It's not fair, it's not right, but it's the reality we face."

Mary spoke quietly. "What kind of documentation would they need?"

Bryn withdrew a list from his pocket. "Birth certificates, church records, marriage documents, anything establishing the family's Spanish origins."

Lupe rose and moved to an ornate wooden chest. "My husband Ramon kept all our family papers. Birth certificates from Andalusia, church records from the cathedral in Seville, immigration documents from when his grandfather came to Mexico." She returned with a leather portfolio. "Will these suffice for your bureaucrats?"

Bryn opened the portfolio and found centuries of carefully preserved family history. "These are remarkable. More than sufficient."

"Good." Lupe's voice carried quiet determination. "Now, what makes you think you can provide for my daughter in these uncertain times?"

After nearly two hours of conversation covering practical matters and family values, Lupe finally rose to her feet. "I believe my husband Ramon would have approved of you, Bryn. He understood that sometimes one must work within unfair systems to protect what matters most." She straightened her shoulders. "You have my blessing."

Chapter 17: Permission to Love

Relief flooded through Bryn like monsoon rain breaking the season's first drought. The formal proposal that followed felt almost anticlimactic after the intense family discussion. But when Alicia said yes and he slipped the sapphire ring onto her finger, the political complications faded into background noise.

"It's beautiful," Alicia whispered, tears in her eyes. "And I love you completely."

"And I love you," Bryn replied, pulling her close. "Whatever bureaucratic hurdles we face, we'll face them together."

Two weeks later, Wellington's approval came through with unexpected speed: "All documentation found satisfactory. Government House raises no objections. Congratulations to you both," Wellington said.

One month later, the green Rolls-Royce stopped before St. John's Cathedral, its polished exterior gleaming in the mid-morning sunlight. Wedding day had finally arrived, and it felt entirely real. In the pews were Lupe, Mary and Greta, along with May Lin from the Golden Phoenix. There too was Bryn servant staff, Ah-Min, and Mrs. Wu, and his colleagues from the Sanitation Department, including Dr. Wellington. With Inspector Jason Lam beside him, Bryn ascended the cathedral steps, his heart pounding. The cool interior enveloped them as they walked down the aisle.

Bishop John James greeted them with a warm smile. "Nervous, my boy?"

"Terrified," Bryn admitted.

"As it should be. Marriage is life's most important decision." The Bishop chuckled. "But I can see in your eyes that you're certain of your choice."

"More certain than I've ever been of anything."

"Good. That certainty will serve you well in the years ahead." Bishop James adjusted his ceremonial robes. "Shall we begin? Your bride awaits."

The processional music began. When Alicia entered on her mother's arm, radiant in her elegant gown, Bryn's breath caught. The cathedral's colored light played across her face as she moved down the aisle, eyes never leaving his. Behind her, Greta and Mary followed, beaming with joy. When the procession reached the altar, Lupe placed Alicia's hand in Bryn's with quiet ceremony. "Take care of her," she whispered.

"With my life," Bryn promised.

Little did he know that promise would be tested repeatedly.

Bishop James began the traditional liturgy, but when they reached the vows, he paused. "I believe you've prepared your own words?"

Bryn turned to face Alicia fully, his voice steady despite his racing heart. "Alicia, when I first saw you at that dance, I knew my life had changed forever. You challenged me, surprised me, and made me want to be worthy of your love." His Welsh accent grew more pronounced with emotion. "I promise to honor your intelligence, respect your strength, and love you with everything I have. In times of joy and times of trial, I will stand beside you. I will be your partner, your protector, and your devoted husband until my last breath."

Alicia's voice remained clear and strong, though tears sparkled in her eyes. "Bryn, you saw me not as an ornament but as an equal. You listened when I spoke, valued what I thought, and loved me for who I am rather than what you wished me to be." She smiled through her tears. "I promise to support your dreams, challenge your assumptions when necessary, and love you through whatever storms may come. I will be your wife, your companion, and your truest friend for all the days of our lives."

"The rings?" Bishop James prompted.

Jason produced the simple gold bands. As Bryn slipped the ring onto Alicia's finger, he said, "With this ring, I thee wed. All that I am, I give to you."

"With this ring, I thee wed," Alicia replied, placing his ring with steady hands. "All that I have, I share with you."

"By the power vested in me by the Church and the Crown, I now pronounce you husband and wife." Bishop James beamed. "You may kiss your bride." When their lips met, the cathedral erupted with applause.

"Ladies and gentlemen," Bishop James announced, "I present to you Mr. and Mrs. Bryn Williams."

Outside the cathedral steps, Dr. Wellington pulled Bryn aside. "A moment, my boy." He thrust a door key and small card into Bryn's hand. "Wedding present from the Colonial Government."

Bryn stared at the key. "I don't understand."

"Your new home on Barker Road in the Mid-Levels. Harold Smith's former residence. Spacious enough for a proper family, and frankly, large enough for your wife's family as well."

"Dr. Wellington... I...I don't know what to say...except thank you."

"You'll need the space. I suspect Mrs. Valenzuela and her daughters will want to be close to Alicia, especially once grandchildren arrive." His eyes twinkled. "Consider it an investment in Hong Kong's future."

Chapter 18

Building a Home

"A house becomes a home not through fine furnishings, but through the love that dwells within its walls, and the courage to defend that love when challenged."

Aunt Eileen

The large multi-passenger car slowly made its way up Barker Road toward the Mid-Levels carrying the newlyweds and Lupe, Mary and Greta. They were to all see their new home for the first time. Bryn had arranged with Ah-Min to have all their belongings and necessary furniture from both Bryn apartment and the Valenzuela home moved the next day. Bryn had been told that Ah-Min and Mrs. Wu had prepared a feast to celebrate for them.

"From a coal miner's cottage to Barker Road represented a journey that sometimes seems like someone else's life," Bryn thought.

As they rounded a bend and drove through ornate iron gates, everyone drew a collective breath. Before them stood a grand colonial mansion, its white façade gleaming in afternoon sun. Wide steps led to a columned porch, while verandas encircled both floors. "My goodness," Lupe whispered. "It's like a palace."

"Dr. Wellington arranged for it to be assigned to us as a wedding gift," Bryn explained as they emerged from the car.

Ah-Min approached carrying an ornate wooden box. "Master, before we enter, there is a Chinese custom that brings good fortune to new homes." Ah-Min opened the box to reveal jade, coins, a mirror, and herbs tied with red ribbon. "These represent prosperity, protection, and harmony. With your permission, I would place them in the four corners of the house."

"How wonderful, Ah-Min, its so thoughtful of you to think of this," Alicia said.

"First," Ah-Min said with gentle humor, "there is another tradition. The husband should carry his bride across the threshold."

Without warning, Bryn lifted Alicia into his arms, eliciting a yelp of surprise. "Bryn Williams! What are you doing?" she laughed, arms wrapping around his neck.

"Tradition. For luck and prosperity and for a lifetime of happiness within these walls," Bryn said, carrying Alicia over the threshold.

"And for love," she added softly. "Above all, for love."

The entrance hall unfolded before them with soaring ceilings and gleaming teak floors. Crystal chandeliers cast prismatic patterns on the walls.

"Look at this staircase!" Greta exclaimed, running her hand along the carved banister. "It's like something from a palace."

"The craftsmanship is exquisite," Mary observed, admiring the woodwork.

They moved into the spacious living room where large windows framed breathtaking views of Victoria Harbour.

"Oh my," Lupe breathed, moving to the windows. "You can see all the way to Kowloon."

Alicia gravitated toward the piano in the adjoining parlor, lifting the cover to reveal ivory keys. "Do you think it's in tune?" She pressed a key, and the sound rang out true.

Upstairs, they explored the bedrooms. The master bedroom was spacious and elegant, with a magnificent four-poster bed draped in burgundy silk. "This bedroom is larger than our entire house in Kowloon," Mary marveled.

"The lotus carvings on the mantel represent purity and rebirth," Ah-Min observed. "Perfect symbols for a new marriage."

By evening, they had settled into routines. As they sat on the veranda for tea, watching sunset paint the harbor in brilliant colors, the political tensions seemed distant.

"Are you happy with our new home?" Bryn asked Alicia.

"It's more than I ever dreamed. But you know what makes it truly special?" She asked.

"What's that?" Bryn answered.

"That we're all here together. That's what makes a house a home," she said.

"The wise ruler governs with compassion," Ah-Min quoted, serving tea with practiced grace. "A house thrives when all who dwell within it feel valued."

The ensuring months saw the entire family settle in to a relaxed, and happy

Chapter 18: Building a Home

existence in their new home, supported by a devoted servant staff. Months later, Dr. Wellington made an unexpected visit. His presence at their home rather than requesting an office meeting suggested something significant.

"I apologize for the intrusion, I won't stay long," Wellington said as they settled in the sitting room, "but I felt this conversation required privacy."

"What's troubling you?" Bryn asked, noting the strain around Wellington's eyes.

"The political situation has developed more rapidly than anticipated. Japanese forces have moved closer to Hong Kong waters. More concerning, there are intelligence operations targeting colonial officials with foreign connections."

"What does that mean for us?" Alicia asked directly.

Wellington turned to her with visible respect. "Not suspicion, Mrs. Williams. Scrutiny. Your marriage approval went through smoothly because we documented Spanish heritage thoroughly. However, renewed security concerns mean ongoing observation."

"Are we under surveillance?" Bryn asked.

"A level of oversight that didn't exist before. Nothing dramatic, but social activities may be noted. Travel requires additional clearance."

"For how long?" Alicia asked.

"Until the political situation stabilizes. Which may be some time." Wellington leaned forward.

After Wellington left, Bryn and Alicia sat on the veranda discussing the implications.

Alicia leaned against Bryn's shoulder. "Our love survived bureaucratic approval. It can survive security clearances.

Bryn turned to look at her. "Are we planning to expand our family?"

She smiled mysteriously. "We might be."

Three months later, Bryn announced that the promotion came through with security clearance approved. The investigation had been thorough but not hostile.

"That's good news," Alicia said, "And I have some more good news. I'm pregnant. You're going to be a father."

She jumped into Bryn's arms, joyfully. He kissed her several times. "You are? That is such good news. I'm so happy for us…and are you feeling alright?"

Alicia kissed him again. "I've never felt better Bryn. I'm so happy."

The ensuring months saw an uneventful pregnancy and happy household preparing for a new family member.

September 1937.

The afternoon light streamed through the blinds of Alice Ho Miu Ling Nethersole Hospital, casting warm stripes across pale blue blankets. Alicia had only been admitted to the maternity ward the day before, as the latter stages of her pregnancy had gone amazingly fast.

In the center of the bed, Alicia cradled their newborn daughter, whose blond hair was still damp from the exertion of labor, which had been only a few hours long, as though the child could not wait to come into the world. The tiny bundle, wrapped in a hospital-issued swaddle, made nearly imperceptible movements: a flutter of eyelids, the subtle rise and fall of her chest.

Bryn stood at the bedside, his stocky frame bent slightly forward as if gravity itself had shifted, pulling him toward this new center of his universe. He hadn't taken his eyes off their child since the nurses had placed her in Alicia's arms twenty minutes earlier. The world outside this room seemed to exist in another dimension now.

"She's so small," he whispered, reaching out with one finger to touch the baby's cheek. His voice caught, thick with an emotion he hadn't anticipated. "I knew she would be, but..."

"She's perfect," Alicia said softly, exhaustion and wonder shining in her eyes. "Look at her tiny fingers."

The baby's hand opened and closed with instinctive grace, each miniature nail perfectly formed, each wrinkle in her palm a testament to the miracle of new life.

"Have you thought about what we'll name her?" Alicia asked.

"What about Patricia?" Bryn asked cautiously.

Alicia studied her daughter's face, as if searching for confirmation in the delicate features. The baby's eyes remained closed, but her expression seemed peaceful, content. "I like Patricia. And Anna as a middle name, after my grandmother."

"Patricia Anna Williams." Bryn tested the name in the air between them, sensing its weight and rhythm. "It's perfect." They embraced gently, aware of the precious life between them. Bryn inhaled the fragrance of Alicia's hair, now blended with the sterile hospital odor and something else: something new and indescribable that seemed to radiate from their daughter.

"Do you think she looks like you or me?" Alicia asked, tracing the baby's

Chapter 18: Building a Home

eyebrow with her fingertip.

"She has your beautiful features but my coloring," Bryn observed, marveling at how Patricia's skin held the same fair tone as his own.

"She has your eyes," Alicia added. "That same blue."

The door burst open and Lupe rushed in, her eyes wide with excitement, bringing with her an energy that seemed to fill the space. "¡*Dios mío!* (My God). Let me see the *pequeña!* (little girl)." Her hands fluttered in the air like birds, hesitant to touch yet eager to hold. Alicia gently shifted the bundle and placed Patricia in her mother's arms. Lupe's face transformed instantly, the lines of worry and excitement melting into pure adoration. "She is so beautiful and so fair," Lupe whispered, rocking gently from side to side, tears streaming down her cheeks. "Your father Ramon would have been so proud."

Lupe was softly rocking Patricia, who started to squirm inside her swaddle. Her tiny face scrunched up as she let out a mewling cry that sounded impossibly loud for such a small creature.

"You'll have lots of time to hold her back home," Alicia said, reaching out her arms. Lupe reluctantly handed the baby back to her daughter, and Patricia instinctively settled into quiet, staring intently at Alicia's face.

"She's strong," Alicia observed, watching her daughter with amazement. "Look how she holds on."

"Like her mother," Bryn replied, stroking Alicia's hair with infinite tenderness.

The sun began to set outside the hospital windows, bathing the room in a deepening golden glow. Hong Kong's skyline sparkled in the distance as the city prepared for night, while inside these walls, their world had irreversibly expanded. As evening settled over Hong Kong, the hospital's sounds formed a gentle symphony around them: the squeak of rubber-soled shoes in distant hallways, muffled conversations, and the soft ping of monitors.

As night fully settled and Alicia's eyes grew heavy with exhaustion, nurses moved gently through the room, checking vitals and offering help. The city lights shimmered through the window like earthly stars, but Bryn's focus stayed on the two most important people in his world. He leaned down and whispered into his daughter's ear, words meant solely for her: "Welcome to the world, Patricia Anna. We've been waiting for you."

As if in response, her tiny fingers wrapped around his, holding on with unexpected strength that seemed to anchor him to this moment, this new reality, this transformed life. Her first promise, her first gift.

Chapter 19

The Last Goodbye

"Love doesn't end when people leave you. It gets passed on."

Aunt Eileen

The letter arrived on a Tuesday morning with the regular post. Bryn recognized Evan's handwriting on the envelope straightaway, that distinctive scrawl his younger brother had never bothered to improve. He carried it to his study before opening it, some instinct telling him he'd want privacy for whatever news it contained.

His hands shook as he unfolded the single page. The words swam before his eyes, refusing at first to make sense.

"Bryn,

I'm writing to let you know that Aunt Eileen passed Thursday. The funeral was held on Saturday at St. David's. It was a nice service. Reverend Morris spoke well of her. There were quite a few people there from the village.

I know you've been writing to her since you left. I thought you should know why she hadn't written back.

Evan."

Bryn read it twice. Then a third time. Each reading made the anger build higher in his chest, a hot pressure that mixed badly with the grief trying to break through underneath.

"She'd died on a Thursday, at least a month ago as the letter arrived by ship. Then they had the funeral two days later. I didn't know Auntie was so close to death. No one let me know. Not the hospital, not any of my family or hers. It's as though it didn't exist!" he said out loud.

He found Alicia in the morning room, mending one of his shirts by the window. She looked up when he entered and must have seen something in his face because she set down her needle straightaway.

"What's happened?"

He handed her the letter. Watched her eyes move across the page, watched understanding dawn and then horror at what the letter didn't say as much as what it did.

"Oh God. Bryn, I'm so sorry." She looked up at him. "When did this arrive?"

"I…I lost track of time." Tears formed in his eyes. "I should have been there to comfort her…" He crumpled up the letter in his fist.

Alicia stood, crossing to him to try to console him, but he moved away to the window, still angry with himself. Outside, the garden stretched peaceful and green under morning sun. Somewhere out there, hundreds of miles away, Eileen lay in a grave he'd never seen. In a churchyard he'd never visit.

"I knew she was dying." The words came out flat. "We both knew. She told me that the doctor had given her six months, maybe less. That's why I'd been writing so often. Every week. Sometimes twice a week." He gripped the window frame. "She stopped answering in August. I thought perhaps she was too weak to write, or that she'd taken a turn. I thought about going to see her but I kept telling myself I'd wait for her to write back first. That I didn't want to impose if she needed rest."

"You couldn't have known Bryn," Alicia said embracing him.

"I should have gone to see her one last time…she was not just my aunt…she was like a mother."

Alicia waited, the letter still in her hands.

"They knew," Bryn said, and the anger he'd been holding back started seeping through. "Evan knew Everyone in that village knew she was dying, And not one of them thought to send word to me before it happened." His voice rose. "A telegram takes hours, Alicia. Hours. They could have wired. But instead, Evan waits to write a letter after she's dead and buried."

He was shaking now, the fury and grief all tangled together. "She raised me. From the time I was fourteen until I was eighteen, when my own father couldn't be bothered, she took me in. She fed me, taught me, loved me like I was her own son. She told me once that she'd have been blessed to call me her son." His voice cracked. "She was more my mother than my own mother ever was."

Alicia came to him then and this time he didn't pull away. She wrapped her arms around him and he buried his face in her shoulder, the anger draining away and leaving only the grief behind, raw and enormous.

"In my last letter to her," he said into Alicia's shoulder. "I told her about the garden, about how well the roses were doing this year. About the painting I'd been

Chapter 19: The Last Goodbye

working on. She loved hearing about my work. She's the one who encouraged it from the start, who told me I had something worth developing." He pulled back, wiping at his eyes.

"She knew you loved her Bryn…she knew." Alicia said.

"Did she? Or did she die thinking I'd abandoned her like everyone else?" He moved away, pacing now. "No visits. Just letters that got less frequent as summer went on because I was busy, because there was always something else that needed doing. And when her letters stopped coming, did I rush to her side? No. I told myself I'd wait. That I'd give her time." He laughed, sharp and bitter. "Time. That's exactly what she didn't have."

He stopped at the window, looking out without really seeing. "I always thought I'd go back one day. Really go back, I mean. Not just for a funeral or a quick visit, but properly. I'd see Evan, spend time with my sisters Mary and Bernice. I'd visit Mam's and Tad's graves too, even after everything. Stand in Eileen's cottage again. Make peace with it all, somehow." His voice grew quieter. "I had this idea in my head that eventually enough time would pass and the anger would fade and we'd find some way to be family again. Not like before, but something."

He turned to face Alicia. "But that was all fantasy, wasn't it? I never went back because I didn't want to face what I'd left behind. Didn't want to see how old Eileen had gotten. Didn't want to walk into that cottage and feel the weight of all those years I'd stayed away." His hands clenched into fists. "And my family... they resent me for leaving, yes. But they also watched me not come back. Year after year. They saw Eileen waiting for me, growing older, and I never came. So perhaps they decided I'd made my choice. Perhaps they're right."

"Bryn..." Alicia whispered.

"No, it's true. There's nothing there for me anymore, but that's partly because I made it so. I can't go back now and stand in that village pretending I cared, pretending I was ever coming back. They buried her without me, and I'm angry about that. But I'd already buried that life years ago. I just didn't have the honesty to admit it." He pressed his palms against his eyes. "This is my home now. Hong Kong. This house. You. And that means Wales stopped being home long ago. It hurts to face that. But it's the truth. The kind of truth that comes too late."

He pulled away gently and went to his desk, pulling out paper. "I need to write this down while it's fresh. Everything I want to say to her. Everything I should have said." He sat and began writing, his hand moving quickly across the page. Alicia watched him quietly, understanding that he needed this.

The letter poured out of him. Memories of that first night at her cottage after his father had expelled him from his family home, how she'd made him tea and sat with him while he cried. How she'd taught him to make proper Welsh cakes, even though hers were always terrible, burnt on the outside and raw in the middle. How she couldn't sew to save her life but her garden was like something from a painting. How she'd found money in her tight budget for paper and pencils when Mr. Clements said he had talent. How she'd never once made him feel small or worthless or like he owed her for her kindness.

When he finished, his hand was cramping and his face was wet with tears. He folded the letter carefully and slipped it into his pocket.

"I'm going to build a cairn for her in our garden, and bury this letter with it," he said. "So she'll have my words, even if she never heard them," Bryn said sobbing.

They stood together for a long time, Alicia's arms around him while he cried the way he hadn't cried since he was a boy. For Eileen, yes, but also for the years he'd had with her and the years he'd lost. For the goodbye he'd never get to say. For the funeral where his chair sat empty.

He found Ah-Min in the servants' hall, polishing the silver tea service with his usual meticulous care. He looked up as Bryn entered, and whatever he saw in Bryn's face made him set down his cloth immediately.

"Master?"

"I need your help along with Alicia with something." Bryn's voice was rough. "Outside. In the garden."

Ah-Min didn't ask questions. He simply nodded and followed, listening to Bryn describe what had happened.

Bryn stood in the far corner of the garden. He walked past the vegetable garden, past the herb beds Alicia tended with such care, past the rose bushes that reminded him of Eileen's own garden back in Wales. All the way to the back corner where the old stone wall marked their property line. Here the ground was rockier, wilder. He'd been meaning to clear. The brambles and wild grass, the scattered stones and weathered wood. It was perfect.

He began gathering stones. Some from the wall itself, where winter frost had crumbled the mortar away. Others from the ground, half buried in decades of soil and moss. Large ones that made his back strain. Small smooth ones that fit in his palm. Each one chosen with care. Each one placed with intention.

Ah-Min worked beside him in silence at first, moving with an economy of motion that spoke of someone who understood the value of physical labor. Together they lifted stones that would have taken Bryn twice as long to move, positioning them with careful precision. After nearly an hour, as Bryn's hands began to blister, Ah-Min finally spoke. "In my village, we say that grief is like water." His voice was quiet, thoughtful. "If you try to hold it in your hands, it will

Chapter 19: The Last Goodbye

slip through your fingers. If you try to build walls against it, it will find the cracks. But if you give it a place to flow, it will move through you and continue on its way."

Bryn paused, a stone heavy in his hands. "I don't want it to move on. I want to remember her."

"The *Tao* teaches us that the soft and yielding overcomes the hard and strong." Ah-Min placed another stone carefully on the growing cairn. "Water wears away stone, not through force, but through persistence. Your love for this woman, it is like water. It has shaped who you are. That doesn't end when she ends."

"It feels like it should have been different." Bryn set down his stone, wiping sweat from his forehead. "I should have been there."

"Perhaps." Ah-Min selected another stone, turning it in his hands to find the right placement. "But we cannot step twice into the same river. What was, was. What is, is. You build this cairn now, in this moment, with these hands. That is what the Tao allows you."

"The Tao." Bryn almost smiled despite everything. "You reckon the Tao cares about a Welsh woman who died hundreds of miles away?"

"The Tao is not a god who cares or does not care. It is simply the way of things. The way water flows. The way stones rest upon each other. The way grief moves through a man's heart and teaches him to be more than he was." Ah-Min met his eyes. "You are angry at your family for their silence. This is natural. But anger is also water. Let it flow through the work of your hands. Let it become something that honors her instead of something that hurts you."

They worked in silence for a while longer. The physical labor was a blessing, giving Bryn's anger and grief somewhere to go besides eating him alive from the inside. Each stone he placed was a prayer, a memory, a way of saying what he'd never get to say at her graveside.

Alicia appeared sometime later, and without a word, she joined them. Then Lupe, Alicia's mother, came out from the house, her dark eyes taking in the scene. She understood straightaway, as mothers do, and began gathering stones from the garden path.

Mrs. Wu emerged from the kitchen, wiping her hands on her apron. The cook was a woman of few words, but she brought an armful of smooth stones and placed them at Bryn's feet with a slight bow of respect. Mei-Lin, the amah, followed with her quiet grace, adding her own stones to the pile.

Mary and Greta, Alicia's younger sisters, came last, curious at first, then solemn as they understood what was being built. They worked alongside the others, and no one spoke much. There was no need.

The cairn grew slowly, taking shape stone by stone. Bryn found himself talking as he worked, mostly to himself, but the others listened. How she'd taken him in when his father had beaten him bloody for refusing to go back down the pit. How she'd let him stay in her cottage for four years, treating him like the son she'd never had. How she'd encouraged his art when everyone else in the village thought drawing and painting was daft for a working-class boy.

"She made the worst Welsh cakes you ever tasted," he said, and surprised himself by laughing. "Like little rocks. Burnt on the outside, raw in the middle. But she'd serve them up with such pride, and I'd eat every one and thank her for them because they were made with love." He placed another stone. "Couldn't sew worth a damn either. Everything she mended came back with crooked seams and wrong thread. But her garden." His voice softened. "Her garden was something to see. Roses and lavender, herbs that smelled like heaven itself. She had a gift for making beautiful things grow."

Lupe was crying quietly. Even Mrs. Wu's normally stern face had softened.

"She was kind. Not the sort of kindness that costs nothing, but the kind that changes lives." He set down the stone he was holding and looked at what they'd built. "And my family couldn't even be bothered to tell me she was gone until it was too late."

The anger flared again, hot and bright. He picked up another stone and placed it harder than he meant to. "My brother Evan. He would have been at that funeral. Standing right there at the grave. And he knew what Eileen meant to me. Everyone in that village knew. But he couldn't take five minutes to send a telegram. Five minutes. That's all it would have taken."

Ah-Min placed a hand on Bryn's shoulder. "The stone that is angry breaks when struck. The stone that accepts its nature endures."

Bryn looked at him, then back at the cairn. He took a breath, steadying himself, and continued working. The fury didn't disappear, but it settled into something he could carry without it consuming him. He worked until the sun hung low and orange over the western trees. By then, the cairn stood as tall as his chest, broad and solid and built with grief and love in equal measure. Not elaborate. Not perfect. Just stone upon stone, each one carrying weight and meaning.

He smiled through his tears. "I wrote long letters about everything and nothing. About this garden, about our family and home, about Patricia. Ordinary things, because I wanted her to know that the life she'd helped me build was good. That her kindness had mattered. That I was happy."

He was gripping the cairn now, his knuckles white. "My family resents me for leaving. For refusing to go down into those mines and ruin my lungs like my father and grandfather before him. For making something of myself beyond what they

Chapter 19: The Last Goodbye

thought I deserved. And so they punished me for it by taking away my chance to say goodbye to the one person in that village who loved me without resentment or conditions."

Alicia's arm came around his waist, steadying him.

"But they can't take away what she gave me. They can't take away the years I had with her, or the lessons she taught me, or the love she showed me when I needed it most." He straightened, looking at the cairn. "They buried her in some churchyard I'll probably never see. But this is hers too. This cairn, in this garden, built with my own hands and the hands of people who care about me. This is my memorial to her. This is where I'll come when I need to remember."

He took a breath, steadying himself. "Eileen Davies. You took in a frightened, angry boy and you taught him how to be gentle. You showed him that kindness wasn't weakness and that wanting more from life wasn't selfishness. You gave him a home when he had none, and love when he'd forgotten what it felt like to be loved." His voice dropped to almost a whisper. "You were my mother of choice. I'm sorry I wasn't there at the end. I'm sorry I didn't come when you stopped writing. I'm sorry for every visit I put off and every letter I meant to write but didn't."

The tears were streaming down his face now. "But I'm not sorry for loving you. I'm not sorry for the years I had with you, or for the man I became because of you. You saved my life, Auntie. Not just that night when you opened your door to me, but every day after. You saved my life by showing me it was worth saving."

He pressed both hands against the cairn. "Rest well, my dear aunt. Rest well, my second mother. Rest well, and know that you were loved. Know that you mattered. Know that the boy you saved grew up to be a man who will remember you every day for the rest of his life."

The silence that followed was complete. Even the birds seemed to have stopped their evening songs. In the gathering dusk, the cairn stood solid and permanent, a marker for memory, a place to hold grief.

Mrs. Wu stepped forward and placed a sprig of rosemary at the base of the cairn. "For remembrance," she said quietly.

One by one, the others came forward. Mary laid down a handful of autumn leaves. Greta placed a smooth stone in the shape of a cross. Mary added a spray of berries from the hedgerow. Alicia picked a single flower from Eileen's cuttings growing by the south wall and wove it between the stones. They stood together as the stars began to appear, as the darkness gathered soft and gentle around them. No one spoke. No one needed to. The cairn said everything that needed saying.

Finally, as the last light faded from the sky, they began to drift back toward the house. Alicia waited, her hand in Bryn's, until he was ready.

"Thank you," he said to her, his voice hoarse. "For helping. For understanding."

"She'd be proud of you," Alicia said. "For this. For how you honored her."

They walked back to the house together, the cairn standing sentinel behind them. Tomorrow would bring the letter that would likely sever what little remained of his connection to his birth family. But tonight, he'd said goodbye to Eileen in the way she deserved. He'd built her something that would last, something that would weather and moss over with time but would stand as long as he tended it. A marker for the woman who had saved him. A place to come when he needed to remember that he'd been loved once by someone who asked nothing in return.

In the morning, he'd find the mist had touched the cairn, silver and sparkling in the weak sunlight. He'd stand there for a long time, and he'd feel something like peace settling over him. Not happiness. Not yet. But peace. The kind that comes from knowing you've done right by someone you loved.

The kind Aunt Eileen would have wanted for him.

Chapter 20

The Gathering Storm

"When empires start explaining why they can't protect their own people, start packing your bags. The explanations always come before the abandonment."

Edward Gibbon, *The Decline and Fall of the Roman Empire*

November 1937

The morning light filtered through the shutters of their Barker Road house, casting gentle patterns across the nursery floor where Patricia Anna slept in her wicker bassinet. Bryn stood in the doorway, still amazed that something so small could have changed his entire world. Her tiny chest rose and fell in perfect rhythm, one miniature fist curled against her cheek as if she were already preparing to fight whatever challenges lay ahead.

"She's beautiful when she's sleeping," Alicia whispered from behind him.

"You should be resting," Bryn said, turning to guide his wife back toward their bedroom.

"I can't sleep while she's sleeping. It feels like such a waste." Alicia let herself be led back to bed, though her eyes stayed fixed on the nursery. "Besides, Mrs. Halston next door stopped by yesterday. She seemed really worried about something."

Bryn felt a familiar knot tighten in his stomach. Mrs. Halston was married to a shipping executive who often had early intelligence about conditions on the mainland. "What did she say?"

"Something about her sister's family in Shanghai. They haven't heard from them since the fighting intensified." Alicia settled back against the pillows, exhaustion evident in every movement. "She asked if we had heard anything through official channels."

The *South China Morning Post* was folded on the nightstand where Bryn had left it earlier, its headlines deliberately out of his wife's sight. The reports from Shanghai got worse each day, but Alicia didn't need that extra worry while she was healing.

"I'll make some inquiries," he said, adjusting her pillows. "The communications are probably just disrupted by the fighting."

Alicia's eyes searched his face with the perceptiveness that first drew him to her. "Bryn, you're worried about something. More than usual, I mean. What aren't you telling me?"

He sat on the edge of the bed, taking her hand in his. How much truth could he share with her? "The situation in China is deteriorating rapidly," he said carefully. "But Hong Kong remains secure. We're a British colony, protected by the Royal Navy."

"That's not what I asked." Alicia's grip on his hand tightened. "I asked what you aren't telling me."

Before he could answer, Patricia Anna's cry echoed from the nursery, the demanding wail of an infant who had discovered that the world didn't always meet her needs right away. Alicia started to rise, but Bryn gently pushed her back.

"I'll get her. You rest."

As he lifted his daughter from the bassinet, her cries faded into the softer sounds of a baby seeking comfort. She was so light, so completely reliant on others for everything. The weight of that dependency had been growing heavier each day as news from the mainland grew darker. After gently rocking her, Patricia returned to her sleep.

"All right," he said quietly when he returned to the bedroom. "The Japanese are advancing faster than anyone expected. Shanghai may fall within weeks. If that happens, they'll control most of the coast between here and Beijing."

"And Hong Kong?" Alicia asked.

"Hong Kong is different. We're a British colony with naval protection." The words felt hollow even as he spoke them. "But I'd be lying if I said there was no risk," Bryn replied.

Alicia absorbed this information with the calm practicality that was a core part of her character. "What kind of risk? And what can we do about it?"

"I don't know yet. That's what I intend to find out today." He moved to the wardrobe, selecting clothes for what promised to be a long and difficult day of conversations. "I'm meeting with some colleagues today at the Hong Kong Club, men who might have better information about our preparedness."

Chapter 20: The Gathering Storm

"Bryn?" Her voice was soft but serious. "If something happens, if we need to leave Hong Kong, how much time would we have?"

The question he'd been dreading. "I honestly don't know right now. But I'll do whatever is necessary to protect you and the family."

An hour later, Bryn stepped onto Queen's Road to find a city altered by unseen currents of fear and readiness. The morning air, usually heavy just with humidity, now carried the electric tension of a place where everyone sensed impending danger but no one wanted to face it directly. The first thing he noticed was the sound. Conversations that should have been casual and unhurried now carried an edge of urgency. Chinese voices called out in rapid Cantonese, with a sharp and worried cadence. Even the clip-clop of horses' hooves seemed more hurried, as if the animals themselves sensed their drivers' anxiety.

A Chinese woman hurried past him, clutching a bundle of possessions close to her chest. Inside the cloth wrap, he caught a glimpse of a jade figurine, family photographs, and what appeared to be gold jewelry. Her eyes briefly met his, wide with the unique terror of someone who had seen armies advance before, then she vanished into the crowd heading toward the harbor. "Mr. Williams!"

He turned to see Thomas Hartwell, a junior clerk from the Colonial Secretary's office, approaching with clear agitation. Hartwell was usually the picture of colonial propriety, but this morning his shirt was wrinkled and his hair uncombed.

"Thomas, you look like you haven't slept," Bryn said.

"I haven't. None of us has. Hartwell looked around nervously before lowering his voice. "We've been processing immigration applications all night. Chinese families seeking exit permits, British subjects requesting passage to Singapore, and even some Portuguese from Macau exploring alternatives."

"How many applications?" Bryn inquired.

"Over five hundred since yesterday morning, and that's just the ones with proper documentation. Hartwell's voice dropped even further. "There are rumors that wealthy Chinese families are paying fishing boat captains to take them south without official papers."

The implications were staggering. If people with resources and connections were already planning to leave, what did that indicate about the confidence level among those who understood the situation best? "What's the official response?" Bryn asked.

"Officially? We're processing applications according to standard procedures and advising people not to panic." Hartwell's laugh held no humor. "Unofficially? Half the staff has been asking about their own families' status for emergency evacuation."

They were interrupted by the sound of hammering from across the street. Wing Liu, who runs a small import business that Bryn passes every day, was boarding up his windows with heavy planks of wood. The rhythmic hammering echoed off the surrounding buildings like a drumbeat of preparation.

"Mr. Liu!" Bryn called out, crossing the street. "Is there a problem with your shop?"

Liu paused his work, hammer in hand, with sweat beading on his forehead despite the cooler morning air. He had always been consistently polite to Bryn, showing the respectful deference expected of Chinese merchants toward British officials in colonial society. "Inspector Williams," Liu said, his English careful but strained. "I am sorry, but shop will be closed for some time. Family business requires travel."

"I'm sorry to hear that. I hope it's nothing serious," Bryn said.

Liu looked directly at Bryn for a moment, as if weighing how much truth to share with a colonial officer. "My brother sends word from Guangzhou. Japanese soldiers ask many questions about Hong Kong. About harbor, about roads, about where British live." He resumed hammering, each blow punctuating his words. "Questions like that mean soldiers plan to visit soon."

Liu's casual delivery of this intelligence made it more chilling than any official briefing. This wasn't speculation or rumor. It was information from someone with family connections across the border, someone who understood the patterns that came before military action.

"Mr. Liu, have you reported this information to the authorities?" Bryn asked.

"Report to who?" Liu's question was genuinely puzzled. "Chinese merchants not welcome at Government House. Chinese police not trusted with important information. So Chinese take care of Chinese, and British take care of British." With that, Liu returned to his lodging, leaving Bryn with the uncomfortable realization that the colony's Chinese majority had been preparing for a crisis through their own networks, while the British administration remained focused on official channels and diplomatic protocols.

Continuing toward the harbor, Bryn saw more signs of a city getting ready for problems it couldn't officially admit. Outside the Hongkong and Shanghai Banking Corporation, a line of European wives had formed despite the early hour. They stood in small groups, their voices quiet but intense as they discussed withdrawal limits and transfer procedures.

Mrs. Henderson from the bridge club stepped away from the line when she saw him. "Mr. Williams, have you heard anything official about evacuation procedures? My husband insists everything is fine, but the Chinese staff at his

Chapter 20: The Gathering Storm

office have been giving notice all week."

"I'm sure it's just precautionary," Bryn replied, though the words felt inadequate. "Has Mr. Henderson mentioned any specific concerns?"

"Nothing official. But he's been staying late at the office every night, and yesterday I found him studying steamship schedules." Her voice dropped to a whisper. "Between us, he's moved most of our savings to an account in Singapore."

Their conversation was broken up by the arrival of a military transport truck, its canvas sides flapping as it navigated the narrow street. Through the open back, Bryn could see stacks of sandbags and what appeared to be radio equipment. Following behind was another truck, this one carrying soldiers in tropical gear who appeared much more alert and serious than the usual garrison troops he was used to seeing.

The convoy paused at an intersection, and Bryn found himself standing close enough to overhear fragments of conversation from the lead vehicle. "...positions along the Gin Drinker's Line by fourteen hundred hours...ammunition supplies still inadequate for extended engagement...civilian evacuation protocols remain classified pending authorization from..."

The trucks moved on before he could hear more, but the brief glimpse into military preparations revealed hurried defensive efforts and incomplete planning. More concerning was the mention of civilian evacuation protocols that remained classified. If the military was planning for civilian evacuation but kept those plans secret, it suggested either unfinished preparations or a deliberate choice to limit panic by withholding information.

The Sanitation Department occupied three floors of a colonial-era building that still carried the optimistic grandeur of an empire confident in its permanence. But as Bryn climbed the familiar stairs to his office, even these surroundings felt different, as if the building itself sensed that the certainties it was designed to represent were crumbling.

His secretary, Miss Chen, looked up from her typewriter with evident relief as he entered. "Oh, Inspector Williams, Dr. Wellington wants to see you immediately, and there have been at least a dozen telephone calls from district Sanitary Inspectors."

"What kind of calls?" Bryn asked

"Requests for emergency medical supplies, questions about evacuation procedures for hospitals, inquiries about water purification in case of supply disruption." She handed him a stack of pink message slips. "And this telegram arrived an hour ago, marked urgent."

Bryn tore open the telegram, his hands trembling slightly as he read the brief message from the Colonial Medical Service headquarters: "PREPARE CONTINGENCY PLANS FOR MEDICAL SERVICE CONTINUITY UNDER EMERGENCY CONDITIONS STOP PRIORITY ONE STOP REPORT READINESS STATUS IMMEDIATELY STOP."

The telegram's clinical language couldn't hide the implications. Contingency plans for medical service continuity involved preparations for scenarios where standard medical infrastructure might be compromised or destroyed. Priority one classification indicated that this wasn't a routine planning exercise.

"Miss. Chen, I want you to start pulling files on emergency medical supply requirements and hospital evacuation procedures," Bryn said.

Wellington's office was a study in controlled chaos. Medical journals lay open alongside official correspondence and what appeared to be military maps of the New Territories. Wellington looked up as Bryn entered, his usually immaculate appearance disheveled and his eyes red-rimmed from lack of sleep. "Ah, Bryn, good. Close the door and sit down. We need to discuss some rather uncomfortable possibilities."

Wellington was a career medical officer who had spent twenty years in various colonial postings. His calm professionalism had seen the Sanitation Department through cholera outbreaks, typhoon damage, and the usual challenges of maintaining European health standards in a tropical climate. But today, that professional composure showed cracks that Bryn had never seen before. "I've just come from a briefing with the Military Medical Service," Wellington said, removing his glasses and rubbing his eyes. "The situation is considerably worse than what's been reported in the newspapers."

"How much worse?" Bryn asked.

"Put it this way: I've been instructed to prepare for the possibility that we might need to maintain medical services without reliable supply lines from the mainland or regular communication with London." Wellington picked up one of the maps, pointing to red circles that had been drawn around various locations. "These are the facilities we would need to keep operational in an emergency. Hospitals, water treatment plants, food distribution centers."

Bryn studied the map, noting that most of the marked locations were on Hong Kong Island itself, with very few in Kowloon or the New Territories. "This looks like a plan for defending the island while abandoning everything else."

"That's exactly what it is." Wellington's voice carried the weight of a man who had been forced to accept unacceptable realities. "The military assessment is that the New Territories and Kowloon cannot be held against a determined assault."

"What about the civilian population in the areas being abandoned?" Bryn

Chapter 20: The Gathering Storm

asked.

Wellington's silence answered the question more effectively than words could have. The briefing continued with increasingly alarming details. Medical supplies enough for about six weeks of normal operations. Water purification chemicals sufficient for three months if carefully rationed. Food stores enough for the civilian population for roughly two weeks without resupply.

"Bryn, you have a newborn daughter. I know what that means." Wellington's clinical tone couldn't mask the personal weight of what he was saying. "Essential personnel will have priority access to whatever evacuation capacity exists. But you need to understand something. If this situation deteriorates as rapidly as the military experts predict, personal considerations may have to be subordinated to maintaining essential services."

Before Bryn could respond, the conversation was interrupted by Miss. Chen's voice through the office intercom. "Dr. Wellington, Mr. Fung from the Water Department is here. He says it's extremely urgent."

Wei-ming Fung entered without waiting for permission, his usual diplomatic courtesy replaced by obvious agitation. Bryn had worked with Fung on various public health initiatives and had never seen the normally composed engineer in such a state. "Dr. Wellington, Inspector Williams, we have a serious problem. I have just received information from my contacts in Guangzhou. Japanese reconnaissance units have been mapping our water supply infrastructure."

"What kind of mapping?" Wellington asked.

"Detailed surveys of the reservoirs, treatment facilities, and distribution networks. They are not preparing to occupy these facilities intact. They are preparing to disable them systematically." Fun spread a hand-drawn map across Wellington's desk. "Every critical junction, every pump station, every storage facility has been documented."

"Bryn, you and I had better have a meeting with the Chief Medical Officer about this report. I'll set it up immediately."

Bryn nodded. "I'll check back in about the meeting. In the meantime, I'm going to the Hong Kong Club to meet with some well-connected friends in government to find out unofficial news that can help us."

The Hong Kong Club occupied a position of privilege both geographical and social, its imposing facade declaring the confidence of an empire accustomed to having its way. But as Bryn climbed the familiar steps, he noticed details that had escaped his attention before. Inside, the atmosphere held the false normalcy of men determined to stick to familiar rituals despite mounting evidence that the world around them was changing. Ceiling fans stirred air thick with humidity and unspoken fears. The familiar ritual of afternoon drinks felt like a performance staged against the encroaching darkness.

Dr. Charles Preston waved him over to a corner table where four other men sat sipping whiskeys in the golden light filtering through tall windows. The shadows cast by the afternoon sun appeared longer today, reaching out like grasping fingers.

"Well, Bryn," Police Inspector Thomas Harrington announced, raising his glass with studied cheerfulness, "I think congratulations are in order. To Patricia Anna Williams. May she grow up in more peaceful times than these."

As the men lifted their glasses, Bryn examined their faces more closely than ever before. These weren't just colleagues having afternoon drinks. They were men whose decisions would impact thousands of lives in the coming weeks, each carrying burdens visible in the lines around their eyes and the tension in their shoulders. "Thank you, gentlemen," Bryn said, his voice thick with emotion. "I never knew I could love someone I've only just met so completely."

Harrington was a seasoned policeman, with twenty-three years on the force, fifteen of those in Hong Kong. His worn face had witnessed riots, typhoons, and the usual violence that comes with maintaining order in a crowded colonial port. But today, his eyes showed a different kind of worry, the look of a man who understands better than most how quickly civilized society can fall apart. "Fatherhood changes everything, doesn't it?" Harrington said, his voice carrying personal weight. "I have two boys of my own back in Yorkshire. Haven't seen them in a year, but I write them every week. Tell them stories about Hong Kong, about the Chinese children I see playing in the streets here." He paused, staring into his whiskey. "Lately, I've been wondering what stories I'll have to tell them about what happens next."

Jack Ramsay from the Colonial Secretary's office adjusted his wire-rimmed spectacles with hands that trembled slightly. Ramsay was the consummate civil servant, a man who had built his career on understanding the subtle currents of colonial administration. His usually pristine appearance showed signs of strain: his shirt collar was slightly wilted, and his normally perfectly knotted tie sat askew. "Children clarify priorities wonderfully," Ramsay said carefully. "Yesterday's policy abstractions become quite personal when you're responsible for someone's entire future." He glanced around the table, lowering his voice. "I've been in closed meetings with the Governor all week. The cables from London..." He paused, clearly struggling with how much to reveal. "Let me just say that paternal instincts and imperial policy don't always align as neatly as one might hope."

Robert Kinsey nodded grimly from across the table. As Secretary for Chinese Affairs, he spent his days balancing between British colonial authority and Chinese interests, a role that had become more unstable as military tensions grew. "The

Chapter 20: The Gathering Storm

Chinese have a saying," Kinsey said quietly. "'When the nest is destroyed, no egg remains whole.' Rather apt, wouldn't you say?" His voice carried the weight of someone who had spent years building relationships with Chinese community leaders, relationships that were now strained by circumstances beyond anyone's control. "My wife is Chinese," Kinsey added so softly that the others had to lean in to hear him. " We married five years ago, despite strong opposition from both communities. She's pregnant with our first child, due in December." His voice wavered slightly. "Yesterday she asked me if our child would be considered Chinese or British if we have to evacuate. I didn't have an answer."

Dr. Preston, always the pragmatist, swirled his gin and watched the ice melt in the amber liquid. Preston had spent his career confronting the practical realities of maintaining health and sanitation in tough conditions. His medical training had stripped away most illusions about human nature and the fragility of civilized society. "Children force us to confront our own mortality," Preston observed clinically. "Before Patricia Anna, Bryn, you were just another colonial officer. Expendable in the grand scheme of imperial calculations. Now you're a father with responsibilities that go far beyond quarterly reports and administrative efficiency."

The conversation was broken up by the arrival of a tall, distinguished man with a pronounced limp. His weathered face and sharp eyes marked him as someone who had experienced action beyond the comfort zone of colonial service. "Mind if I join you, gentlemen?" he asked. "Ralph Meeker, recently arrived from Cairo."

Bryn stood to make introductions. "Ralph's is a friend from my military days in Cairo. Military intelligence background, now running an import business."

Meeker eased into a chair with visible discomfort, his left leg extending at an awkward angle. "Shrapnel from the Somme," he explained, catching Bryn's concerned glance. "Twenty years later, it still reminds me every morning that the universe has a sense of humor about timing."

"What brings you to Hong Kong, Major?" Preston asked.

Business opportunities, officially. The import trade between China and the colonies has been quite profitable. Meeker's expression darkened. "Unofficially, I've been watching Japanese military preparations across the region. Old habits from intelligence work, you understand."

"And what have you observed?" Ramsay asked carefully.

"Gentlemen, may I speak freely?" Meeker waited for their nods before continuing. "I've spent the last six months traveling between Singapore, Manila, and various ports along the China coast. What I've seen suggests that we're facing a much more systematic and immediate threat than official assessments indicate." He pulled out a small notebook and started flipping through pages filled with neat handwriting. "Japanese forces aren't just moving forward randomly. They're executing a carefully planned strategy to control the entire South China Sea. Hong Kong isn't just an afterthought to them. It's a strategic must."

"How so?" Harrington asked, his policeman's instincts engaged.

Control Hong Kong, and you control access to southern China. Control southern China, and you can cut off Western access to Chinese markets and resources. It's not about territory. It's about economic domination." Meeker closed the notebook and looked directly at each man in turn. "And gentlemen, I have to tell you: the preparations I've observed suggest they're planning to move much sooner than anyone in London seems to expect.

"What kind of timeline are we looking at?" Bryn asked, thinking of Patricia Anna sleeping peacefully in her nursery while Japanese forces maneuvered hundreds of miles away.

"Based on the supply movements and troop concentrations I've observed, I'd estimate two years at the most. After they take Shanghai, I think they'll take Nanjin, Wuhan Hankou, Guangzhou and Xuzhou, then move on Hong Kong. When they do move on Hong Kong the weather becomes a significant factor."

Ramsay looked around the table, clearly struggling with how much official information to share. "Gentlemen, what Major Meeker is describing aligns rather too closely with certain classified assessments that have been circulating at the highest levels of government."

"What kind of assessments?" Preston asked.

"The kind that result in quiet preparations for scenarios that officially aren't being considered." Ramsay's diplomatic training made him choose words carefully even with trusted colleagues. "Priority evacuation lists have been prepared. Essential supplies have been relocated to more secure storage facilities. Contingency communication procedures have been established."

"And civilian evacuation?" Bryn asked.

"Jesus," Harrington muttered. "They're planning to abandon us."

"Not abandon," Ramsay corrected carefully. "Strategic withdrawal to defensible positions."

"What's the difference?" Kinsey asked bitterly.

"The difference is that strategic withdrawal sounds better in official reports," Meeker said with dark humor. "I've seen this before, gentlemen. In 1917, when the Western Front was collapsing, staff officers spent weeks drafting memoranda about tactical repositioning while French farmers fled their homes with whatever they could carry."

Chapter 20: The Gathering Storm

Preston leaned forward, his medical training making him focus on practical implications. "What about medical facilities? Hospitals? The infrastructure needed to care for civilian casualties?"

"Civilian personnel, with high priority to Health and Sanitation, would be ordered to remain on duty."

"And the plan is to evacuate all British civilian personnel's wives and children."

"What about the million Chinese residents of the colony?"

Silence provided the answer.

Bryn felt anger rising in his throat, hot and bitter. "So we're talking about abandoning a million people to save a few thousand Europeans and politically connected Chinese?"

"We're talking about maintaining essential services under impossible circumstances," Ramsay said defensively. "The evacuation capacity simply doesn't exist for the entire population."

"Then why haven't we been building evacuation capacity?" Harrington demanded. "Why haven't we been preparing for scenarios that apparently everyone in government considers likely?"

"Because," Meeker said quietly, "preparing for evacuation acknowledges the possibility of defeat. And empires don't like to acknowledge the possibility of defeat, even when that acknowledgment might save lives."

The weight of Meeker's words settled over the table like a shroud. Outside, late afternoon rain began to patter against the windows, streaking the glass and blurring the harbor view. The weather seemed to mirror the emotional atmosphere of their conversation, as if nature itself was responding to the gravity of their discussion.

"Gentlemen," Bryn said finally, his voice tight with barely controlled emotion, "we're talking about our families. My daughter. Kinsey's pregnant wife. Harrington's contacts in the Chinese community. Preston's young wife who wants children. These aren't statistics in a military assessment. These are the people we're supposed to protect."

"And we will protect them," Ramsay said, though his voice lacked conviction. "The contingency plans..."

"The contingency plans prioritize maintaining colonial administration over protecting colonial residents," Bryn interrupted. "There's a difference."

Harrington nodded grimly. "In my twenty-three years on the force, I've learned that when official policy conflicts with protecting innocent people, you have to choose which side of that conflict you can live with."

"What are you saying, Thomas?" Preston asked.

"I'm saying that each of us needs to decide whether our primary loyalty is to the system we serve or to the people we're supposed to protect. Because gentlemen, I don't think we're going to be able to serve both."

The conversation was interrupted by the arrival of a Chinese steward carrying fresh drinks. The man moved with the quiet efficiency that colonial society expected, but Bryn noticed that his hands trembled slightly as he set down the glasses. When he looked up, the steward's eyes met Bryn's for just a moment, and in that brief contact, Bryn saw the same fear and uncertainty that was eating at all of them.

After the steward withdrew, Meeker leaned forward conspiratorially. "Gentlemen, may I offer some advice from someone who has been through similar situations before?"

They nodded.

"Start making private arrangements now. Don't wait for official guidance that may never come or may come too late to be useful." His voice dropped to barely above a whisper. "Establish private contacts with shipping companies. Arrange for emergency supplies to be stored outside official channels. Create alternative communication methods that don't depend on government infrastructure."

"You're talking about circumventing official procedures," Ramsay said nervously.

"I'm talking about survival," Meeker replied bluntly. "Official procedures are designed to maintain order and hierarchy. But when the system itself is failing, order and hierarchy become luxuries that can get you killed."

The gathering began to dissolve as each man retreated into his own calculations and fears. Ramsay promised to share any developments from the Governor's office, though he warned that official information might be increasingly unreliable. Kinsey offered to provide intelligence from his Chinese contacts, relationships that might prove more valuable than official channels. Preston mentioned quietly that certain medical supplies were becoming harder to requisition, a development that spoke volumes about hidden preparations.

Harrington was the last to leave, gripping Bryn's shoulder with the strength of a man who had spent years dealing with crises.

"Bryn, I want you to know something," he said quietly. "If the time comes when we have to choose between following orders and protecting our families, I know what choice I'm going to make. And I hope you do too."

Chapter 20: The Gathering Storm

Rain lashed the club's windows as Bryn stood at the entrance, watching water cascade down glass that blurred the city beyond recognition. The streets had emptied except for the most determined travelers, who splashed through puddles that reflected the neon signs of Chinese businesses shuttering early.

The taxi home took him through streets transformed by the storm. Water rushed along gutters, carrying with it debris from the day's preparations: torn fragments of paper notices, broken wood from hastily constructed barriers, the detritus of a city preparing for troubles it couldn't openly acknowledge. As he approached his home, something made him look back toward the harbor. Through the storm, barely visible in the distance, he could make out lights that didn't belong to the usual merchant vessels or British naval patrols. Ships positioned differently than they had been that morning, anchored as if waiting for something.

Or someone.

The empire's flags still flew from their poles, but they hung limp and sodden in the downpour. At home, Patricia Anna was sleeping peacefully, unaware that the world around her had begun to change in ways that would define her entire life.

"What kind of world have we brought you into?" he whispered into the rain.

The storm was no longer gathering. It had arrived.

Chapter 21

The Burden of Duty

"When the house is on fire, you don't debate the architecture. You save what you can and run."

Winstons Churchill

October 1938

The evening air hung thick with humidity as Bryn Williams stood at the doorway of his house, his shirt clinging to his back despite the approaching sunset. His mind weighed heavy with all the information he'd collected during the day. The headline from the South China Morning Post still burned in his memory: "Guangzhou has fallen. Japanese forces occupy the Pearl River Delta."

The wireless reports from the BBC had been equally sobering throughout the day. His department meetings and conversations with Dr. Wellington only confirmed the troubling discussions he'd had at the Hong Kong Club. The threat to Hong Kong was no longer theoretical.

Wellington's words echoed in his mind: "The health and sanitary services will continue to operate in Hong Kong and will be critical in the event of a Japanese attack. Essential services such as food and water, sanitation, and disease prevention will be vital."

When Bryn asked if civil servants might be drafted into a volunteer militia, Wellington assured him the Governor had said no. Their public health responsibilities would come first.

Taking a deep breath of the heavy air, he climbed the stairs to the front door. He needed to appear calm, though his insides twisted with worry. Already, he could feel the weight loss from months of irregular meals and sleepless nights.

Ah-Min greeted him with his customary efficiency, though Bryn noticed the older man's eyes studying his face with concern. "Welcome home, Master Bryn. I trust you have had a productive day."

"Thank you, Ah-Min," Bryn replied, weariness evident despite his efforts to conceal it. "It's been what I would call an illuminating day."

Ah-Min's eyes met Bryn's, and understanding passed between them. "Madam and her family are in the living room with young Patricia," Ah-Min said softly. "The little one has been quite active today, walking everywhere and getting into mischief. Perhaps you would like your usual before joining them?"

"That would be perfect."

As Ah-Min disappeared to prepare his gin and tonic, Bryn knew the older man sensed his distress. The servants' network probably had better intelligence than the colonial government about what was happening across the border.

From the living room came the sound of a toddler's delighted giggling and Lupe's gentle voice saying, "Patricia, come back here with *abuela's* shoe!"

Bryn paused at the living room entrance to take in the scene. Thirteen-month-old Patricia was tottering around the room with surprising speed, clutching one of Alicia's shoes while her grandmother Lupe tried to coax her back. The toddler's blond hair had grown into soft curls, and her sturdy little legs carried her confidently from furniture piece to furniture piece.

"Patricia Anna Williams, bring that back to Grandmama," Alicia called out, laughing despite herself.

The little girl looked up at the sound of her name, saw her father, and immediately dropped the shoe. "Papa!" she squealed, rushing toward him on legs that have just found out how to walk.

Bryn knelt and caught her up in his arms, spinning her around gently. "There's my little girl! Have you been causing trouble for Mama and Grandmama?"

Patricia babbled something incomprehensible but urgent, patting his face with her small hands.

"She's been quite the handful today," Lupe said with affectionate exasperation. "Walking non-stop, climbing on everything she can reach. She even got into the kitchen and tried to help Mrs. Wu cook."

"She's definitely inherited her mother's determination," Bryn observed, settling into his chair with Patricia on his lap. She immediately began exploring his tie and shirt buttons with intense concentration.

Across the room, Mary and Greta were engaged in animated conversation, their voices carrying excitement that contrasted sharply with the heaviness in Bryn's chest.

Ah-Min appeared with the gin and tonic just as Patricia decided to attempt an escape from her father's lap. "Papa, down!" she demanded with surprising clarity.

Chapter 21: The Burden of Duty

"Someone's vocabulary is expanding," Alicia observed with pride and exhaustion in equal measure.

The conversation turned to Mary and Greta's romantic prospects. Both sisters had found serious suitors: Mary with Captain Lars Lindgren, a Swedish ship's captain from the Jardine fleet, and Greta with George Chisham, whom Bryn knew. The discussion was animated and hopeful, with talk of wedding possibilities and future plans.

But Alicia's eyes remained focused on her husband's face throughout the cheerful chatter. She could read the tension in his jaw, the furrow between his brows that appeared when something troubled him deeply. He was thinner too, she noticed, the stress was taking a physical toll.

Patricia, having tired of her exploration, climbed back onto Bryn's lap and leaned against his chest, thumb finding her mouth in the universal gesture of a sleepy toddler.

When a comfortable quiet settled over the room, Bryn seized the moment he'd been waiting for. "I need to share something important with all of you," he announced, his tone immediately commanding attention. "Ah-Min, would you please ask Mrs. Wu and Mei-Lin to join us? This affects everyone in the household."

The laughter died away. Alicia instinctively moved closer to him, while Lupe reached out to stroke Patricia's hair as the toddler dozed against her father's shoulder.

Ah-Min nodded gravely and left, returning moments later with Mrs. Wu and Mei-Lin. The women's smiles faded as they sensed the gravity of the moment.

Bryn caught Ah-Min's steady gaze and saw the quiet strength that had sustained the older man through decades of upheaval in China. Ah-Min had seen this before: governments falling, armies advancing, families fleeing. Perhaps that was why he remained so calm.

"I know you've heard on the wireless or read in the newspapers that Japan's military has invaded China," Bryn began, keeping his voice measured. "Today I learned that the government here has serious concerns that Hong Kong may become a target."

The room fell silent except for the distant sound of cicadas and the ceiling fan's rhythmic whirring.

"What exactly does that mean?" Lupe asked carefully, her voice barely above a whisper.

"Are we talking about actual war here?" Greta's earlier happiness evaporated.

Bryn held up his free hand, careful not to wake Patricia. "The government hasn't received assurances that Britain will send sufficient reinforcements to strengthen our defenses. They continue to press London, but..." He let the sentence hang unfinished.

"What will we do? Are we safe here?" Greta asked, her voice small. "What about George!"

"Should we leave immediately?" Mary's panic was evident.

"And go where, *mija?*" Lupe questioned steadily. "Hong Kong is our home now."

"I'm not leaving," Greta declared. "I won't abandon George based on fears that may never come true."

Alicia's voice cut through the rising anxiety. "Calm down, everyone. Let's hear what Bryn has to say!"

He paused, steeling himself. "Dr. Wellington informed me that even if the Japanese attack, all health and sanitary personnel must continue their duties. We'll be even more critical with refugees flooding in from the mainland. Bryn took a big breath. "If invasion appears imminent," Bryn continued carefully, "the government is developing plans to evacuate European women and children to Australia."

"European women and children," Alicia repeated slowly. "What about Chinese women? Mixed families like ours?"

Bryn swallowed hard. "At present, the policy covers only British and European civilians."

"Because they're white," Alicia said flatly.

"It appears so, yes," Bryn admitted sadly.

"And what category do we fall into?" Alicia's agitation was growing. "My mother? Mary and Greta? Me?"

"I'm working to get answers. Alicia, because you're married to me, the government considers you eligible. You would qualify for passage."

"But not my mother, and not my sisters?" Alicia asked, her voice shaking.

"Preliminary indications are they are not. I'm fighting for exceptions, for family unity provisions."

Mrs. Wu spoke up quietly. "Master Bryn, what of the household staff?"

"The government has made no provision to evacuate people of Asian or Euroasian descent. If the situation deteriorates, I would release everyone from obligations to me so you can care for your own families," Bryn replied immediately.

Chapter 21: The Burden of Duty

"Your safety is more important than any domestic arrangements."

The questions that followed came in worried bursts, about timing, about ships, about what they could take, about reconnection. Bryn answered as best he could while Patricia slept peacefully against his chest, her small body trusting and warm. Finally, sensing the weight of fear threatening to overwhelm the room, he stood carefully. "I suggest we take a break from this heavy discussion. Perhaps some tea? I'd like to walk in the garden with Alicia and Patricia."

The gathering dispersed slowly, each person retreating into private thoughts. Bryn cradled his sleeping daughter against his shoulder while reaching for Alicia's hand. They walked silently among the bauhinia flowers, their sweet scent mixing with the heavy evening air. The oppressive humidity that had dominated the day was finally beginning to ease slightly. Patricia slept on, her steady breathing a comfort against the uncertainty surrounding them.

"I'm frightened, Bryn," Alicia whispered finally. "What's going to happen to us?"

Bryn stopped walking and turned to face her. "What I know is that you and Patricia can be safe by evacuating. I am convinced that the Japanese will invade and the British forces won't stop them, even though the government officially says the colony can be defended successfully. I know that I am obliged to remain in Hong Kong and continue my duties, or…."

"Or what…?"

"Or I resign from my job and I leave with you, Patricia, your mother and sisters if they want to go. I would have to find private passage."

"Resign! It's not like you to abandon your duty," Alicia said firmly.

"Yes, that's true, but I won't be able to go with you, then," Bryn replied. "I'll do everything in my power try to get your family to safety…if they want to leave. In the meantime, we stay close, support each other, and take things one day at a time."

Alicia leaned against him, kissing him softly before pressing her lips to Patricia's sleeping forehead. "I trust you," she said, though her voice trembled. Still, there was newfound resolve in her eyes. She didn't necessarily believe his reassurances, but she believed in him.

"Whatever comes," he said finally, adjusting his daughter's position as she sighed in her sleep, "we face it together as long as possible."

Chapter 22

Refugees and Resolve

"In times of crisis, you discover who you truly are. The rest is just costume."

Marcus Aurelias

August 1939

Ten months had changed Hong Kong from a nervous colony into a city overwhelmed by desperation. The Japanese capture of Guangzhou had triggered a massive influx of people that tested every system and challenged all assumptions about what the British colony could manage. The colonial treasury was draining funds: refugee aid, emergency medical services, and increased sanitation efforts had nearly bankrupt the administration.

Bryn Williams had also changed. The man who once worried about routine inspections now handled a crisis that worsened each day. His office maps were filled with colored pins marking disease outbreaks, crowded settlements, and contaminated water sources. His white inspector's uniform had permanent stains that no amount of washing could remove, and his face looked gaunt, like a man surviving on too little sleep and irregular meals. During that time, his family changed as well. Greta went to with George to London after he was recalled for "consultations," a diplomatic term that no one was fooled by. While Lupe blessed their decisions, she had lapsed into sadness.

The sharp whistle of the kettle pierced through the stifling August heat lingering over Hong Kong like a heavy blanket. Outside, dawn was breaking over Victoria Peak, but the air already felt thick with humidity, making each breath a struggle. It was Monday, just past five in the morning, and Bryn was already moving with the practiced efficiency of someone who had learned to survive on exhaustion. After six years in Hong Kong, he still woke before sunrise. Refugee faces haunted his dreams, and he often woke up calling out warnings about contaminated water or disease outbreaks. Mrs. Wu was preparing breakfast in the sweltering kitchen, the aroma of freshly baked bread battling the oppressive heat. Ah-Min appeared in his freshly pressed uniform, even though the elderly servant's movements seemed slower in the stifling humidity.

"Good morning, Master," Ah-Min said with a formal nod, dabbing perspiration from his forehead with a handkerchief. "Madam asked me to tell you she will be down shortly."

He went back upstairs, pausing outside Patricia's bedroom where twenty-two-month-old Patricia was already awake, chatting to herself in a mixture of English and Cantonese she'd learned from Mei-Lin. Even in the early morning heat, the toddler was full of energy, building towers with her wooden blocks.

"Papa!" she called out when she spotted him, abandoning her blocks to run to the door. Her vocabulary had expanded considerably, though her pronunciation remained charmingly unclear.

"Good morning, little one," he said, scooping her up for a quick hug before setting her back down. "Be good for Mei-Lin today. It's going to be very hot."

Alicia joined him in the dining room, her black hair limp despite being freshly pinned. Dark circles under her eyes indicated another restless night. She moved carefully, one hand supporting her swollen belly, and kissed him softly.

"You're leaving even earlier these days," she observed, settling heavily into her chair. "This heat is unbearable, and I worry about you working in those settlements all day.

"The new refugee situation in Aberdeen is critical," Bryn replied, gently touching her distended stomach. The baby kicked vigorously under his palm. "David seems as eager to escape this heat as the rest of us."

" Dr. Peterson says the baby should arrive in January, but with this stress and heat..." She trailed off, then forced a smile. "Tell me something good will happen today."

"I'll try to be home earlier. Maybe we can sit on the terrace with Patricia if the evening brings any relief."

"That would be wonderful. She's been asking for her papa more frequently. I think she senses the tension, even at her age."

By seven a.m., Bryn was navigating his government-issued automobile through streets that shimmered with heat waves. The city was already alive with desperate activity: refugees seeking shade, vendors trying to keep food from spoiling in the crushing temperature, and the constant flow of people seeking registration papers or medical attention. The military presence had increased noticeably. More Royal Navy ships crowded the harbor, their metal hulls gleaming like ovens in the

Chapter 22: Refugees and Resolve

morning sun. Royal Air Force planes roared overhead more frequently, and uniformed personnel seemed to wilt in the oppressive heat just like everyone else. "Our defences look more impressive than they are," he thought. "A few ships, some planes, and soldiers who've never fought in this kind of brutal heat against the Imperial Japanese Army that's been conditioning in Asia for years."

The wireless reports that morning had been sobering. Fighting in China was intensifying, and refugee numbers were swelling beyond anything the colony could reasonably handle. At the Sanitation Department offices, the young Chinese clerk greeted him with urgent paperwork and a face flushed from the heat. "Good morning, sir. Dr. Wellington left this folder marked urgent, and there's an envelope from Government House. And sir, the ice delivery didn't come."

Bryn's office had become a furnace despite the ceiling fan that rotated sluggishly overhead. Maps covered every wall, marked with colored pins that seemed to multiply daily: red for disease outbreaks, blue for sanitation crises, yellow for overcrowding emergencies. The maps looked like battlefields painted in sweat and desperation. Each pin represented human suffering that statistics couldn't capture, made worse by heat that turned refugee settlements into potential death traps. He'd barely settled when Jason Lam burst through the door, his usually crisp appearance wilted by the morning heat.

"Please tell me you have good news," Bryn said, though Jason's expression and the sweat stains on his shirt suggested otherwise.

"Three more typhoid cases in Sheung Wan," Jason announced, dabbing his forehead with a handkerchief. "Same pattern as last month, but the heat is making everything worse. People are desperate for any water source."

"The contaminated well again?" Bryn asked.

"I'm afraid so. Despite our warnings, they're still using it. But Bryn, it's not just stubbornness. The heat is driving them to desperation. Alternative sources are either too far away or completely dry."

Jason had been Bryn's most reliable colleague since being appointed Deputy Chief Sanitation Officer. A locally born Chinese who'd been educated at Cambridge, he understood both the Western administrative mindset and the realities of Chinese refugee life in ways that made him invaluable.

"What's our response plan?" Bryn asked, making notes while sweat dripped onto the paper.

"I've dispatched a team with lime and disinfectant, but they're struggling in this heat. Two workers collapsed yesterday from heat exhaustion. We need to permanently seal that well this time, but we also need to provide an alternative water source immediately."

"Agreed. What resources do you need?"

"A full crew, concrete, portable water tanks, and probably some constables to keep the peace. The locals won't like losing their water source, especially in this heat, even if it's contaminated."

Bryn made notes, his shirt already clinging to his back despite the early hour. He remembered the Governor's envelope and opened it, his expression darkening as he read.

"What is it?" Jason asked, noticing the change.

"The Governor wants detailed contingency plans for Japanese military action. Evacuation protocols for hospitals, resource allocation under siege conditions." He looked up grimly. "The financial strain is forcing decisions. The colonial treasury is nearly empty from refugee assistance."

Jason's composure faltered, sweat beading on his forehead. "It's really that close, isn't it? In the Chinese community, families are already packing valuables. Shop owners are talking about burying their merchandise."

"London's attention remains focused on Germany," Bryn replied. "The Governor's requests for reinforcements have been largely ignored. What few troops they've sent aren't acclimated to this climate."

"And if the Japanese do come?"

"We'll be on our own. Military commanders are already discussing how long we might last in this heat with limited supplies." Bryn opened Wellington's folder. "Meanwhile, we still have thousands of new refugees arriving weekly. This report details another settlement near Aberdeen. Five thousand people arrived over the weekend, all seeking shelter."

Wellington's note was characteristically blunt: "Williams, inspect immediately. Sanitation non-existent. Heat creating emergency conditions. Expect disease outbreak within hours if not addressed."

"So, we prepare for war while pretending it won't happen, all while people suffer in this furnace?" Jason asked, pulling out his own handkerchief.

"Chaos, but we have a responsibility to do what we can. Organize the Sheung Wan operation. Full disinfection protocol, emergency water distribution, and this time we seal that well permanently. I'll join you after I meet with Wellington."

Dr. Wellington's office felt like an oven despite two electric fans running at full speed. The Chief Sanitation Officer looked haggard, his tall frame more gaunt than ever, his shirt soaked with perspiration.

"Ah, Bryn. Even more punctual than the heat, I see." Wellington gestured

Chapter 22: Refugees and Resolve

weakly to a chair. "I assume you've read the Governor's request?"

"Yes. How specific do they want us to be with our plans, and how are we supposed to manage in this temperature?"

"Very specific. They want to know how we'll maintain basic sanitation with reduced staff, limited supplies, and potentially thousands more refugees fleeing fighting, all while dealing with the worst heat wave in years."

Wellington moved to the window, looking out at the shimmering streets. "The truth is, Bryn, we're already at the breaking point. The Aberdeen settlement you're inspecting today? It's a disaster waiting to happen. No proper water source, inadequate waste disposal, overcrowding beyond anything we've seen, and now this heat that's turning the place into a potential charnel house."

"What resources can we allocate?"

"That's the problem. The colonial treasury is nearly bankrupt from refugee assistance. The Governor approved emergency funds for additional latrines and water distribution, but it's a fraction of what we need. Every day we delay, the heat makes conditions worse."

"With respect, sir, statistics and reports won't prevent a cholera epidemic, especially in this temperature. We need supplies, manpower, and authority to act decisively."

Wellington returned to his desk, perspiration staining his shirt despite the fans. "I've been making that argument for months. But London expects us to work miracles with depleted resources while managing a humanitarian crisis in tropical heat."

"What's your honest assessment?" Bryn asked.

Wellington lowered his voice. "Off the record? If the Japanese attack during this heat wave, we won't last days, let alone weeks. The Colonial Secretary told me privately that our military commanders are already discussing surrender terms, partly because fighting in this climate would be nearly impossible."

"And the civilian population? The refugees trapped in those settlements?"

"God help them all. The heat alone could kill thousands before any fighting starts."

By midday, the sun was a merciless furnace overhead as Bryn stood at the entrance to the Aberdeen settlement. The sight was overwhelming. Thousands of refugees were crammed into makeshift shelters that offered no protection from the blazing heat. The smell hit him like a physical blow: human waste, rotting food, and unwashed bodies, all amplified by temperatures that made breathing feel like inhaling fire.

"Bryn?" Dr. Sarah Thompson, her face flushed from heat and exhaustion. "Thank God you're here. We're losing the battle against this heat."

"What's the situation, Sarah?"

"Critical beyond anything I've seen. We've got suspected typhoid in the eastern section, but the heat is creating new problems hourly. Dehydration, heat stroke, and the sanitation situation..." She gestured helplessly. "It's a miracle we haven't had a major outbreak yet."

They walked through the settlement together, the sun beating down mercilessly. Bryn's two junior inspectors followed, documenting problems while struggling not to succumb to heat exhaustion themselves.

"How many people are we dealing with?" Bryn asked, his shirt already soaked through.

"Official count is five thousand, but I suspect it's closer to seven," Sarah replied, shading her eyes against the glare. "More arrive daily, all fleeing the fighting and seeking any shelter from this heat. We're running out of everything: space, food, water, shade."

They paused near a group of families clustered under a makeshift awning that provided minimal relief from the sun. An elderly woman looked up hopefully as they approached, her face gaunt from dehydration.

"You are officials?" she asked in broken English, her voice hoarse. "My grandson very sick. Fever for three days, but in this heat, we cannot tell if it is sickness or just the sun."

Sarah knelt beside her, checking the woman's pulse. "Where is he?"

She pointed to a small shelter where a young boy lay listlessly on a mat, his face dangerously flushed.

"We need to isolate suspected cases immediately," Sarah said quietly to Bryn. "But to where? There's no space, and the heat makes any enclosed area potentially lethal."

"We'll create space and find shade," Bryn replied firmly. He turned to his assistants. "Mark this entire section for emergency medical quarantine. We'll need to relocate healthy families to any area with better ventilation."

They continued through the settlement, each step revealing new horrors amplified by the crushing heat. At every turn, the sun created additional problems: a contaminated water barrel that was too hot to touch, raw sewage that had dried into dangerous dust, dead rats that were decomposing rapidly in the heat.

"Inspector!" One of his junior assistants called out, his voice strained. "There's

Chapter 22: Refugees and Resolve

a disturbance near the main entrance."

They hurried over to find chaos erupting around a water distribution point. Desperate people were fighting for access to the few containers of drinking water, their movements sluggish from heat but driven by desperation.

"Everyone back!" Bryn called out in his limited Cantonese, stepping into the crowd despite the blazing sun. "Form lines! Elderly and children first! There's water for everyone if we do this properly!"

A middle-aged man protested weakly, his face a dangerous shade of red from heat exposure. "We've been waiting since before dawn! The sun is killing us!"

"And you'll get your share," Bryn replied firmly, though he felt dizzy from the heat himself.

It took nearly two hours to restore order and complete the distribution. By then, both Bryn and Sarah were showing signs of heat exhaustion, and two refugees had collapsed from dehydration.

"This happens multiple times daily," Sarah explained as they sought shelter under a tarp, both breathing heavily. "Too many people, not enough water, and this heat that makes everything a crisis. We've had six heat stroke cases just this morning."

"What do you need most urgently?"

"Clean water, shade structures, medical supplies, and a way to get people out of this sun. In that order."

"I'll see what can be done immediately."

As the afternoon wore on, Bryn worked with his team to identify the most critical issues while fighting the effects of heat exhaustion. Emergency water distribution, portable shade structures, better ventilation for the sick, and waste removal that wouldn't create additional health hazards in the blazing temperature. His notebook filled with urgent tasks, ink smearing from his perspiration.

By six o'clock, they had completed their assessment while the sun finally began to lose some of its killing intensity. The situation was worse than Wellington had described, and the heat had made every problem exponentially more dangerous.

"Sarah, thank you help, I couldn't do this without you," Bryn said as they prepared to leave, both of them exhausted and dehydrated. "I'll have emergency supplies here by tomorrow morning, including shade structures and additional water."

"And after that?"

"We keep fighting the crisis one day at a time, and pray for cooler weather."

"Be careful yourself, Bryn, make sure you drink lots of water today," she said.

In a moment of friendship and common understanding, they embraced each other.

It was nearly eight when Bryn finally reached home, staggering from heat exhaustion and the emotional weight of what he'd witnessed. His uniform was completely soaked through, and he felt lightheaded from dehydration.

"Master Bryn!" Ah-Min appeared immediately, his face creased with concern. "You look unwell. Madam is on the terrace with Miss Patricia. She was worried about you working in this heat. Come, sit in the shade immediately."

"Thank you, Ah-Min," Bryn managed, loosening his tie with shaking hands. "I need something cold to drink, then perhaps we could sit outside if there's any breeze at all."

"At once, sir. You should know, Madam is not feeling well. This heat is affecting her pregnancy, and your late hours are adding to her stress." Ah-Min saw everything, understood everything. In six years, he had become more advisor than servant, and his concern was genuine.

On the terrace, Bryn found Alicia in a loose cotton dress, fanning herself while Patricia played with wooden blocks nearby. The toddler looked up as he approached.

"Papa hot!" Patricia announced with the matter-of-fact observation of a child, then returned to her blocks.

"Very hot, sweetheart," he agreed, sinking into a chair beside Alicia.

"You look terrible," Alicia said, reaching out to touch his forehead. "You're burning up. How can you work in these conditions?"

"Someone has to. The situation is getting worse daily."

Within minutes, Ah-Min returned with iced tea and a damp cloth for Bryn's forehead. "Master, if I may suggest, perhaps we could sit here where there is at least some evening breeze."

They settled into comfortable chairs as the temperature finally began to drop from unbearable to merely oppressive. Patricia abandoned her blocks to climb onto her father's lap, chattering about her day in her mixture of languages.

"Sit with me for a while," Bryn said to Ah-Min. "I need to talk through some things. The Japanese situation," Bryn began after a long silence, pressing the cool cloth to his neck while Patricia dozed against his chest. "The Governor has us preparing evacuation plans, not if they attack, but when. And this heat wave is making everything infinitely worse."

Chapter 22: Refugees and Resolve

Ah-Min's face remained composed, but understanding flickered in his eyes. At his age, he had survived the collapse of the Chinese empire, civil wars, and natural disasters that had tested human endurance. "You fear for your family, especially in Madam's condition," Ah-Min observed, fanning himself with a paper fan.

"Alicia's pregnant. Patricia's just a toddler. Ships are taking European women and children to Australia, but Alicia refuses to travel in this heat, especially so close to her due date," Bryn said.

"Madam has a strong spirit," Ah-Min noted approvingly, though his voice carried concern. "But wisdom sometimes means accepting help, even when it means separation."

"What about you, Ah-Min? Your family? This heat must be affecting everyone, and the refugees tell horrific stories about Japanese treatment of Chinese civilians," Bryn replied.

Ah-Min was quiet for a moment, his weathered hands folded as he considered his words. "My grandson departed for Chungking last month. He could not bear this heat any longer. My daughter and her husband will follow when the temperature breaks. They want me to come."

"You have my blessing whenever you decide to go. If you need money for passage, or help with arrangements…" Bryn added.

Ah-Min raised his hand gently. "My place is here, Master. For now. Though I confess, this heat tests even my old bones."

"Why stay? You owe no loyalty to the British Crown, especially under these conditions."

A small smile touched Ah-Min's lips. "I have lived eighty-two years, not sixty-two as my papers say." The revelation startled Bryn, although it wasn't surprising. "When you have endured as many seasons as I have, including droughts and heat waves that lasted months, you learn that empires come and go like monsoons, but people, individuals, they endure. The Tao teaches us about cycles," Ah-Min continued, his voice taking on a teacher's cadence as the evening air finally began to cool. "Expansion and contraction. Heat and cooling. Light and darkness. The Japanese advance now, just as the British advanced a century ago. Even this brutal heat will pass. The wheel turns."

"That's rather philosophical comfort when facing bayonets and bombs in hundred-degree heat," Bryn said with a rueful smile, though he felt some relief as his body temperature finally began to normalize.

"Perhaps. But wisdom lies in recognizing what can be changed and what cannot. You cannot stop the Japanese Empire any more than you can stop this heat wave. But you can decide how you will meet whatever comes," Ah-Min said.

"How should I meet it?" Bryn asked.

Ah-Min took a deliberate slow breath. "By doing what you already do each day. Tending to the sick. Protecting the vulnerable. Being a good husband and father." Ah-Min's gaze was steady as the first cool breeze of the evening stirred the air. "The great river does not wonder about its purpose; it flows regardless of drought or flood, carrying life to all it touches."

Bryn sat back, feeling the first real relief from the heat he'd experienced all day. Patricia stirred in his arms, murmuring "Papa" before settling back to sleep.

"You've generously lent me some of your philosophy books," Ah-Min continued, "The Stoics and the Taoists are not so different. Both understand that true strength comes from within, not from external circumstances, whether those are political upheavals or killing heat."

Bryn nodded, taking time to let Ah-Min's words settle on him.

They sat in comfortable silence as the heat finally began to dissipate, listening to the evening sounds of Hong Kong and feeling grateful for any breeze.

"What will you do?" Ah-Min finally asked. "Will you send Madam and Miss Patricia away, despite the heat and her condition?"

"I don't know. The heat makes travel dangerous for someone in her condition. And part of me wants them close, where I can protect them," Bryn asserted

"Not foolish. Human." Ah-Min rose slowly, moving more carefully in the heat. "The future is never certain, Master. But fear, like excessive heat, is a poor advisor. Trust instead in what you have built, not this house or position, but the strength within your family. That cannot be taken, even by an empire or a heat wave."

"You said the wheel will turn for the Japanese. Do you think it has turned for the British Empire?" Bryn queried.

"It began years ago, Master. People didn't notice because the wheel turns slowly, like seasons changing. One day it will stop, and something new will begin," Ah-Min said evenly.

As Ah-Min prepared to leave, Bryn felt compelled to ask one more question. "Do you think Hong Kong will fall?"

The older man paused at the door. "All things must change, empires, weather, everything. But not all change is ending. Sometimes it is transformation. The Hong Kong we have known will disappear, and another will take its place. Perhaps cooler, perhaps warmer. It will endure. But it will never be the same again."

"Thank you, Ah-Min. You have been more than a servant to me. In many ways, you have been family to me. I will help you with whatever plans you make

Chapter 22: Refugees and Resolve

in the coming months. "The admission broke down all remaining barriers between master and servant. In crisis, whether political or natural, people discovered who had really been caring for them. Bryn stood and embraced Ah-Min, both men grateful for the cooler evening air. After a moment's awkwardness, Ah-Min returned the embrace, his eyes reflecting both affection and concern.

"You are a fine man, Master, and it has been an honor to serve you and be your friend," Ah-Min said, his voice carrying the weight of years and genuine emotion.

"Friend." The word transformed everything and would help the coming separation bearable for Bryn.

For the next hour, Bryn sat alone as the temperature finally dropped to bearable levels, reflecting on Ah-Min's words while Patricia slept peacefully in his arms. They were on the precipice of changes that would shake the British Empire and beyond, all while nature itself seemed to be conspiring against them. But as the evening breeze picked up and the oppressive heat finally began to break, something was settling within him, a resolution, perhaps. Whatever happened, he would meet it with dignity, protect what he could, and trust in the strength that Ah-Min assured him already existed within his family.

Outside, the lights of Victoria Harbour twinkled through the heat haze, still beautiful despite everything. Somewhere in those lights were refugee settlements where people were finally getting relief from the killing sun, overcrowded hospitals where heat stroke victims were slowly recovering, families making impossible choices about survival in impossible conditions. Tomorrow would bring new crises, new decisions, new fears, and probably another day of crushing heat. But tonight, as the temperature finally became tolerable, there was still peace in his garden, still love in his home, still hope that somehow they would find a way through whatever came next.

Just as Bryn was preparing to carry Patricia inside, the telephone rang. Through the open window, he heard Ah-Min answer it, then call out urgently: "Master Bryn! It's Dr. Wellington. He says it's urgent. There's been an outbreak at the Aberdeen settlement. Multiple cases of cholera."

The wheel was turning, as Ah-Min had said. But perhaps in the turning, there was also opportunity: for courage, for love, for the quiet strength that let ordinary people endure extraordinary times, even under a merciless sun.

Chapter 23

New Life, Old Wounds

"The hardest choices require the strongest wills, but sometimes the strongest wills break the tenderest hearts."

Found in a Hong Kong government official's diary, 1940

June 18, 1940

A few months earlier, amid a world unraveling into chaos, a new life had entered the Williams family. David George Williams, small, pink faced, and crying fiercely, was born on a stormy January night. Lightning split the sky as Alicia brought him into the world, as if heaven itself acknowledged the miracle unfolding. For a brief period afterward, the world had narrowed to lullabies and feeding schedules. Mei-Lin worked tirelessly with the newborn while Lupe spent hours teaching Patricia to be gentle with her baby brother. "Soft hands, *pequeña*," she would say, guiding Patricia's fingers across David's cheek.

But outside their bubble, chaos erupted faster than anyone expected. Japanese forces swept through southern China like a wave of steel and fire. Guangzhou fell in three days. Shenzhen was burning. Radio reports brought fresh horror each morning: columns of refugees flooding south, villages cleared by bombing, hospitals overwhelmed with civilian casualties. Hong Kong's population had swelled to nearly two million desperate souls. The refugee camps in Kowloon reeked of human waste and despair. Disease spread faster than relief supplies could arrive. Bryn returned home each night hollow-eyed from scenes that would haunt him forever: children separated from their parents, elderly people dying alone on concrete floors, families fighting over scraps of bread. Three weeks earlier, Japanese reconnaissance planes had been spotted over the New Territories. Last week, artillery fire could be heard from across the border. The Royal Navy had quietly moved its main fleet away from Hong Kong harbor, although the government denied any strategic withdrawal.

Evacuation orders had come from London. But only for some. Only for white British and European civilians. Not for the Chinese refugees who had fled

Japanese brutality. Not for those whose blood colonial bureaucrats deemed insufficient for salvation.

The rain had stopped, leaving the scents of earth and jasmine in the heavy midnight air. Bryn rubbed his eyes, feeling exhaustion deep in his bones. His medical bag sat by the door, supplies nearly gone: quinine tablets, sulfa powder, hope itself running low.

He grabbed his journal and wrote: "*They've approved Alicia's departure. Patricia, David to go with her. But not Lupe, Mary, Ah-Min, Mrs. Wu and Mei-Lin. I should feel relief. Instead, I feel like I'm betraying everyone I've sworn to protect. How do you tell the mother of your children that the empire considers her family disposable?*"

Footsteps approached. Alicia and Lupe emerged from the house, both sensing the crisis that had kept him awake. "You received word today?" Lupe asked, settling across from him.

"Evacuation orders. From London." He met her eyes directly. "British and European civilians only. Women and children only."

"But not me, Mary and Greta," Lupe said with calm resignation that somehow made it worse. "Not our loyal household servants. Not our Chinese neighbors who've been here longer than any of us."

"Mama, there has to be an appeal process..." Alicia began, knowing full well that it would amount to an empty exercise.

"*Mija*, I've seen how these decisions work. In Mexico, during the revolution, they chose who lived and who died based on which side of town they were born on. There is no appeal when they draw lines through people's hearts."

Before Bryn could respond, soft footsteps padded across the tiles. Mei-Lin appeared in the doorway, David cradled in her arms, his small face peaceful in sleep. "He wouldn't settle," Mei-Lin said quietly. "I think he senses something." She looked between their faces, reading the grief there. "You're discussing the evacuation."

"You know about it?" Bryn asked.

"Word travels fast in the servant quarters. Mrs. Wu heard it from her sister who works at Government House. We know who is included and who is not." Mei-Lin's voice remained steady, but her knuckles were white where she gripped David's blanket.

Ah-Min emerged from the kitchen, carrying a tray of tea despite the late hour. At his old age, he moved with the careful dignity of someone who had survived floods, famines, and civil wars. "If we are to be left behind," he said matter-of-factly, "we must prepare properly. No use pretending otherwise."

Chapter 23: New Life, Old Wounds

The practical acceptance in his voice somehow made everything more real.

"We can't just leave you," Alicia said fiercely. "You're family. All of you."

"You will go," Lupe said firmly, "because your children need you alive. Patricia and David cannot survive what's coming."

"Tell me about the ship," Mei-Lin said, settling David in Alicia's arms. "How long is the journey?"

"The Empress of Asia. Three days to Manila, though submarine activity could delay us." Bryn's voice grew quieter. "Then onward transport to Australia, eventually."

"Then we have little time to teach you everything," Ah-Min declared. "No wet nurse, no amah, no cook. No mother or husband to help. You must do these things all yourself."

The Next Morning

The household transformed into an urgent school of survival. Mei-Lin began David's care lessons in the nursery while morning light filtered through bamboo blinds. "Never use ship water directly for formula," she instructed, demonstrating with precious condensed milk. "Always boil it first, even if they say it's clean. See how I test the temperature on my wrist? Too hot burns his mouth, too cold gives him stomach cramps."

She showed Alicia how to recognize fever in David's flushed cheeks, how to feel for dehydration by pinching the skin on his hand, and how to position him for feeding when the ship's motion made everything unstable. "If he won't eat, try smaller amounts more frequently. And this," she produced a small tin of rice powder, "mix with the condensed milk if the regular formula upsets his stomach. Ask other women with older children to help."

In the kitchen, Mrs. Wu demonstrated practical magic: how to stretch rations, and how to trade efficiently with other passengers. "You watch the other mothers traveling alone," she said, her weathered hands quick and sure as she divided their remaining food into voyage portions. "The ones with quiet children who don't cry constantly, those are the survivors. You help each other. Survival is never solitary." She pressed a small cloth pouch into Alicia's hands. "Ginger root. For seasickness. Chew small pieces. And this," another pouch, "dried plums. When Patricia gets scared and won't eat, these taste like candy to children."

Meanwhile, Lupe focused on emotional preparation. In the garden, she helped Patricia practice being "mama's big helper" while teaching Alicia the subtle arts of managing a frightened child in public. "Patricia, show me how you can carry David's bottle," Lupe instructed. The three-year-old carefully lifted the glass bottle with both hands, concentrating intensely. "Good girl. Now, when you're on the big boat, if Mama needs to help baby David, what do you do?"

"Stay right here!" Patricia announced proudly.

"That's right. You stay close to Mama, and you hold your doll tight."

Later, when Patricia was napping, Lupe pulled Alicia aside. "She's too young to understand why we can't come, but old enough to feel abandoned. You must watch for signs: refusing to eat, nightmares, clinging behavior. When children feel their world disappearing, they sometimes try to disappear too."

Bryn was in amazement and grateful for how the house staff dedicated their time to helping Alicia and the children make the evacuation less traumatic, all the while knowing they would be left behind.

The bureaucratic machinery of evacuation moved with brutal efficiency. Bryn spent the morning at Government House, navigating the paperwork that would save his family while condemning thousands of others.

Dr. Wellington's office buzzed with activity. Maps covered every surface, marked with evacuation zones and ship schedules. The Colonial Secretary looked like he hadn't slept in days. "Bryn, thank God you're here. We need your medical assessment of the Chinese staff situation." Wellington gestured to a thick file. "London's asking whether we should include 'loyal servants' in the evacuation."

Bryn felt his stomach clench. "What's the current directive?"

"British and European extraction only. No exceptions." Wellington's voice carried the weight of someone implementing orders he didn't entirely agree with. "But some families are refusing to leave without their amahs, their cooks. We're getting pushback."

"What kind of pushback?"

"The Ashford family withdrew their evacuation request when we denied passage for their Chinese staff. Said they'd rather stay and face whatever comes together." Wellington rubbed his temples. "Can't have that kind of sentiment spreading. Bad for morale."

Bryn stared at the evacuation lists, hundreds of names divided into neat categories: Approved, Denied, Pending Review. Under "Denied" he saw familiar names: Ah-Min, and Mei-Lin Chen, listed as "Domestic Staff, Chinese National." Mrs. Wu, whose son served in the Hong Kong Volunteer Defense Corps. Families that had lived in Hong Kong for generations, suddenly classified as expendable.

"Sir, these people have been here longer than most of the British residents..."

"Orders from London, Bryn. I don't like it any more than you do, but we're

Chapter 23: New Life, Old Wounds

not in a position to debate imperial policy." Wellington fixed him with a steady look. "Your family's passage is confirmed. There's nothing more I can do."

That afternoon, Bryn sought out Robert Jenkins at the American consulate. The conversation that would determine his family's immediate future took place in Jenkins' elegantly appointed office overlooking the harbor. Jenkins was exactly as Bryn remembered from the Hong Kong Club: mid-forties, prematurely gray hair, expensive suits that managed to look crisp despite the tropical humidity. But there was something else now, a loneliness that made him almost eager to help since his wife passed away.

"Of course, I remember Alicia," Jenkins said, his eyes brightening. "Quite the most elegant woman at the diplomatic reception. How could I forget?"

Bryn had noticed Jenkins' attention that night, the way his gaze had lingered on Alicia as she moved through the crowd in her emerald silk gown. The American had monopolized her conversation for nearly an hour, discussing art and literature with the intensity of a man starved for intellectual companionship.

"My wife Eleanor would have liked her," Jenkins continued, his voice softening. "They shared a love of poetry. Eleanor passed five years ago. Tuberculosis." He gestured to a photograph on his desk: a slight, blonde woman with intelligent eyes. "The estate feels quite empty now."

"I appreciate your offer to house my family in Manila," Bryn said carefully. "I would feel better if she didn't have to be housed at the American base Fort McKinley . . . I need to be direct about something."

"What is it?"

"That night at the club last year, I noticed your... interest in my wife. I'm not judging it, but I need to know that your motivations for helping are purely humanitarian."

Jenkins was quiet for a long moment, studying his hands. Then he looked up with surprising honesty. "I'm not offended. Your wife is a remarkable woman, but I'm not offering help in hopes of... well, in hopes of anything beyond doing what's right. I just want to help a friend."

He stood and walked to the window overlooking the harbor. "I've seen what's happening in China, Bryn. The refugee reports, the bombing casualties. I may be lonely, but I'm not a predator. Your family will be safe in my home."

"And if Japanese expansion threatens Manila?"

"Then I'll arrange safe transport to Australia." Jenkins turned back to face him. "I give you my word as a diplomat and as a gentleman." He extended his hand and they shook hands vigorously.

"Thank you, I'll accept your word for it," Bryn replied, never losing eye contact with Robert.

The evening brought Bryn's most difficult conversation at home yet. Mrs. Wu joined them in the sitting room, her usually cheerful demeanor subdued. At fifty-five, she had managed the Williams household's cooking functions, including large dinners, with efficiency and creativity.

"I heard about the evacuation from my sister," Mrs. Wu began without preamble. "She works for the Hendersons. They offered to forge papers claiming she was Filipino. She refused."

"Why?" Alicia asked.

"Because forged papers mean hiding who you are forever. If they catch you, it's not just deportation." Mrs. Wu's voice remained steady. "Better to stay Chinese and hope the Japanese do not need to punish us."

The irony hung in the air like incense smoke.

"Mrs. Wu," Bryn said carefully, "if there were another way..."

"There isn't, and we all know it." She straightened in her chair, dignity intact despite the circumstances. "I've been thinking about what happens after you leave. This house will need caretaking. The garden will need tending. If you return, you'll want everything as you left it."

"When we return," Alicia said firmly.

"Yes. When." Mrs. Wu smiled for the first time that evening. "So, we plan for that. Mei-Lin and Ah-Min and I, we'll take care of things. We'll keep your home ready. And Madam Lupe will be with us."

Mei-Lin had been quiet through most of the conversation, but now she spoke up. "I want to give you something for David." She produced a small jade bracelet, its green surface worn smooth by handling. "This was my grandmother's. In China, we believe jade protects children on journeys."

She fastened it carefully around David's tiny wrist. "When he's older, you tell him about the woman who helped raise him. You tell him that love crosses all oceans."

Lupe had been watching the exchange with the keen observation of someone who understood exile. Now she reached into her dress and withdrew the small wooden box she'd shown Bryn the night before.

"This medallion has protected three generations of women in my family," she said, opening the box to reveal the silver Virgin of Guadalupe. "My mother wore it crossing the desert from Sonora. I wore it crossing the ocean from America.

Chapter 23: New Life, Old Wounds

Now you must wear it crossing another ocean."

She fastened the delicate chain around Alicia's neck, her fingers trembling slightly. "The Virgin watches over travelers and mothers. When you feel lost, you touch this and remember: you come from a long line of survivors."

"Oh, Mama, I love you so much. I can't bear to think about leaving you," Alicia burst out with tears.

Their last full day together was spent in quiet preparation and precious normalcy. Patricia played in the garden, memorizing the sound of Lupe's laughter and the feel of Mei-Lin's gentle hands braiding her hair. David slept peacefully in his basket, occasionally opening his dark eyes to focus on the faces bent over him.

That evening, as the sun set over Victoria Harbor for what might be the last time they would see it together, the five women sat in the garden sharing tea and memories.

"I keep thinking of the night you arrived here," Lupe said to Bryn. "So serious, so proper in your white colonial uniform. I wasn't sure you were good enough for my daughter."

"And now?" Bryn asked with a slight smile.

"Now I know that you love her enough to let her go when staying means danger. That is the hardest kind of love." She paused, watching Patricia chase fireflies among the jasmine bushes. "My granddaughter will not remember this garden, but I want her to remember that she comes from women who made impossible choices with grace."

As the evening deepened, they spoke of practical things and precious memories, weaving together the threads of a family that geography would soon scatter but love would somehow hold together. When Patricia finally fell asleep in Lupe's lap, her small fingers clutching the cloth doll Esperanza, the adults stayed in the garden until the last harbor light winked out, holding each other against the approaching storm, memorizing the weight and warmth of love that would somehow have to sustain them across oceans and through whatever darkness lay ahead.

Chapter 24

The Empress of Asia

"In war, love becomes both the heaviest burden and the lightest hope. We carry it across oceans, through darkness, into whatever waits beyond the horizon."

A letter found aboard the Empress of Asia, 1940

Three a.m. at Kowloon dock, and the humid air pressed against them like a wet cloth. The Empress of Asia loomed overhead, her white hull dulled by wartime service, gun mounts visible on her decks like steel promises of the violence they were fleeing. The scene around them was impossible to understand. Thousands of people moved in a coordinated chaos: British naval personnel with clipboards and stamps, Chinese dock workers carrying cargo, refugees holding suitcases, children, and whatever else they could salvage from their lives.

Bryn carried their single large leather suitcase. Inside: three sets of clothes each, Patricia's favorite picture books, sterilized bottles, condensed milk, Alicia's jewelry sewn into a hidden pocket by Ah-Min's careful hands, sixty Hong Kong dollars converted from Bryn's medical practice savings, and Ah-Min's emergency pesos hidden in the lining.

Lupe had insisted on going despite Bryn's protests about the early hour and the chaos they would encounter. She wore her church dress and silver combs, maintaining dignity despite the imperial indignity. Mei-Lin and Ah-Min flanked her, quietly rebelling against the system that considered them unworthy of salvation.

The dock was a clear display of controlled desperation. Military personnel had split the area into zones: British civilians here, Europeans there, Americans in a separate section near the consulate representatives. Chinese workers handled cargo but were strictly barred from the passenger areas. The racial layout of empire had never been more sharply defined.

"Look at all the people!" Patricia exclaimed, her voice bright with excitement rather than fear. At three, she saw adventure where adults saw catastrophe. "Are they all going on our boat?"

Ashes and Dawn

"Some of them, sweetheart," Alicia explained, shifting David to her other hip. The baby had been fussing since dawn, as if sensing the tension radiating from every adult around him.

"Where are the daddies?" Patricia asked, tugging on Alicia's skirt.

"The daddies have to stay and work," Alicia explained, her voice catching.

"Like my daddy?"

"Like your daddy."

Around them, the scene played out in heartbreaking variations. Mrs. Henderson, a banker's wife, argued desperately with a naval officer about her amah's travel documents, while the Chinese woman stood silently behind her, understanding that her fifteen years of service meant nothing in this moment. The Ashford children clung to their ayah, crying as their parents tried to explain why the woman who had raised them couldn't come on their "adventure."

Near the customs checkpoint, they encountered their friends, the Atkins family. Helen Atkins looked haggard, her twin boys clinging to her skirts as she juggled travel documents and luggage.

"Alicia, thank heavens," Helen said, relief evident in her voice. "Are we sharing a cabin? I heard families are being doubled up due to the numbers."

"It appears so," Alicia replied, noting how Helen's hands shook as she spoke. The woman had always been high strung, but the stress of evacuation had clearly pushed her near breaking point.

Helen's elderly mother-in-law stood nearby, her face a mask of stoic acceptance. At seventy, Mrs. Atkins senior had lived through enough crises to understand that survival required adaptation, not sentiment.

"We'll manage together," the older woman said firmly. "Women have been helping each other through hard times since the beginning of history."

They reached the main checkpoint, where a young lieutenant reviewed the Williams family documents with mechanical efficiency. Bryn noted the officer's youth, probably fresh from England, executing orders he likely didn't fully understand.

"Williams, Alicia. Children: Patricia and David. Destination: Manila, private accommodation with American Assistant High Commissioner Jenkins." The lieutenant stamped their papers with crisp authority. "Fifteen minutes for farewells. Then report to Gangway C."

They found a small space near some cargo containers, away from the main crowd. The brief privacy felt precious, almost sacred.

Chapter 24: The Empress of Asia

Mei-Lin knelt first, taking David's small hand in hers. The baby looked up at her with the solemn attention of someone too young to understand words but old enough to sense emotion. She gripped Alicia's shoulders with surprising strength. "You remember what I taught you about surviving with strangers. You watch, you listen, you help others so they help you. And you never, ever let anyone see how much you're carrying in that jewelry pocket."

Patricia had grown unusually quiet, sensing the weight of adult grief around her. Lupe knelt before her granddaughter, producing the cloth doll sewn from scraps of Alicia's old dresses. "This is Esperanza," Lupe said solemnly. "Hope. When you miss your *Abuela*, you hold her tight, and she'll whisper my love to you."

"Will you come on the next boat, *Abuela?*" Patricia asked, clutching the doll to her chest.

"Perhaps, *pequeña*. Perhaps." Lupe's voice didn't waver, though her eyes brightened with unshed tears. "But for now, you must be my brave girl. Can you help Mama take care of baby David?"

"Yes, *Abuela*. I'm a big girl now."

"Yes, you are. The biggest, bravest girl I know."

"Mama, I'm afraid," Alicia whispered.

"Good. Fear keeps you alert, keeps you careful. But do not let it paralyze you." Lupe drew on reserves of strength built over decades of hardship. "You are my daughter. You have survived uprooting, loneliness, the fear of not belonging. You have built a life in a foreign land and created a family that spans cultures. You are stronger than you know."

The ship's horn blared across the harbor: final boarding call.

Lupe stepped back, drawing herself up with dignity that made her seem taller than her small frame. "Go now. Go quickly, before any of us forget to be strong."

Alicia kissed her mother one last time, tasting salt and sorrow and the lingering scent of the jasmine soap Lupe had used for fifteen years. She grabbed Patricia, and with David in her arms, embraced Bryn with all her strength, kissing him several times.

"Fear not my love," Bryn said, tears rolling down his cheeks. "We will be reunited soon."

Then Alicia turned toward the gangway, Patricia clutching her skirts, David stirring restlessly in her arms.

At the gangway's base, a junior officer checked their papers once more, then waved them forward. "Welcome aboard the Empress of Asia, ma'am. Cabin assignments are posted on the main deck. The purser will sort out meal arrangements."

The gangway rose with mechanical finality. The Empress of Asia groaned as tugboats pushed her slowly from the dock. From the deck, hundreds of faces lined the railings, waving handkerchiefs, hats, and bare hands in a collective gesture of goodbye to everything they had known.

Alicia found space at the railing. They waved at the shrinking figures on the dock until they could no longer distinguish individual faces from the crowd.

Bryn remained visible longer than the others, standing motionless as the ship carried away half her heart. Only when the harbor itself began to fade into the morning mist did he finally turn and begin the long walk home to his house, flanked by Lupe, Ah-Min and Mei-Lin.

At Sea

The ship's movements had settled into a nauseating rhythm that seemed designed to punish human equilibrium. Eighteen hundred refugees crammed into spaces meant for half that number created a floating city of desperation and hope in equal measure. Their cabin was a suffocating box shared with the Atkins family: elderly Mrs. Atkins, her daughter-in-law Helen, and Helen's twin boys, James and Peter, age five. The space barely accommodated four adults and three children, with luggage stacked wherever it could fit and privacy reduced to whatever could be achieved by hanging blankets between the bunks. Patricia had attached herself to the Atkins twins with the determination of someone who understood instinctively that survival meant finding allies. She followed them around the deck like a determined puppy, her blonde hair catching in the sea wind as she peppered them with questions.

"Where are we going?" she asked them repeatedly, not understanding their answers about Australia and safety but comforted by their presence. "When will we see Daddy again?" she asked Alicia for the dozenth time, and each time the question cut deeper because Alicia had no answer.

David was struggling more each hour. The formula disagreed with his stomach, causing violent spasms that left him weak and feverish. The ship's motion made feeding nearly impossible, and Alicia found herself constantly cleaning sour milk from her clothes and his.

Dr. Patterson, the ship's physician, was overwhelmed with seasick passengers and had little time for individual consultations. "Try smaller amounts more frequently," he advised during his brief rounds. "And pray the weather holds. Rough seas make everything worse."

Chapter 24: The Empress of Asia

Alicia had found other mothers willing to share when their own children's needs were met, but their charity had limits. Maria Silva, a Eurasian woman traveling with forged papers that identified her as Portuguese, proved most helpful.

"Mix the rice powder with the condensed milk," Maria suggested, offering a small tin from her own carefully hoarded supplies. "Sometimes easier on their stomachs. And this," she produced a cloth pouch, "fennel seeds. Chew them and let the juice mix with your saliva, then put a drop on his tongue. Chinese remedy for colic."

Alicia accepted gratefully. Survival was communal, just as Lupe had taught her, but it required constant negotiation and reciprocity.

The social dynamics of the ship revealed themselves gradually. The first-class passengers, mostly senior colonial administrators' and military personnel's wives and children maintained their sense of hierarchy even in times of crisis. They had better cabins, better food, and better access to the ship's limited medical supplies. In steerage, where most of the refugees were housed, informal networks developed quickly.

Helen Atkins proved to be one of the more fragile passengers. By the second day, she was barely able to care for her own children, spending most of her time retching over a basin while her mother-in-law managed the boys with grim efficiency. "I can't do this," Helen whispered to Alicia during one of her clearer moments. "I'm not strong enough. How are you managing so well?"

"Practice," Alicia replied, thinking of her years learning resilience from Lupe and the household staff. "And no choice. The children need us to be strong, so we find strength somewhere."

Mrs. Atkins senior had organized what she called "the mothers' council," an informal group that met each evening after the children were asleep to share information and resources.

"Word is that Japanese submarines have been spotted in the South China Sea," reported Mrs. Ashford, whose husband worked in naval intelligence. "Captain's been taking evasive routes, which is why we're making such slow progress."

"How much longer?" asked another mother.

"At least another day."

The information circulated through the ship's maternal network, creating both anxiety and solidarity. They were all in the same situation: powerless to control their circumstances but responsible for keeping their children alive.

That night, Patricia woke screaming from nightmares, her small body shaking with terror she couldn't articulate. The cramped cabin amplified every sound, disturbing the Atkins family and several neighboring cabins. "I want Daddy! I want *Abuela*! I want to go home!" she sobbed, her voice carrying the primal anguish of a child who couldn't understand why her world had been torn apart.

"It's alright, sweetheart," Alicia whispered, pulling Patricia into her arms while trying not to wake David, who had finally fallen into exhausted sleep. "We're going on an adventure, remember? To see daddy's friend Mr. Jenkins in the Philippines."

"I don't want adventure! I want home! I want my toys! I want Mei-Lin!" Patricia cried out.

Other passengers stirred restlessly in their bunks, adding exhaustion and irritation to the cabin's emotional atmosphere. Helen Atkins shot Alicia a look that mixed sympathy with annoyance, while Mrs. Atkins senior sat up and wordlessly handed Patricia a small piece of hard candy from her emergency supplies. "For brave girls who miss their families," the older woman whispered, understanding that kindness was as essential as medicine in their current circumstances.

Alicia held her daughter as other passengers settled back into uneasy sleep. David whimpered softly, his fever returning despite Mei-Lin's rice powder remedy. She touched the medallion at her throat and whispered Lupe's words in Spanish: "When the world turns cruel, you must be twice as kind, twice as strong." The night passed slowly, marked by the ship's groaning timbers and the constant background sounds of eighteen hundred people trying to sleep in spaces not designed for human habitation. Alicia dozed fitfully, waking every time David stirred or Patricia whimpered in her sleep.

Day Three - Manila Harbor

Manila Harbor emerged from the morning mist like something from a colonial postcard: palm trees swaying against Spanish bell towers, American military installations gleaming white in the tropical sun, cargo ships and naval vessels creating a forest of masts and smokestacks.

Under different circumstances, Alicia might have marveled at the exotic beauty of it. Instead, she felt only the weight of uncertainty and the exhaustion of three days spent managing two small children in impossible conditions.

The disembarkation process was controlled chaos orchestrated by American military efficiency. Officers with clipboards moved through the ship, checking documents and directing families toward appropriate processing stations. "British civilians report to Station A," announced a young lieutenant with a voice trained to carry over crowd noise. "Americans and Canadians to Station B. Other nationals to Station C for individual processing."

The deck filled with hundreds of exhausted women and children, luggage

Chapter 24: The Empress of Asia

stacked in precarious towers, children crying from hunger and confusion, mothers trying to maintain composure while privately wondering what came next.

"Name and destination?" The processing officer was Filipino-American, his uniform crisp despite the tropical heat already building at nine in the morning.

"Alicia Williams. Children Patricia and David." Her voice sounded stronger than she felt. "Private accommodation with American Assistant High Commissioner Robert Jenkins."

The officer's eyebrows rose slightly. "The Commissioner? You're expected, ma'am. Transportation has been arranged." He stamped their papers and handed her a manila envelope. "Documentation for local authorities and a letter from Commissioner Jenkins."

As they made their way through customs, Patricia clung to Alicia's skirt with one hand and clutched Esperanza with the other. The doll was already showing signs of wear from constant handling, but it remained her primary comfort object. David fussed in Alicia's arms, his small face flushed and sticky with heat. The formula troubles had left him weakened, though his fever had finally broken during the night. The tropical climate was clearly not agreeing with his Welsh constitution.

Through the chaos of refugees, soldiers, and dock workers, Alicia spotted the elegant black Packard limousine parked apart from the military transports. Diplomatic flags fluttered from its front fenders, and a uniformed Filipino driver stood beside it holding a cardboard sign with "Mrs. Williams" written in careful script. The contrast between the limousine and the military trucks loading other refugees toward Fort McKinley was stark. Alicia felt suddenly self-conscious about her disheveled state: hair tangled from days of ship humidity, travel-stained dress clinging unfavorably to her slight frame, children who looked as exhausted as she felt.

"Mrs. Williams?" The driver's accent carried the musical quality of Tagalog mixed with American English. "I'm Alfredo, Commissioner Jenkins' chauffeur. Welcome to Manila." His manner was deferential but warm, and Alicia sensed immediately that he was someone who understood displacement. As he loaded their single suitcase into the car's spacious trunk, she noticed his careful attention to detail, the way he adjusted the passenger seat to accommodate David's carrier.

"Commissioner Jenkins asked me to tell you that lunch will be prepared whenever you arrive, but that you should rest first," Alfredo explained as he started the engine. "The estate has a nursery prepared for the children, and there are staff to help with whatever you need."

The interior of the Packard was blissfully cool and quiet after days of ship noise and crying children. Patricia immediately curled up on the soft leather seats, still clutching Esperanza but finally relaxing for the first time since leaving Hong

Kong.

As they pulled away from the harbor, Alicia got her first real look at Manila. The city was a fascinating mixture of Spanish colonial architecture, American modernization, and Filipino street life. Vendors sold tropical fruits she didn't recognize, children played in fountain squares surrounded by baroque churches, and military personnel moved with the purposeful urgency of an empire preparing for war.

"The Commissioner's estate is about thirty minutes outside the city," Alfredo explained, navigating through increasingly congested streets. "Much quieter than downtown Manila. Better for children."

"Has he had other refugee families staying with him?" Alicia asked.

"No, ma'am. You're the first. The Commissioner has been quite concerned about the situation in Hong Kong. He's followed the news very closely."

As they drove through Manila's outskirts, the urban chaos gave way to green hills dotted with grand estates. Palm trees lined the roadway, and the air carried scents of frangipani and wood smoke from distant cooking fires.

Alicia whispered a prayer of gratitude in Spanish. They had survived the crossing, survived the separation, survived three days of uncertainty and fear. But she knew the hardest part lay ahead: learning to live without the two people who had been the foundation of her life, and finding the strength to rebuild their family in a world that seemed determined to tear it apart. David stirred in her arms, opening his dark eyes to focus on her face with the serious attention of someone too young to understand words but old enough to recognize love. Patricia slept peacefully beside her, Esperanza tucked securely under her arm.

The morning sun beat down mercilessly as they drove toward Robert Jenkins' estate, toward an uncertain future.

Chapter 25

Deception and Escape

"In exile, we learn that sanctuary and prison can wear the same beautiful mask. The gilded cage offers safety, but at what cost to the soul? We trade our freedom for our children's tomorrow, and pray the price was not too dear."

From the diary of Margaret Thornton, British evacuee, Manila 1941

The limousine's interior was a surprise after days of cramped spaces: plush leather seats, shiny wood trim, and a cool breeze from the electric fan near the ceiling. Alicia relaxed into the cushions with a sigh that seemed to let go of weeks of built-up stress. Patricia snuggled against her mother's side while David finally drifted into peaceful sleep.

"Are we going to see Papa?" Patricia asked as Alfredo settled into the driver's seat.

"We're going to the home of a friend of Papa's," Alicia replied, smoothing her daughter's hair. "A very kind man who wants to help us."

As they pulled away from the busy port, Manila revealed itself in layers. The commercial district buzzed with activity: American soldiers in crisp khakis, Filipino businessmen in white linen suits, Chinese merchants bargaining over produce. Street vendors shouted in a mix of English, Spanish, and Tagalog, while calesas (horse-drawn carriages) moved between modern cars.

"First time in Manila, Mrs. Williams?" Alfredo asked, navigating the busy streets with practiced ease.

"Yes, it is. It's quite overwhelming."

"Manila is now home to about 600,000 people: Americans, Spanish, Chinese, Filipino, all mingling but mostly staying in their own neighborhoods. Mr. Jenkins mentioned you might feel comfortable with Spanish?"

"Yes, I grew up speaking it." Alicia gazed out at the passing scenes: children playing in dusty courtyards, women hanging laundry from ornate balconies.

The city's character changed as they moved away from the commercial center. Spanish colonial architecture gave way to tree-lined boulevards and spacious lots with large homes surrounded by well-maintained gardens. As they entered the most prestigious neighborhood, the Packard turned onto Dewey Boulevard, where Manila's wealthiest residents enjoyed sweeping views of the bay.

The Jenkins estate sat on a prime piece of land, its entrance marked by towering gates that led onto a circular driveway lined with royal palms. Alicia's breath caught as the mansion came into view through the perfectly manicured grounds. This was more than just a house; it was a symbol of American power and prestige, a Southern plantation palace transplanted to the tropics with striking flair. The building rose three stories, its immaculate white facade shining against the blue sky, supported by grand Corinthian columns. Wide verandas encircled the entire structure, while French doors offered glimpses into the shadowy elegance inside.

The grounds were a work of landscape art. Manicured lawns extended toward ornamental gardens where flame trees and sampaguita bloomed in a carefully arranged display. Alicia caught a glimpse of a tennis court and the shimmer of water through the trees, suggesting a swimming pool designed for entertaining Manila's diplomatic circles. Alicia suddenly felt acutely aware of her travel-worn dress, her tousled hair, and how exhaustion had drained her cheeks. She was about to enter a world where every move she made would be observed, judged, and perhaps deemed inadequate.

A team of uniformed attendants waited at the entrance: a distinguished Filipino butler wearing an elegant *barong* (formal embroidered shirt), housekeepers in crisp uniforms, and footmen standing at attention. At the top of the marble steps, Robert Jenkins was present himself. Alicia's memory hadn't exaggerated Robert Jenkins; if anything, it had underestimated how strong his presence was. At forty-two, he had a kind of masculine charm that effortlessly opened doors and eased resistance. Tall and broad-shouldered, he moved with the natural confidence of someone born into power and wealth. His dark hair was neatly styled, accentuating features that looked like they belonged in a portrait gallery: a strong jaw, aristocratic nose, and those sharp blue-gray eyes that seemed to observe more than they revealed.

His white linen suit was flawlessly tailored, and he wore it with the relaxed elegance of a man who had never doubted his place in the world. Everything about him reflected old Southern wealth and political ties, the kind of background that guaranteed prestigious diplomatic assignments and the resources to live grandly in the colonies.

As Alfredo helped her out of the car, Jenkins descended the steps with smooth grace. His smile was warm, and welcoming. His eyes moved quickly from Alicia to

Chapter 25: Deception and Escape

her children. "Alicia." He took her hand in both of his. "My dear woman, what an ordeal you've endured. I cannot express how relieved I am that you've arrived safely."

"Robert, thank you for your generosity."

"Nonsense. Bryn is a valued friend, and any family of his is family to me." He turned to Patricia. "And this beautiful little lady must be Patricia." He knelt before the child with practiced charm. "Welcome to Manila, princess. I have a feeling we're going to be great friends."

Patricia smiled shyly. When Jenkins peered under the blanket at David, his expression softened with what appeared to be genuine affection.

"And this little fellow looks like he needs some proper rest and care. We'll have you all feeling better in no time." He straightened, offering Alicia his arm. "Come, let me show you to your rooms."

As they ascended the marble staircase together, the grand mahogany doors swung open quietly, revealing an interior that took her breath away. The foyer stretched out before them like a cathedral of American ambition. The floor was a masterpiece of inlaid marble, but it was the staircase that drew the eye: a sweeping curve of polished *narra* wood that arced gracefully upward to the upper floors, with balustrades carved by master Filipino artisans. A burgundy carpet runner traced the steps like a river of wine flowing upward.

Crystal chandeliers hung from coffered ceilings painted in cream and gold, their light catching and breaking into rainbow prisms that danced across silk wallpaper imported from France. Through open doorways, Alicia glimpsed grand public rooms: a dining room where a table could seat twenty, walls adorned with paintings by Fernando Amorsolo, and a library with floor-to-ceiling shelves of leather-bound volumes.

"Beautiful, isn't it?" Jenkins murmured, his hand still warm against her elbow. "I wanted to create something that would honor both American and Filipino artistry."

"The ballroom is through there," Jenkins indicated toward the double doors of frosted glass. "We host the Commissioner's receptions there, usually about two hundred guests."

Alicia felt Patricia's grip tighten on her hand as they processed this display of wealth and power.

"Your rooms are upstairs," Jenkins continued, guiding them toward the grand staircase. "I've given you the Blue Suite; it has a lovely view of the bay and a connecting room for the children."

The Blue Suite was fittingly named: its walls were adorned with silk wallpaper in the hue of Manila Bay at sunset, and it was furnished with pieces that combined elegance and comfort. French doors led to a private balcony where wicker chairs were set out for morning coffee or evening reflection. The connecting nursery was already arranged with a beautiful mahogany crib for David and a small bed for Patricia, complete with mosquito netting and toys indicating Jenkins had thoughtfully considered their comfort.

"I hope this will suit you," he said, standing perhaps a little too close. "If there's anything you need, anything at all, you have only to ask. My staff has been instructed to ensure your comfort. A young housemaid, Rosa, will be at your disposal. After, we can walk in the garden, and give instructions to our kitchen staff. I've also taken the liberty to bring in a milk supply for the children," Robert said. "And I'm sure you'd like to let Bryn know you've arrived safely."

"Yes, I would like to as soon as I can," Alicia replied.

"You can use the telephone any time," Jenkins replied.

"Thank you so much, Robert, for everything you have done. I am grateful," Alicia replied sincerely.

A Commission assistant appeared and handed Robert some papers, and together they left, just as Rosa, the housemaid, joined Alicia.

"Mrs. Williams, let me show you where to find things in the closets and bathroom. I don't know if you might have been breastfeeding your son David or giving him formula. I have been serving as a wet nurse to other children and can offer that to you as well. I am here to serve your needs and those of your children day and night," Rosa said.

"Oh, Rosa, thank you so much," Alicia said. She took Patricia by the hand and held up David so he could see Rosa. "This is Rosa, she will be helping us while we are staying here. Say hello to Rosa."

Patricia curtsied. "Pleased to make your acquaintance, Miss Rosa."

Rosa let out a big grin. "My goodness, what a lady."

David just stared at Rosa in silence, watching with the solemn intensity that infants sometimes possess.

After helping Rosa settle David in his crib and ensuring Patricia was comfortable, Alicia decided to make the phone call that had been on her mind. The small sitting room was tastefully decorated with a modern black Bakelite telephone. Alicia's hands trembled slightly as she connected the call through the operator, giving Bryn's office number in Hong Kong.

The crackling connection seemed to carry her voice across an ocean of

Chapter 25: Deception and Escape

uncertainty before Bryn's familiar baritone filled the line. "Alicia? My darling, thank God. I've been beside myself wondering if you've arrived safely."

The sound of his voice nearly undid her composure. "Bryn, we're safe. We're here at Robert's house, and it's like a palace. The children are well, though exhausted."

"And you? How are you holding up, my love?" Bryn asked.

Alicia closed her eyes, letting his concern wash over her. "I'm managing. Patricia has been so brave, and David is beginning to settle. But Bryn, this house and Robert's hospitality is overwhelming."

"Much better than the army barracks at Fort McKinley where most of the other evacuees are, I can assure you," Bryn said.

"The luxury is almost shocking after what we've been through. The children have their own nursery, and Robert has even arranged for a wet nurse, one of the housemaids named Rosa who seems genuinely caring."

"A wet nurse? That's thoughtful of him. You've been under such strain, darling. Perhaps it would be good for you to have that help."

"I think so too. Bryn, how are you managing? How is Mama and the house staff?"

His voice grew heavy. "Mama is fine, although feeling a bit lost, like me, missing you. Ah-Min, Mrs. Wu and Mei-Lin have been wonderful, taking care of us. Conditions in the colony are rapidly deteriorating. I can't keep up with dealing with health and sanitation problems."

"And how are you, dear?" Alicia asked, with emphasis on you.

"I'm managing. The hardest part is being away from you and the children," he replied through crackling on the telephone receiver.

They talked for nearly thirty minutes, sharing details of her journey, his work, their fears, and hopes for the future. When Alicia finally hung up the phone, she felt both comforted and melancholy, connected to Bryn yet separated by an ocean that seemed to grow wider each day.

Returning to her suite, she discovered Rosa had laid out a silk nightgown and matching robe in the softest shade of blue. David was fussing in his crib, and Patricia was sitting up in the bed, rubbing her eyes.

"Mama, I'm hungry," Patricia announced with the straightforward honesty of childhood.

"And Master David is ready for his feeding," Rosa added with a smile. "Shall we try the arrangement we discussed?"

Alicia nodded, settling into a comfortable chair while Rosa lifted David from his crib. "Rosa, tell me more about your experience as a wet nurse. David has been taking both breast milk and formula, but the journey has been so difficult."

Rosa's expression grew understanding and professional. "I have been wet nurse to two children in the past two years, Mistress. My own son is now walking and no longer needs me, so my milk is still good and strong. If Master David will take to me, it would be my honor to help."

Alicia felt a wave of gratitude wash over her. "I think that would be a blessing, Rosa."

David immediately bonded with Rosa, his small hands reaching for her blouse with natural hunger. As Rosa helped him nurse, Alicia experienced a mix of relief and sadness, thankful for the assistance but feeling somehow diminished by her inability to meet all of her son's needs.

"There now, little master," Rosa crooned softly in accented English mixed with gentle Tagalog phrases. "You drink and grow strong."

While David nursed contentedly, Alicia helped Patricia from the bed. "Let's get you properly bathed, sweetheart. The journey left us all rather grubby."

The bathroom connected to their suite was another marvel of American engineering and Filipino craftsmanship. A deep porcelain tub took center stage in the marble-tiled space, with fixtures of polished brass and towels thick enough to wrap a child completely. Alicia ran warm water, adding bath salts that smelled of sampaguita and jasmine.

"This soap smells like flowers, Mama," Patricia observed, holding a bar of imported French lavender soap to her nose.

"It does indeed. Shall we use it for your bath?" Alicia asked softly.

As Alicia gently washed her daughter's hair and scrubbed away the dust and salt of their journey, Patricia chattered about the grand house, the beautiful gardens she could see from the windows. "Are we going to live here forever, Mama?" Patricia asked as Alicia wrapped her in a towel soft as down.

"No, darling. This is just until Papa can join us and we find our own home. Mr. Jenkins is being very kind to let us stay here."

"I like Miss Rosa. She smells nice and her voice is soft."

When Patricia was clean and dressed in a fresh nightgown, Alicia prepared for her bath. David had finished nursing and lay drowsy and content in Rosa's arms. "He took to you beautifully," Alicia observed with genuine gratitude.

"Children know when they are loved and cared for, Mistress. It is my joy to

Chapter 25: Deception and Escape

help." Rosa said.

Alicia's bath was a luxury she hadn't enjoyed in days. The water was perfectly warm, and the soap produced a rich lather that washed away not only the dirt from her trip but also some of the stress she had been holding onto for weeks. She soaked until the water started to cool, then dried herself with towels that felt like silk against her skin. The nightgown Rosa chose fit perfectly, its silk cool and soothing against skin still warm from the bath. As Alicia emerged from the bathroom, she saw Patricia already drowsy on the big bed, while Rosa had settled David back into his crib with a small night light casting gentle shadows on the nursery walls.

"Thank you, Rosa. For everything. I don't know how to repay such kindness," Alicia said appreciatively.

"It is what we do for family, Madam. Master Jenkins has made it very clear that you and your children are to be treated as family."

Alicia settled into the luxurious bed beside Patricia, her daughter instinctively curling against her. The silk sheets were cool against her skin, and the mattress was perfectly supportive after weeks of sleeping on ship bunks and uncomfortable chairs. As sleep started to take her, Alicia's mind floated between thankfulness and doubt. They were safe, cozy, and cared for, but at what cost? Robert Jenkins' kindness felt real, yet felt excessive. Tomorrow would bring new struggles and questions about their future. Her thoughts of Bryn and her mother never completely left her mind, nor the chaos of war and separation.

Now, her children were safe and sleeping peacefully. Bryn's voice still echoed in her memory, serving as a lifeline across the vast waters. And for the first time in weeks, Alicia Williams fell into deep, dreamless sleep, her daughter's warm weight against her side and the sound of the tropical night filtering through the French doors, a lullaby of safety in a world torn apart by war.

Alicia had been at the Jenkins estate for more than a month when she realized that her host's generosity had gone beyond simple hospitality. It began with small gestures: fresh orchids were placed daily in her sitting room, French chocolates appeared on her nightstand, and silk scarves were draped over her chair with handwritten notes expressing hope that she would find them "suitable for Manila's climate."

One morning marked the most extravagant gesture yet: a full wardrobe hanging in her armoire, each piece chosen with obvious care and intimate knowledge of her measurements. Afternoon dresses in flowing silk, evening gowns suited for Hong Kong's most exclusive social events, and delicate French lace undergarments that made her cheeks burn with embarrassment.

Rosa appeared in the doorway as Alicia stood frozen in front of the display of finery. Over the past three weeks, the young Filipina woman had become more than just a servant; she was Alicia's confidante, the one person in this gilded world who seemed to understand her growing unease with their host's attention. "Master Jenkins thought you might need proper attire for this evening's reception, Mistress. The American business community will be here, nearly a hundred guests." Rosa's tone was carefully neutral, but Alicia caught the worried glance she cast toward the elaborate wardrobe.

"Rosa, this is too much." Alicia's fingers traced the emerald silk of an evening gown that probably cost more than most Filipino families saw in a year. "I cannot accept such personal gifts."

Rosa closed the door quietly behind her and moved closer, her voice dropping to barely above a whisper. "Mistress Alicia, may I speak freely?"

Alicia nodded, grateful for the one person who still treated her as a woman rather than a prized ornament.

"The other servants, they talk. Master Jenkins, he has never shown such attention to any lady guest before. Even the beautiful wives of important men who stay here for diplomatic visits. This is different."

"It doesn't feel right," Alicia said quietly. "But what can I do? We have nowhere else to go, and Bryn is still in Hong Kong."

"I feel you are a good woman, *Señora*. I see how you pray each morning and how you speak of your husband with love, even when you are sad…" Rosa said softly. Then nervously she looked at the door. "But I must say this…Master Jenkins is not himself…something is not right. Even Alfredo has noticed the change in Master Jenkins. Yesterday, when he drove you to the market, he said to me that he has never seen Master Jenkins so possessive about a guest."

Alicia felt a warmth rise within her at the mention of Alfredo. Over the past three weeks, their drives around Manila had become the bright spots in her increasingly uncomfortable situation. Alfredo was probably fifty, a dignified Filipino man who had worked as Robert's driver for nearly a decade. Unlike the other staff, he seemed to understand her delicate position without judgment, offering quiet observations about the city, gentle questions about her children, and most importantly, a sense that she could speak openly without fearing her words would be reported back to Robert.

"Alfredo sees much from the front seat," Alicia murmured.

"He is a good man, *Señora*. He has been asking me if you are well, if you need anything. I think he worries about you." Rosa's expression grew more serious. "Just be careful tonight. And remember, if you ever need someone who sees the truth of things, I am here. And Alfredo can be trusted."

Chapter 25: Deception and Escape

Before Alicia could reply, the sound of children's laughter drifted up from the garden below. Through the window, they saw Robert kneeling on the well-kept lawn with Patricia her how to feed breadcrumbs to a family of ducks that had wandered up from the ornamental pond.

"Robert, look! The baby duck likes me!" Patricia's delighted voice carried clearly through the morning air.

"The children like him," Alicia murmured watching Patricia curtsy prettily when Robert praised her for being gentle with the ducks as she gently rocked five-month-old David in her arms.

"Children see kindness, not calculation," Rosa observed quietly on another occasion. "But *Señora*, I have served in this house for two years. I have never seen Master Jenkins spend time with children before. He usually finds them inconvenient."

Rosa's comments and her reference to Alfredo's perception were beginning to worry Alicia. She did feel that Robert's attentions to her and the children seemed to be not "normal" and excessive at times.

"Mama!" Patricia's voice called from below. "Come see the ducklings!"

Alicia forced a smile and waved from the window. "I'll be down in a moment, darling!"

Alicia felt the weight of her situation settle in her chest. Whatever his motives, Robert genuinely appeared to care for her children. They had never experienced such luxury, such devoted attention from a father figure. How could she explain to a three-year-old that the man who gave her picture books and played duck-feeding games might not always have their best interests at heart?

The reception that evening was a whirlwind of introductions and polite conversations, but Alicia gradually felt like she was playing a part she hadn't auditioned for. Robert's hand never left her elbow, and his pride in introducing her to Manila society was clear and possessive. She endured curious looks from other wives, aware of whispers that followed behind them.

When the last guest departed near midnight, Robert suggested they retire to his private dining room for a late supper. "Just something light," he said. "We have much to discuss."

Alicia's instincts told her to refuse, but Rosa had already taken the children upstairs hours earlier, and refusing might lead to the confrontation she wanted to avoid. The dining room was cozy, lit by candles and set for two. A bottle of expensive wine was open on the sideboard along with covered dishes, showing that the servants would not be serving them.

"You were magnificent tonight," Robert said, pouring himself a generous glass. He had already loosened his tie, his formal demeanor beginning to slip. "Every man in that room envied me."

"That's exactly what concerns me, Robert." Alicia accepted only water, keeping her voice level. "I don't want to be envied. I want to be respected."

"Respect." He took a long drink, his eyes never leaving her face, slurring his words. "Do you think Bryn respects you, Alicia? Leaving you to flee Hong Kong alone with two small children? Letting you depend on the charity of other men?"

"Bryn had no choice. The government ordered it."

"There's always a choice." Robert's voice was growing harder, the wine loosening his carefully maintained control. "He chose his precious government job over his family's safety. What kind of man does that?"

Alicia felt anger flare in her chest. "A man who was trying to secure our future. A man who trusted his friend to protect his family until he could join us. A man who swore an oath to help the people of Hong Kong."

"And here you are. Protected. Provided for. Cherished." Robert rose from his chair, stumbling around the table toward her. "Tell me, Alicia, when was the last time you felt truly desired? When did Bryn last look at you the way I look at you?"

"Robert, you've had too much to drink. Let's have this conversation tomorrow," Alicia replied nervously.

"No." His hand fell heavily on her shoulder, preventing her from rising. "We'll continue it now. Tonight. I've been patient, Alicia. More patient than any man should have to be." The candlelight flickered across his face, revealing something predatory hidden beneath weeks of careful courtesy.

Alicia's heart started racing as she realized the real danger she was in. "I think I should check on the children."

"The children are fine. Rosa is with them." His grip tightened on her shoulder. "It's time you and I came to an understanding about your position here. About what I expect in return for my generosity."

Alicia tried to stand, but his hand forced her back into the chair. "Robert, let me go. This isn't what I want."

"What you want?" His laugh was bitter. "What any of us wanted stopped mattering the day the Japanese started their march south. This is about survival now, Alicia. About making the best of impossible circumstances."

He leaned in closer, his breath heavy with wine and something darker. "I can give you everything. Security, comfort, and a future for your children. All I ask in

Chapter 25: Deception and Escape

return is what any man has a right to expect from the woman in his household."

"I am not the woman in your household. I am Bryn Williams' wife, and I will remain so," Alicia snapped defiantly.

"Bryn Williams is half a world away, and will probably end up dead in a ditch somewhere while Hong Kong burns." Robert's mask finally slipped completely. "I'm here. I'm real. I'm offering you a life."

Alicia managed to free herself and ran toward the door, but Robert was faster. What followed would haunt her dreams for years: the sound of fabric tearing, her own voice crying out in the empty house, and the crushing weight of inevitable doom as all her protests were dismissed by a man who believed his desires mattered more than her humanity.

When it was done, Alicia lay still on the dining room floor, her beautiful dress wrecked, her dignity shattered. Robert stood over her, breathing hard, his own clothes messy. For a moment, she saw a hint of regret cross his face.

"Alicia, I didn't want this." He reached toward her, then stopped. "You have to understand, I couldn't let you keep refusing. I couldn't."

He didn't finish his sentence but instead collapsed face down on the floor, dead drunk.

Chapter 26

Sanctuary

"Freedom begins the moment someone says: you are safe here."

Filipino Proverb

October 28, 1941 - Late Evening

Gathering the torn remnants of her dress around herself, Alicia hurried upstairs to her room, her bare feet silent on the marble floors that once seemed luxurious but now felt cold and treacherous beneath her. Every surface in this house seemed to conspire in her captivity. She locked the door behind her and collapsed against it, trembling uncontrollably.

The beautiful silk nightgown Rosa had laid out now seemed to mock her. She sat on the edge of the bed, staring at her reflection in the vanity mirror. The woman staring back at her had hollow eyes and finger-shaped bruises on her arms, but beneath the shock, Alicia saw something unexpected: determination.

Jenkins had shown her exactly who he was. Now she knew exactly what she had to do. She quickly put on her own clothes.

Rosa appeared within minutes, slipping through the door like a shadow. She must have been listening from the servants' quarters, waiting for the sounds of struggle to end. She took one look at Alicia's torn dress crumpled on the floor, her bruised arms, her hollow expression, and asked no questions. Instead, she simply knelt beside her mistress and whispered, "We leave tonight."

"The children."

"I will get them. You must pack only what is necessary." Rosa's voice carried absolute certainty.

Alicia nodded, unable to speak. The simple conviction in Rosa's voice was like a lifeline thrown to someone drowning. Here was someone who saw the truth and was willing to act on it, regardless of the personal cost. "Rosa, why are you helping me? If Jenkins discovers what you've done, he could have you arrested, deported, worse."

Rosa paused in her efficient movements, her hands stilling on a child's dress. "Because I have seen what men like Jenkins do to women who have no choices. Because someone must stand against this evil, even if we are only servants and refugees."

The word "refugees" hit Alicia like cold water. In Jenkins' eyes, that's exactly what they were: displaced people dependent on his charity, with no rights and no recourse. But Rosa had just reminded her of something crucial: even powerless people could choose to resist.

Rosa moved with quiet efficiency, first checking on the sleeping children. Patricia stirred as Rosa gently lifted her from the bed.

"Rosa? Where are we going?" Patricia asked sleepily, using the Tagalog word for older sister that she had learned from the other servants.

"We're going to visit my family, *pequeña princesa,* (little princess)," Rosa whispered. "Like in your fairy tales. But we must be very quiet, like the mice in Cinderella."

Alicia knelt beside her daughter, her heart breaking at the confusion in those innocent blue eyes. How could she explain that the man who had given Patricia picture books and played games with her was not who they thought he was? "We're going to meet Rosa's mama and papa. They have chickens, remember? And you love chickens."

"But what about Uncle Robert? Will he be sad we didn't say goodbye?" Patricia's voice was small, worried. Three-year-olds understood absence as abandonment.

Each innocent question felt like a knife in Alicia's chest. Her daughter had no understanding of what had happened, no idea why they were fleeing in the darkness. "Uncle Robert will understand," Alicia managed, though the lie tasted bitter.

Rosa had wrapped David in his softest blanket, and miraculously, the toddler stayed asleep despite being lifted from his crib. He had just begun saying "Mama" and "Papa," but he was still small enough to sleep through their midnight escape.

As they gathered the few essential items they could carry, Alicia watched David sleep peacefully in Rosa's arms. The little boy who had learned to trust Jenkins' daily visits, who reached chubby arms toward the man whenever he appeared, would never understand why that familiar face had vanished from his life. Within minutes, they slipped through the darkened hallways like shadows. Patricia held Alicia's hand tightly, her bare feet silent on the marble floors, while Rosa carried David with the practiced ease of someone who had cared for younger siblings. The house felt different at night: larger, more menacing, full of corners where Jenkins

Chapter 26: Sanctuary

might be lurking.

As they reached the servants' entrance, Patricia whispered, "Mama, why are we sneaking? Are we playing hide and seek?"

"Something like that, darling," Alicia managed, her voice barely steady. "We're going on an adventure, but it's a secret adventure."

Alfredo was waiting with the car at the servants' gate, his weathered face grim but determined in the moonlight. He helped them into the vehicle without questions, his movements efficient and protective. At fifty-five, he had worked for wealthy Americans for most of his adult life, and his expression suggested he had seen this situation before.

"Are you hurt, Mrs. Williams?" noticing a bruise on her arm.

"I will survive, Alfredo. How did you know to be here?" she replied.

"Rosa and I, we have been watching, planning for when this night would come. Men like Jenkins, they always reveal themselves eventually." His voice carried the weight of experience. "And women like you, you always find the strength to leave when you must. But the risk you are taking..." Alfredo said.

"Madam," Rosa interrupted gently, "in my country, we have a saying: *'Ang hindi marunong lumingon sa pinanggalingan ay hindi makararating sa paroroonan.'* (Those who do not know how to look back to where they came from will never reach their destination. We know where we came from. We remember when people helped our families. Now we help yours."

As they drove through Manila's empty streets toward Binondo, David began to stir in Rosa's arms, making soft baby sounds. Patricia curled against Alicia's side, clutching the small bag Rosa had packed with her most treasured possessions: a wooden doll, a picture book, and a seashell from their journey.

"Mama, I forgot my tea set. Uncle Robert gave it to me," Patricia whined.

Alicia's breath caught. The tea set was beautiful, imported from England, something Jenkins had presented to Patricia with great ceremony just days earlier. But it was also a chain, a way of binding them to him through her daughter's gratitude. "We'll get you a new tea set, sweetheart. An even prettier one."

The Jenkins limousine moved quietly through the narrow streets of Binondo as dawn approached. The Chinese district was just beginning to stir: vendors setting up breakfast stalls, early workers heading to the docks, the eternal rhythm of a community that survived by adaptation and hard work.

"My family lives just ahead," Rosa whispered, pointing toward a two-story wooden house with carved balconies and flowering vines. The structure was modest but well maintained, painted in soft colors that caught the early morning light. "Mama will have heard the car. She has been expecting us."

Alicia's stomach clenched with anxiety. "Rosa, someone will remember seeing Jenkins' car in this neighborhood. The risk to your family..."

"My family understands risk, Mrs. Williams. During the Philippine Revolution, they hid Spanish loyalists from insurgents. During the American occupation, they hid Filipino resistance fighters from the Americans. We know how to protect people who need protection."

A woman appeared in the doorway before they had even stopped. Maria Santos was clearly Rosa's mother: the same intelligent dark eyes, the same quick, efficient movements. She wore a simple cotton dress and had obviously dressed quickly, but when she saw Rosa emerge from the car with a baby in her arms, her expression shifted to immediate understanding. Behind her appeared Carlos Santos, Rosa's father. Shorter and stockier than Alfredo, with work worn hands and graying hair, he surveyed the scene with the calm assessment of a man who had faced difficult situations before. His eyes took in the limousine, the well-dressed woman with a child, his daughter's urgent posture, and he stepped forward without hesitation.

Rosa spoke rapidly in Tagalog to her parents, her words urgent but respectful. Alicia caught fragments: *"ginawa niya sa kanya"* (what he did to her), "*kailangan namin siyang tulungan"* (we need to help her), "*hindi siya ligtas doon"* (she's not safe there). The conversation was brief but comprehensive, Rosa painting the essential picture without unnecessary details.

Carlos's expression darkened as he understood what had driven them here in the middle of the night. His weathered hands clenched into fists, but when he spoke, his voice was controlled. *"Halika,"* he said to Alicia, then switched to careful English. "Come. You and your children are welcome here. No questions, no conditions."

Maria approached Alicia with open arms, her face radiating the universal warmth of a mother recognizing another mother in distress. "I am Maria Santos. My husband, Carlos. Rosa has told us much about you and your beautiful children."

The simple acceptance brought tears to Alicia's eyes. Here was kindness without calculation, help offered freely to someone in need.

Carlos gently lifted Patricia from Alicia's arms, his weathered face softening when the little girl looked at him with sleepy confusion. Despite his work-roughened hands, his touch was infinitely gentle. "*Ganda mo naman,*" he said softly to Patricia, then translated: "You are so beautiful, little one. Like a princess in our stories."

Chapter 26: Sanctuary

Patricia studied this new adult with the frank curiosity of a three-year-old. "Are you Rosa's papa?"

"Yes, little princess. And you are Patricia, who loves to read books. Rosa tells us you are very smart," he answered.

The fact that Rosa had shared such details about their daily life, carrying stories of her children's personalities even while witnessing their danger, brought unexpected tears to Alicia's eyes. In her growing isolation at Jenkins' estate, she hadn't realized how much Rosa had truly seen and cared.

Maria moved to take David from Rosa's arms, cooing softly in a mixture of English and Tagalog. The baby immediately settled against her, as if recognizing the universal comfort of a grandmother's touch. "*Ay, ang laki na niya (*oh, how much he has grown*)*" she observed, noting how David held up his head alertly despite being barely awake.

As they settled Alicia and the children into a small but spotless room on the second floor, the weight of what Rosa and Alfredo had accomplished became clear. They had extracted the family of one of Manila's most powerful Americans using his own resources, and now they needed to return and face whatever consequences awaited.

"Be careful when you go back," Alicia urged as Rosa prepared to leave with Alfredo. "Don't let him suspect anything. Your safety is more important than protecting me."

Rosa squeezed Alicia's hand, her young face showing determination beyond her twenty years. "Madam, men like Master Jenkins succeed because good people do nothing. We will not be good people who do nothing."

Carlos placed a protective hand on his daughter's shoulder. "Rosa is strong, like her mama. She knows when to bend and when to stand firm." His expression grew steel hard. "And if Jenkins tries to blame her for his own sins, he will find that not all Filipinos are as powerless as he believes."

The quiet threat hung in the air. Not violence, but something potentially more damaging to a man who relied on Filipino labor and goodwill for his comfort and status: the withdrawal of cooperation, the silent resistance of people who could make his life very difficult in small, untraceable ways.

The drive back to Forbes Park passed in careful planning. Rosa and Alfredo rehearsed their story: Rosa in the kitchen preparing morning feeds, then retiring to her quarters before midnight. Alfredo maintaining the car in the early hours, testing the engine after hearing concerning noises during yesterday's driving. Neither had seen Mrs. Williams or the children after Rosa helped them upstairs following dinner. When they arrived at the estate, it was exactly as they expected: windows blazing with light, Jenkins' voice echoing from inside, growing more agitated as the alcohol wore off and reality set in.

"Alicia! Where are you? We need to finish our conversation!"

The slurred words made Rosa and Alfredo exchange glances before entering through the servants' quarters. They moved quickly to establish their presence: Rosa in the kitchen preparing what appeared to be formula for David, Alfredo in the garage checking fluid levels and making notes in his maintenance log.

Nearly an hour passed before Jenkins found them, appearing in the kitchen doorway like a man waking from a nightmare. His formal clothes were wrinkled and stained, his hair disheveled, his eyes carrying the wild confusion of someone whose carefully constructed reality had suddenly collapsed. "Rosa! Where is Alicia? Her room is empty, the children's rooms too."

Rosa continued her work at the stove, her movements calm and measured. "I do not know, Master. I have been preparing food for the children. Their favorites."

Jenkins' gaze sharpened, suspicion cutting through his confusion. "When did you last see her?"

"Last night, Master. After dinner, I helped her settle the children for sleep. She said she would not need me again until morning," Rosa replied calmly.

"Did she seem... upset about anything?" Jenkins asked.

Rosa paused, as if considering the question carefully. "Madam, has seemed sad since arriving, Master. Missing her husband, worried about the war. Perhaps homesick for Hong Kong." It was a masterful response: truthful enough to be believable but offering an explanation that had nothing to do with Jenkins' assault.

For the rest of the morning, Jenkins questioned every servant, his growing panic barely concealed beneath his diplomatic training. Each gave variations of the same response: they had seen nothing unusual, heard nothing suspicious, and knew nothing about where Alicia and the children might have gone. When he summoned Alfredo to the study, the driver stood at attention with military precision, his maintenance log visible in his shirt pocket. "You drive her everywhere," Jenkins said, his voice dangerous with barely controlled rage. "Did you take her anywhere last night?"

"No, Sir. I have not driven Mrs. Williams anywhere since yesterday afternoon when we returned from the market," Alfredo replied evenly.

"Then where the hell were you? I heard the car engine early this morning," Jenkins questioned aggressively.

Alfredo pulled out his maintenance notes with the calm efficiency of a professional. "Master, I was concerned about a rattling sound in the transmission.

Chapter 26: Sanctuary

The car has been working hard with all the recent social engagements. I took it out to test the engine while the streets were empty, around four this morning."

Jenkins studied the maintenance log, looking for any inconsistency. "How long were you gone?"

"Nearly an hour, Master. I drove through Escolta and Malate, testing different speeds and road conditions. When I returned, the house was quiet. I assumed everyone was sleeping…if Madam is missing, should we not be contacting the police to assist?"

The idea of involving the police hung between them like an unexploded bomb. Both men understood what it would mean: calling authorities would require explaining why a guest had fled so suddenly, answering questions about the nature of their relationship, possibly facing an investigation that could damage Jenkins' diplomatic career.

"No," Jenkins said finally, his voice tight with controlled fury. "No authorities. This is a private matter."

By afternoon, Jenkins' rage had transformed into something uglier: bitter rationalization that allowed him to salvage his bruised ego. "Ungrateful woman," he declared to his reflection in the study mirror, raising his glass in a mock toast. "After everything I offered her, everything I was willing to give those children. Let her try to survive in a war zone with her precious principles."

Back in Binondo, Alicia spent her first full day observing the rhythms of the Santos household. Despite their modest circumstances, there was a warmth and dignity here that Jenkins' mansion had lacked for all its luxury. The house served three generations: Carlos and Maria, Rosa and her two younger brothers Miguel and José, plus Carlos's elderly mother who spent her days on the front balcony watching street life and offering commentary in rapid Tagalog. The family functioned as a unit, each member contributing according to their abilities.

"You have such a beautiful family," Alicia told Maria as they sat in the small garden behind the house, watching Patricia play with Rosa's brothers while David napped in Maria's lap.

"Family is not only blood," Maria replied, her weathered hands busy with mending. "Family is who feeds you when you're hungry, who stands with you when you're afraid, who helps you find strength when you think you have none. You and your children, you are family now."

The simple declaration opened something in Alicia's chest that had been locked tight since the assault. She found herself able to speak about what had happened, not in detail, but enough for Maria to understand.

"Men with too much power and too little conscience," Maria said quietly, her needle never pausing in its work. "They exist in every generation. But so do women who refuse to accept what they try to do to us."

That evening, as the family gathered for dinner around their simple wooden table, Carlos raised his glass of water in a toast. "To Alicia Williams, who chose courage over comfort, truth over safety. And to Rosa, who remembers that our strength comes from helping others find theirs." The words hit Alicia like a physical blow, tears streaming down her face as she realized that someone finally understood. She hadn't been foolish or ungrateful. She had been brave.

As the days passed, Alicia found herself growing stronger. The constant tension that had marked her time at Jenkins' estate began to ease. Patricia laughed again, playing with the other children Miguel and José and helping Maria feed the chickens that wandered freely in their small yard. David babbling in an attempt to speak. But underneath the healing, Alicia's resolve was building. She could not stay here forever, no matter how welcome the Santos family made her feel. She had to find a way back to Hong Kong, back to Bryn, back to the life that was truly hers.

"You are thinking of leaving," Rosa observed intuitively one evening as they sat together watching the children play.

Alicia nodded slowly. "I can't stay here, Rosa. This isn't my home, and my husband doesn't even know if we're alive. Every day I remain here is another day he thinks he might have lost us forever."

"But the journey back to Hong Kong, with the war coming..." Rosa said carefully.

"There's danger everywhere now," Alicia interrupted. "There was danger with Jenkins. At least in Hong Kong, I'll have Bryn to protect us. And we can face danger together."

Rosa was quiet for a long moment. "If you are determined to do this thing, then we will help you do it safely."

November 2, 1941

Carlos returned from the docks that evening with more than his usual small gifts. "I have spoken to Captain Reyes of the Sampaguita," he announced quietly. "A good man. He's been running cargo between Manila and Hong Kong for fifteen years. He understands that sometimes good people need help."

Alicia felt her heart leap with hope and terror. "Carlos, I couldn't ask you to arrange..."

"You are not asking. I am offering." His voice carried the quiet authority of a man accustomed to making difficult decisions. "Captain Reyes has sailed through

Chapter 26: Sanctuary

worse waters than these. He can get you home safely."

"When?" Alicia asked.

"In five days. The Sampaguita will be carrying medical supplies to Hong Kong. Captain Reyes can be trusted," Carolos answered.

The next four days passed in careful preparation. Maria packed food for the journey: dried fish, rice cakes, preserved fruits that would keep well at sea. Rosa helped Alicia decide what few belongings they could manage, focusing on practical items rather than sentimental ones. Carlos made final arrangements with Captain Reyes, vouching for Alicia's character and her husband's ability to pay passage upon arrival. On their last evening together, the Santos family gathered around their table for what everyone knew would be their final meal together.

"To courage," Carlos said, raising his glass to Alicia. "And to the wisdom to know when that courage must carry us home."

"To family," Maria added, "and to love."

That night, as Alicia packed their few belongings, Patricia appeared in the doorway wearing the simple cotton nightgown Maria had sewn for her. "Mama, I don't want to leave. Lolo Carlos tells good stories, and Lola Maria lets me help with the chickens."

Alicia knelt beside her daughter, taking her small hands in her own. "They are wonderful people, sweetheart. But we have our own family waiting for us. Papa is in Hong Kong, and he must be so worried about us."

"Will we ever see them again?"

"I hope so, darling. But even if we don't, we'll always remember their kindness. Love doesn't disappear just because we can't see the people we love."

Tomorrow would bring new challenges and the uncertainty of a sea voyage in increasingly dangerous waters. But tonight, surrounded by the Santos family's love and her own children's trust, Alicia Williams felt stronger than she had in months. She was no longer a victim seeking shelter. She was a woman taking control of her destiny, determined to reunite her family and reclaim the life that Jenkins had tried to steal from her.

Chapter 27

Homecoming

"The heart knows no distance when it comes to protecting what matters most. A mother will cross any ocean, brave any storm, to bring her children safely home."

Captain Eduardo Reyes

November 7, 1941 - Evening

The harbor churned with restless energy as storm clouds gathered over Manila Bay. Ships strained at their moorings while dock workers moved with the urgent efficiency of people who sensed time running short. The political situation had grown more tense each day, with rumors of Japanese troop movements and American military preparations creating an atmosphere of barely controlled anxiety.

Carlos guided them along the crowded docks, their small group moving carefully between stacks of cargo and hurrying stevedores. The air smelled of salt, diesel fuel, and the particular tension that precedes conflict. Everywhere, people were preparing for something, though nobody spoke openly about what that something might be.

The Sampaguita occupied a berth between larger vessels, her weathered hull and patched paintwork making her nearly invisible among the more impressive ships. She was clearly a working vessel, built for cargo rather than comfort, her single stack belching black smoke into the heavy evening air.

Captain Reyes waited at the gangplank, his lean frame wrapped in an oilskin coat as the first drops of rain began to fall. At perhaps fifty, his sun-darkened face showed the weathering of decades at sea, but his eyes were sharp and alert as he assessed his unusual passengers.

"Captain Reyes," Carlos called, raising his voice over the harbor noise.

The captain nodded, his gaze taking in Alicia with David balanced on her hip and Patricia pressed against her side, obviously overwhelmed by the chaos around them. "Mrs. Williams. You understand this won't be a pleasure cruise. My ship carries medicine and supplies, not passengers. Rough seas ahead, and the political situation makes everything uncertain."

Alicia lifted her chin, meeting his direct gaze. "I understand, Captain. But I need to get my children home to their father."

Something in her tone, perhaps the quiet determination beneath the obvious fear, made Reyes nod with approval. "Family comes first. I respect that. Does your husband know you are coming home?"

"No. My attempts to contact him by telephone have failed. I can't get through…" Alicia replied.

The captain nodded. "All communication now is being disrupted. I too have had difficulty confirming with my business contacts in Hong details of my departure."

Carlos pressed a small cloth bag into her hands. "For Captain Reyes, for his kindness." Alicia saw see the paper money poking out of the bag.

"Oh, Carolos, from the bottom of my heart, thank you," as she embraced him warmly.

The ship's whistle sounded, its deep note echoing across the harbor like a farewell. Patricia clung to Alicia's skirt, her small face upturned with worry. "Are we really going on the big boat, Mama?"

"Yes, darling. It's going to take us home to Papa Bryn."

"Will the boat be scary?"

Before Alicia could answer, Rosa knelt beside Patricia. "Sometimes the bravest princesses in the stories have to go on boat adventures. And you, *pequeña princesa*, are the bravest girl I know."

Patricia considered this gravely, then nodded. "Will you remember me, *Ate* Rosa?"

"Always, little one. And when you're grown up and have your own babies, you can tell them about the brave adventure you took when you were small."

The farewell was brief but intense. Maria Santos embraced Alicia like a daughter, whispering a prayer in Tagalog for safe travel and quick reunion. Carlos shook her hand with the formal dignity of a man who understood the weight of the moment. Rosa hugged the children, her eyes bright with unshed tears.

As the Sampaguita pulled away from the dock, Alicia stood at the rail with Patricia in her arms and David balanced on her hip, watching the Santos family grow smaller in the distance. Their figures remained visible until the harbor lights

Chapter 27: Homecoming

blurred together, four people who had risked everything to help Alicia find her way home and ask nothing in return.

At Sea

The Sampaguita proved to be exactly as challenging as Captain Reyes had promised. Their quarters consisted of a tiny cabin with two narrow bunks and a porthole that showed nothing but endless gray water. The space was clean but cramped, barely large enough for Alicia to change David's diaper without bumping into Patricia.

The first two days were brutal. A storm system that had been building over the South China Sea caught them in its grip, sending the cargo vessel pitching and rolling with nauseating consistency. The ship's hull groaned and creaked with each massive wave, while everything loose in their cabin slid from one side to the other in an endless, chaotic dance.

David cried almost constantly, his small body unable to adjust to the violent motion. His usual sunny disposition disappeared, replaced by the miserable wailing of a toddler in distress. Patricia tried to be brave but succumbed to seasickness on the second day, lying pale and listless in the lower bunk while Alicia held a basin and tried to keep fluids in her daughter.

"Mama, I want to go home," Patricia whimpered during a particularly violent series of waves that sent their few belongings flying across the cabin.

"We are going home, sweetheart. This is just the way we have to get there," Alicia replied.

"I don't like this boat. I want to see *Lolo* Carlos," Patricia said petulantly.

The longing in her daughter's voice broke Alicia's heart. Patricia was too young to understand why they couldn't stay with the Santos family, too young to grasp the larger forces that had shaped their journey. She only knew that she had been taken from people who loved her and put on a frightening boat that made her sick.

On the third day, the storm finally broke. The violent motion gradually calmed to a steady roll, and blessed sunlight streamed through their small porthole. The children, resilient as only the very young can be, began to recover. David's appetite returned, and he started babbling again, pointing at the porthole and saying "Wa-wa" for water. Patricia managed to keep down some rice and broth that the ship's cook brought them.

Captain Reyes, perhaps feeling sorry for his small passengers, allowed them short periods on deck when the weather was calm. The Filipino crew showed unexpected gentleness with the children, taking turns entertaining Patricia with simple songs and helping David practice his walking on the ship's steady deck.

Captain Reyes studied her with those weathered eyes that had seen too much of the world's uncertainty. "Mrs. Williams, you have remarkable courage for someone who admits she doesn't know what comes next. That's the kind of strength that sees people through impossible situations."

"I don't feel courageous. I feel terrified most of the time," she replied.

"Courage isn't the absence of fear, ma'am. It's doing what must be done despite the fear. You've already shown more bravery than most people manage in a lifetime," Reyes answered.

The conversation stayed with Alicia as the Sampaguita continued its steady progress toward Hong Kong. She had been thinking of herself as someone running away, fleeing from Jenkins and his assault. But perhaps Captain Reyes was right. Perhaps she was actually running toward something: toward the life she wanted for her children, toward the man she loved, toward a future she could live with.

Patricia had made friends with another crew member, an older man named Juan who carved small animals from driftwood. He was teaching her the names of sea birds in Tagalog, and she delighted in pointing at the sky and calling out "*Ibon!*" (bird) whenever gulls appeared.

Watching her children adapt and find moments of joy even in their difficult circumstances, Alicia felt something shift inside her chest. The constant fear that had gripped her since the assault began to ease slightly. She was still afraid of what they would find in Hong Kong, still worried about Bryn's reaction to their unannounced return, but underneath the fear was something stronger: determination. She had brought her children this far. She would see them safely home.

November 12, 1941 - Morning

On the morning of the fifth day, Captain Reyes found her at the bow, David balanced on her hip while Patricia stood beside her at the rail.

"Hong Kong ahead," he announced simply.

The morning mists parted like curtains, revealing the island rising dramatically from the South China Sea. Victoria Peak towered above the harbor, its slopes dotted with the white mansions of the colonial elite. The harbor itself was busier than Alicia remembered, crowded with military vessels, cargo ships, and smaller craft moving with purpose between the larger ships. The docking process took longer than expected, with British authorities boarding the Sampaguita for inspection before they were allowed to tie up. Alicia watched nervously as uniformed officials checked cargo manifests and questioned Captain Reyes about his passengers, but their documentation was in order, and eventually they were

Chapter 27: Homecoming

cleared to disembark.

Captain Reyes helped them onto the dock, refusing any payment beyond what Carlos had already arranged. "Mrs. Williams, you take care of those children. And remember, whatever happened to you in Manila, it doesn't define who you are. You're stronger than you know."

The taxi ride through Hong Kong's winding streets felt both familiar and strange. The driver, a elderly Chinese man who spoke careful English, confirmed what she had observed from the ship: the city was preparing for war. "Many changes since summer, missus. Army everywhere, people very nervous. But still safe for now, still home for people who belong here."

As they climbed toward the residential areas where colonial families lived, Alicia's heart began beating faster. What if Bryn wasn't there? What if he had been reassigned? What if everything had changed while she was gone? The house appeared around a familiar curve in the road, and Alicia felt tears spring to her eyes. It looked exactly the same: white columns gleaming in the morning sun, wide veranda wrapped around the front, garden carefully maintained despite the uncertain times. Home. They were really home.

"Is that our house, Mama?" Patricia asked, pressing her face to the taxi window.

"Yes, sweetheart. That's our house," Alicia replied.

Before Alicia could pay the driver and gather their few belongings, the front door opened. Ah-Min, appeared on the steps, his usually composed face showing pure shock. Mrs. Wu stood beside him, dish towel forgotten in her hands as tears welled in her dark eyes. *"Aiya!* Madam come back!" Mrs. Wu called out, her voice breaking with emotion. "We think... we think maybe you never come back!"

Alicia stepped out of the taxi with David in her arms and Patricia holding tightly to her hand. The familiar faces of their household staff, people who had cared for them for years, made the reality of their return finally sink in. They were truly home. "Ah-Min, Mrs. Wu, Mei-Lin," she called, her voice thick with emotion. "We're back. All of us."

Ah-Min descended the steps with unusual haste, his formal dignity forgotten in his relief. "Madam, the children, why have you come back...are you and the children alright?"

"We had to return Ah-Min, and that is a long story... is Bryn here?"

"Master Bryn is at the office or on his rounds. He said he would be home for dinner. He..." Ah-Min paused, searching for the right words. "He is very worried since you left. He works all the time, with no rest."

The house enveloped them like an embrace. Everything was exactly as she remembered: the polished wood floors, the Chinese vases filled with fresh flowers, the family photographs arranged on familiar tables. Mrs. Wu bustled around them, exclaiming over how much the children had grown, insisting they must eat immediately to restore their strength.

Patricia ran through the familiar rooms with squeals of delight, rediscovering toys she had forgotten and claiming her old bedroom as if she had never left. David toddled around the sitting room, his confident steps carrying him to windows where he could see the harbor spread below.

"Mama, my rocking horse!" Patricia called from her bedroom. "He missed me!"

Watching her children reclaim their home, Alicia felt a profound sense of rightness. This was where they belonged. Not in Jenkins' mansion with its cold luxury and hidden dangers, not even with the Santos family despite their loving kindness. Here, in this house, with their own people who had worried about them and waited for their return. As afternoon faded into evening, Alicia found herself standing at the front window, watching the garden path for any sign of Bryn's familiar figure. Patricia played quietly with her toys, while David napped in his old crib, exhausted by the day's excitement.

At six thirty, she saw him. Bryn walked slowly up the path, his medical bag heavy in his hand, his shoulders bowed with exhaustion. He looked thinner than she remembered, his clothes hanging loose on his frame, his fair hair dulled by worry and overwork. Heart pounding, Alicia moved toward the front door. She opened it just as Bryn reached for the handle, and he froze, staring at her as if she were a vision that might disappear at any moment.

"Alicia?" His voice broke on her name.

"It's us," she said softly, drinking in the sight of his beloved face. "We're home, Bryn. All of us."

His bag dropped to the veranda with a heavy thud as he reached for her, his hands trembling as they framed her face. His blue eyes searched hers, looking for confirmation that this was real, that his family had truly returned to him. "How? I thought... there was no word from Manila, no communication..." He pulled her against him then, holding her as if she might vanish if he loosened his grip. She felt the rapid beating of his heart, the way his whole body shook with relief and disbelief. He buried his face in her hair, breathing deeply as if memorizing her scent. "I dreamt of this," he whispered. "Night after night, I dreamed you would come home, but then I'd wake up and the house would be empty and I'd remember..."

"I'm here. We're all here. Patricia, David, all of us safe."

Chapter 27: Homecoming

He drew back to study her face more carefully, and she saw the moment when he registered the changes: the new lines around her eyes, the way she held herself differently, the wariness that hadn't been there before. "Alicia, what happened?"

"Go see the children first. Then I'll tell you everything," she said, tears in her eyes.

Hand in hand, they climbed the stairs to the nursery where Patricia was arranging her dolls on the small bed and David was just waking from his nap. When Patricia saw her father, she shrieked with joy and launched herself into his arms. "Papa! Papa!"

Bryn caught her against his chest, tears streaming down his face as he held his daughter. "My princess. Look how big you've gotten. Did you take good care of Mama while you were away?"

"I was very brave, Papa. Even on the scary boat. And Mama was brave too."

When Bryn knelt beside David's crib, the little boy studied him with the serious concentration that toddlers bring to important moments. Then recognition dawned, and David's face lit up with a wide grin as he reached up with both arms.

"My boy," Bryn whispered, lifting David from the crib and kissing him on both cheeks.

They settled in the sitting room while the children played, and Alicia told Bryn everything. About Jenkins' escalating attentions, his sense of entitlement, the assault, and their escape with Rosa and Alfredo's help. She spoke quietly and factually, watching Bryn's face grow pale, then flush with barely contained rage.

When she showed him the faded bruises still visible on her arms, his hands clenched into fists. "Jenkins," he said, the name coming out like a curse. "I trusted him with the most precious things in my life, and he..." His voice broke. "Alicia, I failed you. I should have seen what kind of man he really was."

"You couldn't have known. He was very skilled at hiding his true nature," she replied.

"I should have come with you. Should have resigned my position and kept my family together," Bryn said with regret.

"No," she said firmly. "Your work here is important. Lives depend on what you do. Jenkins is responsible for his own actions, not you."

"But if I had been there..." Then a darkness crossed his face. "One day when the time is right, I'll pay a visit to Robert Jenkins, and he'll account for his actions."

"Oh Bryn, don't do anything…" she said.

"Not to worry my love, five years in the coal mine and seven years in the

British Army taught me there should be consequences to bad behavior, and how to deliver them," Bryn replied calmly but with intensity.

"I was rescued by two of the servants, Rosa, an *ahma*, and Alfredo the driver, and Rosa's family gave me shelter and took me into their home with love. I would never have made it back without them."

"I am so grateful for them. One day I'll find the right way to thank them," Bryn replied.

That night, after the children were settled in their own beds and the household staff had finally stopped exclaiming over their return, Alicia and Bryn sat together on their veranda, watching the harbor lights twinkle in the darkness.

"Tell me about the situation here," Alicia said. "Captain Reyes warned me that Hong Kong might not be the safe haven I was expecting."

Bryn's expression grew grave. "It's deteriorating rapidly. Intelligence reports suggest Japanese forces are massing for an invasion. Some estimates say we have weeks, maybe days, before they move against us."

"Then perhaps I brought the children into even greater danger," Alicia said.

"In one way yes, but I've heard from my intelligence friends that Manila and Singapore are next," Bryn said firmly, taking her hand. "You brought them home. Whatever happens, we'll face it together, as a family. That's worth any risk."

They talked long into the night, sharing the details of their separation. Bryn spoke of the flood of refugees from China, the growing certainty that war was coming, his own guilt and worry about sending them away. Alicia told him about Rosa's courage, the Santos family's incredible kindness, Captain Reyes and his crew's dedication to getting them home safely.

"I love you," Bryn said simply. "I love your courage, your strength, your determination to bring our family back together against impossible odds."

"I love you too. And I'm grateful for a husband who trusted me to make the right choices, even when they seemed dangerous."

Sitting in their garden on their last free evening before the siege began, watching Patricia chase fireflies while David continued to babble as though he was determined to say words. Alicia looked at her children with wonderment, amazed at their strength and resiliency, something that would hold them in good stead in the days to come.

Alicia reflected on her journey. She had survived assault, engineered an escape, crossed dangerous seas, and brought her children safely home to their father. She was not the same woman who had left Hong Kong months earlier, trusting in others to protect her family. She was stronger now, more self-reliant, more aware of her own capacity for courage and survival. Whatever challenges lay ahead, she carried with her the knowledge that she had allies in unexpected places and strengths she had never imagined possessing. Her family was complete. That was enough. That was everything.

And when the dark days of internment arrived, bringing hunger, uncertainty, and the constant threat of violence, Alicia would realize that her experience with Jenkins had prepared her for something crucial: she knew how to identify predators, how to protect her children from those who would exploit the vulnerable, and how to find the inner strength needed to resist evil while keeping her humanity. The woman who had fled Hong Kong in fear returned as someone who could face whatever came next with courage, wisdom, and an unshakeable conviction that some things, love and family and dignity, were worth any sacrifice to preserve.

Chapter 28

Fortress of Paper

"The most dangerous moment for any empire comes not when it appears weak, but when it still believes itself strong."

Lieutenant General Sir Mark Young, Governor of Hong Kong, 1941

December 8, 1941

The sky over their home was still dark when Bryn stepped into the cool December air, leaving a quiet note beside sleeping Alicia and lingering longer than usual over Patricia and David's beds, as if some premonition had taken hold of him. The familiar weight of his leather satchel felt heavier this morning, filled with the unspoken understanding that everything was about to change.

The streets were unusually quiet for a Monday morning. Fewer Chinese vendors had set up their stalls, and those who had looked nervous, frequently glancing at the northern horizon. The usual chatter of early commuters was replaced by an uneasy silence, broken only by the distant hum of aircraft engines overhead that seemed too numerous for a peaceful dawn.

At 7:30 am, the windows of his Sanitary Department office shook like leaves in a storm. A dull, rolling explosion echoed through the city, soon followed by another, louder and closer. Bryn's pen halted mid-sentence as air raid sirens began their piercing wail. Through his office window, he observed smoke rising from Kai Tak Airport in dark clouds against the dawn sky. Japanese planes flew low over the harbor, their engines roaring as they targeted Royal Navy ships and police stations with surgical precision. The feared invasion had begun with the careful efficiency that characterized everything about the Imperial Japanese military.

"Sir! What's happening?" Liu, his young assistant, burst through the door with wild eyes and trembling hands.

Bryn rushed to the window, where the harbor he had gazed upon peacefully for six years was now a theater of war. Ships burned while planes dove through curtains of anti-aircraft fire. "The Japanese have begun their attack." He was now working and sleeping in his office twenty-four hours a day.

The phone rang nonstop, each sharp tone signaling a new crisis. Reports flooded in from across the colony: explosions at the Royal Navy dockyard, fires at government buildings, fighter planes strafing civilians mercilessly. Every call brought news of Britain's defenses crumbling faster than anyone had expected.

Across the city, Alicia heard the first explosion while she was dressing David for breakfast. The windows rattled in their frames, and David began crying from the loud noises. Patricia hurried down the hallway clutching her stuffed bear, her small face pale with confusion. "Remember what we practiced?" Alicia said, gathering her daughter close while her voice remained steady despite her racing heart. "We're going to the shelter now."

The loyal household staff moved with practiced efficiency. Mrs. Wu appeared with emergency water bottles and medical supplies, her weathered face grim but determined. Ah-Min checked their shelter preparations with his usual calm dignity, while young Mei-Lin helped Patricia gather her few treasured belongings.

The walk to Barker Road shelter took them past neighbors emerging in various states of undress. The social hierarchy that normally governed colonial life had dissolved in minutes, replaced by the simple arithmetic of survival. Barefoot women carried infants while elderly men in silk dressing gowns hurried alongside Chinese shopkeepers and British clerks, all reduced to the same fundamental need for safety. Inside the concrete shelter that reeked of dust and human fear, families huddled together in ways that would have been unimaginable under normal circumstances. Alicia found a spot against the wall with David sleeping restlessly against her shoulder and Patricia pressed against her side, while Lupe held their small bag of essential supplies.

"The Japanese will never take Hong Kong," declared an elderly British gentleman with the confidence of someone who had never seen an empire fall. "The colony is impregnable."

A woman nearby snorted softly, her voice carrying bitter wisdom. "My brother works at Government House. They know we cannot hold. The Japanese have been preparing for years, while we prepared excuses."

The hours in the shelter dragged by painfully slow. Children whined and cried, adults whispered prayers in different languages, and the elderly sat in stoic silence, showing they had survived other disasters. Outside, the sounds of war grew louder: the whistle of falling bombs, the crack of anti-aircraft guns, and the rumble of collapsing buildings. When the all-clear finally sounded, families emerged blinking into daylight that seemed different somehow, as if the world itself had fundamentally changed in the space of a few hours.

Chapter 28: Fortress of Paper

December 9, 1941

Bryn was managing emergency water distribution when Jason Lam arrived at his office, his usually tidy appearance disheveled and his eyes showing the hollow look of someone who had seen the impossible. "Bryn, they've taken Tai Po intact." Jason's voice shook, his careful English accent cracking under stress. "Walked right in and turned the taps back on for themselves. It's like they had blueprints of our entire system."

The implications struck Bryn like a physical blow. The enemy had been studying Hong Kong's vulnerabilities while the British had been relying on assumptions of imperial superiority. "Our backup systems?"

"Completely stuffed. We've got half of Guangdong Province trying to drink from puddles because our brilliant planners never imagined this many refugees." Jason ran his hands through his hair, leaving it standing at odd angles. "Three camps showing dysentery already. It'll be cholera next, mark my words."

Dr. Wellington's voice crackled through the damaged phone lines with news that confirmed their worst fears. The man spoke in the clipped tones of someone who had seen too many crises to waste words on diplomacy. "Shing Mun's finished. Twelve hours, start to finish." Wellington's Scottish accent became more pronounced under stress. "Japanese used local guides. Knew every bloody path through terrain we thought was impregnable. Our lads trained for conventional war, not this ghost-and-shadow business."

"Sir, what's the word from Government House?" Bryn asked.

"His Excellency informs us that essential services must continue regardless of who's signing the paychecks." Wellington's bitter laugh carried clearly through the static. "Seems we're expected to hand over functioning systems to our new masters. Rather thoughtful of us, don't you think?"

Bryn reflected grimly that they were being ordered to prepare for their own defeat, to ensure the smooth transition from one empire to another as if public health were somehow independent of politics.

The next several days blurred together in a nightmare of collapsing infrastructure and mounting desperation. Reports filtered through even the most hardened administrators. The systematic killings had begun, intended to terrorize the civilian population into submission. At Blue Pool Road, approximately thirty civilians had been executed, including Chinese businessmen and government officials. The killings were methodical and deliberate, sending a clear message about the cost of resistance.

The medical situation deteriorated with each passing hour. Canosa Relief Hospital had been destroyed, forcing medical staff to establish aid stations in schools and private homes. The smell of gangrene competed with the overwhelming stench of sewage as sanitation systems collapsed and disease began its silent work alongside the bombs. "We're seeing cholera symptoms in Western District," Wellington reported during one of their increasingly brief telephone conferences. "Without proper sewage treatment, we're looking at epidemic conditions within days."

Bryn understood the implications. Disease would kill more people than Japanese bullets, given time. But time was something they no longer had.

December 15, 1941

The family's routine had become a grim dance with death. They rushed to the shelter when sirens wailed, returned home during brief respites to check for damage and gather supplies, and barricaded doors against both bombs and the gangs of looters who emerged after each attack like scavengers following a storm.

Triad members sporting crude Rising Sun armbands appeared on the streets, documenting government officials' faces and demanding protection money from frightened civilians. The social fabric that had held Hong Kong together was unraveling rapidly.

During one of his increasingly rare visits home from his offices, Bryn found Alicia organizing their remaining supplies with military precision. Mrs. Wu had performed her usual miracle, creating a nutritious meal from rice and preserved vegetables, while Mei-Lin entertained the children with gentle songs that somehow masked the sounds of distant artillery.

"How long do we have?" Alicia asked quietly while Patricia played with her remaining toys.

"Not long enough," Bryn admitted, the weight of certainty heavy in his voice. "If I can't contact you, the phone lines might be cut. I'll get word to you somehow."

Alicia gripped his hands with desperate strength. "We'll wait. No matter what happens, we'll wait."

December 18, 1941

A messenger arrived on foot, his bicycle having been requisitioned by retreating British forces. The hastily scribbled note from Wellington was brief and devastating: "Military command estimates twenty-four to forty-eight hours before complete collapse. Maintain essential services. Prepare for occupation protocols."

That evening, Bryn took what he thought might be his last trip home through the dark streets of a dying colony. The house was dark when he arrived, following

Chapter 28: Fortress of Paper

blackout protocols that had become second nature. Alicia met him at the door, her face pale but composed in the candlelight that had replaced electric lighting.

"It's almost over," he said simply. "Wellington estimates two days before surrender."

She nodded as if she had been expecting this news, as if some part of her had been preparing for this moment since the first bombs fell. "What happens to us then?"

"I don't know. The Japanese may keep essential service personnel, such as me, working at least temporarily." The admission felt like another kind of defeat. "Or they may decide that foreign experts have nothing to offer them. Do you regret coming back? We could have arranged for you to leave some other way," Bryn asked the question he had been afraid to voice.

Alicia considered this carefully, weighing not just the question but all the choices that had brought them to this moment. "No. Whatever comes, we face it together. That's what marriage means. Not just the good times, but the impossible times too."

December 19, 1941

The sounds of battle grew nearer throughout the day, a steady drumbeat signaling the final collapse of British resistance. By evening, Japanese forces had broken through the last defensive line with overwhelming force. Government House prepared to surrender as officials destroyed sensitive documents that could jeopardize those who had served the empire loyally.

Bryn spent his day at the offices ensuring that water treatment facilities remained operational and medical supplies were secured for the civilian population. Not because he believed the Japanese would appreciate these efforts, but because people would need clean water regardless of which flag flew over Government House.

December 20, 1941

Bryn awoke to discover that the telephone lines to the Mid-Levels district had gone completely dead overnight. A young Chinese clerk from the telephone exchange found him at the water distribution point near Government House, his face carrying the weight of unwelcome news.

Bryn's hand froze as he poured water into a cracked teapot. The last thread connecting him to his family had been severed. In a city under siege, distance was no longer measured in miles but in the impossibility of communication, the growing silence that separated love from knowledge.

Chapter 29
Silent Night, Violent Night

"Christmas Eve, and all through the colony, not a creature was stirring, except for the bombers overhead and the prayers whispered in shelters below."

Anonymous entry found in the ruins of St. John's Cathedral, Hong Kong, 1941

December 24, 1941

On Christmas Eve morning, Bryn was overseeing the distribution of water to a growing line of desperate civilians when a military police officer arrived with urgent orders. The man's khaki uniform was stained with soot, and his face showed the hollow look of someone who had seen too much death. The sharp smell of burning buildings mixed with something worse, something organic and terrible that spoke of bodies left unburied in the tropical heat.

The water line stretched around the block, a gathering of people stripped down to their most basic needs. An elderly Chinese man held an empty cooking pot with arthritic hands, maintaining his dignity despite circumstances that could have broken younger spirits. Behind him, a British expatriate woman still wore her colonial manners like armor, her pearl necklace somehow surviving while the world fell apart around her.

"Inspector Williams? You're needed at the Colonial Secretariat immediately."

Bryn handed the measuring cup to Mrs. Chen, the reliable woman who had helped him countless times before. "Make sure everyone gets their fair share," he told her, then turned to address the queue. "Mrs. Chen will continue the distribution. Please be patient with one another."

The walk to the Colonial Secretariat took him through streets that had become foreign territory in just two weeks. Bomb craters filled with stagnant water reflected the gray sky like dark mirrors. Shop windows gaped like empty eye sockets, their contents scattered across pavements that crunched with broken glass

Ashes and Dawn

and debris. The elegant Hong Kong of tea parties and cricket matches had been replaced by something from a nightmare.

At the Colonial Secretariat, Dr. Selwyn-Clarke hunched over a desk cluttered with evacuation lists and medical supply inventories. The Director of Medical and Sanitation Services looked as if he had aged years in days, his usually spotless appearance replaced by wrinkled clothes and bloodshot eyes that revealed sleepless nights spent trying to save lives while watching civilization collapse. "Williams, you made it here safely," Selwyn-Clarke said, looking up from papers that chronicled systematic destruction. "I'm assembling a skeleton team to maintain essential services after the inevitable occurs. Governor Young will likely surrender within forty-eight hours."

The clinical detachment in his voice couldn't hide the weight of what he was saying. The British Empire in the Far East was about to fall, and they were being asked to help it pass away with dignity. "My main concern is preventing mass casualties from disease outbreaks afterward," Selwyn-Clarke continued. "When the Japanese military administration takes control, we'll need operational systems. But Williams, with communication systems failing, if your family isn't exactly where you expect them to be, finding them will be nearly impossible."

The words hit Bryn like a physical punch. He thought of Alicia and the children, safe in their house the last time he'd been able to contact them. But that was yesterday, and in a city under siege, yesterday might as well have been a lifetime ago.

"So, what am I to do?" Bryn asked.

"What I told Dr. Wellington. Wait until the surrender. British authorities will negotiate with the Japanese what services will continue, if they continue at all. We're hoping they will. The Japanese should have an interest in maintaining health conditions while they occupy Hong Kong, I imagine."

"Alright, I'll await further instructions from Dr. Wellington," Bryn replied.

Returning to the water distribution point, Bryn moved through a landscape changed by war. Bodies lay twisted in doorways, soldiers and civilians alike struck by bombs or bullets. The smallest figures were the hardest to see, their tiny hands still reaching for mothers who would never answer. Feral dogs roamed in larger packs, their eyes hungry and desperate, some still wearing collars that marked them as family pets turned scavengers by circumstances beyond anyone's control. Near Government House, civilians had gathered around a makeshift water tank, forming orderly lines despite their desperation. The social contract that held civilization together was unraveling, but hadn't entirely broken apart.

"Form a line, please," Bryn called out, trying to maintain some semblance of normal procedure. "Everyone will get water."

Chapter 29: Silent Night, Violent Night

Mrs. Patterson, a volunteer, approached with trembling hands, holding a cracked teapot with the careful dignity of someone clinging to the rituals of a vanishing world. "My husband is very ill. Could you spare just a little extra?"

"Of course," Bryn said, filling her container generously.

As he continued distribution, a man in a torn suit approached nervously. Bryn recognized him as from the telephone exchange, though the man looked as if he'd aged a decade in two weeks. "Inspector Williams, I have news about the telephone service." His voice carried the weight of unwelcome tidings. "The lines to the Peak and Mid-Levels districts went dead an hour ago. The Japanese hit the relay station."

Bryn's hand froze mid-pour, water spilling from the ladle onto the pavement. The last thread connecting him to his family had been severed. Distance was no longer measured in miles but in the impossibility of communication, the growing silence that separated love from knowledge.

It was then that the air raid siren began its wail, but this time the bombers were already overhead, their engines screaming as they dove toward the city center. "Everyone down!" Bryn shouted, but Mrs. Patterson was still standing, confused and frightened, clutching her teapot like a talisman. The explosion lifted him off his feet with tremendous force. Bryn felt something tear through his shoulder and side, a sensation like being stabbed with hot iron. He hit the ground hard, his head cracking against the pavement. His vision exploded into stars and then everything went dark. When awareness returned, he was lying on his side in debris, his mouth full of dust and the metallic taste of blood. His right arm throbbed with sharp pain, and something warm and sticky was spreading across his shirt. The world seemed to tilt and spin when he tried to lift his head, waves of dizziness making him immediately nauseous.

Mrs. Chen's face appeared above him, her mouth moving, but her words sounded like they were coming from underwater. She was pulling at his good arm, trying to get him to stand, but his legs felt disconnected from his body and the dizziness was overwhelming. "Can't..." he mumbled, the word slurring. "Everything's spinning..."

More hands grabbed him, and pain shot through his shoulder. He may have screamed. The journey to Queen Mary Hospital passed in fragments: being half carried, half dragged through streets filled with smoke, the jouncing agony of being loaded into a cart, Mrs. Chen's worried face swimming in and out of focus. Every bump and jostle sent fresh waves of nausea through him, and he lost consciousness twice before they reached the hospital.

At the hospital, chaos ruled. The main building had been bombed and partially damaged, forcing all operations into the basement levels. Wounded soldiers and civilians lay on stretchers in the corridors, some moaning, others ominously silent.

The air reeked of blood, antiseptic, and something worse that made Bryn's stomach lurch.

A harried nurse with blood on her apron looked him over quickly. "Shrapnel wounds, conscious, concussion likely," she called out to someone Bryn couldn't see. "Bed seven when it's available."

"How bad?" Bryn managed to ask, though forming words felt like tremendous effort.

"You're alive," she said curtly, already moving to the next patient. "That's all I can tell you right now."

Hours passed before Dr. Miner could examine him properly. By then, Bryn was shivering uncontrollably despite the humid heat, his clothes soaked with sweat and blood. The pain had intensified to a constant, grinding agony that made thinking difficult. Every time he tried to sit up, the room spun violently.

Dr. Miner worked by the light of two kerosene lamps, his hands steady despite obvious exhaustion. He had been operating for eighteen hours straight, and it showed in every line of his face. "Shrapnel fragments in the shoulder and side," he said, probing carefully while Bryn gritted his teeth against waves of nausea. "Not too deep, fortunately. I can get to all of them." He paused, shining a light in Bryn's eyes. "But you've got a concussion. Your pupils aren't responding evenly. Hit your head when you went down?"

"Don't remember," Bryn managed. "Everything's blurry."

"That's the concussion talking." Dr. Miner continued his examination. "How many fingers am I holding up?"

Bryn squinted. The doctor's hand seemed to multiply. "Three? No, two?"

"It's four." Dr. Miner made some notes. "The head injury is my main concern right now. You need to stay still and let that brain settle down. Any vomiting?"

"Twice. On the way here."

"Not surprising. You took a hard knock." He gestured to a nurse. "We'll get these metal pieces out first, then you need complete rest for at least a week. No getting up, no moving around. Concussions are tricky. Push yourself too soon and you could have serious problems."

The morphine they gave him helped, though it was carefully rationed. Dr. Miner worked methodically, extracting each piece of shrapnel and cleaning the wounds with precious iodine. Bryn drifted in and out of consciousness during the procedure, grateful for the fog that dulled the worst of the pain. "Got them all," Dr. Miner finally announced. "The wounds themselves aren't too serious. Clean cuts, no major blood vessels or nerves damaged. But that head of yours took a

Chapter 29: Silent Night, Violent Night

beating. You're going to need time to heal properly."

Dr. Miner cleaned the extraction sites and began bandaging with strips torn from what had once been hospital bed sheets. "The shrapnel wounds should heal well enough if infection doesn't set in. We're low on sulfa powder, but I've cleaned everything thoroughly. The real issue is your concussion."

"How bad?" Bryn asked weakly, though even talking made his head pound.

"You need rest. Complete rest. A week minimum, possibly longer depending on how you respond." Dr. Miner's voice was firm. "I've seen men ignore concussions and end up with permanent problems. Seizures, blindness, worse. Your brain needs time to recover from the trauma."

"A week?" Bryn tried to sit up, but the room spun violently and he immediately lay back down. "My family..."

"Mr. Williams, you can't help anyone if you're unconscious or having seizures." Dr. Miner's voice was gentle but unyielding. "The dizziness and nausea should improve over the next few days, but you need to stay in that bed. No walking, no sitting up for more than a few minutes at a time. Let your body heal."

As Dr. Miner worked, word came that made the entire ward fall silent. A young orderly, barely sixteen years old, stumbled in with news that drained the color from every face. "Doctor," he said, his voice breaking, "the Japanese hit St. Stephen's College. The field hospital there..."

"How many casualties?" Dr. Miner asked without stopping his work, though his hands had tightened almost imperceptibly.

"All of them, sir. They killed everyone. Doctors, nurses, support staff, volunteers, wounded soldiers, patients. Raped and then bayoneted the nurses. Shot the doctors."

The silence that followed was broken only by the distant rumble of artillery and the occasional moan from the wounded. Several patients began to weep quietly. The systematic atrocities had escalated beyond anyone's worst fears.

Dr. Miner finished Bryn's bandages with mechanical precision, but his face had gone gray. "That was Dr. Black's unit," he said quietly. "Good man. Good surgeon." He paused, staring at his bloodstained hands. "They're not following the Geneva Convention. Medical personnel, wounded prisoners... it doesn't matter to them."

Bryn tried to focus through the haze of pain and fog. "My family... they're in a shelter. The phone lines are down. I can't..."

A British sergeant in the next bed spoke through gritted teeth. "My wife's somewhere in Wan Chai. Haven't heard from her in three days. The waiting's worse than the pain."

But Bryn barely heard the conversation. The concussion made coherent thought difficult, and fever from the wounds was starting to take hold. His thoughts scattered into disconnected pieces. Alicia's face swimming in his vision. Patricia's laugh blending with the sound of sirens. David's small hands reaching for him through a fog of pain and morphine.

Dr. Miner returned to check his dressings later. "Temperature's rising slightly, but that's normal after this kind of trauma. The concussion is what worries me most. I've seen strong men die from head injuries that seemed minor at first, and I've seen broken men survive the impossible." He leaned closer, lowering his voice. "Keep fighting, Williams. Your family needs you to keep fighting. But fighting means resting right now. Let your body do its work."

Over the next several days, Bryn's condition slowly improved. The dizziness gradually subsided, though sudden movements still made the room spin. The shrapnel wounds were healing cleanly, showing no signs of infection. By the fourth day, he could sit up without feeling nauseous. By the sixth day, he could walk short distances with only minor dizziness.

Dr. Miner examined him on the seventh morning. "Your pupils are responding normally now. The wounds are healing well. You're fortunate, Williams. Another few days and you should be able to leave, but remember, no strenuous activity for at least another week. Your body's been through trauma. Respect that."

Bryn nodded, though his mind was already racing ahead to finding his family. Nearly a week had passed. Nearly a week of lying helpless while they were somewhere in the chaos, waiting for him.

Through the small barred windows, they could hear the sounds of the city's death throes: explosions, rifle fire, the occasional scream that drifted through the humid night air. Each sound reminded Bryn that somewhere in that burning maze of streets, families waited in shelters, separated by forces beyond their control.

Meanwhile, across the burning city…

Alicia knelt in their garden with her mother and the children, trying to maintain some semblance of normalcy while chaos closed in around them. The familiar ritual of tending flowers seemed almost absurd given the circumstances, but it was something to hold onto, a small act of faith that the world might still have room for beauty.

"Mama, why are we cutting the flowers when the planes are so loud?" Patricia asked, her small hands carefully arranging fallen petals.

"Because gardens need tending, sweetheart, even when the world seems upside

Chapter 29: Silent Night, Violent Night

down," Alicia replied, though her eyes kept scanning the sky for signs of approaching aircraft.

Lupe hummed softly as she worked, an old Mexican lullaby that seemed to create a small pocket of peace amid the chaos. *"Mija,* you're very quiet today. What troubles you beyond the obvious?"

"Everything troubles me, Mother. Bryn's been gone since dawn, the bombing is getting closer, and I keep thinking we should have evacuated when we had the chance."

"But this is our home," Patricia protested, looking up from her flower arrangement. "Papa said we're safe here."

Alicia exchanged a glance with her mother, both women understanding the weight of promises made in peacetime that war had rendered meaningless. "Papa is very smart, darling. He knows what's best."

"Where is Papa today?" Patricia continued with the relentless curiosity of a four-year-old.

"He's helping people in the city. Making sure they have clean water to drink."

"Even with the bad planes flying?"

"Especially with the bad planes flying. That's when people need help most."

The drone of aircraft grew louder, different from the usual patrols. Deeper. More menacing. The sound that had become the soundtrack to their nightmares.

"Come here, quickly," Alicia said, reaching for Patricia just as the first explosions rattled the hillside.

The initial blast shook the ground, sending dirt cascading down like lethal confetti. David began wailing in his basket, his small fists reaching desperately for his mother. Patricia covered her ears, her four-year-old body trembling with fear that no child should have to understand.

Lupe pulled both grandchildren close as Alicia looked up to see a dark object falling toward the other side of the house, followed by a deafening blast that lifted the earth beneath them and transformed their world in the space between one heartbeat and the next. When the roaring subsided, Alicia lifted her head cautiously. Debris continued raining down like deadly snow, each piece carrying the weight of their destroyed life. Where their house had stood, where six years of careful domesticity had created a sanctuary from the complexities of colonial life, only smoke and emptiness remained.

"Oh no!" Alicia screamed, the words torn from her throat. "Ah-Min! Mrs. Wu! Mei-Lin!" She called their names again and again, her voice breaking with each repetition.

"Mama, where's our house?" Patricia asked, her voice small and bewildered. "Where's Mei-Lin?"

Alicia ran toward the smoking crater, stumbling over debris, calling desperately into the ruins. "Mrs. Wu! Can you hear me? Ah-Min!" But her voice echoed back unanswered, swallowed by the acrid smell of destruction and something worse that made her stomach turn.

She found fragments scattered everywhere, each one a knife to her heart: Patricia's toy elephant that Mei-Lin had mended just last week, its blue velvet body torn and stained dark. Mrs. Wu's beloved porcelain tea set, the one she'd used to serve them breakfast every morning for six years, now glittering like deadly stars among the rubble. Ah-Min's reading glasses, cracked and bent, still holding a fragment of the newspaper he'd been reading when the world ended.

"Mama, why aren't they answering?" Patricia had followed her, and now stood frozen, staring at the devastation. "Where's Mei-Lin? She was going to braid my hair today!"

"Mama, keep the children back out of the way while I look for them." Alicia clawed through the wreckage with bleeding hands, searching for any sign of life, any hope that somehow they had survived. But she found only pieces of the people who had been family: Mrs. Wu's apron, still tied as if she had just stepped away from the kitchen; Mei-Lin's hairbrush with its delicate ivory handle; Ah-Min's worn prayer book, pages scattered like autumn leaves.

The reality hit her like a physical blow. These weren't just servants who had died; these were the people who had raised her children, welcomed her into their daily routines, and formed the foundation of their family life. Mrs. Wu, who had taught Patricia to count in Cantonese and always saved the best pieces of fruit for the kids. Ah-Min, whose gentle wisdom had guided them through every household crisis, who had carried David when he was colicky and sang him Chinese lullabies. And Mei-Lin, sweet Mei-Lin, barely eighteen herself, who had become Patricia's constant companion, teaching her songs and games, braiding her hair each morning with infinite patience.

"Mei-Lin!" Patricia suddenly screamed, the full horror finally penetrating her four-year-old understanding. "MEI-LIN!" She began running toward the rubble, tears streaming down her face. "She's hiding! She's playing hide-and-seek!"

Alicia caught her daughter, pulling her back from the dangerous debris. "Patricia, no, sweetheart, it's not safe."

"But Mei-Lin is in there! She needs me! She was scared of the loud noises!" Patricia fought against her mother's arms, sobbing with the abandonment of a child

Chapter 29: Silent Night, Violent Night

whose world had shattered. "I have to find her! She doesn't like to be alone!"

Lupe approached, tears streaming down her weathered cheeks. She had loved Mrs. Wu like a sister, the two older women bonding over their shared devotion to the children and their quiet strength. "Mija," she whispered to Alicia, "they're gone. All of them."

Patricia's sobs grew more desperate. "But Mei-Lin was teaching me the butterfly song! We didn't finish! She has to finish teaching me!" She turned to her grandmother, her small face twisted with anguish. "Abuela, make her come back! Make them all come back!"

Lupe knelt beside her granddaughter, her own voice thick with grief. "*Mijita*, sometimes when the bad planes come, good people have to go to heaven. Mei-Lin, Mrs. Wu, and Ah-Min, they're all together now, watching over us."

"But I don't want them in heaven!" Patricia screamed, her voice hoarse. "I want them here! I want Mei-Lin to sing to me! I want Mrs. Wu to make my rice! I want Ah-Min to tell me stories!"

Alicia held her daughter tightly, tears streaming down her face. She had tried to stay strong, but seeing Patricia so devastated broke something inside her. These people had been the heart of their home, the ones who made Hong Kong feel like home instead of just another colonial posting. They loved her children unconditionally, celebrated every small milestone, and were there for every scraped knee and childhood fear.

"I know, darling," she whispered into Patricia's hair. "I want them back too. Mrs. Wu was going to teach you how to make moon cakes for Chinese New Year. And Mei-Lin was so excited about the new songs she'd learned. And Ah-Min was teaching you to write Chinese characters."

David, sensing the anguish around him, began crying in. The sound seemed to pierce through Patricia's hysteria, reminding them all that they had to survive this, had to keep going for his sake.

The sound of approaching aircraft grew louder. More planes, more bombs coming.

"We have to go to the shelter," Alicia said, her voice breaking. "We have to go now."

"I won't leave them!" Patricia cried, clinging to a fragment of Mei-Lin's favorite dress. "They'll be scared without us!"

"They're not scared anymore, sweetheart," Lupe said gently, taking Patricia's hand. "They're safe now. But we have to keep ourselves safe too, because that's what they would want. Mei-Lin would want you to be safe, wouldn't she?"

Patricia nodded through her tears, still clutching the scrap of fabric. "She would want me to take care of baby David."

"That's right, *mija*. We take care of each other now."

As they hurried away from the ruins, Patricia looked back repeatedly, calling "Goodbye, Mei-Lin! Goodbye, Mrs. Wu! Goodbye, Ah-Min!" as if she could somehow ensure they heard her.

Alicia's heart felt as shattered as the porcelain scattered in the rubble. They had lost more than their home and possessions. They had lost the people who had made their family complete, who had bridged the gap between British colonial life and Chinese tradition, and who had loved her children as if they were their own.

The sound of bombs grew closer, forcing them to run, but Patricia's sobs echoed behind them, a child's grief for the people who would never braid her hair again, never sing her to sleep, never be there when she woke from nightmares. In just minutes, the safe world of childhood was destroyed as completely as their house, leaving only memories and the terrible knowledge that love couldn't always protect the people who mattered most.

In the Underground Refuge

The air raid shelter on Barker Road was a concrete tomb filled beyond capacity. Bodies pressed against each other in the stifling heat, the air heavy with the smell of unwashed humanity, fear, and something worse from the makeshift latrine buckets in the far corner. Mrs. Smith waved desperately from her small section of wall, her weathered face slick with sweat.

"Alicia! Here, quickly!" She gestured to a space barely large enough for two people, let alone a family of four plus Lupe.

"That's not enough room," snapped Mr. Wilson a red-faced shipping clerk who had been guarding his family's territory like a fortress. "We were here first. These people can find somewhere else."

"There is nowhere else," Mrs. Smith said firmly. "We make room. That's what civilized people do."

A Chinese shopkeeper nearby muttered something in Cantonese that made his wife hiss at him to be quiet. The racial tensions that polite colonial society usually kept beneath the surface were beginning to surface in the pressure cooker of the shelter.

Alicia squeezed into the tiny space with David in her arms as Patricia immediately started wailing at the top of her lungs. "I want Mei-Lin! I want to go home! I want Mei-Lin!" Her screams echoed off the concrete walls, blending with

Chapter 29: Silent Night, Violent Night

the noise of crying babies, worried conversations in different languages, and someone retching in the corner.

"Patricia, please, sweetheart..." Alicia tried to soothe her daughter, but the child was beyond reasoning, her small body rigid with grief and terror.

"Can't someone shut that child up?" complained Mrs. Henderson, a colonial wife whose usual composure had cracked after six hours underground.

"She's lost everything," Lupe said sharply, her protective instincts flaring. "Show some compassion."

"We've all lost everything," Mrs. Henderson shot back. "That doesn't give her the right to disturb everyone else."

Mr. Fortescue, the shelter warden, a thin man with a bureaucrat's obsession with order, pushed through the crowd. "Ladies, please! We must maintain discipline. Mrs. Williams, please try to console your daughter."

"She's four years old and traumatized," Alicia said, her voice tight with exhaustion and grief. "I'm doing my best."

"Perhaps she needs to sit in the corner until she can compose herself," Fortescue suggested with the tone of someone who had never dealt with children.

"She's not a naughty child," Lupe said, her voice dangerously quiet. "She's a baby who watched her home destroyed and her family killed. Maybe you need to sit in the corner until you find some humanity."

The temperature in the overcrowded space had risen to almost unbearable levels. People had stripped down to undergarments, abandoning colonial modesty for basic survival. Mrs. Patel fanned herself with a soggy piece of cardboard while her husband argued with Fortescue about water rations.

"Two cups per family per day," he insisted, guarding the communal water supply. "That's all we have."

"Two cups?" Mrs. Patel's voice rose in desperation, looking around at almost one hundred people who had crowded into the shelter. "My children are dehydrating!"

"Everyone's children are dehydrating," Fortescue, replied coldly. "Rules are rules."

Patricia had progressed from screaming to a heartbreaking whimper, curled in Alicia's lap and rocking back and forth. "Mei-Lin sang to me when I was scared," she whispered brokenly. "She made the bad dreams go away. Why can't she come back? Why can't she come back?"

David, sensing the tension and his sister's distress, began crying with the relentless wail of an overwhelmed infant. Other babies joined in sympathy, creating a chorus of misery that made conversations impossible.

"For God's sake!" shouted a man Alicia didn't recognize, his face flushed with heat and frustration. "Can't anyone control these bloody children?"

"Watch your language!" Mr. Fortescue commanded.

"Watch my language? I've been sitting in my own sweat for hours listening to screaming brats while bombs fall outside! You watch my language!"

A fight nearly broke out between two Chinese families over space near the single ventilation shaft. Mrs. Wong, an elderly woman who had been sitting in dignified silence, suddenly spoke up with bitter authority.

"You want to know what's outside? My nephew works at the morgue. The Japanese are executing civilians in the streets. Whole families lined up and shot. We sit here fighting over inches of floor and drops of water while our neighbors die."

The shelter fell silent except for the persistent crying of children and the distant rumble of artillery.

An argument erupted between several families about the latrine arrangements. The single bucket system was breaking down, creating sanitation problems that would soon become health crises. The smell was becoming overwhelming, and people were starting to get sick.

Patricia had stopped crying but now sat in complete silence, staring at nothing, occasionally whispering "Mei-Lin" under her breath. Her withdrawal was almost more frightening than her screaming had been. "Mama," she finally whispered, her voice hollow, "are Mei-Lin and Mrs. Wu and Ah-Min cold? They don't have blankets where they are."

Alicia's heart broke again at the question. "No, sweetheart. They're not cold. They're somewhere warm and safe now."

"But I'm cold. And I want them to come back and make me warm."

Young Mrs. Taylor, whose own baby had finally fallen asleep, leaned over carefully. "Sometimes when people we love go to heaven, they send us love to keep us warm. You just have to close your eyes and feel for it."

Patricia considered this seriously, then shook her head. "I can't feel anything."

The hours dragged on with agonizing slowness. People dozed fitfully, woke with starts when explosions shook the building, argued over diminishing resources, and tried to maintain some semblance of human dignity in increasingly impossible conditions. Mrs. Smith shared her last rice cake with Patricia, though the child only

Chapter 29: Silent Night, Violent Night

picked at it listlessly. An elderly Chinese man offered his jacket to Lupe when he saw her shivering. Small kindnesses emerged alongside the growing tensions, humanity asserting itself even in the worst circumstances. But the shelter was a pressure cooker of fear, discomfort, and loss, and everyone inside it was being tested beyond their normal limits. The neat social structures of colonial life had dissolved into the basic arithmetic of survival: too many people, too little space, and too much fear.

The bombing stopped several hours later, and Mr. Fortescue gave them the all-clear to leave the shelter. Alicia and her family walked away and then stopped in the middle of Barker Road. "We don't have a home to go back to now," Alicia said, her voice trembling. "What are we to do?"

"We can go to Mary's home in the lower Mid-Levels. If her home hasn't been destroyed, I know she'll be there," Lupe replied with confidence.

"Then let's go, now!" Alicia replied, gathering her children close to her and began to walk down Barker Road.

Christmas Morning in the Hospital Ward

In the basement of Queen Mary Hospital, dawn arrived without fanfare. Dr. Miner continued his rounds by lamplight, moving between beds where wounded soldiers and civilians shared their common humanity in the face of suffering.

"Nurse," called a voice from the shadows, "what time is it?"

"Just past dawn. It's Christmas morning."

"Merry Christmas," someone said with bitter irony.

"No," Dr. Miner said firmly, looking up from his patient with eyes that had seen enough suffering to understand what truly mattered. "Merry Christmas indeed. We're alive, we're together, and we're still caring for each other. That's what Christmas means."

Sergeant Mills, a young Canadian soldier with bandaged ribs, propped himself up on his elbow. "Half my unit didn't make it out of Stanley. Boys who'll never see another Christmas."

"They died protecting people," said a local volunteer whose own family was somewhere in the burning city. "That has to count for something."

"Does it? When does the enemy execute prisoners and medical staff?" the soldier said.

Dr. Miner paused in his work, reflecting on the question that had no simple answer. "It matters because we choose to make it matter. Every life we save here, every kindness we show, proves that something good endures even in the worst conditions."

Through the small barred windows, they could hear the sounds of the city's transformation: distant explosions, rifle fire, and the occasional scream that drifted through the night air. Each sound served as a reminder that families waited in shelters throughout the colony, separated by forces beyond their control but bound together by the simple human capacity for hope. Even in the basement ward, listening to the death throes of an empire, Bryn clung to faith. Somewhere beyond the smoke and rubble, love awaited to reunite what war had torn apart. Christmas had come to Hong Kong with bombs instead of bells, but in the underground shelters and basement wards, people still chose hope over despair, kindness over cruelty.

As Christmas morning neared, Bryn lay in the humid basement ward, battling fever and infection while Hong Kong fell apart around him. Whether he would survive to see his family again depended on factors far beyond any doctor's control: the unpredictable response of damaged tissue, the availability of increasingly scarce medical supplies, and the stubborn refusal of the human body to give up to circumstances that logic said should be fatal. Perhaps that was the real Christmas miracle: not the absence of suffering, but the presence of love and kindness in the midst of it.

Chapter 30

Safe Harbor

"Safety was a relative concept in a city under occupation, and whatever protection we found would be temporary at best. Still, after days of uncertainty and fear, even temporary safety felt like a gift beyond measure."

"Diary of the Displaced," Hong Kong Civil Defense Records, 1942

The journey through Hong Kong's wounded streets felt like walking through a graveyard where the dead still moved. Alicia held David closer to her chest as they slipped from shadow to shadow, his small body warm against her heart, a living reminder of what she had to protect. Patricia's hand stayed tightly in hers, like a child who had learned that letting go meant losing everything.

Each step brought memories flooding back. Here was the corner where they had bought ice cream on Sunday afternoons, now marked by a crater that had swallowed the vendor's cart and probably the vendor himself. There was the pharmacy where she had collected David's medicine when he was teething, its windows blown out and inventory scattered like confetti across the broken pavement.

The silence may have been the most unsettling part of their journey. Hong Kong had always been a city full of sounds: vendors shouting their wares, children playing in alleys, and the constant hum of commerce that signaled a busy port. Now, those familiar sounds were replaced by the occasional rumble of military vehicles and the distant crack of rifle fire that cut through the morning air like a broken clock marking time in a world that no longer made sense.

The sharp smell of smoke lingered in the air, mingled with brick dust that coated everything in a thin gray film. David's weight felt heavier with each step, and Alicia could sense sweat forming under her arms despite the cool morning breeze.

They had been walking for nearly an hour when Patricia stumbled, her small legs finally giving out. Alicia knelt immediately, balancing David in one arm while steadying her daughter with the other, fully aware of how vulnerable they were in the open street.

"I'm tired, Mummy," Patricia whispered, her voice small and shaky.

"I know, darling. We're almost there." Alicia smoothed Patricia's tangled hair with gentle fingers, noting how much thinner her daughter's face had become over the past week. "*Tía* Mary is waiting for us. She'll have food and warm beds."

"Will Papa be there?" The question came out hopeful, and Alicia felt her chest tighten with the familiar combination of love and uncertainty that had become her constant companion.

"I don't know, sweetheart. But if he's not there yet, he will be soon. Papa is very smart, and he knows we need him." The words felt fragile even as she spoke them, but they were the only comfort she could offer.

Patricia nodded and struggled to her feet, taking her mother's hand again. "Okay, Mummy. I can walk more."

The sight of Mary's building, whole and untouched, felt like a miracle after the destruction they had seen. Alicia stood on the street corner for a long moment, just staring at the familiar structure with its unbroken windows and untouched roof tiles. It seemed impossible that anything could have survived the systematic bombing that had wrecked so much of the city, yet here was proof that some things lasted. "Look, Patricia," she said, her voice thick with relief. "*Tía* Mary's house is still here. The windows still have glass, and I can see lights inside."

But even as she spoke the words, Alicia sensed how fragile this hope was. Safety was a relative idea in a city under occupation, and any protection Mary's house might provide would only be temporary at best. Still, after days of uncertainty and fear, even fleeting safety felt like a priceless gift.

Lupe moved slowly beside them, her weathered hands gripping Alicia's arm for support. The journey had been especially tough for the older woman, but her presence offered a steadying force that helped Alicia keep her composure. "She prepared," Lupe observed, studying the building with the practiced eye of someone who had survived previous disasters. "Look at how the windows are covered, how carefully the front door is secured. Mary saw what was coming and made ready for it."

Alicia approached the front door carefully, hyperaware of how exposed they were standing on the street. She knocked softly using the signal they had created as kids, three quick knocks, then two, then one, a code from games played in their home in Hermosillo.

The silence that followed felt endless. Then Alicia heard it: the careful sound of multiple locks being undone, the cautious shuffle of feet on wooden floors. The door opened just a crack, revealing one dark eye peering out with the wariness of

Chapter 30: Safe Harbor

someone who had learned that survival depended on being careful about who you trusted.

"Alicia?" Mary's voice was barely a whisper, as if saying the name too loudly might shatter whatever magic had brought her sister to her door.

"It's us, Mary. Mama and the children and me. We need help," Alicia said exhausted.

The door flew open so suddenly that Alicia stumbled backwards. Mary stood there, changed by weeks of stress and isolation. Her normally neat appearance had shifted to practicality; her hair was pulled back in a simple bun, and she wore a faded house dress instead of her usual elegant clothes. Dark circles shadowed her eyes, and her face showed signs of weight loss, indicating voluntary rationing. Mary's hands shook as she reached for them. "*Dios mío,*" she breathed, her voice cracking. "I thought, Alicia, I was so afraid you were dead. I've been watching the street every day, hoping, but after the bombing got so bad..." Mary pulled them quickly inside, her movements gentle but urgent. The moment the door closed behind them, Alicia felt something in her chest loosen, a tension she hadn't even realized she was carrying.

The interior of Mary's apartment revealed the extent of her preparations. Every surface was covered with supplies: bags of rice, canned goods, bottles of water, medical supplies, even toys and books for children. She had turned her home into a fortress against catastrophe.

Mary wrapped her arms around Alicia carefully, mindful of David, who was pressed between them. Then she was on her knees, gathering Patricia into her arms while the little girl began to cry, not tears of fear this time, but tears of relief.

"*Tía* Mary," Patricia whispered against her aunt's shoulder. "I missed you. I missed you so much."

"I'm here, *mi niña,*" Mary murmured. "I'm here. You're safe now, all of you."

Lupe settled into a chair with visible relief, while Alicia remained standing, David still in her arms, taking in the miraculous normalcy of Mary's home. After days of uncertainty and fear, the sight of familiar furniture and family photographs felt like evidence that their previous life had been real. "You've been preparing for this," Lupe observed. "You saw what was coming."

Mary nodded, helping Patricia out of her thin coat. "I watched what happened after the Japanese landed. I could see which way things were headed. I spent every dollar I had on rice, canned goods, powdered milk for babies. I've been living like a hermit since Christmas Eve, rationing everything, hoping my family would find me."

The meal Mary made felt like a feast after days of eating shelter rations. Real rice with vegetables, fresh milk for David, and some preserved fruit that Patricia eagerly ate. As they ate, Alicia watched her children with a mix of relief and heartbreak. They were safe for now, well-fed and warm, but she could see how the past week had changed them. Patricia was quieter, more cautious, her usual chatter replaced by careful watchfulness. David seemed smaller somehow, as if the stress had stolen some of his baby fat and replaced it with premature seriousness.

"We can stay here, can't we?" Alicia asked, trying to keep the desperation out of her voice. "At least until we can figure out what's happened?"

"Of course," Mary replied immediately. "This is your home for as long as you need it. I have enough supplies to last us several weeks if we're careful."

That evening, as they settled into the first comfortable beds they had experienced in weeks, Alicia felt overwhelmed by conflicting emotions. Gratitude for Mary's generosity, relief at being safe and well-fed, but beneath it all was a constant, gnawing anxiety she couldn't suppress. They had found sanctuary, but they still felt incomplete. Somewhere in this wounded city, Bryn was either searching for them or beyond all searching. And until she knew which, this safety would remain fragile and temporary.

Chapter 31

The Weight of Silence

> *"The cruelest torture is not the infliction of pain, but the withholding of knowledge. To love someone whose fate remains unknown is to live suspended between hope and grief, unable to mourn and afraid to celebrate, trapped in a limbo that corrodes the soul one silent hour at a time."*

From "Letters to the Missing" by Dr. Carmen Rodriguez, 1947

During her first two days in Mary's sanctuary, Alicia realized that safety carried its own kind of suffering. Having been freed from the immediate fight for survival, her mind could now fully focus on the growing question that haunted every quiet moment: Where was Bryn?

The not-knowing had become a weight in her chest, pressing against her lungs and making each breath feel shallow. Eleven days. Eleven days since he'd kissed her goodbye on Christmas morning and walked out their front door with the confidence of a man who always comes back home. Eleven days of silence from someone whose dependability was the cornerstone of their marriage, whose punctuality was so reliable that she could set her watch by his arrivals.

The psychological impact was unlike anything she had gone through before, even during the terrifying days of bombing and displacement. Grief followed a structure: rituals of mourning, stages of acceptance, and a community of sympathy that acknowledged loss. Fear had a sense of urgency: immediate threats that required action, clear choices between safety and danger. But this pause between hope and despair had no set rules, no established route through the wilderness of uncertainty.

Alicia found herself developing troubling habits of thought. She would catch herself listening for his footsteps on Mary's stairs, holding her breath whenever men's voices echoed in the street below. She created detailed scenarios where he would appear at the door with logical reasons for his absence, then moments later, she found herself mentally rehearsing what to say to Patricia about why Papa was never coming home.

The constant cycling between these emotional states was more exhausting than physical deprivation. Her body could recover from hunger and cold, but her mind was wearing itself thin on unanswered questions.

She started noticing small changes in herself that alarmed her. Her hands trembled constantly now, a fine tremor that made simple tasks like buttoning Patricia's dress or spooning porridge into David's mouth require focus. She would begin sentences and lose track of what she was saying halfway through, her thoughts scattering like leaves in the wind. Sleep, when it arrived, brought dreams where Bryn was always just around the next corner, always calling her name from another room she could never quite reach.

During the day, she could lose herself in the rhythms of caring for her children. The simple mechanics of daily life provided anchor points in the drift of uncertainty. Washing faces, preparing meals from Mary's carefully hoarded supplies, and reading stories from books that smelled faintly of lavender and better times all helped ground her. But in quiet moments, when Patricia napped and David played contentedly with toys he hadn't seen in weeks, the silence would expand to fill the space where her husband should have been.

"You're not sleeping," Mary observed on their second morning, settling beside Alicia at the kitchen table. Steam rose from their cups of real tea, another small miracle of Mary's foresight. The porcelain was delicate against Alicia's palms, thin enough that she could feel the warmth through the cup's walls, a sensation that seemed almost foreign after weeks of metal camping cups and uncertain water.

"I close my eyes," Alicia replied, noting absently how the bones in her hands now showed through skin that had grown translucent from stress. "I rest. But sleep feels like giving up somehow. Like if I stop watching and waiting, I might miss him coming home."

Mary's face showed the careful expression of someone trying to provide comfort without offering false hope. "This not-knowing is eating you alive. I can see it in your face, in the way you hold yourself."

The observation was sharp and painful because it was accurate. Alicia had caught glimpses of herself in Mary's mirror: a woman she barely recognized, gaunt and brittle, aging years in the space of weeks.

"What am I supposed to do, Mary? How am I supposed to act when I don't know if my husband is alive or dead? When I don't know if I should be hoping for his return or preparing for widowhood?" The questions burst out with mounting desperation. "I watch Patricia playing with her toys, and part of me thinks I should tell her that Papa might not be coming back, that she needs to prepare herself. But then I think, what if he's alive and searching for us right now? What if I destroy her faith in his return just days before he walks through that door?"

Chapter 31: The Weight of Silence

Mary reached across the table and took her sister's hands, feeling how thin they had become, how the wedding ring now slipped loose around Alicia's finger.

"And David," Alicia continued, her voice breaking, "he's so young he barely remembers what his father looks like. If Bryn is dead, David will grow up with no memories of the man who sang him to sleep every night. But if Bryn is alive and I start acting like he's dead, am I betraying both of them?"

The impossible mathematics of hope and despair had become Alicia's daily calculation. Mary could see her sister fragmenting under the pressure of holding contradictory emotional states while trying to make decisions that might determine her children's future well-being.

"There's something else," Alicia said, her voice dropping to barely above a whisper. "Something I haven't told you because I'm ashamed of thinking it."

Mary waited, understanding that some confessions required patience.

"Part of me is angry at him." The words came out in a rush, as if she needed to expel them before she lost courage. "I know it's not rational, I know it's not fair, but I'm angry that he left us to face this alone. I'm angry that he made promises about always coming home and then disappeared without explanation. I'm angry that he's made me into someone who doesn't know whether to hope or grieve."

The admission hung between them, weighted with guilt that Alicia had carried alone. Being angry at someone who might be dead felt like a betrayal of everything she believed about love and loyalty. But the anger was real, and denying it was using energy she couldn't spare. "And then I feel terrible for being angry," she continued, tears beginning to flow freely now, "because if he's lying wounded somewhere, if he's trying to get back to us and can't, then my anger is just another burden he doesn't deserve. But if he's dead, then I'm angry at a ghost, and that feels even worse."

Mary gripped her sister's hands more tightly, feeling that Alicia's mental strength was about to give way. The stress from the bombing, displacement, caring for two young children, and now the overwhelming uncertainty about Bryn—it was more than anyone should have to endure. "You're not terrible for being angry," Mary said firmly. "You're human. You're a woman who has been abandoned in the middle of a war with two babies to protect, and you don't know why. Anger is a reasonable response to an unreasonable situation."

But even Mary's understanding couldn't resolve the core problem that was eroding Alicia's ability to function. The uncertainty was becoming intolerable, affecting her capacity to be the mother her children needed.

On their third morning in Mary's house, as golden morning light filtered through curtains that had somehow survived the bombing, Alicia made a decision that had been building despite every argument against it. "I have to try to find him," she announced, settling David on her hip while Patricia arranged wooden blocks into careful towers on the sitting room floor. "I can't live with this uncertainty anymore. I need to know what happened to Bryn."

Mary's reaction was immediate and worried. "Alicia, absolutely not. The streets are more dangerous than you can imagine. The Japanese are conducting systematic searches for British nationals. You'd be walking right into the hands of people who want to arrest you."

"But what if he's lying in some hospital ward, wondering where his family is?" Alicia continued, her voice gaining strength as she articulated thoughts that had been tormenting her for days. "What if he's trapped somewhere, unable to get word to us? What if he's been taken prisoner and is depending on me to find him?"

The conversation showed how uncertainty had started to cloud Alicia's judgment. Her logical mind knew that going into occupied Hong Kong would be suicidal, but her emotional stress was overwhelming her ability to think clearly about danger and consequences.

"Listen to me," Mary said, reaching for Alicia's free hand with an urgency that spoke of genuine fear for her sister's safety. "I understand your need to act, your need to do something rather than just wait. But think about what you're risking. If you're captured, what happens to Patricia and David? How does it help Bryn if you disappear too and leave the children orphaned?"

The argument was logical and devastating. Alicia's primary responsibility was to her children, and any action that endangered her also threatened their survival. But the psychological toll of inaction felt nearly unbearable.

"Then what am I supposed to do?" Alicia asked, her voice carrying the desperation of someone trapped between impossible choices. "How am I supposed to just sit here wondering whether the man I love is alive or dead? How am I supposed to make decisions about our future when I don't know if there's going to be a future that includes him?"

Mary saw her sister balanced on the edge of a precipice, caught between hope and despair, reason and reckless action. The uncertainty about Bryn's fate was eroding Alicia's ability to function, but acting out of that desperation would almost certainly lead to capture and separation from her children. "Give it a few more days," Mary pleaded. "Let the situation stabilize. Maybe we'll hear something, maybe someone will bring news. In a few days, we might have a better understanding of which areas are safe, which hospitals are still functioning."

Alicia wanted to argue, to rush out into the streets immediately and start searching every hospital, shelter, and government office where Bryn might be held. But she looked at David sleeping peacefully in her arms for the first time in weeks,

Chapter 31: The Weight of Silence

at Patricia finally playing with the focused attention that showed she felt safe, and knew Mary was right. "Two days," she said finally, her voice carrying the stubborn determination that Mary recognized from childhood. "I'll give it two more days. But then, Mary, I have to try to find him. I can't live with myself if I don't at least try. The not-knowing is killing me slowly."

"Not alone," Mary said quietly. "If you're determined to do this, we'll figure out how to do it as safely as possible. We'll plan it properly, gather information, minimize the risks. But I won't let you go out there by yourself."

That evening, as shadows gathered in the corners of Mary's sitting room and they prepared for what they hoped would be another peaceful night, their sanctuary received an unexpected visitor. Mary's Chinese servant Lin appeared in the doorway, his face tight with barely controlled anxiety. "Madam," he said, his English more formal than usual, "I need to tell you something urgent. There are military trucks and Japanese soldiers three streets over, moving systematically from house to house. They appear to be conducting organized searches, and they're heading in this direction."

The words settled into their cozy evening like stones dropped into still water, sending ripples of fear across the room. Mary moved quickly to the window, pulling back the curtain just enough to peer into the darkening night. In the distance, they could all hear it now. The rumble of engines growing steadily louder, punctuated by the sharp sound of boots on pavement and occasional shouts in Japanese.

"How long do we have?" Alicia asked, her voice steady despite the fear that was making her hands shake.

Lin's expression was grim, the look of someone who had been watching this process unfold across the city. "But madam, you should know: they're not just conducting general searches. They appear to be looking for specific people. Specific families."

The sanctuary they had found was about to come to an end. Their time of waiting, of hoping, of pretending the war might pass them by, was over. Whatever came next would determine not just their immediate fate, but possibly their chances of ever reuniting with Bryn.

Alicia pulled her children closer, feeling the familiar surge of protective instinct that had kept her moving through every crisis of the past weeks. The question of Bryn's fate would have to wait. The uncertainty that had been tormenting her would be set aside in favor of immediate survival. Whatever happened, they would face it together. And somewhere in this wounded city, she had to believe that Bryn was alive and would find them, no matter where they were taken or how impossible the search seemed.

Chapter 32

The Roundup

"They came with clipboards and categories, sorting human lives into neat administrative columns. What struck me most was not their cruelty, but their efficiency. How quickly love becomes a logistical problem when viewed through the lens of occupation."

From "Witness Accounts: Hong Kong Under Siege," compiled by the Red Cross, 1943

The soldiers arrived at dawn, their approach precise and methodical, as if they'd done this countless times. Alicia woke to the distant sound of truck engines, steadily getting closer like approaching thunder, and she knew immediately that their brief refuge was coming to an end.

Mary was already at the window, her face pale in the gray morning light as she watched the convoy move through their neighborhood. "They're stopping at every house with foreign residents," she whispered, her voice tight with fear. "Lin was right. This isn't random. They have lists."

Alicia sat up carefully, mindful of David sleeping against her chest, and felt the familiar surge of protective instinct that had become her main emotional drive. Whatever was about to happen, she would face it with as much dignity as she could muster for her children's sake. Her hands moved automatically to check David's breathing and to smooth his hair—small gestures of protection that had become unconscious habits.

Patricia was awake too, though she lay still and silent beside her mother, her large brown eyes reflecting an understanding that had aged her far beyond her four years. She had learned to read the subtle signs of adult fear, how voices change pitch and movements become more careful. The bombing had taught her that silence could mean survival.

"Mummy," she whispered, her voice barely audible, "are the soldiers coming for us?"

The question was asked with such careful control that Alicia felt her heart break all over again. Patricia was trying to be brave, trying to make it easier for the adults around her by not showing the terror that must be be running through her small body.

"I don't know yet, darling," Alicia said honestly, smoothing Patricia's hair with gentle repetition. "But whatever happens, we'll face it together. Remember what I've taught you about being brave?"

Patricia nodded solemnly. "Being brave doesn't mean not being scared. Doesn't it mean also, mama, doing what you have to do anyway?"

"That's exactly right, sweetheart. And you've been so brave already, braver than most grown-ups I know," Alicia said.

The sound of boots on stairs echoed through the building, accompanied by sharp voices speaking Japanese and the occasional cry of fear or protest from other apartments. Each sound felt like a countdown, marking time until their turn arrived. Alicia found herself noting details of Mary's sitting room: the way morning light fell across the worn carpet, the faint scent of jasmine tea still lingering in the air, the particular creak of the floorboards near the kitchen door. She wanted to remember this space that had sheltered them, however briefly.

Lupe emerged from the kitchen, her weathered face set with a calm determination that had carried her through decades of crisis. She had been awake for hours, preparing whatever food she could and organizing their few possessions in case they needed to leave quickly. Her movements were deliberate and economical, the actions of someone who had learned to function under pressure.

"The children should eat something," she said quietly, settling into a chair near Alicia with the careful movements of someone whose joints protested every motion. "Whatever comes today, they need their strength."

It was such a grandmotherly thing to say, so perfectly practical and loving, that Alicia felt tears threaten despite her efforts to stay composed. In a world where everything familiar had been taken away, Lupe's insistence on maintaining basic care felt like an act of defiance against chaos itself.

Mary continued her vigil at the window, her usual elegant composure replaced by the tense alertness of someone who knew that their next few hours could decide everything. She held the curtain back just far enough to observe without being obvious, her posture stiff with focus. "They're being thorough," she reported quietly. "Taking time with each apartment, checking documentation, making lists. This is going to take a while."

The delay was both a blessing and a curse. It gave them more time to prepare emotionally, but also allowed fear to grow and multiply in the confined space of waiting. David stirred against Alicia's chest, making small sounds that suggested he

Chapter 32: The Roundup

was waking, and she began the familiar routine of gentle touches and soft humming that usually kept him calm.

When the knock finally sounded, it wasn't a polite tap of a social visitor but the forceful, commanding beat of authority demanding immediate response. Three sharp knocks that seemed to reverberate through the apartment like gunshots, followed by stern voices speaking rapid Japanese.

Mary looked at Lin, who had been waiting near the door with the patient resignation of someone who understood his role in the upcoming drama. He nodded and stepped forward to answer, his movements deliberate and cautious as he approached what might be the end of their temporary safety.

Alicia could hear Lin speaking in Cantonese, his voice calm and respectful as he addressed whoever was outside their door. The conversation was brief, conducted in the careful diplomatic language that had become necessary for survival in occupied Hong Kong. Then the voices grew sharper, more insistent, and she heard the unmistakable sound of the door being pushed open despite Lin's polite resistance.

They were inside.

The soldiers who entered moved with practiced efficiency, their movements showing men who had performed this type of operation many times before. Their uniforms were clean but bore the signs of active service, and their expressions carried the businesslike focus of professionals executing a plan they knew well. They spread through the main room with military precision, positioning themselves to control all exits while their leader assessed the situation.

The officer in charge seemed to be in his thirties, with sharp eyes that surveyed every detail of the room and its occupants. His gaze shifted from Lin to Mary to Lupe, briefly pausing on each face as he observed features and made mental notes. There was nothing personal in his inspection, nothing indicating he saw them as individuals rather than categories to group.

David whimpered softly upon seeing the uniformed strangers, and Alicia instinctively pulled him closer, one hand gently cupping his head against her shoulder where he couldn't see the rifles and stern faces that had suddenly filled their sanctuary. Patricia pressed against her leg, her small body trembling with the effort of staying silent as she had promised.

The officer's examination was thorough and detached, his focus finally resting on Alicia and the children with a calculating look that hinted he was categorizing them in his mind. She could almost imagine him taking mental notes, comparing them against whatever criteria he had been given for this operation.

He spoke to his subordinates in rapid Japanese, words that Alicia couldn't understand but whose tone suggested discussion and decision-making. Then he addressed the room in English that was functional despite its careful pronunciation.

"All persons present will show identification documents. Now."

Mary stepped forward with the dignity that years of colonial social life had instilled in her, her upbringing showing even in this moment of powerlessness. "I am Mary Valenzuela. This is my residence." She moved to the sideboard with careful composure, retrieved her passport from the drawer where she had placed it in preparation for this situation, and handed it to the officer.

The officer examined the documents with professional thoroughness, his eyes shifting between Mary's face and the photograph in her passport while he spoke to one of his men in Japanese. Alicia could see him noting Mary's features, making judgments based on appearance and documentation that would determine her immediate fate.

"Documents for all residents," he said, his voice cutting through the room's tense silence.

Alicia stepped forward slightly, David's familiar weight in her arms giving her a sense of purpose amid the swirling uncertainty. "My home on Barker Road was destroyed in the bombing," she explained, her voice as steady as she could keep it. "All our identification papers were destroyed in the attack."

The explanation was accurate but seemed inadequate given the circumstances. She watched the officer's face for any sign of sympathy or understanding, but his expression stayed neutral, focused on categorization rather than the human tragedy behind their missing documents.

The officer's scrutiny grew sharper as he examined Alicia's appearance, noticing her lighter skin, the shape of her features, and how she carried herself and spoke. Years of living in colonial Hong Kong had taught her to recognize when someone was making assumptions about her background, social status, or her place in the racial hierarchy that had defined their world before. Then his attention shifted to Lupe, and Alicia watched as he examined her mother's clearly indigenous Mexican features and reached whatever conclusion his training had prepared him to make about her nationality and importance to his mission.

"State your name and relationship," he said to Alicia, pulling a small notebook from his breast pocket.

"I am Alicia Williams. Lupe is my mother, and Mary is my sister. I am married to Bryn Williams, who serves as Deputy Chief Sanitation Officer for the Hong Kong government. These are our children, Patricia and David."

The explanation seemed both completely accurate and utterly insufficient.

Chapter 32: The Roundup

Bryn's role with the colonial administration, once a source of pride and security, now made her family targets for whatever policies the occupation authorities decided to enforce regarding former government officials and their families.

The officer's questions were asked in careful English, but their intent was unmistakably clear. Where was her husband currently? What exactly was his role in the colonial government? How long had she lived in Hong Kong? Were the children considered British subjects? Alicia answered honestly, her voice steady despite the fear that made her hands shake, while David pressed against her shoulder and Patricia stayed pressed against her leg like a small, frightened shadow.

Throughout the interrogation, she kept studying the officer's face for clues about his intentions, trying to interpret the bureaucratic calculations that would decide their fate. His expression stayed professionally neutral, revealing nothing about the decisions being made or the criteria being used. He wrote in his notebook with the mechanical precision of someone filling out forms, turning their lives into administrative data.

Finally, he stepped back and addressed his men in rapid Japanese. The conversation was brief but seemed to involve some kind of consultation or confirmation. Then he turned back to face the room, his expression unchanged as he delivered his verdict.

"You," he said, pointing directly at Alicia with the kind of certainty that suggested the decision had been predetermined rather than made in the moment. "You and your children will come with us. British subjects must report for registration and processing."

Alicia's heart started pounding against her ribs, but she had been mentally preparing for this possibility since the soldiers entered. Her marriage to Bryn alone would have marked her as someone the occupation authorities wanted to control, and her own background only strengthened their resolve to include her in whatever system they were implementing.

" All British subjects must be processed. No exceptions," the officer repeated curtly.

The words seemed to reverberate in the sudden silence that followed. Alicia felt the world tilt around her, as if the ground had become unstable beneath her feet. She had mentally prepared for internment, even accepting that she might be separated from Mary and Lupe. But the thought of Patricia and David being dragged into whatever system the Japanese had built to control civilian populations felt like a violation of every natural law meant to protect children from the consequences of adult conflicts.

"Please," Alicia said quickly, her voice rising despite her efforts to remain calm, "the children are too young for any kind of registration. They need care, they need..."

"Children will come," the officer snapped, his tone carrying the finality of someone who was not interested in negotiation or discussion. "Orders must be followed. No exceptions."

Mary stepped forward, her voice urgent with the desperation of someone watching her family be torn apart. "Sir, please consider that the children are Mexican citizens through their grandmother. They shouldn't be classified as British subjects requiring registration."

The officer's cold stare silenced her protest before it could gain momentum. "Children of British father are British subjects under occupation law. All will be processed. You and elderly woman will remain here. Not required for registration."

The racial categories that once defined colonial Hong Kong were being reshaped by the occupation authorities, creating new hierarchies that separated families along lines that had previously been just biographical details. Alicia felt a piercing clarity as understanding washed over her: she and her children were being sorted into one category, while Mary and Lupe were placed in another, based purely on assumptions about blood and belonging that had nothing to do with love or family ties.

"May I bring supplies for the children?" Alicia asked, her voice barely controlled as she struggled to focus on practical concerns rather than the panic that was building in her chest like flood water.

The officer nodded curtly. "Twenty minutes. Essential items only. No delays."

As soldiers spread through the apartment to conduct their search, Alicia knelt beside her children, David still clinging to her while Patricia watched with eyes that held far too much understanding for someone not yet four years old. The little girl had stopped trembling and now stood with the stillness that comes when children realize that resistance is futile.

Alicia's hands moved swiftly but carefully as she gathered their belongings, each choice weighed with the knowledge that what she selected now could determine their comfort and survival in whatever place they were being taken. She packed a change of clothes for each child and herself, diapers for David, the precious powdered milk that Mary had saved, and Patricia's small doll that had somehow survived every crisis. Her journal, in which she had been writing letters to Bryn, was placed in her smaller bag along with the little money she had remaining.

"We're going on another journey," Alicia told Patricia, her voice as calm as she could make it while her heart hammered against her ribs with the force of terror and protective instinct combined. "Just the three of us for now. We need to be

Chapter 32: The Roundup

very brave and very quiet, just like we practiced."

"What about *Tía* Mary?" Patricia's voice was so small it barely carried across the space between them. "What about *Abuela* Lupe?"

Alicia's throat constricted with the effort of not breaking down completely in front of her daughter. "They have to stay here and take care of the apartment. But we'll see them again soon." The lie tasted like poison on her tongue, but it was the only comfort she could offer. "And remember what I told you about Papa? He'll find us wherever we are. Papa is very smart, and he loves us more than anything in the world."

Patricia nodded with the solemn acceptance of a child who had learned that adult promises were fragile and easily broken by forces beyond anyone's control. But she reached out and took her mother's hand with a trust that was both heartbreaking and empowering.

Mary and Lupe stood watching, tears streaming down their faces in silent flows that revealed grief too profound for words. The soldiers' decision was based solely on appearance and documentation: Alicia's European features and marriage to a British official marked her for internment, while Mary and Lupe's darker skin and Mexican heritage offered them protection from this particular fate.

"Alicia," Mary whispered, her voice breaking with the weight of watching her sister disappear into an uncertain fate, "I'm so sorry. This isn't right. Families shouldn't be separated like this."

"You saved us when we had nowhere else to go," Alicia replied firmly, though her own tears were falling now, hot tracks down her cheeks that she couldn't stop. She shifted David to one arm so she could embrace Mary briefly, desperately. "Take care of each other."

With the few minutes remaining, Alicia took paper and pen and wrote a message to Bryn. "I believe Bryn will look for us here. Tell him what happened, and give him this letter," she said, handing it to Mary.

"Yes, I will Alicia, and we'll tell him what happened," Mary replied.

When the twenty minutes were up, the officer reappeared with the punctuality of someone for whom efficiency was a matter of professional pride. "Time finished. Come now."

Alicia stood, with David secured in her arms, and Patricia's small hand tightly in her own. As they approached the door, she could hear voices from the street outside: other families being separated, children crying, and women trying to hold their composure for those who depended on them.

Outside, the harsh January air bit at their faces with a cold that felt like it carried the weight of winter and war together. The gray sky pressed down on them like a physical burden, and the familiar sounds of Hong Kong had been replaced by the mechanical noise of military operations. A military truck waited at the curb, its canvas covering flapping in the wind like the wings of a mechanical predator. Other civilians were already seated in the back: women with children, elderly couples, single men, all sharing the same look of fear mixed with resignation, understanding their powerlessness.

David started crying as the cold wind hit his face, his tiny voice joining the chorus of distress filling the air around the truck. Alicia quickly wrapped her coat around him, using her body to shield him from the worst of the weather while Patricia squeezed her hand with desperate strength.

"Mummy, I'm scared," Patricia whispered, her voice nearly lost in the wind and the general commotion.

"I know, darling," Alicia replied, her voice steady despite the fear that was threatening to overwhelm her. "But we're together, and that's what matters most. And remember, Papa will find us. He promised he would always find us, no matter where we are."

A soldier helped Alicia climb into the truck bed with practical movements rather than gentle ones, then lifted Patricia up afterward. David's cries grew louder as they sat down on the rough wooden bench, his small body trembling with cold, fear, and the increasing hunger that had become their constant struggle.

Alicia arranged herself carefully, trying to shield both children from the wind while generating as much warmth as possible with their limited clothing. She started humming softly to David, the same Mexican lullabies her mother had sung to her, while gently stroking Patricia's hair, the repetitive motion always offering comfort.

As the truck started to move, Alicia took one last look at Mary's house through the truck's canvas opening. At the window, she saw Mary and Lupe watching behind the curtains, their faces filled with grief and helplessness that would stay with her. They were alone now, three family members torn apart by forces beyond their control or understanding. But they were alive, together, and somewhere in this wounded city, Alicia had to believe that Bryn was searching for them with the same desperate determination that would carry her through whatever lay ahead.

The truck rumbled through Hong Kong's streets, past shuttered shops and bombed-out buildings, past groups of Japanese soldiers on patrol, past the remnants of the life they all knew before the world changed overnight. But Alicia no longer saw the destruction as proof of an end. She saw it as the terrain Bryn would search across until he found them.

That hope would have to sustain them through whatever came next.

Chapter 33

Searching the Ruins

"Love in wartime becomes both navigation and destination. When the familiar world has been erased, when every landmark has been destroyed, the heart becomes the only reliable compass pointing toward what must not be lost."

From "Finding Home in Chaos: Personal Narratives of the Hong Kong Occupation," by Dr. Elena Vasquez

The discharge papers from Queen Mary Hospital crumpled in Bryn's hand as he pushed through the heavy doors into Hong Kong sunlight that felt different from anything he remembered. Three weeks of forced inactivity in that narrow hospital bed had been torture for a man whose family was missing somewhere in the chaos of occupation. The doctors had been inflexible about his recovery time. Now, finally released, he felt the crushing weight of lost time like a physical burden.

The city that greeted him wore the face of his former home but moved like a stranger. Streets he had walked confidently for six years as Deputy Chief Sanitation Officer now required navigation by stealth and memory. Japanese soldiers moved through familiar neighborhoods with mechanical precision. Their boots echoed off broken pavement in rhythms that communicated absolute authority. Their eyes scanned every face with the calculation of men who knew they were surrounded by potential enemies.

Bryn pulled his hat low and adopted the posture of defeat that seemed expected of Hong Kong's civilian population. Each step toward Barker Road felt like a prayer whispered in desperation, though he tried to prepare himself for what he might find there. Jason Lam had told him during one of his hospital visits that the house had been destroyed. Hearing about destruction and witnessing it were entirely different forms of devastation.

The journey revealed the scope of the bombing. Entire blocks had been reduced to rubble, their former purposes unrecognizable except for occasional fragments. A child's toy buried in concrete. A family photograph fluttering from a tree branch. A cooking pot sitting intact amid what had once been someone's kitchen.

But the silence disturbed him most. Hong Kong had always been a symphony of urban life. Vendors calling their wares, children playing in alleys, the constant hum of commerce and conversation that marked a thriving port city. Now the familiar rhythms had been replaced by the occasional rumble of military vehicles and an underlying quiet that spoke of a population learning to make itself invisible.

When he finally reached his neighborhood, Bryn had to stop and orient himself using landmarks that no longer existed. Street signs had been replaced with Japanese characters. So many buildings had been destroyed that the very geography of the area had been altered. He found himself using the placement of trees and the contours of the land to navigate toward what had once been his home.

The elegant colonial house where Alicia had arranged fresh flowers every morning, where Patricia had played with her dolls in the garden while David napped in his crib, where they had shared countless meals and quiet evenings was gone. In its place stood a crater filled with twisted metal and charred timber.

Bryn's knees gave way and he crumpled to the ground. "Oh, no…no…"

Memory flooded through him. He could see Alicia in their kitchen on Christmas morning, humming while she prepared breakfast, sunlight streaming through windows that no longer existed. He could hear Patricia's laughter echoing from the garden where she had chased butterflies between flowers that were now ash. He could feel the weight of David in his arms during their evening walks around the property, the baby's small hand gripping his finger with unconscious trust.

The loss was personal in a way he hadn't anticipated. This wasn't just the destruction of property. This was the obliteration of the physical spaces where his family's happiness had been created and sustained. Every room held memories now accessible only through the painful process of remembrance.

But Jason had been clear during his hospital visits. The family had not been in the house when the bomb fell. They had made it to the air raid shelter, had survived the initial bombing, had been alive when last seen. This destruction, complete as it was, didn't mean they were dead. It meant their refuge had been destroyed, but they had found refuge elsewhere.

Bryn forced himself to stand and begin searching through the wreckage. If his family had returned to the house after the bombing, if they had been caught here during a subsequent attack, there would be evidence. He had to know. The rubble was treacherous, shifting under his weight as he picked his way through what had once been rooms filled with love and laughter. His injured shoulder protested every movement, sending sharp reminders down his arm and into his ribs. The pain was nothing compared to the emotional weight of searching through the remains of his previous life. The dining room where they had celebrated Patricia's third birthday was now an open pit. The nursery where he had read bedtime stories while Alicia nursed David had been erased so completely that he couldn't determine where it had been. The sitting room where they had entertained friends was marked only by a fragment of their sofa, its fabric burned beyond recognition. But in the area that had once housed their servants' quarters, he found what he had been dreading.

The bodies were barely recognizable after weeks of exposure, but love provided recognition that transcended physical identification. Ah Min's brass spectacles caught the afternoon light like a beacon. Mrs. Wu's jade bracelet lay beside what remained of hands that had prepared countless meals with love and skill. And there, weighted down by debris but still visible, was a fragment of Mei Lin's blue cotton dress.

Bryn collapsed beside them. His shoulders shook.

These weren't just employees who had worked for his family. They had been the foundation of his household's daily happiness, people he had come to love and respect over years of shared meals and celebrations and the quiet intimacy of domestic life. Ah-Min had been the wise one, full of stories about old China and patient advice about everything about life. He had taught Bryn more about dignity and resilience than any formal education could provide. Mrs. Wu had treated them all like her own children, fussing over their health and happiness with fierce protectiveness. Her dumplings had been legendary among their neighbors. Her concern for Patricia and David had been constant and genuine. And Mei-Lin. Barely twenty-four years old. She had possessed the kind of gentle spirit that made everyone around her feel more hopeful about the world. She had giggled at Patricia's attempts to speak Cantonese and spent endless patient hours teaching her Chinese characters, treating the little girl like a beloved younger sister.

They deserved better than to be forgotten casualties of someone else's conflict.

"I'm so sorry," he whispered to the ruins. His voice broke. "You deserved to live long lives, to see your grandchildren grow up, to die peacefully in your beds surrounded by family who loved you." He remained there until the sun began to set, building small stone cairns over each spot where they lay. The work was physically demanding. His hands bled from moving sharp rubble. His shoulder screamed with each lifted stone. But it felt necessary, a ritual that honored their service and his grief while providing the kind of structure that loss requires to become bearable.

For Ah-Min, he constructed a dignified mound of stones and placed the old man's spectacles on top as a marker that would catch the light. For Mrs. Wu, he arranged her jade bracelet among carefully selected stones, creating a shrine that honored both the woman who had worn it and the grandmother who had given it to her. Mei-Lin's grave he marked with the fragment of her blue dress, weighted down with smooth stones so it would flutter in the wind like a prayer flag. As he worked, he spoke to them quietly, making promises he wasn't sure he could keep but needed to make nonetheless. "I will find your families. I will tell them how much you meant to us, how you died as part of our family. They will know that you were honored in our house and that you are honored still."

The air raid shelter on lower Barker Road was his next destination, though he suspected it would yield no more information than Jason had already provided. The concrete structure stood intact, but it felt like a tomb when he entered it. Stale air thick with the smell of fear and unwashed bodies filled his lungs. His ribs ached with each breath. Empty water buckets sat in corners. Scattered belongings told the story of families who had abandoned this refuge for something that seemed safer. He called their names softly, his voice echoing off concrete walls.

"Alicia! Patricia! David! It's Papa!"

Only silence answered.

The anger came then, sudden and hot. Why hadn't anyone left a message? Why hadn't Alicia scratched something into the walls, left some sign of where they had gone? But the anger dissolved just as quickly. She had been terrified. The children had been crying. She had been doing the best she could with impossible choices.

As darkness began to fall, Bryn noticed a flicker of candlelight in the distance, coming from the direction of what had been the Richardsons' house. The sight of that small flame in so much darkness felt like a miracle. Proof that someone had survived.

The approach required careful navigation through rubble. But as he drew closer, he could see that someone was living in the partially destroyed structure. Hope began to build in his chest. "Hello?" he called softly. "Is anyone there?"

A curtain moved at what remained of a window. Moments later the door opened to reveal Li Wong, one of the Richardsons' servants. Her face, which he remembered as perpetually cheerful, was gaunt and shadowed by weeks of survival under impossible conditions. But she recognized him immediately. Her eyes widened. "Master Bryn!" She pressed her hand to her mouth. "You are alive! When you didn't come home, when the bombs fell, we thought..." She shook her head. "We all thought you were dead."

Relief flooded through him at seeing a familiar face. Li Wong had always been popular among the neighborhood children, known for her kindness and her willingness to help with small emergencies. "Li Chen, thank God you survived." He stepped closer, lowering his voice. "My family. Alicia, the children, Lupe. Have you seen them? Do you know where they went?"

Chapter 33: Searching the Ruins

Her expression shifted immediately. She twisted her hands in a gesture he remembered from times when she had accidentally broken something valuable.

"Please," he said. "I need to know everything."

She looked around nervously, then opened the door wider. "Come inside. Not safe to talk in the street."

The interior of the Richardson's' house was dim, lit only by the single candle. She led him to what remained of the sitting room and gestured for him to sit. "They came here after the bombing," she said quietly. "Madam Alicia, she was very scared. The children, they were crying."

"When was this? How long ago?"

"Three days after Christmas, maybe four. Little Patricia, she kept asking for Papa." Li Chen's voice softened. "She kept saying, 'When will Papa come home? Is Papa hurt?' Madam Alicia, she didn't know what to tell her."

The image of Patricia crying for him was almost unbearable. He had promised his daughter that he would always come home. The broken promise felt like a wound. "They stayed here?" he asked.

"One night only. Madam Alicia's sister Mary, she lives on Wellington Street. Madam Alicia, she said they must go there, be safe with family."

Bryn leaned forward. "Did she say anything else? Did she leave any message in case I came looking?"

"She said..." Li Chen hesitated. "She said if you were alive, you would find them. That you always kept your promises." Her eyes filled with tears. "But Mr. Bryn, you must be very careful now. Japanese soldiers, they come to many houses. Taking British people, taking anyone they think might be troublemaker."

"What do you mean, taking them where?"

"We Chinese servants, we share information about these things. We try to warn people." She lowered her voice further. "They make all British people register. Some they let go home. Some they take away in trucks. We don't know where."

Ice went through his veins. A woman married to a colonial government official, with two half British children, would be exactly the kind of person the occupation authorities would want to control.

"When did they start these roundups?"

"Maybe one week ago. They post notices all over city. All British and European civilians must report to Murray Parade Grounds for registration." She looked at him with real fear in her eyes. "You should not go there, Mr. Bryn. They have lists.

They know names and positions from before the war. You were Deputy Chief Sanitation Officer. They will know this."

"I have to get to Mary's house," he said, standing despite the exhaustion pulling at him. "I have to find out if my family is there."

"Wait." Li Chen disappeared into the back of the house and returned with a bundle of clothes. "These belonged to Mr. Richardson. He was taller than you, but better you look like refugee than government official. Change your appearance. Walk different. Don't stand so straight."

She was right. His bearing, his way of speaking, even his posture marked him as someone who had held authority. Those same qualities that had once commanded respect now made him a target. "Thank you," he said, taking the clothes. "I won't forget this kindness."

"Just find your family, Master Bryn. And be careful."

The journey across Hong Kong to reach Central District took hours because he had to take a circuitous route through back alleys and bombed out buildings, avoiding the main thoroughfares where Japanese patrols maintained their surveillance. Every sound caused him to freeze against walls still warm from fires that had burned days earlier. The loose clothing Li Wong had given him chafed against his wounded shoulder. Sweat ran down his back despite the cool night air. His ribs ached with every careful step.

The city that had once felt like home now seemed designed to trap him. Streets he had walked confidently for six years now required navigation by stealth and fear. The Hong Kong of afternoon tea and cricket matches and orderly colonial administration had been replaced by something altogether more dangerous. When he finally reached Mary's neighborhood, his heart was pounding so loudly he could barely hear his own footsteps. The area had suffered less damage than his own district, but signs of occupation were everywhere. Japanese language signs posted on buildings. Military vehicles parked at strategic corners. The general atmosphere of a population learning to live under foreign authority.

Mary's apartment building still stood intact. Bryn felt his knees go weak at the sight of unbroken windows and an undamaged roof. Light flickered behind curtains. Someone was home. He approached the front door with a mixture of hope and terror. Using the coded rhythm that Alicia would recognize from their courtship days, he knocked. Three quick taps, then two, then one. They had created this signal during their early days together, a private joke about secret meetings that had become a permanent fixture of their relationship.

For a moment, nothing happened. Then he heard careful footsteps approaching, the cautious movement of someone who had learned not to trust unexpected visitors.

Chapter 33: Searching the Ruins

The door opened just a crack. Mary's eye appeared in the gap, brown and familiar but shadowed with wariness. For several seconds, she stared at him. "Bryn?" The word was so quiet he almost didn't hear it.

Then the door flew open and she was in his arms, sobbing against his chest. The familiar scent of her perfume brought back memories of family gatherings and holidays, of the normal life that had existed before. "Bryn, you're alive!" Mary's voice was muffled against his shirt. He could feel her tears soaking through the fabric. "We thought you were dead! Alicia waited and waited for you to come home. She couldn't get any information about what had happened to the government buildings, couldn't reach anyone who might know if you were safe or..."

Behind Mary, Lupe appeared. Tears streamed down her weathered face as she crossed herself and murmured thanks in Spanish. "*Dios mío*, Bryn, thank heaven you've come back to us." Lupe embraced him. "But you can't stay here long, *mijo*. The soldiers come through regularly, checking houses, asking questions. If they find you here..." Her embrace pressed against his wounded ribs. Bryn couldn't suppress a sharp intake of breath. "You're wounded," Lupe said immediately. Her maternal instincts took over as she pulled back to examine him. "What happened to you? Where have you been all this time?"

"Shrapnel from an explosion near Government House. I've been in Queen Mary Hospital for over three weeks. Unconscious for part of that time, then recovering. The doctors said I was fortunate."

"*Lo siento, mijo*. We had no way of knowing you were hurt." Lupe's hands fluttered over him with the instinctive need to heal.

"Where are Alicia and the children?" he asked.

The silence that fell over the room provided the answer he dreaded.

Mary's tears came harder. "The soldiers took them, Bryn."

His breath stopped.

"Three days ago," Mary continued. Her voice shook. "They came in the morning. Very polite at first. They said all British civilians had to come with them for registration and processing. They put Alicia and the children in trucks with other British families."

Each word hit him like a physical blow. Three days ago. While he had been lying in a hospital bed, growing stronger and planning his search, his family was being loaded into military vehicles. "Why didn't they take you?" he asked. "Why didn't they take you and Lupe?"

"They said only British and European civilians were required for registration."

Mary's voice carried the guilt of those who are spared when others are taken. "They looked at our papers. They looked at our faces. They decided our Mexican heritage meant we weren't included in their orders."

Alicia's European features and marriage to a British official had marked her for internment. Mary and Lupe's darker skin and Mexican citizenship had provided them with protection.

"Did they say where they were taking her?" His voice was barely under control.

"No specific destination." Mary wiped her eyes. "But several days before they came for Alicia, notices had been posted around the city. All British and European civilians were ordered to report to Murray Parade Grounds for registration. Alicia decided it was too dangerous to comply voluntarily."

"She was right to be afraid," Lupe said quietly.

"But it didn't matter in the end," Mary continued. "They found her anyway. They took the children too. I argued that Patricia and David were too young to be considered threats to anyone. The soldiers just ignored me."

Bryn sank into the nearest chair. His hands were shaking. While he had been unconscious and recovering, his wife had been making impossible decisions about their family's safety. She had tried to protect their children by avoiding the registration. The occupation authorities had been systematic in their search. "Tell me exactly what happened," he said. "From the beginning. I need to know everything."

Mary and Lupe exchanged glances. Then Mary sat down across from him. "They came at dawn. Four soldiers and an officer. The officer spoke some English. He was very polite, very formal. He said the Imperial Japanese Army required all British and European civilians to be registered for their own safety and protection."

"What did Alicia say?" Bryn asked

"She asked if she could have time to pack belongings for the children. The officer said they could bring one small bag each. Nothing more." Mary's voice broke. "Patricia was so scared, Bryn. She kept asking where they were going. If Papa would be there. Alicia told her you would find them soon. That Papa always found them when they got separated."

The image of his daughter's frightened face was unbearable.

"What about David? How was he?"

"Crying. Lupe had just fed him before the soldiers came. He was upset by all the commotion, all the strange voices. The soldiers guns." Lupe's tears fell freely now. "I tried to take him from Alicia, said I would keep him safe until this was over. The officer said no. Children must stay with mothers."

Chapter 33: Searching the Ruins

"Did they hurt anyone? Did they threaten?" Bryn asked.

"No," Mary said. "That's what made it so terrible. They were businesslike. Loading women and children into trucks like it was the most normal thing in the world."

"Did Alicia leave any message? Anything at all?" Bryn queried, barely holding his emotions in check.

Mary stood and went to a drawer. She pulled out a folded piece of paper and handed it to him with shaking hands. "She wrote this the night before. She seemed to know what was going to happen. She made me promise to give it to you if you came looking."

Bryn unfolded the paper. Alicia's familiar handwriting covered the page.

"My dearest Bryn,

If you are reading this, then you are alive and you have found your way to Mary's house. Thank God. We have been so worried about you, not knowing if you survived the bombing, if you were injured, if you were somewhere thinking we had abandoned you.

The soldiers are here now. They say we must go with them for registration. I don't trust this, but I have no choice. I have our children to think of, and they have made it clear that resistance is not possible.

Patricia asks for you constantly. She wants to know when Papa is coming home. I tell her soon. I tell her Papa always keeps his promises. Please let that be true.

David is too young to understand what is happening, but he senses my fear. I try to be brave for them, but inside I am terrified.

I need you to know that I love you. That whatever happens, wherever they take us, you are the first thought in my mind every morning and the last thought before I sleep. You are the compass that points me home.

Find us. I know you will try. But please, my love, be careful. Don't let them take you too. Our children need at least one parent to survive this.

All my love, forever, Alicia

P.S. Patricia wanted me to tell you that she still has the seashell you gave her from our trip to Repulse Bay. She carries it everywhere. She says it reminds her of Papa's voice, how you held it to her ear and told her the ocean was saying hello."

Bryn read the letter three times. His vision blurred. The seashell. He remembered that day perfectly. Patricia had been two years old, delighted by everything she saw. She had held that shell to her ear for hours, insisting she could hear the ocean talking to her. "I have to find out where they took them," he said. His voice sounded distant to his own ears. "I need to get to my office, contact Dr.

Wellington if possible. He might know something about where they're holding civilian internees. He has connections with relief organizations."

"The city is crawling with Japanese patrols," Mary warned. "And they've taken over many of the government buildings. If they recognize you from your work with the Colonial Secretariat..."

"I know every maintenance tunnel and service route in this city. Six years of sanitation inspections taught me how to move through Hong Kong without using the main roads. I can avoid the areas where they're most likely to have heavy patrols."

"Not tonight," Lupe said firmly. She grasped his arm with gentle firmness. "First, you need food and rest. A few hours to build up your strength. You'll need everything you have for what's ahead."

He wanted to argue. Wanted to run immediately into the night and begin searching every prison, every camp, every place the Japanese might be holding civilian internees. But one look at his mother in law's face, at the exhaustion settling into his bones, told him she was right. His shoulder throbbed. His ribs ached. His hands were still bleeding from building the cairns. If he collapsed from exhaustion before finding his family, he would be useless to them. "You're right, Lupe, and while I rest, we'll decide how to stay in communication. If Alicia somehow manages to escape or get word to us, I need to know immediately."

Lupe disappeared into the kitchen. The smell of rice and vegetables being warmed filled the small house. Mary brought him water and helped him remove the bloodied shirt so she could examine his wounds.

"These need to be cleaned properly," she said, looking at the still healing shrapnel injuries. "You're fortunate they're not infected."

While Mary cleaned and bandaged his wounds with supplies she had managed to hide from the soldiers, Bryn asked more questions about the days leading up to Alicia's capture. He learned that his wife had been frantic with worry. That she had made the decision to avoid voluntary registration only after consulting with other families in the neighborhood, many of whom had heard rumors about people who registered and then disappeared.

"She was trying to do the right thing," Mary said quietly. "Trying to keep the children safe. She talked about you constantly, Bryn. About how you would know what to do, how you would find a way to protect the family if you were here."

The weight of that faith was almost unbearable for Bryn.

Lupe returned with food. Simple rice and vegetables, but Bryn realized he hadn't eaten properly in days. The hospital food had been minimal, and he had been too focused on getting out to worry about meals. Now his body demanded

Chapter 33: Searching the Ruins

fuel for what lay ahead.

As he ate, Mary told him more about the occupation. About the curfews and checkpoints. About families who had been separated. About rumors of internment camps being established in various locations around Hong Kong. About the fear that permeated every interaction, every decision. "Some people say they're taking British civilians to Stanley," Mary said. "Others say there are camps at Sham Shui Po. But nobody knows for certain. The Japanese don't give information. They just come and take people away."

"She will likely be at Stanley Camp," Bryn said. "They have designated Stanley for civilians and Sham Shui Po and North Point Camps for military personnel."

"You can't just walk up to a prison camp and ask if your wife is inside," Lupe said. Her voice was gentle but firm. "You need a plan. You need information. You need to be smart about this."

She was right, Bryn thought. Desperation would get him captured or killed. He needed to be strategic.

After he finished eating, exhaustion hit him like a physical force. Mary led him to a small room at the back of the house and insisted he lie down. The bed was narrow but clean. He could smell lavender in the pillowcases, a scent that reminded him of Alicia.

"Sleep," Mary said. "Just a few hours. Then you'll decide what you will do."

He wanted to protest. Every minute he rested was a minute his family spent wherever the Japanese had taken them. But his body betrayed him. The moment his head touched the pillow, darkness claimed him. He dreamed of Patricia holding her seashell to her ear, smiling up at him with absolute trust. He dreamed of David's small hand gripping his finger. He dreamed of Alicia in their kitchen, humming while she prepared breakfast. When he woke, dawn light was filtering through the curtains. He could hear Mary and Lupe talking quietly in the kitchen. The smell of tea filled the air. He pulled Alicia's letter from his pocket and read it again. Her words steadied him.

"You are the compass that points me home."

He would find them. He didn't care how long it took or what he had to do. He would bring his family home. Because in the end, when everything familiar had been stripped away, when the world had been reduced to rubble and fear, love remained the only thing worth fighting for. The search would begin this morning.

Chapter 34

Hell's Antechamber

"They took us to a place where even the walls remembered shame. We learned that there are worse things than being imprisoned. Being imprisoned in a place designed to destroy dignity is one of them."

From "Seventeen Days: A Mother's Account" by Alicia Williams, unpublished memoir, 1946

Day One: January 4th, 1942

The convoy of trucks stopped and Alicia heard water. Seagulls. Shouted commands in Japanese.

"Out! Everyone out! Move quickly!"

She climbed down with David heavy in her arms, Patricia clinging to her skirt. Nearly three hundred people pressed around them, confused and frightened. An elderly woman stumbled and no one was allowed to help her up. The building in front of them was two stories, paint peeling, windows grimy.

The woman's face had gone white. "That's the Lily Hotel. Or it was. Before the war it was a... it was a brothel, Mrs. Williams."

The smell hit them the moment they crossed the threshold. Alicia's stomach clenched. Unwashed bodies. Stale perfume. Alcohol. And underneath it all, something worse.

David started screaming immediately. Alicia pressed her hand gently over his nose and mouth, trying to filter the air. Around them, other children were crying too. "Mummy, it smells bad," Patricia whispered, her hand over her own nose.

"I know, darling. Just breathe through your mouth. Papa will find us soon." The words felt like lies.

They were processed quickly. Names. Ages. Family relationships. Men separated from women. Husbands torn from wives. An elderly couple tried to hold hands and a soldier struck the man's arm with a rifle butt. The woman collapsed, sobbing. "Upstairs! All women and children upstairs!"

The staircase was narrow and the walls closed in. Alicia struggled to keep David balanced while holding Patricia's hand. The wood groaned under their weight. Behind her, Mrs. Henderson was breathing hard, barely able to climb. The second floor was worse. Tiny rooms, each with a single narrow bed. Barred windows painted black years ago. The air was thick and foul.

"In here." A soldier pointed Alicia toward a room that already had six women and children inside. The space was perhaps eight feet by ten feet. Two thin mattresses on the floor, stained with things she didn't want to think about. No other furniture. No privacy.

Mrs. Henderson claimed a corner near the window. Two young sisters, neither older than twenty, sat holding a sickly infant. A Russian woman named Rose rocked in the opposite corner, arms wrapped around her knees, eyes vacant. Mrs. Winston from their neighborhood was trying to comfort her twin boys.

Alicia put David on one of the mattresses and pulled him back when he started crawling toward the edge.

"Will Papa know we're here?" Patricia asked.

"Papa is very smart," Alicia said. "He'll find a way."

The room had no ventilation beyond the painted window. With ten people inside, the air became unbreathable within an hour. Three hours later, a soldier appeared with a metal pot. "Food," he said, and left. They stared at the pot. The liquid inside was nearly transparent. A few pieces of something that might have been cabbage floated on top. No bowls. No spoons.

Mrs. Henderson stood up. "We'll manage. Children first."

They used cupped hands. Alicia scooped the watery substance and held it to Patricia's mouth. Her daughter lapped at it, the liquid running down her chin. Most of it spilled through Alicia's fingers before Patricia could drink. David wouldn't take any. He pushed her hands away, crying, looking for his bottle. "Please, mi niño," Alicia begged. "Please try."

When the adults finally shared what remained, each person got perhaps half a cup of liquid. Alicia's stomach was empty and cramping. Patricia looked at her with hollow eyes. "I'm still hungry, Mama."

"I know, darling. Tomorrow will be better."

Night came and sleep was impossible. Ten people sharing two mattresses in a room without air. Children crying constantly. The smell of human waste from the toilet down the hall. Alicia lay on her side with David against her chest and Patricia

Chapter 34: Hell's Antechamber

pressed to her back. Her daughter's body was hot. Fever. "Mama, I'm thirsty."

Alicia had no water. She wet her fingers with her own saliva and pressed them to Patricia's lips.

In the darkness, Mrs. Henderson's voice came soft. "Mrs. Williams? Are you awake?"

"Yes."

"My husband died three years ago. Cancer. I thought that was the worst thing I would ever experience." She made a sound like a suppressed sob. "But this is worse. Because at least then we had morphine. Clean sheets. Dignity."

Then Alicia spoke. "My husband is a sanitation inspector. He knows what happens in places like this." She was crying now, silently, tears running into the mattress. "If he's alive, he's going insane thinking about us here. And I hate him for not finding us yet. I hate him even though I love him."

"Because you're human," Mrs. Henderson said. "And humans contain contradictions." No one answered that. They all lay in the darkness with their impossible questions and no way to resolve them.

Day Five: January 8th

"Mrs. Williams. Wake up."

Alicia opened her eyes. Mrs. Henderson was kneeling beside her.

"Your daughter needs water. She's burning up."

Patricia's fever had grown overnight. Her lips were cracked and her eyes unfocused. When Alicia tried to wake her, she barely responded. "Patricia, sweetheart. Look at Mummy."

"Thirsty," Patricia whispered. "So thirsty."

Mrs. Wellington held out a tin cup with perhaps two inches of liquid in the bottom. "This is all I have left. Take it."

Alicia held the cup to Patricia's lips. Her daughter drank in gulps, choking, desperate. The water was gone in seconds.

In the corner, David lay listless. He'd stopped crying two days ago. Rose, a young Russian woman who volunteered to help Alicia, sang to him softly in Russian, rocking him like the baby she'd lost.

Mrs. Wellington crawled over to Alicia. "How long has he been refusing food?"

"Three days now."

"My cousin had a baby like that. She had to force feed him. Hold his nose until he has to open his mouth."

Alicia felt sick at the thought. "I can't do that to him."

"Then watch him starve. Those are your choices." Mrs. Wellington's voice was kind despite the harsh words. "That's what mothers do. The things they have to."

The days blurred after that. Each morning brought the same watery soup. Each night brought the same airless darkness. The children grew thinner. The women grew quieter. Mrs. Henderson developed dysentery. The Russian woman never stopped rocking.

Day Nine: January 12th

Mrs. Winston was sitting on the mattress crying.

"What happened?" Alicia asked.

"My husband. Someone saw him downstairs. He tried to call up to me but the guards hit him. Beat him for trying to speak to his wife." She sobbed harder. "I couldn't even call back. The boys heard his voice and I had to cover their mouths." The other women gathered around her. There was nothing to say. They just sat close, sharing the grief, the helplessness, the rage that had nowhere to go.

That night, Alicia lay in the darkness listening to children whimpering, women crying. And somewhere inside herself, under the fear and exhaustion, she felt fury building. White hot and pure. She was angry at the Japanese for doing this. Angry at the British for abandoning them. Angry at God for allowing it. And underneath it all, a terrible anger at Bryn.

Where was he? Why hadn't he found them? She'd spent nine days telling the children Papa was coming, Papa would save them, Papa never broke his promises. But Papa wasn't here. The children were starving and Papa wasn't here. She hated herself for thinking it. But the anger was there anyway, burning in her chest, giving her something to hold onto besides despair.

Day Twelve: January 15th

David looked like a skeleton. His lips were cracked. His skin was gray. Rose sat with him for hours, singing Russian lullabies, telling him stories he was too weak to hear.

"He's still fighting," Rose said quietly.

Mrs. Henderson tried organizing a story time for the children who could still

Chapter 34: Hell's Antechamber

focus. Four children sat in a loose circle, their eyes dull.

"Once upon a time," Mrs. Henderson began, her voice cracking, "there was a beautiful princess who lived in a castle by the sea."

"Was she hungry?" one of the children called out.

Mrs. Henderson paused. "No, darling. She had plenty to eat."

Mrs. Winston crawled over to where Alicia sat with David. "I heard something from one of the guards. We're being moved soon. Stanley. The peninsula. They're setting up a proper internment camp there next to the prison."

Alicia felt something stir in her chest. "When?"

"Maybe a few days. Maybe tomorrow."

"A place with a name," Alicia whispered. "A place that Bryn can find."

Day Seventeen: January 21st

"All prisoners! Pack belongings! Move out immediately!"

The soldiers were in the corridor, shouting. Alicia shook Patricia awake. "Wake up, darling. We're leaving." She gathered their few possessions. The wooden cross from Lupe. Bryn's photograph. Her journal.

Mrs. Henderson stood in the corner, swaying. "I don't think I can walk."

"You have to," Alicia said, grabbing her arm. "We need you." Mrs. Winston took the older woman's other arm. Together they helped her down the stairs.

The march through Hong Kong's streets felt endless. Alicia carried David, his body limp against her chest. Patricia held onto her skirt with both hands, stumbling every few steps.

The city had changed. Japanese flags everywhere. Enemy soldiers on every corner.

"Almost there, sweetheart," Alicia said. Another lie. She had no idea how far they had to walk.

Mrs. Henderson was struggling beside her. "I can't... I need to rest."

"You can't rest. They'll shoot you if you fall." Mrs. Winston's voice was urgent but kind. "Just a little further."

Patricia was crying quietly. "Mummy, I can't walk anymore."

"I can take her for a bit," a woman named Sarah said. "I don't have children. My arms are free." Sarah picked up Patricia, settling the little girl on her hip. "We're all mothers now. All of us. Every woman here is mother to every child. That's how we survive."

At the docks, they were loaded onto a ferry. Alicia found a space against the wall and collapsed there, both children in her lap.

Stanley was still on Hong Kong Island. Bryn knew Stanley. He'd worked there, inspecting facilities. If he was searching for them, Stanley was a place he would know about. A place he could find. She looked down at David. His eyes were half open but unfocused. His breathing was shallow. "We're going to Stanley," she whispered to him. "Papa knows Stanley. He'll find us there. I promise."

The boat moved away from the dock. Alicia watched Hong Kong recede, the city she'd loved now occupied and strange. Patricia leaned against her, too exhausted to be sick this time. David lay still. Seventeen days. They had survived seventeen days of hell. And now they were going somewhere new. Somewhere with a name. Somewhere that could be found on a map. Somewhere Bryn could find them. She had to keep telling herself that to live. She had to believe that. Because without that belief, there was nothing left but surrender. And she wasn't ready to surrender. Not yet. Not while her children were still breathing, still fighting, still alive. She held them both close as the ferry carried them around the island toward their new prison. Toward Stanley. Toward whatever came next.

Chapter 35

Against All Odds

"The reunion we had dreamed of during those long weeks of separation bore no resemblance to the reunion we experienced. There was joy, yes, but it was inseparable from horror at what had been done to the people we loved. We found each other again, but we were not the same people who had been torn apart. The camp had already changed us in ways we were only beginning to understand."

From "Letters from Stanley" by Elizabeth Fortescue, internee, written 1946

Bryn's hands trembled as he packed the canvas rucksacks. The powdered milk went in first, that large valuable container that had cost him nearly everything. Bandages and iodine. Two tins of condensed milk, wrapped carefully. A wool blanket. And hidden at the bottom, sewn into the lining, Hong Kong dollars and Japanese Yen. He worked quickly, forcing his mind to stay focused. Each item could mean the difference between life and death.

Dr. Wellington arrived just before dawn with the documents. The old Scotsman looked exhausted, his face drawn. "These papers identify you as a government sanitation inspector," Wellington said, handing over the official documents. "They'll get you through the gates. After that, you're on your own."

Bryn studied the stamps, the signatures. They looked genuine because they were genuine, though their purpose was entirely fabricated. "Thank you. I know what you've risked to help me."

Wellington gripped his shoulder. "Find them. Bring them whatever hope you can."

As dawn broke over occupied Hong Kong, Bryn moved through the rubble filled streets toward the docks. Wong Ah Fook was waiting beside his battered Ford truck, its paint scratched, its fenders dented from weeks of navigating roads torn apart by war.

"You have money?" Wong's English was heavily accented, each word carefully formed.

Bryn handed over a roll of Hong Kong dollars. More than the truck driver would normally earn in six months. "Half now. Half when we reach Stanley."

Wong examined the bills, then nodded. "Very dangerous for British man. Soldiers at checkpoints hate British people. If they find you, I cannot help. They will kill you. Maybe kill me too."

"I understand."

"You hide in back. Under rice sacks. No talking. No moving when truck stops."

Bryn climbed into the truck bed where burlap sacks of rice were stacked from floor to ceiling. Wong helped him create a narrow hiding spot, then covered him with more bags and a tarpaulin. The space was cramped and airless. The truck lurched forward. Through gaps in the tarpaulin, Bryn caught glimpses of the city. Japanese flags hanging from government buildings. Enemy soldiers patrolling in pairs. Chinese civilians hurrying with their eyes down, shoulders hunched. At the first checkpoint, Bryn held his breath as a Japanese soldier thrust his bayonet randomly into the rice sacks. One blade pierced the tarpaulin inches from his face. He watched the steel catch the morning light, saw it withdraw, heard it plunge in again slightly to his left. Every muscle screamed to move away from the weapon, but he remained frozen. The voices faded. The truck moved again. At the second checkpoint, the guards were more thorough. Bryn heard Wong being questioned aggressively. A soldier climbed into the truck bed and started moving sacks aside, working methodically toward Bryn's hiding spot. He could smell cigarette smoke on the man's uniform. The guard was so close that Bryn could have reached out and touched his boot. Then Wong called out something in Japanese. The guard cursed and climbed down to check the delivery documents. After several tense minutes, the truck was waved through. The military checkpoint at the base of Stanley Peninsula loomed ahead with concrete barriers and machine gun emplacements. Through the tarpaulin, Bryn watched soldiers moving with the casual confidence of men who held absolute power.

Wong's voice rose in pitch as guards began their inspection. This time they didn't just check the sacks. They started removing them entirely, tossing them onto the ground. Bryn realized they were about to unload the entire truck bed. In seconds, they would find him anyway. He had one chance to control this. Before the soldiers reached his hiding spot, Bryn pushed aside the remaining bags and sat up with his hands raised. "Excuse me," he said, keeping his voice steady and authoritative. He reached slowly for the papers inside his jacket. "I am Bryn Williams, government sanitation inspector. I have documents authorizing my entry to Stanley Camp."

Chapter 35: Against All Odds

The soldiers immediately raised their rifles, shouting in Japanese. Bryn kept his hands visible as he offered the papers to the senior officer. The Japanese officer examined the documents with a deep frown, turning them over, studying the official stamps. Bryn forced himself to stand calmly despite his racing heart.

"I need to inspect the sanitation conditions at Stanley Camp," Bryn said. "After my inspection, I will remain with my family who are already interned there. My wife and children."

The officer grunted, clearly uncertain. Finally he spoke in broken English: "You go to camp. Guards at gate will check papers again." The barrier lifted. Wong drove through, his knuckles white on the steering wheel. As they approached the main camp, Bryn saw the walls of Stanley Prison rising ahead with St. Stephen's College buildings beyond. His stomach tightened. Somewhere inside those walls were Alicia, Patricia, and David. The truck stopped before the main gate. Guards surrounded the vehicle immediately. Bryn climbed down with his rucksacks on both shoulders and presented his papers to the Japanese officer.

This officer was younger, his English better, his questions more pointed. He studied Bryn with cold calculation. "Why does government inspector come to camp? What is real purpose?"

"I am here to assess sanitation conditions. After completing my inspection, I will remain here with my wife and children rather than return to Hong Kong."

"You want to stay in camp?" The lieutenant's eyes narrowed. "British man wants to be prisoner?"

"Yes. Mrs. Alicia Williams and my children, Patricia and David. I request permission to remain with them."

The guards spoke rapidly in Japanese. The lieutenant gestured sharply toward Bryn's rucksacks. "Show contents."

Bryn opened the bags and laid everything on a nearby table. When the guards found the powdered milk, one held it up with suspicion. "This is for my children," Bryn explained. "My son is barely a year old. Babies need milk to survive."

The lieutenant's face hardened. "British people think they deserve special treatment. Even in defeat." He confiscated one tin of condensed milk, the soap, and half the medical supplies. "You are prisoner now. Same as all others. You will learn respect for Imperial Japanese authority."

But Bryn had achieved his goal. He was being admitted.

As the gates opened, a British internee approached. The man was thin, perhaps in his fifties, wearing the remnants of what had once been a good suit. "You're new," the man said. "I'm Robert Thornton."

"I'm looking for my family." The words came out more urgently than Bryn intended. "Alicia Williams and two children, Patricia and David. They would have arrived in late January."

Something shifted in Thornton's expression. A kind of pained reluctance. He glanced away, then back. "Williams. Yes. I know them." He paused, seemed to struggle with his words. "They're in the married quarters, Block 13. But Mr. Williams, I need to tell you something before we go there."

Bryn's throat tightened. "Tell me what?"

"The children here. They're not doing well. The rations." Thornton's voice dropped. "There's barely any protein. The babies especially. They're not getting what they need. And your son, he's been ill. Your wife has been doing everything she can, but."

The world seemed to tilt slightly. "Take me to them. Now."

Bryn followed Thornton through the camp, past buildings converted into overcrowded dormitories. The smell hit him first. Unwashed bodies, sickness, inadequate sanitation. Then the faces. Hollow eyes. Protruding bones. Children sitting too quietly in patches of shade. Building 13 was on the eastern edge of the camp, a former dormitory now housing families. Thornton led him up to the second floor. "Room Seven," he said quietly. "At the end of the hall. I'll leave you to it."

The room had once been designed for perhaps four students. Now twenty people lived in that space. Thin mattresses covered every inch of floor. The single window, its glass replaced with boards and canvas, provided the only ventilation. And there, in a corner by the window, he saw them. Alicia sat on a thin mattress, her back against the wall, holding David close to her chest. Patricia was curled against her mother's side. Bryn couldn't move. Couldn't breathe. The shock of finally seeing hit him like a physical blow.

Alicia looked up. For a long moment she simply stared at him. Her face went through a series of expressions so rapid he could barely track them. Confusion. Disbelief. Recognition. Then something broke open in her eyes. "Bryn." His name came out as barely more than a whisper, as if she was afraid he might disappear if she said it too loud. She tried to stand, her movements clumsy and uncertain, still holding David against her chest. Patricia looked up at her mother, then followed her gaze to the doorway.

"Papa?" Patricia's voice was small, hesitant, as if she couldn't quite trust what she was seeing.

Then Alicia was moving toward him, stumbling slightly, and Bryn crossed the room in three strides. He caught her, pulled her and David into his arms. The

Chapter 35: Against All Odds

moment his hands touched her, he felt the shock of how thin she'd become. He could feel every rib, every sharp angle of her shoulder blades through her dress. She felt breakable, as if holding her too tightly might snap something vital.

Alicia made a sound against his chest, something between a sob and a gasp. Her whole body started shaking. "You're here. You're real. You're really here."

He buried his face in her hair. It smelled different. Unwashed, yes, but also something else. The sharp metallic scent of fear and deprivation. "I'm here. I found you. I found you."

Patricia was pulling at his shirt, making small desperate sounds. He released Alicia with one arm and scooped Patricia up, holding both his wife and daughter. The little girl wrapped her arms around his neck so tightly he could barely breathe. "Papa came back," Patricia said, her voice muffled against his shoulder. "Mummy said you would. She said every day."

Alicia pulled back to look at him, her hands coming up to touch his face as if to confirm he was solid and real. Tears were streaming down her cheeks. "I thought. Sometimes I thought." She couldn't finish the sentence.

David stirred weakly in her arms, making a small sound. Bryn looked down at his son and felt his heart stop. The baby looked like a shadow of himself. His face was gaunt, his eyes too large in his thin face. At thirteen months, David should have been plump and active, pulling himself up on furniture, babbling constantly. Instead he lay limply in Alicia's arms, his small body unnervingly still. "David." Bryn touched his son's cheek gently. The skin felt papery, too warm.

"He's been so sick," Alicia said, fresh tears spilling over. "The food. There's barely any food. And what they give us, it's just rice and thin soup. Nothing for babies. Nothing with protein or fat. I've been giving him my portions but it's not enough. He needs milk. He needs." Her voice broke completely.

Bryn set Patricia down gently and reached into his rucksack with shaking hands. When he pulled out the container of powdered milk, Alicia's face crumpled. "Oh God. Bryn. Yes."

She found a chipped cup with trembling fingers and mixed a small amount of the precious powder with water from their daily ration. She cradled David carefully, trying to get him to take small sips. At first the baby turned his head away weakly. Then the taste seemed to register and he began to drink slowly, his tiny hands grasping at the cup with what little strength he had. "There," Alicia whispered, her tears falling onto David's face. "Drink, *mi niño*. Get strong."

Bryn sank down onto the mattress beside them, his arm around Alicia's shoulders, watching his son drink. Patricia climbed into his lap and pressed herself against his chest. Around them, other internees watched quietly. An elderly woman was crying openly.

"I knew you'd come," Alicia said softly, leaning her head against his shoulder. "I told the children every single day. Papa will find us. Papa never breaks his promises."

"I will never leave you again," Bryn said, holding them all as tightly as he dared. "Never."

They sat like that for a long time, the four of them together again, while the afternoon light shifted through the barred window. Other people in the room moved quietly around them, giving them space, respecting the sacredness of this reunion.

Eventually Patricia lifted her head. "Papa, I was good. I helped Mummy with David."

"I know you were, darling. You're such a brave girl."

After some time, Mrs. Wellington approached quietly. "Mr. and Mrs. Williams," she said with gentle understanding, "why don't you take a walk together? I'll watch Patricia and David with my boys. You need some time."

Alicia looked up at Bryn, her eyes asking the question. He nodded. They needed to talk, just the two of them, about what came next. They slipped away from Building 13, stepping into the warm evening air. After the suffocating atmosphere of the crowded room, even the camp's limited space felt like relief. Alicia took Bryn's hand and guided him along the narrow paths between buildings. "This is our world now," she said quietly. "Everything is contained within these walls." She pointed north. "That's Stanley Prison. We're forbidden to look at it, but the Japanese use it for criminals. Sometimes we hear screaming at night." They walked past the main administration building. "That's where they make all the decisions about our lives," Alicia said. "How much rice we get. Who receives medical attention. Who gets punished."

Finally they walked around the eastern side of Building 13 to a small terrace overlooking Stanley Bay. The view was breathtaking. Water shimmered silver in the moonlight. Distant lights twinkled along the coastline.

Alicia leaned against the low wall. Bryn put his arm around her shoulders, feeling how small she'd become. "I used to stand here every evening," she said. "Watching the water and wondering if you were alive. Wondering if you would ever find us."

Bryn turned her to face him, his hands cupping her face gently. "I couldn't look for you…I was in the hospital."

She brushed his cheek. "Why? Are you injured? Are you alright?"

Chapter 35: Against All Odds

He motioned to his shoulder and back. "Shrapnel and a concussion from being too close to a bomb explosion. They patched me up, and the dizzy spells from the concussion are finally gone. I had to find you."

"She looked up at him, her dark eyes reflecting the moonlight. "But Bryn, what now? How do we survive this? How do we keep our children alive?"

He traced her cheek with his thumb, wiping away a tear. "Together. We do it together."

Alicia stood on her toes and kissed him. The kiss spoke of desperate love and hard won hope. When they broke apart, she rested her forehead against his. "I love you," she whispered. "I've loved you every day we've been apart."

"And I love you. You and Patricia and David. You're my whole world now."

Bryn held Alicia, his mind was racing with fears he couldn't speak aloud. David's labored breathing. The way Patricia's eyes had looked too old, too knowing. He thought about all the ways his family could be taken from him even now, even after he'd found them. "We're going to survive this," he said, putting conviction into his voice that he didn't feel. "We're together now.

Alicia pressed closer against him, and he wondered if she could feel his heart hammering, if she knew how terrified he really was.

As they walked back to Building 13 hand in hand, Bryn felt determination growing alongside the fear. He had found them. He had kept his promise. Now he would find a way to keep them alive, even if he didn't yet know how. Even if the odds seemed impossible. He would find a way. He had to.

Chapter 36

The Work of Survival

"In the camp, idleness was not merely uncomfortable but dangerous. Those who found purpose in organizing, teaching, or healing fared better than those who simply waited for liberation. We learned that survival required more than food and shelter. It demanded that we remain useful to ourselves and to each other."

From "Stanley Remembered" by Margaret Watson, former internee, 1947

Bryn woke from restless sleep on the concrete floor of Block 13, instinctively tightening his arm around Alicia as gray dawn light seeped through the grimy windows. David lay curled between them, his small body finally still after a night of crying from hunger. Patricia pressed against Alicia's other side, her fever having broken but leaving her pale and weak. Three weeks. They'd been in Stanley Camp for three weeks now. February 15th, and every day felt longer than the one before.

Alicia stirred beside him. As she turned, her elbow accidentally pressed against his left side where the shrapnel wound was still tender. Bryn couldn't suppress a sharp inhale. "Oh, Bryn, I'm so sorry."

He caught her hand and brought it to his lips. "It's healing well."

But her fingers were already gently exploring the area through his shirt, her touch tender and careful. "You've been so focused on taking care of all of us. You haven't been taking care of yourself. Does it still hurt much?"

"Only when beautiful Mexican women accidentally elbow me in my sleep," he said, earning a soft laugh from her despite their circumstances.

She traced her finger along his jawline, a gesture so intimate and familiar that it brought tears to his eyes. "I love you, Bryn Williams," she whispered. "Whatever happens here, I need you to know that. You've given me everything."

Bryn felt his throat constrict. "You saved me from a life half-lived. Before you, I was just going through the motions, following duty and routine. You taught me what it means to truly love someone."

Alicia's eyes filled with tears. "Promise me something. Promise me that if something happens to me, you'll get the children out of here. You'll find a way to give them the life we dreamed of."

"Nothing is going to happen to you," Bryn said fiercely. "We're going to survive this together. All of us."

For a moment, they lay there in the gray dawn light, foreheads touching, sharing the quiet intimacy that had carried their marriage through eight years.

"Papa," Patricia whispered. "I'm hungry."

Bryn's heart clenched. He looked down at his daughter's hollow cheeks, her eyes too large in her thinning face. "I know, my darling. Papa will find a way to make things better. I promise you that."

Patricia reached up and touched his face with her small hand. "Papa, why do the Japanese men not like us?"

"Some people make very bad choices, sweetheart. But that doesn't mean there isn't still love in the world. Look." He pointed to Alicia. "Mama loves us. I love you and David more than all the stars in the sky. Love is stronger than hate."

David woke and pulled himself up using Bryn's shirt, wobbling on his little legs. Some color had returned to his cheeks since they'd been feeding him the powdered milk. "Da da," David said softly, reaching his arms up.

Bryn lifted his son, feeling how light he still was, how his tiny ribs showed through his thin shirt.

Mrs. Wellington was already awake in the corner with her twin boys. She caught Bryn's eye and nodded toward the door. "There's talk of a meeting today. About organizing ourselves better. Setting up committees to handle things the Japanese won't do."

Bryn's pulse quickened. "When and where?"

"This afternoon. Near the old Prison Officers' Club. Anyone interested in helping organize."

Alicia squeezed his hand. "You should go. You know how to make things work. These people need someone who understands administration."

After their meager breakfast of rice congee that was more water than grain, Bryn knelt to Patricia's level. She was sitting quietly in the corner, trying to play with a small doll that Alicia had sewn from scraps of cloth. "Patricia, Papa has to go to a meeting with some other grownups today. We're going to try to make things better here."

Chapter 36: The Work of Survival

Patricia looked up at him with those serious dark eyes. "Will you make the bad smell go away, Papa?"

"I'm going to try, sweetheart. Papa is going to work very hard to make things cleaner and safer for you and David."

"And for Mama too?"

"Yes, darling. For Mama too." Bryn kissed her forehead. "Can you be my brave girl and help Mama take care of David while I'm gone?"

Patricia nodded solemnly. "I'll sing to him if he cries."

The meeting was held in an open area near what had been the Prison Officers' Club. Bryn was surprised by the turnout. Nearly two hundred internees had gathered, representing Hong Kong's former British, American, Dutch and other European communities. Benjamin Wylie called the meeting to order. Bryn recognized him from before the war. The director and general manager of the South China Morning Post had a reputation for clear thinking and strong organization. "Ladies and gentlemen," Wylie began, his voice carrying across the gathering. "We're here because it's become clear that the Japanese have no intention of providing us with the basic necessities of life. If we're to survive this ordeal with our health and dignity intact, we must organize ourselves." L.R. Nielsen stepped forward. "I propose we establish formal committees to handle different aspects of camp life."

A voice called out from the crowd. "Who's going to lead these committees? And what makes you think the Japanese will let us do anything?"

Nielsen nodded. "Fair questions. We need people with relevant expertise. As for the Japanese, they've already indicated they expect us to manage our own internal affairs. They don't want to deal with day to day problems."

"That's because they don't care if we live or die," someone else said bitterly.

"Perhaps," Wylie said. "But that also gives us room to operate. If we can improve conditions without requiring Japanese resources, they may allow it."

Bryn raised his hand. Nielsen nodded to him.

"Bryn Williams. I was Deputy Chief Sanitation Inspector for Hong Kong before the war. I would like to volunteer for any committees related to health and sanitation. Since arriving here, I've been observing the conditions. We're facing serious risks of epidemic disease if we don't implement proper hygiene measures immediately." A murmur of approval spread through the crowd. Several people nodded.

Dr. Dennis Utley spoke up from the side. "I'm one of the camp's physicians. Williams is absolutely right about the health risks. I've already seen dysentery cases increasing. Poor sanitation in confined populations leads to epidemics. We need someone with government experience to implement proper systems."

A woman near the front raised her hand. "Mr. Williams, what exactly would you propose doing? We have no materials, no tools, barely any water."

"We have skilled workers among the internees," Bryn replied. "Engineers, construction supervisors, other sanitary inspectors. We can salvage materials from damaged buildings. Organize labor gangs. Establish maintenance protocols. It won't be perfect, but it will be better than what we have now."

"And the Japanese will just let us do this?" another man asked skeptically.

"That's something we'll need to negotiate," Bryn said. "But if we present it as internees taking responsibility for our own conditions, not as demands for their help, they may approve it. Especially if we emphasize that disease outbreaks could affect their soldiers as well."

Wylie consulted his notes. "Mr. Williams, I understand you also have experience with administrative coordination?"

"Yes, the last six years. I know how to navigate bureaucracy and implement large-scale projects with limited resources."

"Then I'd like to put you forward for the main organizing committee and also to lead a sanitation subcommittee. Does anyone object?"

Silence, followed by several voices calling out support.

A tall man in his sixties stood up. "Robert Thornton. I was a teacher at St. Stephen's. I want to propose an education committee for the children. They can't just sit idle for however long we're here."

"Excellent suggestion," Nielsen said.

For the next hour, committees were formed and responsibilities divided. Housing. Food distribution. Medical care. Sanitation. Education. Recreation. Each group would report to the main council, which would coordinate with Japanese administration. As the meeting broke up, Dr. Utley approached Bryn. "Williams, I'd like to work with you on that sanitation inspection. My medical perspective combined with your engineering knowledge could give us a comprehensive picture."

"I was hoping you'd say that," Bryn said. "When can we start?"

"Tomorrow morning. I'll bring my medical bag and notes. You bring whatever measuring equipment you have."

James Fraser and H.R. Butters joined them. Fraser had been Defense Secretary before the war. Butters, the Financial Secretary. "Good to see some government

Chapter 36: The Work of Survival

representation on these committees," Fraser said. "We're going to need careful coordination between the Japanese administration and our internal organization."

"It's a delicate balance," Butters added. "The Japanese want us to be responsible for internal camp management, but they also want to maintain absolute control. Any initiatives we propose have to be presented in ways that serve their interests."

"I understand," Bryn said. "I've dealt with difficult bureaucracies before. The key is framing proposals so they solve problems for the administrators, not create new ones."

Fraser gave him an appraising look. "You might be exactly what we need, Williams. The previous attempts to negotiate with the Japanese have been... unsuccessful. Perhaps a fresh approach will work better."

The following morning, Bryn met Dr. Utley at the camp's makeshift administrative building. Utley was stocky, in his fifties, with graying hair and wire rimmed glasses that he kept adjusting as he reviewed his patient notes. "I've been treating the symptoms," Utley said, showing Bryn his handwritten list. "Dysentery cases are rising daily. Respiratory infections are widespread. Clear signs of malnutrition in the children. But we need to focus on causes, not just effects."

Bryn pulled out his journal. "Where should we start?"

"The worst overcrowding is in the former Indian Quarters. Let's begin there."

They walked together through the camp. Utley carried his medical bag and notebook. Bryn brought his measuring tape, sketching supplies, and the systematic method he'd developed during years of sanitary inspections. At the Indian Quarters, they stopped outside a room where a family of six had hung makeshift curtains for privacy.

"The Andersons," Utley said quietly. "Grandmother, parents, three children, and an infant. This room was designed for two people at most. Maybe two students."

Bryn pulled out his measuring tape. "Help me with this."

They measured the space together. Twelve feet by eight feet.

"That's ninety-six square feet total," Bryn calculated aloud. "Six people. Sixteen square feet per person."

"What's the regulation?" Utley asked.

"Hong Kong housing code requires a minimum of sixty square feet per person. This is about a quarter of that."

Utley shook his head. "No wonder respiratory infections are spreading so quickly. They can't even turn over without touching each other."

They moved to the latrine facilities. The smell hit them before they reached the door. "This is a breeding ground for cholera," Utley said, standing outside the single toilet serving the second floor. "Fifty-seven women and children are using one toilet that hasn't been properly cleaned since the camp opened."

Bryn examined the plumbing while Utley took notes. "The pipe system is completely inadequate for this volume. Look at this." He pointed to the connections. "This was designed for maybe eight to ten users maximum. We're looking at six times the intended capacity."

"Can it be fixed?"

"We'd need to add additional facilities. Run new pipes. Install proper ventilation." Bryn sketched the layout in his journal. "The question is whether we can salvage enough materials and whether the Japanese will allow construction."

They spent two days conducting a comprehensive inspection. At each location, they worked together, with Bryn analyzing the structural and engineering problems and Utley evaluating the medical risks. On the second evening, they sat in a corner of the Prison Officers' Club reviewing their findings. "The water system is the most critical," Bryn said, showing Utley his diagrams. "Peak usage times in the morning and evening cause pressure to drop so low that the upper floors get almost nothing. People are reusing dirty water because they can't get enough clean water."

"That explains the dysentery cases," Utley said, making notes. "If they're washing food or drinking water that's contaminated..."

"We need to install holding tanks on the roof of each building. Gravity feed. It's basic, but it would provide consistent pressure throughout the day."

"Where would we get the tanks?"

"Salvage them. The old air raid shelters have metal water containers. Some of the damaged buildings have intact plumbing we could cannibalize. We have engineers among the internees who could design the systems."

Utley leaned back and removed his glasses, rubbing his eyes. "This is all assuming the Japanese cooperate. What if they refuse?"

"Then we do what we can without their permission and deal with the consequences later. But I think if we present this correctly, they'll approve it. They don't want an epidemic any more than we do."

"I hope you're right."

The next day, they presented their findings to the British Communal Council.

Chapter 36: The Work of Survival

Nielsen and Wylie sat at a makeshift table with Fraser and Butters. Several other committee heads had been invited to hear the report. Bryn laid out his diagrams and charts. "We've identified three critical areas requiring immediate intervention. First, the latrine facilities. Second, the water distribution system. Third, waste disposal and drainage."

Nielsen studied the documents. "Walk us through each problem and your proposed solution."

"The latrine situation is straightforward," Bryn said. "We have one toilet per fifty to sixty people in most buildings. That's far beyond safe capacity. We need to construct additional facilities using salvaged materials from damaged buildings."

"Where would you put them?" Wylie asked.

"Here, here, and here." Bryn pointed to his sketches. "We can add facilities at the end of each floor, running new pipes down to the existing main drainage line."

"And you think we can do this without Japanese materials?" Fraser asked.

"We have three qualified plumbers among the internees," Bryn replied. "We can salvage pipes and fixtures from the bombed out buildings. The main limitation is labor, but we can organize work gangs."

Butters frowned. "What about the Japanese? They'll need to approve any construction."

"That's where presentation matters," Bryn said. "We don't ask them for help. We inform them that we're taking responsibility for sanitation to prevent disease outbreaks that could affect their soldiers. We emphasize that we're using our own labor and salvaged materials."

"You think that will work?" Nielsen sounded skeptical.

"I think it's our best approach. The Japanese want us to manage our own internal affairs. They don't want to be bothered with daily problems. If we frame this as us solving a problem rather than creating demands, they're more likely to approve."

Dr. Utley spoke up. "And if they don't approve, we're looking at major epidemics within months. Dysentery is already spreading. Once we get into the warmer months, we could see cholera, typhoid, possibly worse."

"All right," Nielsen said finally. "Bryn you have council authorization to approach the Japanese administration. But be careful. The officers there are unpredictable, and the civilian administrators are rigid bureaucrats. One wrong word could get you punished or get all of us punished."

"I understand the risks."

"And take Fraser with you," Nielsen added. "He has experience dealing with Japanese officials."

Fraser shook his head. "Actually, I think Williams should go alone. My previous interactions with them haven't been productive. Sometimes a fresh face has better luck."

Bryn looked around the room at the faces watching him. These people were depending on him to negotiate with men who held absolute power over their lives. "I'll go tomorrow morning," he said. "I'll present the report as a professional courtesy, not a request. And I'll make sure they understand that preventing disease serves their interests as well as ours."

"Be careful, Bryn," Wylie said quietly. "We need you alive and functional. Don't be a hero. If they refuse, accept it and come back. We'll find another way."

That evening, Bryn returned to Block 13 as the sun was setting. Alicia was teaching Patricia to draw simple words in the dirt. David was sleeping in her lap, his breathing steady.

She looked up as Bryn entered, and her smile faded when she saw his expression. "What happened?"

"The council approved my plan. Tomorrow, I meet with the Japanese administration to get permission for the sanitation improvements."

Alicia's hand went to her mouth. "Bryn, that's dangerous."

"I know. But it's necessary." He sat beside her and pulled her close. "If we don't improve the sanitation, people will start dying. Children will start dying. I have to try."

Patricia looked up from her writing. "Is Papa going to talk to the bad men?"

"Yes, darling. But Papa will be very careful and very respectful. And then Papa will come back to you."

Alicia held him tightly. "Promise me you'll be careful. Promise me you won't do anything that might make them angry."

"I promise. I'll bow when I'm supposed to bow. I'll keep my eyes down. I'll speak respectfully. I'll do everything right."

But as he held his family that night, listening to the quiet breathing of the other families in their crowded room, Bryn understood that no amount of careful behavior could guarantee safety. The Japanese guards and administrators could punish any of them at any time, for any reason or no reason at all.

He would do his best. He would be smart, cautious, and diplomatic. And he would hope that was enough.

Chapter 37

Negotiating with Shadows

"Every interaction with our captors carried the weight of consequences we could not predict. A man could bow correctly and still be struck. He could speak with perfect deference and still be punished. Yet we had to keep trying, keep negotiating for small mercies, because in those tiny victories lay the difference between survival and surrender."

From "Notes on Captivity" by Franklin Gimson, Colonial Secretary, Stanley Camp, 1942

The next morning, Bryn walked across the camp to the buildings that housed the Japanese administrative offices. He'd carefully prepared for this moment. His report was neatly organized in a folder. He wore the cleanest clothes he could find. He'd rehearsed his approach multiple times.

The guards at the entrance looked at him with suspicion.

"I am Bryn Williams, Deputy Chief Sanitary Inspector for Hong Kong Government," he said in formal English, presenting his credentials. "I represent the Camp British Governing Committee and I request a meeting with camp administration regarding urgent health matters."

One of the guards disappeared into the building. Several minutes passed. Then the guard returned with Lieutenant Fukui.

The lieutenant was compact, with cold, calculating eyes. His reputation for cruelty was well known in the camp. His hand rested casually on the grip of his sword. "What is this?" Fukui demanded, snatching Bryn's credentials and inspecting them with suspicion. "Professional sanitation report for camp administration. Notification of internee health initiatives."

Fukui's eyes narrowed as he studied Bryn. "You think you are important man? Government official?" He stepped very close, invading Bryn's space. His hand moved to his sword, fingers drumming on the hilt. "You are nothing. Prisoner. Defeated."

Bryn kept his voice level and his eyes down, showing respect without showing fear. "I am a qualified sanitary inspector, sir. My report addresses sanitary conditions that impact all residents, including your men."

Fukui's hand rose suddenly, stopping inches from Bryn's face. Bryn forced himself not to flinch. The lieutenant held his hand there for a long moment, then lowered it slowly, his cold smile never reaching his eyes.

"Mr. Saito will see you. I will watch," Fukui said acidly.

Bryn was escorted into a small office where a stern faced Japanese civilian administrator sat behind a desk piled with paperwork. Mr. Saito wore a dark civilian suit but carried himself with rigid formality. Lieutenant Fukui positioned himself near the door, arms crossed, watching.

An interpreter stood beside Saito's desk. A young man, probably in his late thirties, who looked uncomfortable with his role. Saito spoke in Japanese. The interpreter translated: "You are sanitary inspector?"

"Yes, sir. Dr. Utley and I have conducted a thorough inspection of camp facilities. I submit this professional report documenting current health conditions and internee plans for improvements using our own labor and materials." Bryn placed his report on the desk and waited while Saito examined it. The administrator's face revealed nothing as he turned the pages.

After several minutes, Saito spoke again. The interpreter translated: "You request materials? Supplies?"

"No, sir," Bryn replied carefully. "We request only permission to proceed with improvements using internee labor and salvaged materials. We understand that camp administration has no obligation to provide comfort for civilian internees."

Saito set the report aside. He spoke at length in Japanese, his tone curt and bureaucratic. The interpreter translated: "Civilian internees have no status under international law. Japanese authorities provide what is necessary for existence. Nothing more is required. Camp administration has no responsibility for internee comfort."

"Understood, sir. We ask only that administration not interfere with internee efforts to maintain basic hygiene standards. Disease outbreaks in confined populations can spread rapidly. Such outbreaks could affect camp security and potentially impact your men stationed here," Bryn replied politely.

When Bryn mentioned the Japanese soldiers, Saito's expression shifted slightly. He picked up the report again and scanned it more carefully, stopping at certain pages. Lieutenant Fukui spoke sharply from his position by the door. Saito replied. They had a brief exchange in Japanese. Bryn caught a few words. Disease. Soldiers. Risk. Finally, Saito spoke again. The interpreter translated: "Internees are

Chapter 37: Negotiating with Shadows

responsible for their own conditions. Do not request Japanese assistance. Do not expect Japanese materials or tools. You may use salvaged materials found within the camp to make improvements. However, you must submit detailed plans to me for approval before beginning any construction. Any construction that proceeds without approval will be stopped and those responsible will be punished."

"Thank you, sir. We will submit detailed plans for your review," Bryn said.

Lieutenant Fukui stepped forward as the meeting concluded. "I will be watching you, sanitary inspector." His smile was cold. "Japanese authorities do not forget troublemakers. You will follow all rules precisely. Any violation will be dealt with severely."

"Yes, sir. I understand," Bryn said compliantly.

As Bryn walked back across the camp, he allowed himself a moment of satisfaction. Not much had been accomplished on the surface, but permission to proceed was crucial. Now they could begin actual work. Near Building 9, he saw a man kneeling in the dirt, his hands on his head. A Japanese guard stood over him, barking orders. The man had apparently been there for some time. His face was gray with exhaustion. Other internees walked past quickly, eyes averted. Bryn kept walking, understanding instinctively that stopping to look would only make things worse for the kneeling man.

Returning to Block 13, he found Alicia teaching Patricia simple Chinese characters in the dirt with a stick. David slept fitfully in her lap. When she saw Bryn's expression, she smiled. "Good news?"

"Very good news. We got approval to make improvements. They won't help us, but they won't stop us either. We're going to make this place more livable," Bryn replied.

Patricia looked up from her writing. "Papa is going to fix the bad smell?"

"Yes, darling. Papa and some other people are going to work very hard to make things cleaner and safer," Bryn said stroking Patricia's hair.

Alicia reached for his hand, her eyes searching his face. She could see the tension there, the things he wasn't saying. "Be careful. Don't give them any reason to notice you."

"I'll be careful. I promise." He thought of the man kneeling in the dirt, of Fukui's raised hand, of the old man slapped at the gate. "I saw some things on the way back. We need to be very careful about how we move around the camp. How we behave near the guards."

"I know," Alicia said quietly. "We've learned. Mrs. Wellington's boy Peter didn't bow fast enough last week. The guard made him stand in the sun for three

Ashes and Dawn

hours." She squeezed his hand. "We teach the children to look down when Japanese soldiers pass. To bow immediately. To never question anything."

That evening, as the February air grew cool and the children finally settled into restless sleep, Bryn wrote in his journal by the dim light of a small candle stub:

"Today marked a turning point. I have been accepted into camp leadership and gained cooperation of the Japanese administration for essential sanitation improvements. Alicia grows thinner each day, but she remains strong. The children suffer, but they survive. I have found my purpose here. To use my skills and connections to keep us all alive until freedom comes. And it will come."

Outside their window, lights from the Japanese administrative building glowed in the darkness. But here, in this crowded room filled with the quiet breathing of sleeping families, Bryn felt something he hadn't experienced in weeks. Hope for tomorrow. The work would begin immediately. Lives depended on it.

Chapter 38

Bread, Rice and Resolve

"In captivity, a man's garden becomes his defiance. Each seed planted is a refusal to surrender, each harvest a small victory over those who would reduce us to numbers and rations. The soil remembers what we were before the wire, and promises what we might become again."

From "Cultivating Hope: A Gardener's War Diary" by James Mitchell, Stanley Internment Camp, 1943

March 1942

The faint morning light streamed through the single window of their cramped quarters, casting shadows across the concrete floor they shared with the Wellington family and two other families. Mrs. Wellington rested on her thin mattress, still weak from dysentery, while her husband quietly mended a torn shirt with thread salvaged from worn garments.

Bryn carefully unwrapped the bundle he'd managed to get the night before. Real rice, not the watery gruel they'd grown used to, lay in a small mound alongside a piece of salted fish and a few wilted vegetables that still held the promise of vitamins their bodies desperately needed. He had set up a steady route to the black market outside the camp. The Chinese civilians who remembered his fair treatment were willing to trust him.

"Is there enough to share?" Alicia whispered, her eyes moving toward their roommates.

Bryn nodded, understanding her unspoken question. "Mr. Wellington, Mrs. Wellington, please join us. We have a bit extra today."

The elderly man's eyes filled with gratitude as he helped his wife sit up slowly. "That's very kind, Bryn. Very kind indeed."

"Papa, is that fish?" Patricia whispered, her eyes wide with wonder at the sight of protein they hadn't tasted in weeks.

"It is indeed, little one," Bryn smiled, carefully dividing the meager portions with surgical precision.

Alicia moved closer to help distribute the food, her once elegant dress now hanging loose on her diminished frame. "See how David sits up now for his food," Alicia remarked with pride.

"*¡Comida!*" David blurted out in his enthusiastic baby's voice.

The six of them shared the modest feast, with Bryn and Alicia ensuring the children ate first. The rice felt like a banquet after weeks of subsisting on thin soup.

"Tell us about your work with the sanitation committee, Bryn," Mr. Wellington said quietly.

"I finally got approval for some basic improvements. Additional latrines in Block C, and permission to dig a drainage ditch near the kitchen areas," Bryn replied. "But Lieutenant Fukui made it clear that any further requests would be viewed as unreasonable demands."

Alicia set down her portion and looked around their small shared space. "Speaking of authority, have you all heard about the new regulations they've implemented?"

"The roll calls?" Mrs. Wellington asked.

"Twice daily now," Alicia confirmed. "Seven in the morning and seven at night. And we must all be back in our building areas by eight in the evening, no exceptions."

Mr. Wellington shook his head grimly. "Lights out by eleven, and the guards are patrolling all night. Mrs. Smith from Block A told me they're holding the building chairmen personally responsible if anyone is missing during the counts."

"It's because of the escape attempt last week," Bryn said quietly. "They're tightening security across the entire camp."

Alicia reached over to check if David was still eating, her maternal instincts constantly watching her children's intake. "The children adapt, but it's harder on the elderly and infirm. Two roll calls daily, plus the restriction on evening movement. It feels like the walls are closing in even more."

"At least we have each other," Mrs. Wellington said softly, managing a weak smile. "And generous neighbors who share their good fortune."

They ate in contemplative silence for a while, the weight of their new restrictions settling over the small room like a heavy blanket. Bryn noticed how the conversation itself had become more guarded, even among trusted roommates. The increased surveillance made everyone more cautious about what they said and

Chapter 38: Bread, Rice and Resolve

when they said it.

The months passed in the rhythm of survival. June brought the departure of nearly four hundred Americans on the Asama Maru, exchanged for Japanese nationals held in the United States. Bryn and Alicia stood at the fence with other British and Canadian internees, watching their friends board ships bound for freedom. The ache of those departures settled into their bones and stayed there.

By autumn, food rations had decreased further. The Japanese provided barely enough to prevent starvation: eight ounces of rice, three ounces of meat or five ounces of fish, less than an ounce of sugar per family. Vegetables arrived spoiled or contaminated. Children grew thin. The elderly began to die. Bryn claimed a small plot of land near Block 13 and began to dig.

December 1942

On a hot December afternoon, Bryn knelt in the dry soil of his garden, hands caked in dirt and sweat. The small patch he had claimed was scarcely larger than a dining table, yet it had become his family's lifeline beyond the meager communal rations.

His fingers, calloused from months of this work, scraped the ground with a makeshift wooden tool. Every movement felt like a battle against stubborn earth. Each seed planted was its own small victory.

The sun hung low and fierce. Bryn's shirt clung to his back. His stomach twisted with familiar hollow ache. The daily rations barely kept him functional. He settled into work with the meditative rhythm that had carried him through military service. Ah-Min's voice came to him unbidden. *"Patience, young master. All things grow in their proper season."* That patience felt harder now, with Patricia's ribs showing through her dress and David's eyes too large in his small face. But forcing growth never worked. He had learned that much. Control what you can control, as the Stoics taught. He could not command the soil to be richer or the sun to be gentler, but he could work with what existed, bending without breaking.

A shadow fell across his plot. Bryn looked up to see Thompson and Miller approaching, two burly American internees whose faces showed the strain of men pushed to their breaking point. Both had arrived in the camp after the repatriation. Thompson had been classified as a businessman rather than a civilian, while Miller had been rejected for the exchange due to some minor criminal conviction in his past. Both men had the soft look of those who had lived comfortable lives before the war. Thompson had been an insurance executive in Shanghai, Miller a construction foreman in Hong Kong. But months of internment had hardened them, creating the desperate edge that Bryn recognized from other hungry men in tight quarters.

Thompson's eyes flicked toward Bryn's plants with the calculating gaze of a predator sizing up prey. "Nice little setup you've got here, Williams," Thompson said, his Boston accent still clear despite months of internment. "Heard some of the married quarters are doing pretty well for themselves." The words carried resentment. Single men lived in overcrowded bachelor quarters where competition for resources was fierce, while families in the married quarters had developed support networks that helped them survive more effectively.

Bryn slowly straightened, his body relaxed but ready. His martial arts training, learned from a Gurkha sergeant in Cairo, had taught him to read intentions from stance and the tension around the eyes. "It's for my family," Bryn replied evenly, noting how Miller had positioned himself slightly to the left. Classic pincer movement. Amateur. "Like the other plots are for their families. Don't you have your own garden space?"

Miller stepped closer, his worn boots crunching on the dry earth. "We don't have kids to feed," Miller said, his voice tinged with resentment. "Just ourselves. But we're all starving here, mate. Don't see why your little ones should eat while grown men waste away."

"They're children, not competitors," Bryn said quietly. "You're grown men with the strength to work for your own food. The Japanese allow garden plots for anyone willing to claim and work them. Get your own."

Thompson's lips curled into a sneer. "We don't have time to play farmer while you live like a king. Maybe we'll just help ourselves to what you've got growing." He lunged toward the nearest plant, his hand outstretched greedily toward a bok choy that represented hours of careful cultivation. Bryn moved with fluid precision, not the brutal efficiency he'd learned in military combat, but the economy of motion that years of internal martial arts practice had ingrained in his muscle memory.

He intercepted Thompson's arm at the wrist, applied gentle but irresistible pressure to the nerve cluster just below the palm, and guided the American smoothly to his knees. The movement was so controlled that Thompson found himself kneeling before he understood what had happened.

"Enough!" Bryn said, his voice carrying quiet authority. The wooden tool in his free hand hovered inches from Thompson's face, not threatening but simply present. "You're desperate. I understand that. We all are. But touch my garden again, and you'll discover I learned more than farming during my army service."

Thompson clenched his teeth, Bryn's grip sending sharp warnings up his arm. "All right, all right! Let me go!"

Bryn released him with a gentle push that sent the American stumbling backward into Miller's waiting arms.

Chapter 38: Bread, Rice and Resolve

"You'll regret this, Williams," Thompson muttered, rubbing his arm where pressure points still tingled.

"Perhaps," Bryn said, returning to his plants with deliberate calm. "But the Japanese provide garden plots for those willing to work. The soil is poor, the tools are makeshift, but the vegetables will grow if you tend them properly. I'd be happy to show you the techniques I've learned."

The offer was genuine, though Bryn suspected it would be rejected. These were men who wanted easy solutions to complex problems.

Thompson spat in the dirt. "Keep your charity."

But Bryn noticed that Miller paused for a moment, his eyes examining the careful arrangement of plants and the improvised irrigation system made from tin cans and scavenged wire. Perhaps there was hope for that one.

As the two Americans walked away, muttering threats and complaints, Bryn settled back into his meditative state. Epictetus came to mind now, lessons from another lifetime. "We cannot choose our circumstances, but we can choose how we respond to them." The Stoics understood something essential about control. He could not control the hunger, the guards, the wire. But he could control his hands in the soil, his response to provocation, his choice to plant rather than despair.

He knelt once more among his plants, fingers digging into soil that offered hope of sustenance, however small. The vegetables he cultivated here could add vitamins to their diet, helping ward off the diseases that increasingly claimed the elderly and weak among the internees.

With careful hands, Bryn began harvesting what was ready. Three small bok choy leaves, a handful of bean sprouts, and two tiny radishes no bigger than his thumb. Each piece was valuable, potentially making the difference between health and the slow decline he noticed in too many faces around the camp. He wrapped the vegetables gently in a piece of cloth, protecting them carefully. The walk to Block 13 led him past other garden plots. Some thrived under careful tending, while others had been abandoned by internees who lacked patience for gardening.

Alicia looked up from where she sat mending a tear in David's small pants. Even after months of meager rations, she maintained the quiet dignity that had first attracted him during their courtship in Hong Kong's colonial society. Her dark hair, now kept short for practicality, framed a face grown thin but not yet gaunt. Her eyes, the deep brown he remembered from better days, lit up when she saw the bundle in his hands.

"The garden was good to us today," Bryn said quietly, mindful of their roommates who pretended not to watch as he unwrapped the vegetables with careful ceremony.

Alicia set aside her mending and came to examine the small harvest, her fingers gentle as she touched each leaf. "Oh, Bryn," she whispered, her voice filled with genuine wonder. "Look at these beautiful radishes. And the bok choy is perfect." She held up one of the leaves to catch the fading light from their single window. "Patricia will be so excited. She's been asking about green vegetables for days."

Their daughter, now almost five years old, was playing quietly in the corner with David, who at nearly two had learned to contain his boyish energy within the constraints of their shared space. Both children had grown thin, their clothes hanging loose despite Alicia's constant alterations, but their eyes still held the brightness that spoke of resilience and hope.

"Mama, is that food from Papa's garden?" Patricia asked, abandoning her game of making dolls from scraps of fabric and bits of string.

"Yes, darling. Real vegetables that Papa grew just for us," Alicia smiled at their daughter, though Bryn caught the worried glance she gave him over Patricia's head. They both knew how precarious their situation remained, how each day was a small victory against circumstances designed to break them.

Alicia carefully rewrapped the vegetables in the cloth. "I'll take these to the communal kitchen early tomorrow morning," she said, her voice adopting the practical tone Bryn recognized as her way of planning and calculating. "Mrs. Kowalski showed me how to stretch vegetables. If I add them to whatever rice we can get, along with some vegetable scraps that other families might be willing to share, I can make a stew that will last us three, maybe four days."

"See if you can get some extra water to wash the vegetables first," Bryn suggested. "One of the Japanese guards, Yuto, knows you and might be willing to help if you ask nicely."

Alicia nodded, understanding the unspoken web of small favors and careful alliances that made survival possible.

Bryn settled onto their sleeping mat. He opened his arms to the children. Patricia immediately curled against his side, her small body warm and trusting, while David, still holding onto some of his boyish independence, sat close enough to touch but far enough away to assert his growing autonomy.

Outside their window, the lights of distant boats drifted across Stanley Bay, and somewhere beyond the horizon, a world still at war continued to fight for the freedoms they had lost. But here, in this crowded room filled with the quiet breathing of sleeping families, hope grew in small steps. A shared meal, a successful harvest, and the stubborn belief that love could endure even in places built to destroy it.

Chapter 39

The Price of Integrity

"They offer us bread for betrayal, rice for our silence, meat for our complicity. But what sustains the body can poison the soul. In this place where everything has been taken from us, integrity remains the one possession our captors cannot confiscate unless we surrender it willingly."

From "Moral Choices in Extremis" by Franklin Gimson, Stanley Internment Camp, 1945

September 1943

Months had passed. Winter brought cooler weather but no relief from hunger. Spring arrived with storms that battered the garden plots. Bryn replanted what was lost. Ah-Min had taught him that a gardener accepts what the seasons bring and works with what remains. Resistance, the old man had said, was not always loud defiance. Sometimes it was simply continuing to plant seeds when destruction seemed certain.

By summer, rumors circulated through the camp about increased Japanese paranoia. Talk of a secret radio. Whispers about who might be involved. Bryn kept his head down and tended his garden, but he felt the tension growing like pressure before a storm.

Now, on this September afternoon, the sun cast long shadows across the camp as Bryn walked the perimeter with his family. Their daily exercise was now a slow shuffle that conserved energy. Alicia's arm rested lightly on his, and he could see how thin she had become beneath her patched cotton dress. Patricia held his other hand, while three-year-old David rode on Bryn's shoulders, his weight no longer the burden it once was.

"Papa, why are the Japanese soldiers digging near Block 18?" Patricia asked, her voice carrying the seriousness that camp life had taught all the children.

Bryn glanced toward the Indian Quarters, where he saw soldiers overseeing

Indian guards with shovels. His stomach clenched. "I don't know, sweetheart. Perhaps they're looking for something." Those trenches looked all too familiar.

Alicia caught his eye with a worried look. They both understood what "looking for something" probably meant in Stanley Camp. Rumors had been spreading for weeks about increased Japanese surveillance, surprise searches, and whispers about resistance activities. The recent arrests of several key internees had created a tense atmosphere that hovered over the camp like the humid September air.

"Bryn Williams." The harsh voice cut through the afternoon stillness like a blade.

Bryn turned to see Lieutenant Yamamoto approaching, his heavyset figure unmistakable even from a distance. The Japanese officer's uniform was tidy despite the heat, and his wooden baton gleamed in the sunlight. Behind him walked two guards, their faces blank but alert.

"Lieutenant Yamamoto," Bryn replied carefully, bowing and keeping his voice neutral as he gently lifted David from his shoulders and set him down beside Alicia.

Yamamoto's small eyes narrowed as he examined Bryn's family. The silence dragged on before he spoke again. "The Commandant wants to talk to you."

"About what?" Bryn asked, immediately regretting the question.

Yamamoto's face darkened, and he quickly raised his baton in a threatening motion. Bryn automatically stepped forward, placing himself between the officer and his family, and gave a slight bow while maintaining eye contact. The gesture was just enough to acknowledge Japanese authority without appearing servile. "You don't ask the questions. We do." Yamamoto's voice carried barely contained violence. He pointed toward the administrative building with his baton. "Now."

Bryn felt Alicia's hand brush his arm in reassurance. "I'll be back soon," he murmured to his family, trying to sound confident even though uncertainty gnawed at him. "Why don't you go to our garden plot and see how the radishes are doing?"

"We'll see you soon," Alicia replied. "Come on, Patricia and David, let's see how our garden is doing." She took the children by the hand and walked slowly away, glancing once at Bryn.

The walk to the administrative office felt longer than usual. His mind raced. *"What was this about? Had someone reported his conversations with other internees about camp conditions? Had vegetable gardens somehow violated regulations? Or was this connected to the recent escapes that had angered the Japanese and put everyone on edge?"*

The administrative building had once served as the officers' quarters in the prison and still exuded an air of institutional authority, which the Japanese had

Chapter 39: The Price of Integrity

reinforced with their symbols of power. Outside the Commandant's office, Yamamoto signaled for Bryn to wait as he went inside. Through the thin walls, Bryn could hear muffled voices speaking rapidly in Japanese. After what felt like an eternity, Yamamoto finally emerged and jerked his head toward the office. "Go."

Commandant Nakazawa sat behind a heavy wooden desk that loomed over his slight frame. In his early forties with prematurely gray hair, he exuded an air of cultured intelligence that made him more dangerous than the brutish Yamamoto. Unlike his subordinate, Nakazawa spoke perfect English and grasped the subtle dynamics of camp life. "Mr. Williams, please sit." Nakazawa's voice was nearly gentle, a sharp contrast to Yamamoto's stern commands. He gestured toward a wooden chair facing his desk. "I trust your family is well?"

Yamamoto had positioned himself directly behind Bryn, blocking the door.

"As well as can be expected, given the circumstances," Bryn replied cautiously, settling into the chair while staying alert.

Nakazawa nodded sympathetically. "Yes, these are difficult times for everyone. I understand your daughter has been quite ill recently?"

"She's recovered, thank you," Bryn replied.

"And your wife? The rations are difficult for maintaining proper nutrition, especially for women and children."

The observation lingered in the air. Bryn stayed silent, sensing this was heading somewhere specific.

Nakazawa leaned back in his chair, studying Bryn with calculating eyes. "You know, Mr. Williams, I have been watching you since your arrival in camp. You are not like some of the others. You don't complain constantly or make unreasonable demands. The other internees respect you. They listen when you speak."

"I try to help when I can," Bryn said carefully.

"Exactly." Nakazawa smiled, but the expression never reached his eyes. "This is why I wanted to speak with you privately. I have heard disturbing rumors recently. Whispers about certain activities that are serious violations of camp regulations."

"Here it comes," Bryn thought. *"Accept what comes. Do not waste energy resisting what has already occurred."*

"What kind of activities?" He asked.

"There are rumors of prisoners making a radio, which is strictly forbidden and punishable by death," Nakazawa said.

"I see," Bryn managed to say, his mouth suddenly dry.

Nakazawa leaned forward, his voice becoming more personal. "I believe you understand the seriousness of this situation. These men, if they exist, are not just risking themselves but the entire camp. When such activities are discovered, the consequences go far beyond the offenders. Because of your respected position among the internees," Nakazawa continued, "people trust you. They share information they might not tell others. This puts you in a unique position to help us prevent a tragedy."

Nakazawa paused. "In return for your assistance in keeping me informed about any such activities," Nakazawa added, his tone becoming almost businesslike, "your family would receive extra food rations. Fresh vegetables, perhaps some meat, definitely more rice. And clothing. Undoubtedly, your wife's and your children's clothing is getting quite worn, and your children will need warmer garments for the coming winter."

Bryn's mind raced. He thought of Patricia's thin arms, David's prominent ribs. But once reading ancient philosophy the words of Epictetus came back to him . *"If you would not be a slave to circumstances, do not value what circumstances can take away."* Integrity could not be bartered, not for rice, not even for his children's comfort. Once sold, it could never be recovered.

"I can tell you right now, I don't know anything about a radio or the men that might be involved in making one," Bryn said.

Nakazawa nodded. "I believe you. But if you come across any information, no matter how insignificant it seems, I want you to come see me immediately. Your family will be rewarded, as I have said."

"I need to think about this," Bryn said finally, his voice carefully controlled.

Nakazawa nodded as if he had anticipated this response. "Of course. But don't think too long, Mr. Williams. Events are moving quickly, and I fear that if this radio situation isn't resolved soon, the consequences will be severe for everyone."

Bryn stood to leave, his legs feeling unsteady. "How long do I have to decide?"

"Twenty-four hours. That should be enough time to weigh your family's welfare against vague loyalties that might cloud your judgment," Nakazawa answered.

Bryn bowed and walked slowly out of the office without another word, with Yamamoto close behind.

Alicia took one look at his face when he returned. "Play quietly," she told the children firmly. "Help Papa and me by digging some more holes for new seeds to be planted. Papa and I need to talk."

Chapter 39: The Price of Integrity

Bryn related the entire conversation in whispers. Alicia's face grew pale as he described Nakazawa's offer and the implicit threats.

"The children," she whispered, glancing toward Patricia and David. "They're so thin, Bryn. David's ribs show when he bathes, and Patricia barely has energy to play anymore."

Bryn nodded. Despite his efforts to supplement their diet with vegetables from their small garden, tomatoes, sweet potatoes, and greens grown in soil scraped from hillsides, none of them were getting enough nutrition. The official rations provided by the Japanese were barely enough to prevent starvation.

"What if you report this to Gimson?" Alicia suggested, referring to Franklin Gimson, the Colonial Secretary who served as representative of the internees.

"If there's an informant on the camp committee, word could get back to Nakazawa. That would put us in an even worse position," Bryn replied.

They sat in silence for a few minutes, watching their children play. The sounds of other families nearby created a constant background of human struggle. Privacy was a luxury none of them could afford.

"The radio," Alicia whispered finally. "Do you think it's real?"

"Probably," he admitted. "And if it is, they're already in terrible danger."

Alicia reached for his hand, her fingers thin and cold despite the warm evening. "What are we going to do?"

Bryn looked at his children. Patricia, whose bright intelligence had been dulled by malnutrition and the constant stress of camp life, and David, who was so young he would have no memory of the world before barbed wire and guards. The choice was not just about moral convictions. It was about their survival. "I don't know," he admitted. "I have only twenty four hours to give Nakazawa an answer. But I know one thing. Whatever we decide, we decide together. And we protect our family first."

Outside their window, the sun was setting over Stanley Bay, painting the sky in brilliant oranges and reds that seemed to mock the gray desperation of camp life. In the distance, they could hear the guards calling roll for the evening count, their voices harsh and commanding. Time was running out, and a choice would define everything that followed.

The evening passed in restless tension. They fed the children their meager portion of rice, played quiet games, and went through the familiar rituals of bedtime. But beneath the surface calm, the weight of the decision pressed down like a physical force. Bryn lay awake long after the other families in their room had settled into sleep. He listened to the breathing of his children, the soft rustling of blankets, the distant footsteps of guards on patrol. His mind turned over the problem again and again, searching for a solution that did not exist.

Marcus Aurelius had written about difficult choices. "Choose not to be harmed, and you won't feel harmed. Don't feel harmed, and you haven't been." But this was not about perception. The harm was real. Children were starving. The danger was immediate. Yet the Stoics also taught that virtue was the only true good. External things like food, clothing, even life itself were neither good nor bad in themselves. What mattered was how one used them, whether one lived according to reason and principle.

Ah-Min's voice came to him again, gentler than the stern Roman philosophers. "The Tao that can be spoken is not the eternal Tao. The way reveals itself not through grasping, but through letting go." What did that mean here? Let go of the desire to control outcomes? Accept whatever came with equanimity?

But Bryn was not a sage meditating in a monastery. He was a father watching his children grow thinner each day. Philosophy offered frameworks for thinking, but it could not make the choice for him.

In the middle of the night, clarity came. Not through argument or reasoning, but through a simple recognition. He knew what he was going to do. "I've decided. I won't cooperate with Nakazawa. I can't betray our fellow internees and become an informant. But that means we won't get his offer of better food and clothing. I want to make sure you agree."

Alicia was quiet for a long moment. Then she hugged him tightly. "I knew you would decide that, darling. Integrity and service run deep in you. I'm in agreement. We will make do. We will survive. Together."

He looked deeply into the eyes of the woman he loved with admiration and respect for her strength and resilience. Ah-Min had taught him that the Tao valued simplicity, honesty, naturalness. To betray others for personal gain would be to lose his way entirely. Better to remain hungry and whole than fed and fractured. "If we become the kind of people who trade others' lives for our comfort," Bryn whispered, "what are we teaching our children? What kind of world are we creating?"

"The only world worth fighting for," Alicia replied. "One where people can still trust each other, even here."

They held each other in the darkness, drawing strength from their shared conviction. Outside, Stanley Camp settled into another night of uneasy sleep, unaware that in just weeks, the discovery of the secret radio would lead to one of the most brutal episodes in the camp's history.

The next morning, Bryn went to the administrative building. He found

Chapter 39: The Price of Integrity

Nakazawa in his office, reviewing papers with the same cultured calm he always displayed.

"Mr. Williams," Nakazawa said, setting down his pen. "I trust you have considered my offer?"

"I have," Bryn replied, keeping his voice steady. "And I must respectfully decline. I don't know anything about a radio, and I don't believe I would hear anything useful. I'm not in a position to provide the information you're seeking."

Nakazawa studied him for a long moment, his expression unreadable. "That is disappointing, Mr. Williams. I had hoped you would see the benefit to your family."

"My family benefits most from having a father with integrity," Bryn said.

"Very well," Nakazawa said. "You may go. But remember, Mr. Williams, when the consequences come, they will affect everyone. Your choice today may seem noble, but nobility is a luxury in times like these."

October brought arrests in the pre-dawn darkness. Seven men dragged from their beds by the Kempeitai, the Japanese military police. John Fraser, the Defense Secretary. Thomas Scott, the former Police Chief. Hugh Murdoch, a former Navy Captain. Four others whose names Bryn knew from camp committees and shared meals. Taken to Stanley Prison.

The camp lived in suspended terror for three weeks, waiting for the inevitable conclusion.

Chapter 40

Thirty-Three

"There are moments when evil reveals itself so completely that witnessing becomes a sacred duty, even when that witness carves wounds in the soul that never fully heal. We become guardians of memory for those who can no longer speak their own names, and in that guardianship lies both our burden and our purpose."

From "The Weight of Seeing" by Franklin Gimson, Stanley Internment Camp, 1943

October 29, 1943

The shouting started at dawn, harsh Japanese voices echoing across the camp. Bryn jolted awake in his narrow bunk, Alicia stirring beside him while the children stayed mercifully asleep. Through the thin walls of Block 13, he could hear other internees murmuring in confusion and fear.

"All leaders from the camp's four councils report to the assembly area immediately!" The announcement blared over the camp loudspeaker in clipped English, followed by rapid Japanese.

Alicia's eyes met his in the gray morning light. "Trouble?"

Bryn nodded. "Stay with the children," Bryn said quietly, pulling on his worn shirt. As an assistant block leader and committee head, he was required to attend whatever the Japanese had planned.

The assembly area was already crowded when Bryn arrived. Franklin Gimson, Colonial Secretary and chairman of the camp's British Communal Council, stood at the front, his face ashen but composed, while other camp leaders gathered in small, nervous groups. Commandant Nakazawa waited with military precision, flanked by Lieutenant Yamamoto and a squad of guards. Yamamoto's sword gleamed at his side, freshly polished.

"Camp leaders," Nakazawa began, his refined voice easily reaching the quiet crowd. "You are here as witnesses. What you observe today will be reported to your fellow internees as a lesson in the consequences of resisting Imperial Japanese authority."

Bryn's stomach clenched. The elaborate ceremony, the forced witnesses, the theatricality. This was not military justice. This was terror.

"The condemned have conspired against the Empire," Nakazawa continued. "They built instruments of espionage, tried to communicate with enemy forces, and jeopardized the security of this facility. Under military law, the punishment is death."

A truck rolled into view from the direction of Stanley Prison, its engine coughing black smoke into the morning air. Through the open back, Bryn could see more than thirty hooded figures bound and blindfolded. His breath caught. Not just seven. Thirty or more.

"My God," whispered Dr. Talbot beside him. "What have they done to them?"

The condemned emerged from the truck slowly, guards shoving them roughly into line. Fraser, once a strong administrator, moved like a broken scarecrow. Scott's uniform hung in tatters, dark stains marking places where wounds had bled through. All of them showed signs of systematic brutality. Swollen faces, missing teeth, carefully methodical damage.

"They were made to confess," Gimson murmured, his voice barely audible. "God knows what they endured."

Bryn counted silently as they were lined up. Seven Stanley internees he recognized. But there were twenty-six others. Chinese men and women in civilian clothes. Indians. A Eurasian man. A woman, small and frail looking. These were not all camp prisoners.

"Resistance workers," someone whispered behind him. "From the British Army Aid Group network."

Of course. The Japanese had uncovered more than just a radio in Stanley Camp. They had found threads connecting to the larger resistance operation in Hong Kong. People who had smuggled food and medicine into the camps. All of them were connected somehow to the radio operation. Thirty-three people in total. The Japanese were going to execute them all at once, in front of the assembled witnesses, to send a message that would echo far beyond Stanley Camp.

The condemned were marched past the assembled witnesses toward the trenches near Block 18. The same trenches Patricia had asked about just weeks ago. Graves dug by fellow internees who had been told they were drainage ditches.

Yamamoto stepped forward, his hand resting on his sword hilt with clear anticipation. His face displayed an expression Bryn had seen before on men in

Chapter 40: Thirty-Three

Cairo, soldiers who discovered they enjoyed killing more than duty required. "The Emperor's justice is swift and absolute," Nakazawa announced. "Let all who witness this understand the price of defiance."

Yamamoto drew his sword with ceremonial flourish, the blade catching the morning sun. His first victim was Fraser, who faced death with quiet dignity that seemed to enrage the Japanese officer. The sword work was clumsy and brutal. Bryn had seen enough combat to recognize incompetence when he saw it. Yamamoto lacked the skill for precise executions. A trained executioner could deliver death with a single stroke. This was butchery. Each blow seemed calculated to prolong suffering rather than end it swiftly. When Yamamoto's blade failed, guards finished the wounded with rifle shots, the crack of gunfire echoing off the hills around Stanley Bay.

This was not Bushido. Bryn had read enough about Japanese warrior traditions to know the difference between honor and this perversion. True Bushido emphasized compassion for the defeated, a clean death delivered with respect. The samurai code valued mercy even in execution. What was happening here dishonored everyone involved, executioners and witnesses alike. The historical samurai would have been appalled by this display. They spoke of "cutting kindness," the responsibility of the executioner to end suffering quickly and cleanly. Yamamoto was doing the opposite, prolonging agony, taking visible pleasure in incompetent brutality. This was not the way of the warrior. This was sadism dressed in ceremony.

The process repeated. Again and again. Chinese resistance workers who had risked everything to bring food to starving prisoners. Indians who had helped internees communicate with the outside world. The American, Chester Bennett, who could barely walk on his infected leg but held his head high. The woman, Lau Tak Oi, whose only crime was being married to a resistance leader.

Each execution revealed more of Yamamoto's character. By the tenth victim, even the guards looked uncomfortable. By the twentieth, the sword had dulled and the executions became even more prolonged. Some victims had to be finished with multiple rifle shots. Thirty-three times the sword rose and fell. By the end, even some of the Japanese guards looked sick, but Yamamoto's enthusiasm never faltered. His face showed something beyond duty, beyond even cruelty. It showed pleasure.

Marcus Aurelius came unbidden to Bryn's mind. "*The universe is change, our life is what our thoughts make it.*" But how could thought transform this? The Stoics spoke of accepting what lay beyond one's control, but they also spoke of virtue, of justice, of living according to reason and natural law. There was nothing natural in what Yamamoto had become. This was a man who had poisoned his own spirit so thoroughly that cruelty had become indistinguishable from joy.

The Japanese invoked Bushido to justify their actions, but they had stripped away everything that made the warrior code honorable. Loyalty without wisdom became fanaticism. Duty without compassion became brutality. They had taken the form of their traditions and emptied them of meaning, creating a twisted shadow that served power rather than principle.

From his military experience, Bryn understood what he was really witnessing. Not strength, but weakness. A professional army maintained discipline through respect, through shared purpose, through adherence to established rules of war. What he was seeing was the breakdown of military order, replaced by brutality that served no tactical purpose. Executions in war had clear objectives. Maintaining unit cohesion. Deterring desertion. Upholding the articles of war. But forcing witnesses to watch prolonged torture served no military goal. It was psychological warfare aimed at destroying the spirit of captives who posed no military threat. In Egypt, when the British Army executed deserters, it was done privately, swiftly, with as much dignity as such an act allowed. The goal was justice according to military law, not terror. What was happening here bore no resemblance to legitimate military justice. The Japanese military had become something monstrous, using the language of honor to justify dishonor, invoking tradition to legitimize barbarism. Yamamoto's pleasure in the killing revealed the truth. This was not the reluctant execution of duty. This was corruption made manifest.

"Remove the bodies," Nakazawa ordered when the killing was finished. "The witnesses will remain."

As guards dragged the corpses toward the prepared trenches, Nakazawa turned to face the assembled camp leaders. His cultured voice remained steady, as if he had just overseen a routine administrative matter. "Prisoners, you have seen Imperial justice. These thirty-three individuals chose defiance and met the inevitable consequence. Seven were from your camp. Twenty-six were Chinese, Indian, and other nationals who conspired with them against the Greater East Asia Co-Prosperity Sphere. You will return to your blocks and explain to your fellow internees exactly what befalls those who threaten the security of this facility." He paused, his gaze moving slowly across each face. "There will be no memorial services. No public displays of mourning. No gatherings to honor these criminals. Anyone who violates these restrictions will join them in the ground."

Other men swayed with shock and revulsion. Dr. Selwyn-Clarke had turned completely white.

"Furthermore," Nakazawa continued, "this camp will understand that the security of every internee depends on absolute compliance with regulations. Any future acts of resistance, any attempts to communicate with enemy forces, any violations of camp discipline will result in collective punishment. The next time, it will not be thirty-three who die."

Chapter 40: Thirty-Three

The threat hung in the air. Each person's survival depended on the absolute submission of everyone else.

"Lieutenant Yamamoto will conduct random searches of all quarters," Nakazawa added. "Anyone found in possession of contraband materials, any evidence of unauthorized communication, any suggestion of organized resistance will be dealt with immediately."

Yamamoto smiled at this, blood still speckling his uniform. His enjoyment of the morning's work was evident.

"You are dismissed," Nakazawa concluded. "Report to your blocks and inform the internees."

The walk back to Block 13 felt endless. The sounds echoed. Metal on bone. Screams cut short. The wet thud of bodies falling. Thirty-three times. Bryn found himself thinking of Ah-Min again. What would the old man have made of this horror? "*Violence begets violence, young master,*" Ah-Min had often said while they worked together in the garden. "*The wheel of karma turns for all, but suffering is not the way of enlightenment.*"

The Japanese claimed to follow Buddhist traditions, yet what happened this morning was the antithesis of Buddhist compassion. Where was the mercy, the understanding of suffering, the recognition of common humanity? The Tao spoke of *wu wei*, action through non-action, achieving goals through harmony rather than force. Ah-Min had demonstrated this principle countless times, solving problems through patience and understanding rather than confrontation. "*The soft overcomes the hard, young master. Water conquers stone not through force, but through persistence and finding the natural way.*"

Yet the Japanese had taken the ceremonial aspects of warrior traditions and stripped them of their underlying philosophy of restraint. They had taken thirty-three lives, not because it served justice, but because it served their own psychological need to demonstrate dominance.

"*When we act from anger, we create more suffering,*" Ah-Min had taught him. "When we act from fear, we multiply that fear in others." There was no compassion in what happened this morning. Only fear expressed through overwhelming violence designed to terrorize captives into absolute submission.

What marks were the Japanese leaving on their own souls? Yamamoto's obvious pleasure in the killings suggested a man whose spirit had already been corrupted beyond recognition. The ceremonial aspects, the sword polishing, the ritual stances, seemed like attempts to sanctify what was essentially spiritual suicide.

"Bryn." Gimson's voice stopped him outside the block entrance. The Colonial Secretary looked like he had aged a decade in the past hour. "I need to speak with you privately."

They found a quiet corner near the defunct tennis court, where overgrown weeds provided some illusion of privacy. Gimson's hands shook as he lit a cigarette, one of his weekly rations. "Thirty-three people," Gimson said finally. "Only seven from Stanley, but they made us watch all of them die. They wanted us to understand that this goes beyond our camp. Anyone who helps us, anyone who resists them, meets the same fate."

"Someone talked," Bryn said quietly. "The timing was too precise."

"Or broke under torture," Gimson replied. "I've heard about Kempeitai methods. No one can be expected to withstand that."

They stood in silence, watching smoke from Gimson's cigarette dissipate in the still air. Stanley Camp was waking up to a new reality, one where any whispered conversation, any act of mutual aid, or any attempt to maintain dignity could be construed as resistance worthy of death.

"What do we tell the others?" Bryn asked finally.

"The truth," Gimson replied. "That thirty-three people died this morning. Seven from our camp, twenty-six from outside who tried to help us. And that we're all walking on the edge of a knife now."

Gimson took another drag on his cigarette. "Nakazawa approached you last month, didn't he? Tried to recruit you as an informant?"

Bryn nodded slowly.

"I'm glad you refused," Gimson said. "Whatever else happens, we need to know we can still trust each other. The moment we start betraying our own, they've won everything that matters."

"But thirty-three people are dead," Bryn said.

"And if you had informed, would it have been different? Or would they have simply had their informant and still executed everyone they wanted to execute?" Gimson shook his head. "The Japanese decided months ago who would die. They were just looking for an excuse to justify it."

Bryn paused outside Block 13, taking a moment to center himself before facing his family. He breathed deeply, feeling the weight of thirty-three deaths pressing against his consciousness. In this moment, surrounded by barbed wire and guard towers, Ah-Min's philosophical consolations felt impossibly distant. The reality was thirty-three people dead, their families destroyed, and a camp full of people living in terror. But perhaps that was the point. Philosophy was not meant to make horror disappear. It was meant to provide a framework for surviving horror without becoming monstrous yourself. The Stoics taught that you could not

Chapter 40: Thirty-Three

control events, only your response to them. The Taoists taught that one could bend without breaking and adapt without surrendering one's essential nature.

He had refused to become an informant. That choice had not saved the thirty-three, but it had saved something else. His integrity. His ability to look his children in the eye. His place in a community that still tried to hold onto human decency in a place designed to destroy it.

The radio was silent now, its voices forever stilled. The true test would be whether the Japanese could kill not just bodies, but the spirit of resistance that had driven men and women to risk everything for connection to the world beyond the wire.

Back in their shared room, Bryn found Alicia waiting with barely controlled anxiety. The children were still asleep, mercifully unaware of the morning's horror.

"How bad?" she whispered.

Bryn pulled her close, breathing in the familiar scent of her hair, now lank and unwashed, but still comforting. "Worse than we imagined. Thirty-three people. They made us watch it all." He described the execution in quiet, clinical terms, trying to drain the emotion from the facts. But he couldn't hide the tremor in his voice when he spoke of the scale of it, the deliberate cruelty, the way Yamamoto had taken obvious pleasure in prolonging suffering.

"And now?" Alicia asked.

"Now we survive," Bryn said. "We keep our heads down, follow every rule, and try to protect our children from becoming the next example."

Throughout the day, news of the executions spread through the camp. Not seven men, but thirty-three people. Chinese resistance workers. Indians who had helped smuggle supplies. An American. A woman. And seven Stanley internees. Conversations turned to hushed whispers.

That evening, as Bryn tucked Patricia and David into their narrow bunks, his daughter looked up with solemn eyes that had seen too much for her six years.

"Papa, why are people so sad today?"

Bryn smoothed her hair, searching for words that could explain incomprehensible brutality to a child's mind. "Some people made choices that got them in trouble, sweetheart. Very serious trouble."

In the darkness of Block 13, surrounded by the soft breathing of his family, Bryn made a silent promise to the dead. *"I will survive. I will protect my children. And someday, when this nightmare ends, I will bear witness to what happened here, to the courage of those who died and the cruelty of those who killed them."*

Chapter 41

The Long Wait

"In the architecture of tyranny, every small comfort removed is a brick added to the wall of despair. Yet even in the most perfectly constructed prison, the human heart finds ways to build secret gardens where love can still grow."

From "Letters Never Sent" by Alaine Wellington, Stanley Internment Camp, 1944

November, 1944

Bryn Williams woke before dawn to the sound of boots in the corridor, the daily inspection that Captain Tanaka conducted with predatory precision. "Time to get up," he whispered to his wife Alicia, who stirred beside him on their thin mat.

"Patricia, David," he called softly to his children. Seven-year-old Patricia was already sitting up, automatically smoothing her hair. Four-year-old David rubbed his eyes but moved quickly, understanding that slowness invited trouble.

They arranged themselves in the prescribed manner as the door swung open. Tanaka's eyes swept the room, looking for any infraction that would justify his cruelty. Finding none, he moved on without a word, leaving behind the familiar mixture of relief and exhaustion.

"Another day," Alicia murmured, leaning against Bryn for a moment before they had to face the food queue.

The change from civilian to military control brought Lieutenant Colonel Tokunaga and his second-in-command, Captain Tanaka. Under the previous civilian commandant, Mr. Nakazawa, there had been grudging respect for internee self-governance. Nakazawa had been educated, even cultured. The new administration brought systematic intimidation and arbitrary cruelty.

The morning congee line stretched around the courtyard, at least forty people ahead of them. Mrs. Truman, the widow from Block 17, stood behind them and kept her voice low. "They cut the rations again. Third time this month."

Dangerous talk with guards positioned nearby, but everyone felt it. The gnawing hunger that never left, the way clothes hung looser each week, the children's faces growing gaunt despite parents' efforts to shield them.

Alicia swayed slightly, and Bryn steadied her with his hand. "Are you all right?"

"Just tired. I'll be fine," Alicia replied.

But he noticed she had been tired more often lately. Small signs he tried not to worry about in a place where worry was as constant as breathing. After they collected their meager portions and returned to their room, Alicia sat heavily on the mat.

Patricia moved close to her mother, and Bryn saw the protective instinct that had developed in his daughter over three years of imprisonment. "Mama, you should eat more," Patricia said, trying to push some of her rice toward Alicia's bowl.

"I'm fine, sweetheart. You need to grow."

But Alicia ate very little, and when the children weren't looking, she ran to the communal toilet and was sick.

That night, after Patricia and David had fallen asleep, Bryn found Alicia sitting outside their door in the warm darkness. When he sat beside her, he saw tears on her face. "You've been nauseous frequently now," he said quietly. "How long has it been like this?"

She looked at him, and in the dim light he saw both fear and something else. Determination, perhaps. Or defiance. "Two months, I think. Maybe a little more. I'm pregnant for sure," she said, needing to speak it aloud to make it real.

The words settled into Bryn's chest like a stone. Pregnant. Here, now, with conditions deteriorating and their own survival uncertain. He felt a complex rush of emotions. Joy that life persisted. Terror at what this meant. Guilt that they had created this situation. "Oh sweetheart," Bryn said softly, "I...didn't realize..."

Her voice was barely a whisper. "Bryn, I'm so sorry. I know the timing is terrible, I know we can barely feed the children we have, I know..."

"It's alright," he said, pulling her close. "I am happy, but worried for you...for both of us. Your health is so delicate now." But his own heart was racing. Another mouth to feed. Another child to protect in a place designed to break them. Another person he could lose. "This isn't something to apologize for."

"But the food situation, and with the military administration, and everything getting worse..." She pressed his free hand to her face. "What kind of world are we bringing a baby into?"

Chapter 41: The Long Wait

"The same world that has Patricia and David," Bryn said, trying to convince himself as much as her. "The same world where Mrs. Henderson had her baby two years ago. The same world where people still find ways to be human."

"I'm afraid," Alicia finally said.

"I know. So am I."

Later, after Alicia had fallen into restless sleep, Bryn lay awake staring at the ceiling. His mind raced through calculations he couldn't control. How to get more food for Alicia. How to keep her healthy enough to carry a baby. What would happen during delivery with Dr. Stanton's supplies nearly exhausted.

He thought about the baby growing inside his wife and felt a confusing tangle of emotions. Love, already, for this child they hadn't planned. Fear that threatened to choke him. And underneath it all, a terrible thought he immediately felt guilty for having resentment. Bryn turned on his side and watched his wife sleep, her thin frame barely visible beneath their threadbare blanket. He reached out and touched her belly gently, feeling nothing yet but knowing life was there. "Please," he whispered into the darkness, not sure who he was praying to. "Please let her survive this."

December, 1944

Word spread through the camp quickly. Alicia Williams was expecting. In a place where privacy barely existed, where families shared single rooms and walls were thin, secrets were impossible to keep.

The reactions varied. Some offered quiet congratulations. Others looked at Alicia's thin frame and said nothing, their silence more eloquent than words. Mrs. Wilson, whose husband had died in the cholera outbreak of 1943, began hoarding tiny amounts of sugar in a carefully hidden tin.

"For when the baby comes," she told Bryn one morning, pressing the tin into his hands. "Every child should have something sweet."

Bryn felt his throat constrict with emotion. "Thank you. This means more than you know."

"We take care of each other," Mrs. Wilson said simply. "That's how we survive."

But survival felt increasingly precarious. Bryn found himself waking at three in the morning, his heart pounding with nameless dread. He would lie there in the darkness, listening to his family breathe, and feel terror washing over him in waves. Alicia could die. The baby could die. They could both die, leaving him alone with Patricia and David in this place.

Ashes and Dawn

The Housing Committee meetings continued to be exercises in managed frustration. Lieutenant Sato announced another consolidation of living spaces in mid-December, and Bryn found himself speaking up despite the risk. "Lieutenant, my wife is expecting a child. We need some privacy for her condition."

"Pregnancy is not a special circumstance," Sato said flatly. "Many women are pregnant. They share rooms."

"With respect, sir, my wife is not well. The morning sickness is severe, and the close quarters..."

"Are you questioning military judgment?" Sato's voice went cold, and Bryn felt every person in the room go still.

"No, sir," he said quietly. "I'm not questioning military judgment."

But after the meeting, Bryn found himself in the small space behind the library, alone, and something broke inside him. He sank onto a broken bench and put his head in his hands. His body shook with silent sobs he had been holding back for weeks. The fear, the helplessness, the grinding certainty that he could not protect his family no matter what he did.

"Bryn? Are you alright?"

He looked up to find Reverend Hartwell standing a few feet away. The elderly Anglican chaplain had been a quiet presence in camp, holding services and offering comfort where he could.

Bryn wiped his face quickly. "I'm fine."

"You're not fine." Hartwell sat beside him. "And you don't need to pretend you are."

The kindness in his voice undid what little composure Bryn had regained. "My wife is pregnant. She's already malnourished, and now she's trying to grow a baby, and I can't protect her. I can't get her more food. I can't make this place safer. I can't do anything except watch and hope it's enough."

"You're doing what you can," Hartwell said. "That's all any of us can do."

"What if it's not enough? What if she dies? What if the baby dies? What if I lose both of them?" The words came faster now, desperate. "I keep waking up in the middle of the night convinced she's stopped breathing. I can't eat because I'm so afraid. And the worst part is, sometimes I..." He stopped, unable to say it.

"Sometimes you resent the baby," Hartwell finished gently. "For putting Alicia at risk."

Bryn looked at him, shocked that someone had named the thought he could barely acknowledge. "Yes. And then I hate myself for thinking it."

Chapter 41: The Long Wait

"You're human," Hartwell said. "Fear makes us think terrible things. The fact that you feel guilty about it shows you're a good man and a good father."

"I don't feel like either right now."

"The mark of a good man isn't the absence of fear or doubt. It's continuing to love and protect your family despite them." Hartwell paused. "Alicia is strong. I've seen her strength. Have you talked to her about how you're feeling?"

"I can't. She's already terrified. If she knows I'm losing faith..."

"She probably already knows. Women usually do." Hartwell stood, placing a hand on Bryn's shoulder. "Talk to her. You're in this together. Carrying it alone will break you."

That night, after the children were asleep, Bryn lay beside Alicia in the darkness. She was awake too, he could tell from her breathing. "I'm afraid," he said quietly. "Afraid of losing you."

She turned to face him, and even in the dim light he could see tears on her cheeks. "I'm afraid too. Every day I feel this baby growing and I wonder if my body has enough strength for both of us."

"I keep having terrible thoughts," Bryn admitted. "About the baby. About resenting the risk."

"So do I," Alicia whispered. "Sometimes I think about how much easier it would be if I weren't pregnant. And then I feel like a monster."

"You're not a monster. Neither am I," he replied softly.

"I want this baby," Alicia said fiercely. "Despite everything, I want him. I already love him."

"So do I," Bryn realized as he said it. "I love him and I'm terrified for him and for you, and I don't know how to hold all these feelings at once."

"We hold them together," Alicia said, taking his hand and placing it on her belly. "We're not alone in this, Bryn. We have each other. We have Patricia and David. We have this whole camp watching out for us."

They lay there in the darkness, hands joined over the life growing between them, and for the first time in weeks, Bryn felt something other than pure terror. Not quite hope, but perhaps the possibility of hope.

Christmas came with its usual bitter irony. Three years since Hong Kong had fallen. Someone had managed to save a few decorations, and the children made ornaments from scraps of paper and tin. The adults tried to make it festive, singing carols in the courtyard while guards watched with expressions ranging from boredom to contempt.

Alicia sat with her hand resting on her barely visible belly, trying to imagine a Christmas when they would be free.

"What are you thinking about?" Bryn asked, settling beside her.

"Next Christmas," she said. "When we're home. When Raymond is here."

"Raymond?"

"For my father. If it's a boy." She looked at him. "Do you mind?"

"I think it's perfect," Bryn said. "A strong name for a fighter."

"He'll have to be," Alicia said quietly. "To survive this place."

January 16, 1945

The morning started like any other. Food queue, morning inspection, the careful navigation of another day under military rule. Alicia was nearly four months pregnant now, her belly just beginning to show beneath her loose dress. The morning sickness had eased slightly, but she was constantly exhausted.

Bryn was in the courtyard when the air raid sirens began to wail.

"Everyone inside!" the guards shouted. "Away from windows!"

Bryn sprinted toward their room where Alicia would have gathered the children. The American planes came in low and fast, their engines screaming. Then came the explosion. The sound was massive, a physical force that knocked Bryn off his feet. He scrambled up and ran toward the smoke rising from what had been Bungalow 5. The building had taken a direct hit, walls collapsed, debris everywhere. Bryn joined the rescue effort, his hands soon bloody from moving broken concrete and twisted metal. Bodies emerged from the wreckage. By afternoon, they knew the full cost. Fourteen dead.

Bryn found Alicia with the children behind their building, where they had sheltered. She was pale and shaking, one arm around Patricia, the other holding David close. "Are you hurt?" he asked urgently, running his hands over her arms, checking for injuries.

"No. We're fine. But the explosion..." She looked toward the rising smoke. "We could have been there. Any of us."

Bryn pulled his family close, feeling Alicia's body trembling against him. His own heart was hammering so hard he thought it might break through his ribs. They could have died. All of them, gone in an instant. Alicia and the baby and the children, wiped out by a bomb dropped by their own side.

That night at the vigil for the dead, Bryn couldn't stop his hands from shaking.

Chapter 41: The Long Wait

Even hours later, sitting with his family among the flickering candles, the tremor persisted. He kept looking at Alicia, at Patricia and David, needing to confirm they were still there, still alive.

"Papa, why are you shaking?" David asked.

"Just cold, son." But it wasn't cold. It was the delayed shock of how close they had come.

After the children were asleep, Alicia wept in his arms. "I can't do this anymore," she said into his shoulder. "I can't keep being strong. I'm so tired, Bryn. I'm so tired."

"I know. I know," he replied, softly stroking her cheek.

"What if the baby comes and we're still here? What if I die in childbirth? What if..." Her voice broke. "I don't want to die here."

"You're not going to die," he reassured her. "You are too strong to die. You've proven that."

"Promise me something," Alicia said, pulling back to look into his eyes. "If I don't make it, if something happens during delivery, promise me you'll tell the children I loved them. That I fought to stay with them."

"Alicia, please..."

"Promise me, Bryn. I need to hear you say it."

He looked at his wife's face, saw the terror and determination warring there, and made a promise he hoped desperately he would never have to keep. "I promise. But you're going to survive. You and Raymond both."

Alicia embraced Bryn tightly, feeling like she couldn't let go.

March, 1945

The cough started small, a tickle in Alicia's throat that she tried to ignore. By mid-March, when she was nearly six months pregnant, it had become persistent enough that Bryn couldn't pretend it was nothing.

"You need to see Dr. Stanton."

"It's just a cough. Everyone has a cough."

"Alicia, please."

She relented, more to ease his worry than from genuine concern. But when she returned from the medical building, her face was ashen.

"What did she say?" Bryn asked, though something in him already knew.

"Diphtheria." The word fell between them like a stone. "She's almost certain. There's a gray membrane forming in my throat."

Bryn felt the world tilt. Diphtheria. A disease that killed healthy adults. In a malnourished pregnant woman, the chances were... "What can you do?"

"Treat symptoms. But without antibiotics, there's no cure. My body has to fight it." Alicia sat heavily on their mat. "She says the pregnancy complicates everything. My immune system is already compromised. The strain on my body..."

She didn't finish, but she didn't need to. Bryn saw it in her face. She might die. The baby might die. They could both die.

"I'm going to talk to Dr. Stanton," he said. "I don't doubt what you said, but I have questions…"

The doctor was frank with him in a way she hadn't been with Alicia. "The diphtheria is serious. Add the malnutrition and pregnancy, and frankly, Bryn, the odds aren't good. If she's still fighting the disease when she goes into labor..." Dr. Stanton shook her head. "I've been a doctor for twenty years. This is one of the worst combinations I've encountered."

"But there's a chance."

"There's always a chance. Your wife is a fighter. But you need to prepare yourself for the possibility that you might lose her. Or the baby. Or both."

Walking back to their room, Bryn felt numb. His mind kept trying to imagine life without Alicia and couldn't. But that evening, sitting with Patricia and David while Alicia slept fitfully, Bryn couldn't find the words. He looked at their faces, still so young despite everything, and felt paralyzed.

Patricia solved it for him. "Mama's really sick, isn't she? Not just a cough."

Bryn took a breath. "Yes. She's very sick."

"Is she going to die?" Patricia's voice was steady, but her eyes were huge.

Every instinct screamed at him to lie, to protect them, to say everything would be fine. But Fitzgerald was right. They deserved truth. "She might," he said, and the words felt like tearing something inside himself. "The doctor is doing everything she can, but Mama has a disease called diphtheria. It's very serious, especially with the baby coming."

David's face crumpled. "But she can't die. She's Mama."

"I know, son. I know." Bryn pulled them both close, feeling David start to sob against his chest. Patricia was rigid, not crying, her body tense as wire.

"What happens to us if Mama dies?" Patricia asked. The practical question hit

Chapter 41: The Long Wait

Bryn like a blow.

"Then we take care of each other. You, me, David, and the baby Raymond if he survives. We stay together."

After he got them settled for sleep, Bryn sat outside their door with his head in his hands. The conversation had gutted him. Looking at their faces, telling them their mother might die, seeing their world crack apart.

That night, after the children slept, Bryn lay beside his wife in the darkness. She was awake, feverish, her breathing rough.

"I told the children," he said quietly. "That you might not survive."

"How did they take it?" she said weakly.

"About as well as you'd expect. David cried. Patricia asked what happens to you after your death."

Alicia made a sound that might have been a laugh or a sob. "She's so practical."

"She's terrified. They both are." Bryn turned to face her, finding her hand in the darkness. "I'm terrified."

"I know. I can feel it." Alicia's grip was weak but insistent. "I'm terrified too. Every time I swallow and it hurts, every time I can't catch my breath, I think this might be how it ends."

"I don't know what I'd do without you," Bryn said, a tear bursting from his eye.

"You'd survive. You'd take care of the children. You'd grieve me and eventually you'd find a way to live again." Her voice was fierce despite its weakness. "But you won't have to. Because I'm not dying. Not here, not now, not before I hold Raymond and see our family safe," she replied with surprising strength in her voice.

Bryn held her carefully, feeling how fragile she had become, feeling the baby moving between them, feeling his own fear threatening to drown him. "I love you," he said. "I've loved you from the moment I met you, and I'll love you until my last breath."

"Then keep breathing," Alicia said. "And help me keep breathing too."

Chapter 42

The Fight

"The hardest choices require the strongest wills, but sometimes the strongest wills break the tenderest hearts."

Found in a Hong Kong government official's diary, 1940

April, 1945

Bryn's hands shook as he tried to button his shirt. The third time he fumbled the same button, he gave up and left it undone.

"Papa, are you cold?" David asked, watching from across the room.

"No, son. Just clumsy today." But it wasn't just today. The tremor had been getting worse for weeks. His body was betraying him, shutting down in ways he couldn't control.

In the food queue that morning, Mrs. Truman stared at him openly. "Good Lord, Bryn. When did you last eat a full meal?"

"Yesterday," he replied.

Bryn collected his rice ration and walked away before they could say more. Back in their room, he sat beside Alicia and tried to eat. She was propped against the wall, her throat so swollen she could barely swallow broth. Watching her struggle made each bite feel like betrayal.

"You need to eat that," Alicia said, her voice a rough whisper.

"I will."

"Bryn." She reached for his hand. "You're giving everything away again, aren't you?"

He didn't answer.

"I can see it in your face. You're starving yourself."

"You need it more," he said.

"And when you collapse? Who takes care of the children then?" Her fevered eyes held his. "You can't pour from an empty cup."

That afternoon, his new friend Tom Fitzgerald found him in the courtyard and pulled him into the shade of a building. "We need to talk."

"I don't have time right now Tom," Bryn answered hurriedly.

"Make time." Tom's usual humor was gone. "You're killing yourself. Don't try to deny it. Everyone can see it."

"Alicia is dying and you want me to worry about whether I'm eating enough?" Bryn heard his voice rising and didn't care. "The diphtheria is getting worse. She can barely breathe. The baby is due in three months, and the doctor worries about her survival. So forgive me if I'm not particularly concerned about my own health right now."

"If you die, who takes care of Patricia and David? Who holds Alicia's hand through this? You think you're helping her by destroying yourself, but you're just creating more people for her to worry about," Tom asked.

Bryn turned away, his jaw clenched. "I can't eat while she starves. I can't sleep while she fights for every breath. Don't you understand? Every moment I'm not suffering feels like I'm abandoning her."

"That's not love. That's guilt," Tom said bluntly.

The words hit like a slap. Bryn spun back. "What?"

"You feel guilty that you're not the one who's sick. So you're punishing yourself, trying to suffer as much as she does. But it doesn't help her. It just means two people are dying instead of one."

"You don't understand Tom."

"I understand perfectly. I watched my brother do the same thing when his wife was dying. Refused to eat, refused to rest, convinced himself that suffering alongside her was somehow noble. You know what happened? She died anyway, and he was too weak to take care of his children. Is that what you want?"

Bryn felt something crack inside him. His legs gave out and he slid down the wall to sit on the ground. Tom sat beside him.

"I'm so tired," Bryn said. "I can't remember the last time I slept more than two hours. Every time I close my eyes I see her dying. I wake up in panic making sure she's still breathing. And when I do sleep, I have nightmares."

"What kind of nightmares?"

"She's dead and I'm holding the baby and the children are asking me what we

Chapter 42: The Fight

do now, and I don't have an answer." His voice cracked. "Or worse. Sometimes I dream the baby lives and she dies, and I'm looking at him and all I can feel is hate. Because he's the reason she's gone."

"That's your fear talking Bryn."

"What if it's not just fear? What if that's who I really am?" Bryn put his head in his hands. "What if I can't love him if she dies because of him?"

Tom was quiet for a moment. "You already love him. I can see it when you talk about Raymond. When you touch Alicia's belly. That love is real. The fear is real too, but it doesn't cancel out the love."

"How do you know?" Bryn asked.

"Because I know you. You're one of the best men I've ever known. Fear makes you think terrible things. It doesn't make you a terrible person."

They sat in silence. Bryn felt the tremor in his hands, the hollowness in his belly, the exhaustion in his bones. His body was screaming at him to rest, to eat, to stop this slow self-destruction. But accepting care while Alicia suffered felt impossible.

"What if I can't save her?" Bryn asked quietly. "What if all of this is for nothing?"

"Then you'll grieve her and eventually you'll heal. But she's not dead yet. Give her the chance to fight without worrying about you collapsing."

Bryn reached out and embraced Tom fiercely. "Thank you Tom, thank you."

That evening, Patricia brought him half her rice ration. She set it beside him without speaking, then sat down and waited.

"I can't take your food," Bryn said.

"Mama says you're not eating. She made me promise to make sure you eat this," Patricia said, assertively.

"When did she tell you that?" Bryn asked.

"This morning. When you went to the meeting." Patricia's voice was matter of fact, but her eyes were worried. "She says you're sick too, only your sickness is in your head. That you're so worried about her you forgot to take care of yourself."

Eight years old and she sounded forty. Bryn looked at his daughter's serious face and felt something shift. He picked up the rice and forced himself to eat it, every bite an act of will. "Thank you, sweetheart."

"Mama also said to tell you something else," Patricia said.

"What?"

"She said if you die because you're too stubborn to eat, she'll be very angry with you. Even in heaven," Patricia replied with conviction in her voice.

Despite everything, Bryn laughed. That sounded exactly like Alicia. Fighting for her life while still managing to worry about him. After Patricia left, he went to see Dr. Stanton at the medical building. She was organizing what little supplies remained. "I need to know the truth," he said without preamble. "No gentle words. No protecting my feelings. What are Alicia's actual chances?"

Dr. Stanton set down the bandages she was counting. "Of surviving delivery? Maybe thirty percent. Maybe less."

Bryn appreciated her direct honesty. "And after delivery? If she lives through it?"

"The recovery will be critical. Her body will be at its weakest point. Infection, hemorrhage, complications from the diphtheria." Dr. Stanton paused. "Even if everything goes perfectly during labor, she could still die days or weeks later."

"So this might not end when the baby is born," Bryn said.

Dr. Stanton nodded. "It might not end for months. You need to prepare yourself for a long fight."

Bryn felt the weight of those words settle on him. Months more of this. Months of watching her suffer, of fearing every breath might be her last, of holding himself together for the children while falling apart inside. "I don't know if I have months in me," he admitted.

"You do." Dr. Stanton's voice was firm. "You're stronger than you think. But you have to take care of yourself. That's not optional. If you collapse, everything gets harder for everyone…and you need to believe. Alicia is one of the strongest women I have ever met. Believe in her. I'll be here with her when the time comes. I believe in her."

Bryn clasped Dr. Stanton's hands. "Thank you…thank you for believing."

That night, after the children slept, Bryn lay beside his wife in the darkness. She was awake, her breathing rough and labored. "Tom told me I'm killing myself," he said.

"They're right." Alicia's voice was weak but certain.

"I can't eat while you starve."

"Then we'll eat together. Or starve together. But this thing where you refuse food while I'm trying to survive?" She turned her head to look at him. "It makes everything harder. I'm worried about the baby, worried about the children, worried

Chapter 42: The Fight

about myself. I can't worry about you too."

Bryn nodded. "I thought I was helping."

"I know. But you're not." She reached for his hand. "I need you strong. I need you healthy. Because when this baby comes, whether I survive or not, someone has to take care of our children. That's you. You can't do that if you're half dead from starvation."

"What if I can't save you?" The question came out broken.

"You can't save me. That's not your job. Your job is to be here, to love me, to take care of yourself so you can take care of our children. The saving part is up to me and Dr. Stanton and God, if He's listening."

Bryn felt tears on his face. "I don't know how to just watch you suffer and do nothing."

"You're not doing nothing. You're here. You're holding my hand. You're raising our children. You're keeping yourself alive so our family has a future, whatever happens to me." Her grip tightened. "That's everything, Bryn. That's all I need from you."

They lay together in the darkness, and for the first time in weeks, Bryn felt the crushing weight lift slightly. Not gone, but bearable. Alicia was right. He couldn't save her by destroying himself. He could only be there, love her, and trust that she would fight with everything she had. "I'll try to do better," he promised. "I'll eat. I'll rest."

"Good. Because I'm planning to survive this, and when I do, I want my husband intact. Not some hollow shell who forgot how to take care of himself."

Despite everything, Bryn smiled. Even now, even fighting for her life, Alicia was still taking care of him. That was who she was. Fighter, mother, partner. Refusing to surrender. He fell asleep holding her hand, and for the first time in months, he slept for more than two hours without waking in panic.

June, 1945

Alicia entered her ninth month barely able to stand without help. Speaking was agony. The gray membrane in her throat was so thick that Dr. Stanton worried about complete airway obstruction.

"We may need to perform an emergency tracheotomy if her breathing becomes too compromised," the doctor explained to Bryn. "But I don't have proper equipment. It would be crude, dangerous, and might not work."

Patricia had taken over many household tasks with quiet competence that broke Bryn's heart. She washed clothes, watched David, brought water from the communal pump. At eight years old, she was functioning as an adult.

One evening, she asked him the question he had been dreading. "Papa, if Mama dies when the baby comes, will we keep him?"

Bryn looked at his daughter's serious face and felt something twist in his chest. "Of course we'll keep him. He's our family."

"But what if he's why Mama dies? What if having him is what kills her?"

"Patricia..." Bryn pulled her close. "Even if that happens, which I don't think it will, it wouldn't be Raymond's fault. He's an innocent baby. We would love him and raise him and never blame him for something he couldn't control."

"Would you be able to love him? If he's why Mama died?"

The question was devastating in its perceptiveness. Bryn had been asking himself the same thing in his darkest moments. Could he look at the baby and not see the pregnancy that had killed Alicia? Could he hold his son without feeling that terrible mix of love and resentment?

"I already love him," Bryn said, and realized as he spoke that it was true. "I love him because he's part of Mama, because he's your brother, because he's ours. Nothing will change that."

"Promise?"

"I promise."

But after Patricia fell asleep, Bryn sat with his head in his hands and prayed to a God he wasn't sure existed anymore. Please don't make me choose between them. Please don't make me face that question in reality instead of just imagining it. Please let them both survive.

In early June, Bryn made his desperate attempt to get antibiotics from Commandant Saito The meeting was brief and brutal. "My wife is dying," Bryn said without preamble. "She has diphtheria and she's about to give birth. I know you have antibiotics. I've seen them used on your soldiers. Please. I'm begging you to help her."

Yamamoto's expression hardened. "Military medical supplies are for military personnel only."

"She's going to die without treatment. Our baby will die."

"That is unfortunate, but regulations are clear. Internees are not entitled to Japanese military medical resources."

Bryn felt rage rising, dark and murderous. For one terrible moment, he

Chapter 42: The Fight

imagined lunging across that desk, wrapping his hands around Yamamoto's throat. The impulse was so strong he had to grip the chair to stop himself. But he thought of Ah-Min's teachings, of Taoist principles about non-resistance to calm himself. He thought of Alicia waiting for him, of Patricia and David who needed their father. He thought of the baby coming into this brutal world.

"I understand," he said finally, the words like swallowing glass.

"Many people die in war, Mr. Williams," Saito said with cold finality. "Your wife is not the first. She will not be the last."

Bryn walked out of that building and kept walking until he was alone. Then he screamed. The sound ripped from his throat, primal and anguished, three years of accumulated fury and helplessness finally finding voice.

That night, Bryn crawled into bed beside Alicia and held her carefully. She was so thin now, so fragile. He could feel every bone in her body. The baby moved between them, strong kicks that seemed impossible given how little nutrition Alicia could provide.

"I went to see Saito today," he told her quietly. "Asked him for antibiotics."

"What did he say?"

"No. He said many people die in war and you wouldn't be the first or last."

Alicia was quiet for a moment. "Then we do this on our own. With Dr. Stanton and this community. Like we've done everything else."

"I wanted to kill him," Bryn admitted. "I've never wanted to hurt someone so badly in my life."

"But you didn't."

"Because it wouldn't have saved you."

"Because you're stronger than hate," Alicia corrected. "Because you know what matters."

"What matters is keeping you alive."

"What matters," Alicia said, her voice fierce despite its weakness, "is all of us surviving together. You, me, Patricia, David, Raymond. That's what I'm fighting for. Not just my own life, but all of ours."

Bryn held her as gently as he could, feeling her heart beating against his chest, feeling the baby moving, feeling time running out. "I'm so afraid," he whispered.

"So am I. But we're afraid together. And somehow, that makes it bearable."

Chapter 43
The Miracle

"In the midst of winter, I found there was, within me, an invincible summer."

Albert Camus

July 15, 1945

The pains started in the middle of the night. Alicia woke Bryn with a gasp, her hand clutching her belly.

"It's time," she said.

Bryn's heart slammed against his ribs. Time. The moment they had been dreading and hoping for simultaneously. The moment when they would learn if Alicia's stubborn will and Dr. Stanton's skill would be enough. He ran through the dark camp to the camp's Tweed Bay Hospital, his breath coming in gasps that had nothing to do with exertion and everything to do with terror. Dr. Henderson appeared.

"It's my wife. The baby's coming."

"How far apart are the contractions?"

"I don't know. Maybe five minutes?"

"And her breathing?"

"Bad. Very bad."

They moved Alicia on a makeshift stretcher, carrying her carefully through the sleeping camp. Her face was gray in the moonlight, her breathing labored even before labor truly began.

At the hospital entrance, Dr. Henderson stopped him. "You'll need to wait outside. The isolation protocols are strict."

"But..."

Ashes and Dawn

"I know. But this is how we keep everyone safe."

Dr. Stanton appeared, looking exhausted before the work had even begun. She pulled Bryn aside. "I need to be honest with you one final time. The odds are not good. The diphtheria, the malnutrition, the physical strain of labor. Her body shouldn't be able to do this. If both she and the baby survive, it will be..." He paused. "It will be a miracle."

"Then we'll have a miracle," Bryn said.

"Go be with your children. We'll send someone if there's news," Dr. Stanton said.

Bryn watched the door close behind his wife, and for a moment he couldn't move. This might be the last time he saw her alive. That moment of her disappearing through the door might be his last memory of her.

His friend Tom Fitzgerald appeared, and touched his arm. "Come on. The whole camp is gathering. You're not doing this alone."

And it was true. Word had spread in that mysterious way news always traveled through Stanley. By dawn, dozens of internees had gathered in the courtyard outside Tweed Bay Hospital. Someone had saved a candle. Others appeared with what little they had to offer.

Mrs. Wilson stood beside Bryn, her hand on his shoulder. "She's going to make it. Both of them."

"How do you know?" Bryn asked.

"Because I've watched that woman for three years. She doesn't break. She bends, she struggles, but she doesn't break."

Reverend Hartwell led prayers. Professor Wynne Jones stood nearby. Tom Fitzgerald stayed at Bryn's side through the long hours. Patricia and David were there too.

"Is Mama going to be okay?" David asked, clinging to Bryn's hand.

"She's fighting very hard to be okay," Bryn said, because it was the only truth he could offer.

The sun rose. Morning inspection happened around them, the guards looking uncertain about the gathered crowd but not interfering. Hours crawled past. Bryn counted seconds, minutes, heartbeats. He heard sounds from inside the hospital, muffled voices, movement, but nothing clear.

At one point, Patricia looked up at him. "Papa, if Mama dies, I'll help you with the baby."

Chapter 43: The Miracle

The casual acceptance in her voice, the adult comprehension of mortality in an eight-year-old, broke his heart. "Thank you, sweetheart. But let's believe she's going to live."

"I believe it too, Papa." Patricia said seriously.

Bryn pulled her close, this daughter who had been forced to grow up far too fast, and tried not to cry. More hours passed. The wait became unbearable. Bryn's mind invented a hundred disasters, each worse than the last. Alicia hemorrhaging on the table. The baby stillborn. Both of them dying while he stood helplessly outside. Then, as afternoon heat baked the courtyard, he heard it. The sharp, indignant cry of a newborn baby. Bryn was on his feet immediately, moving toward the door before Fitzgerald caught his arm. "Wait. Let them stabilize."

The minutes that followed were the longest of Bryn's life. The baby was alive. But what about Alicia? Why was no one coming out? Why was there still silence beyond that one cry?

Finally, after what felt like geological ages, the door opened. Dr. Stanton emerged, her face exhausted but showing something like wonder. "Bryn," she said softly. "You have a son. Raymond is alive. He's breathing well, and his lungs are strong."

"And Alicia?" His voice barely worked.

Dr. Stanton's face split into a tired smile. "Alive. Weak, very weak, but alive. Bryn, I'm not sure how to explain it. By every medical calculation, she shouldn't have survived. But somehow, her body found the strength."

"She's alive?" Bryn could barely process the words.

"They both are," she replied.

The sound that rose from the gathered internees was part cheer, part sob. Bryn felt his knees buckle, felt Tom catch him, felt tears streaming down his face. Alive. Both of them alive. Against impossible odds, against every medical prediction, they had survived.

Dr. Stanton embraced Bryn. "In all my years of medicine, I've never seen anything quite like it. The odds were overwhelmingly against them both. By rights, we should have lost at least one of them, probably both. But that woman in there..." She shook her head in amazement. "She made a promise, and she kept it. That's the only explanation I have. She simply refused to die."

When Bryn was finally allowed into the isolation ward, Alicia lay propped in bed, still gaunt and drawn, but her eyes were clear. In her arms, wrapped in a tiny knitted blanket, was their son. Raymond was small, his skin pale from months of insufficient nutrition. But he was beautiful.

Ashes and Dawn

"He's here," Alicia said, her voice rough but filled with fierce joy. "I told you I'd keep my promise."

Bryn approached slowly, hardly daring to believe what he was seeing. He touched Raymond's tiny hand, and the infant's fingers wrapped around his with surprising strength. Then he looked at his wife, really looked at her, and something broke open in his chest.

"Alicia," he said, his voice cracking. He sat carefully on the edge of the bed and took her free hand in both of his. "What you just did. What you've been doing for nine months. I don't have words for it."

"We did it together," she started, but he shook his head.

"No. Listen to me." Tears were streaming down his face. "I've watched you fight for this baby every single day. I've watched you force down food when swallowing felt like swallowing glass. I've watched you sit up when your body was screaming to lie down. I've watched you comfort our children when you could barely speak." His voice broke. "You were dying, Alicia. The doctors said you couldn't survive. Every medical calculation said it was impossible. But you refused. You simply refused to let death win."

Alicia's eyes filled with tears.

"You're the strongest person I've ever known," Bryn continued. "Not because you didn't feel fear. You were terrified. I know you were. But you felt that fear and kept fighting anyway. You made a promise to our children, to Raymond, to me, and you kept it even when keeping it should have been impossible." He brought her hand to his lips. "I am in awe of you. Do you understand? I am humbled and amazed and so deeply grateful that you're the mother of my children, that you're my wife, that you chose to fight this hard to stay with us."

"I couldn't leave you," Alicia whispered.

"But you could have. Your body was giving you every reason to surrender. The pain, the starvation, the disease. Any of those things alone would have been enough to break most people. But not you." He touched her face gently. "You have a will like iron, Alicia. A courage I can barely comprehend. You looked at death and said no. You looked at impossible odds and said you would beat them. And you did."

"I'm not brave," she said, tears spilling over. "I was so afraid. Yet…down deep I knew…"

"That's what makes it brave. Courage isn't the absence of fear. It's fighting despite the fear." Bryn looked down at Raymond, then back at his wife. "This baby is alive because you refused to give up. I'm sitting here with both of you because your will to live, your love for our family, was stronger than diphtheria, stronger

Chapter 43: The Miracle

than starvation, stronger than anything this place could throw at you."

"Bryn...I…"

"Let me say this," he insisted. "Because I need you to know. When this war is over, when we're home and life is normal again, I will never forget what you did here. How you fought for our family. How you kept your promise against impossible odds. You're a warrior, Alicia. The fiercest fighter I've ever known. And I love you more in this moment than I thought it was possible to love another person."

Alicia was crying fully now, clutching his hand. "I love you too. So much."

"I know you do. I felt it every day. Every time you forced yourself to eat another bite, every time you sat up to comfort the children, every time you whispered in the dark that you were going to survive. That was love, Alicia. The kind of love that refuses to surrender. The kind that fights death itself and wins."

He leaned forward carefully and kissed her forehead, then looked down at their son. "Raymond is going to grow up knowing his mother is the strongest woman who ever lived. And he's going to be right."

Alicia smiled through her tears, shifting Raymond slightly so Bryn could see him better. "He looks like you."

"He has your strength," Bryn said. "I can feel it. Both of you, you beat death together."

They sat in silence for a moment, the three of them, and Bryn felt a peace he hadn't experienced in nine months. His wife was alive. His son was alive. Against every prediction, every calculation, every medical certainty, love had won.

After spending precious minutes with Alicia and Raymond, a nurse gently reminded Bryn that others were waiting. He kissed his wife's hand one more time, touched Raymond's tiny fingers, and walked out of the isolation ward on legs that felt unsteady.

The crowd in the courtyard had grown larger. Several hundred people now, maybe more. When Bryn stepped through the door, every face turned toward him. The silence was absolute, everyone holding their breath.

Tom Fitzgerald moved forward. "Well?"

Bryn's face broke into a smile, the first genuine smile he had worn in months. "She's alive. They're both alive." His voice grew stronger. "Alicia survived. And you have all just witnessed the birth of Raymond Williams."

For a heartbeat, no one moved. Then Patricia and David rushed forward, and Bryn scooped them up, holding them tight.

"You have a brother," he told them, his voice breaking. "A healthy baby brother. And your mama is going to be fine."

Mrs. Wilson started crying openly. Reverend Hartwell closed his eyes in prayer. And then, from somewhere in the back of the crowd, old Mrs. Samson's voice rang out, strong and clear.

"It's a miracle! The baby's a miracle!" The words seemed to hang in the air for a moment. Then Mrs. O'Brien, the Irish nurse, took them up. "The miracle baby! Both of them, they're miracles!" "Miracle baby!" someone else shouted. The phrase spread through the crowd like wildfire, people repeating it, passing it along, their voices growing louder. "The miracle baby! Raymond Williams is a miracle baby!"

Within minutes, internees who hadn't been at the vigil were emerging from buildings, drawn by the noise. "What's happening?"

"Alicia Williams had her baby! Both of them survived!" "It's a miracle!" "They're calling him the miracle baby!"

Bryn stood in the center of it all, holding his children, watching the joy spread through a community that had known so much suffering. It had been more than a year since the last child was born, and he and his mother had died, too weak to survive the ordeal of childbirth. The camp that had been holding its breath for months was suddenly alive with celebration. People were hugging, crying, laughing. Some were singing. Others just stood with smiles on their faces, soaking in the simple goodness of life triumphing.

By nightfall, everyone in Stanley Camp had heard. Alicia Williams, who had been dying of diphtheria while pregnant, had survived delivery. The baby, who should never have made it to term, had been born alive and healthy. Against all medical probability, against the crushing odds of disease and starvation and captivity, both mother and child had lived.

And throughout the camp, in whispered conversations and tearful embraces, in prayers of thanksgiving and expressions of wonder, people spoke of the miracle baby. Raymond Williams, born into suffering but somehow embodying hope. Proof that even in the darkest places, even when death seemed certain, life could still find a way to win.

Offerings poured in from people who had almost nothing. Mrs. Patterson brought a tiny knitted blanket. Old Mr. Samson offered his monthly Red Cross chocolate ration. The Murphy family volunteered to help with Patricia and David. Everyone wanted to contribute something to the miracle.

That evening, when Bryn returned to see Alicia and Raymond, he found his wife awake, the baby sleeping peacefully in her arms. "The whole camp is calling him the miracle baby," he told her.

Chapter 43: The Miracle

"I heard." She smiled. "It suits him."

"It suits both of you." Bryn sat beside the bed again. "You gave everyone hope today, Alicia. In a place designed to strip away hope, you proved that will and love can triumph. Everyone out there needed to see that life could win. You showed them."

"We showed them," Alicia corrected. "This whole community. Mrs. Wilson saving sugar. The vigil. Everyone praying and believing. That's what saved us."

Bryn looked at his wife holding their miracle baby, and he knew she was right. Love had won. Not sentiment or wishful thinking, but fierce, stubborn, refusing-to-surrender love. The kind that fought through nine months of impossible pregnancy. The kind that kept a community together through years of captivity. The kind that looked at death and said no.

"We're will survive this place," Bryn said. "It will not take us."

"I know," Alicia replied, her eyes meeting his. "We didn't survive this just to fail now."

Outside, the celebration continued into the night. In a camp where joy had been rationed more strictly than food, where hope had become a dangerous luxury, the internees of Stanley celebrated life persisting against impossible odds. The miracle baby and his warrior mother. Evidence that even in the worst circumstances, the human spirit could refuse to surrender.

The night settled over the camp with unusual gentleness. Guards completed their patrols without incident. The children's laughter faded into sleep. And in the isolation ward at Tweed Bay Hospital, Raymond Williams dreamed his first dreams, unaware that his very existence had become a symbol of hope for nearly three thousand people still waiting for their liberation.

Chapter 44

Liberation

"Freedom is not the absence of chains, but learning to walk again after they're removed."

Welsh Proverb

August, 1945

Bryn woke to silence. After forty-four months of Stanley Camp, silence meant something was wrong.

The usual morning sounds were absent. No guards shouting in Japanese. No clang of the rice pot signaling breakfast formation. No shuffle of two thousand eight hundred people beginning another day of captivity. Just his own breathing and Raymond's soft snuffling against Alicia's chest.

Something had happened.

He sat up carefully on the narrow cot, every movement calculated to avoid waking his family. Patricia lay curled at the foot of the bed, her eight-year-old body small enough to fit in spaces that would have been impossible before the war. David slept against the wall, one hand clutching the worn stones he carried everywhere, his other arm wrapped protectively around his sister. Through the gaps in the shutters, early morning light painted thin lines across the floor. Bryn's joints ached as he stood. Forty-four months of poor nutrition and hard labor had added decades to his thirty-nine years.

Outside in the corridor, whispers. Not the usual sounds. Different. Urgent.

Bryn moved to the door, pressing his ear against the rough wood. Footsteps. Multiple people moving quickly but quietly, like they were afraid sound itself might shatter something precious.

"Have you heard?" A woman's voice, breathless. Mrs. Pemberton from down the hall.

"Heard what?" Someone else, male, cautious.

"They're saying Japan has surrendered. They're saying the war is over."

The silence that followed was heavier than any sound. Bryn felt his heart hammering against his ribs, felt the sharp intake of breath that could have been hope or terror or both. It couldn't be true. They'd had rumors before.

Behind him, Alicia stirred. He turned to see her eyes open, dark and enormous in her gaunt face. She held Raymond closer, the baby's fragile body barely making an impression against her chest.

"Bryn?" Her voice was barely a whisper. "What is it?"

"People are saying the war's over. Japan's surrendered." He watched her process the words. Four years of captivity had taught them both not to hope too easily. Hope was dangerous. Hope could break you worse than hunger.

"Do you believe it?" she asked.

Bryn thought about the changing behavior of the guards over the past weeks. Less aggressive. Some disappearing from their posts. The way one of the guards had looked at them during the last rice distribution, something almost like shame in his eyes.

"I don't know," he said honestly. "But something's different."

Within the hour, the call came. All internees to the courtyard. Mandatory assembly.

Bryn helped Alicia to her feet. Six weeks since Raymond's birth and she still moved like an old woman, her body ravaged by years of malnutrition and the diphtheria that had nearly killed her. The baby was a month old and looked half that, his skin translucent, his eyes too large in his small face. If this was real, if they were really free, Raymond would never remember this place. He would grow up knowing food and safety and peace.

Patricia woke when Alicia lifted Raymond from his makeshift cradle. The little girl's eyes were sharp with intelligence beyond her years. "Are we leaving, Mama?" she asked, her small hand finding Alicia's skirt.

"I don't know, darling. But we need to go outside," Alicia replied.

David was harder to wake. The six-year-old had retreated somewhere inside himself over the past months, speaking less, watching more. When he finally opened his eyes, he simply nodded and began putting on his worn shoes without asking questions.

The courtyard could barely contain the mass of skeletal figures emerging from the overcrowded buildings. Bryn had seen this gathering place every day for forty-four months, but today it looked different. The light seemed sharper. The air felt

Chapter 44: Liberation

charged with something electric and dangerous.

Alicia swayed on her feet, and Bryn quickly wrapped his arm around her waist, feeling every rib through her thin dress. Raymond made a small sound, not quite crying, as if the baby sensed the collective tension of nearly three thousand people holding their breath.

The Japanese guards stood at attention along the perimeter. Their faces were unreadable masks, but something about their posture had changed. They looked smaller somehow. Diminished. Lieutenant Colonel Tokunaga emerged from the main building, his uniform crisp despite the heat. Captain Tanaka followed, the man who had served as translator for the past three and a half years, who had announced deaths and punishments and the steady erosion of their rations. The commandant spoke in Japanese first, his words clipped and formal. Then Tanaka translated, his English halting but clear enough. "The Imperial Japanese Government has accepted the terms of surrender under the Potsdam Declaration. The war is over. You will remain in camp until proper arrangements can be made for your disposition."

For one heartbeat, two, three, the courtyard remained silent. Then sound erupted like something physical, like a wave breaking against stone. People were crying, cheering, collapsing to their knees. An elderly man near Bryn simply sat down hard on the ground, his face blank with shock.

Bryn felt nothing. This should feel like something. This should be the greatest moment of his life. But his body felt numb, his mind disconnected. He watched people embrace, watched children laugh, watched grown men weep openly, and felt like he was observing it all from very far away.

"Bryn?" Alicia's voice pulled him back. She was looking up at him, tears streaming down her cheeks, and he realized his face was wet too. He was crying without feeling it, his body responding to something his mind couldn't quite process.

"Are we free, Papa?" Patricia asked, tugging at his shirt. "Can we go home now?"

Home. The word felt foreign, like something in a language he used to speak but had forgotten. "Soon, sweetheart," he managed. "Soon."

Raymond started to cry, overwhelmed by the noise and chaos. Alicia rocked him gently, murmuring words Bryn couldn't hear over the sound of two thousand eight hundred people discovering that their nightmare might actually have an end. But when did a nightmare really end? When you woke up? Or when you stopped flinching at shadows?

The days that followed had a surreal quality, like living in a dream where the rules kept changing. The guards became less visible. Some disappeared entirely, slipping away in the night to whatever uncertain future awaited them. Others remained at their posts but without the aggressive authority that had defined their presence for so long. Bryn watched them with something cold and hard forming in his chest. Every time he saw a Japanese soldier, he thought about the rice rations that had been cut again and again. Thought about Alicia's fever, her near death, the way she had wasted away while the guards remained well-fed. Thought about Raymond's fragile body, born small because his mother had been starving. He could kill them. He knew how. Sergeant Evans had taught him in Wales. Quick, efficient, the kind of violence that ended things. The thoughts came unbidden and sharp as broken glass. He would see a guard's neck and think about how easy it would be. See their backs turned and imagine the satisfaction of violence answered with violence.

It frightened him, this rage. He had been angry before, had fought his father in the Welsh mines, had struggled with the moral compromises of colonial service. But this was different. This was a fury that felt bottomless, ancient, like something that had been compressed under pressure for so long it had transformed into something dense and dangerous. The Chinese man with his quiet wisdom and Buddhist philosophy who had helped Bryn understand that working in Hong Kong meant more than imposing British ideas on Chinese people. "Anger is like holding a hot coal," Ah-Min used to say, his weathered face serene despite the chaos of an outbreak investigation. "You intend to throw it at another, but you are the one who gets burned." And another time, when Bryn had been frustrated with a corrupt merchant who was endangering public health: "The wheel of karma turns for everyone, Master. Our job is not to punish. Our job is to prevent suffering. If we focus on revenge, we become part of the cycle of suffering rather than breaking it."

Standing in Stanley Camp, watching the Japanese guards who had ruled over them for forty-four months, Bryn heard Ah-Min's voice in his memory. He would have told Bryn that carrying this rage would only poison his own life, his own family. That the guards would face their own consequences through the natural workings of the world, and Bryn's job was to focus on healing rather than harming.

"Bryn." Alicia's voice, soft as prayer. Her hand on his arm, pulling him back from wherever his mind was wandering. "Look at Raymond. Look at our son."

He forced his eyes away from the Japanese soldier crossing the courtyard. Raymond lay in Alicia's arms, his tiny chest rising and falling in the rhythm that had become Bryn's anchor through the darkest days. The baby's eyes were open, dark and solemn, watching his father's face with an intensity that seemed impossible for a month-old child. This was what mattered. Not revenge. Not rage. This. "I'm all right," he said, though they both knew it was a lie.

Chapter 44: Liberation

"No, you're not." Alicia shifted Raymond to one arm so she could take Bryn's hand. Her grip was weak but determined. "None of us are. But we will be."

The rage didn't disappear. It settled into his bones like coal dust, like something he would carry forever. But looking at his son, at his wife who had survived the unsurvivable, Bryn understood that some things were worth more than satisfaction. Some things were worth swallowing the fury and choosing to live forward instead of backward. He would never forget. He would never forgive. But he would not let it consume him.

On the second day after the surrender announcement, planes from the aircraft carrier HMS Indomitable circled overhead. Bryn stood in the courtyard with hundreds of others, watching parachutes blossom against the blue sky like flowers blooming in fast motion.

David pressed against the fence, pointing excitedly as colorful silk canopies floated down carrying crates of food, medical supplies, and other essentials. "Look, Papa!" His voice was stronger than it had been in months. "They're like colored mushrooms falling from heaven!"

Patricia laughed, the sound so unexpected and pure that it made Bryn's chest ache. When had he last heard his daughter laugh? This was what they had been fighting for. These small moments of joy. These children who should never have had to learn what they'd learned.

One parachute landed just outside the camp perimeter, tantalizingly close. A group of internees gathered by the fence, watching as Japanese soldiers approached the crate with obvious hesitation. The irony wasn't lost on Bryn. Their captors now handling supplies meant for their prisoners, uncertain about their own future.

Alicia managed a weak smile as she watched the children's excitement. "It's really happening, isn't it?" she murmured. "We're going to get through this."

"Yes," Bryn said, though he wondered what "getting through" really meant. Would they ever be the people they were before? Could you lose four years of your life, watch your children starve, give birth in a prison camp, and emerge unchanged? They were going to survive. But they were going to be different. Broken in places they couldn't see yet.

August 28th arrived hot and bright. Bryn heard the commotion before he understood what caused it. Voices calling out, people rushing toward the main gates, a sound like collective breath being drawn in ripples through the camp. "The British are here!" someone shouted. "The Royal Navy! We're really free!"

Bryn helped Alicia to her feet. She was stronger now, the condensed milk from the airdrops helping her recover some strength. But she still moved carefully, like someone testing whether the ground beneath her feet was solid.

Ashes and Dawn

They made their way through the crowd with Patricia, David and Raymond. The children clung close, overwhelmed by the sudden energy after years of enforced stillness. When Bryn finally saw the British naval officers walking through the gates, the contrast was so stark it felt like looking at creatures from another planet. Their white tropical uniforms were impossibly clean, their brass buttons gleaming in sunlight. Behind them, Royal Marines in full dress uniform followed, weapons ready but faces kind as they surveyed the gaunt figures pressing forward.

Admiral Harcourt himself led the contingent, his bearing upright and commanding. He looked around the camp with an expression that shifted between horror and determination. He was seeing what they had become. What Empire's failures had created.

Bryn looked down at his own body, at the rags that passed for clothing, at his skeletal hands and stick-thin arms. Looked at Alicia, beautiful Alicia who had danced in Hong Kong's best halls, now so thin her wedding ring hung loose on her finger. Looked at the children who had forgotten what it meant to run and play and simply be children. Shame washed over him, hot and unexpected. Not shame for surviving, but shame at being seen like this. At having to be rescued. At being reduced to something that needed pity. He had been Deputy Chief Sanitation Officer for Hong Kong. He had managed public health for a city of over a million. He had served in Egypt. He had fought his way out of the coal mines. And now he stood here in rags, unable to feed his own family.

A ceremony began. Simple but deeply moving. Someone produced a flag, the Union Jack that had flown over Government House when Hong Kong surrendered. A member of the Government House staff had hidden it for the entire war, smuggled it into Stanley, kept it safe for this moment. As the flag unfurled in the humid breeze, a sound rose from the assembled internees. Someone started humming "God Save the King." The melody grew until thousands of voices joined in, cracking with emotion and malnutrition but singing nonetheless.

Bryn tried to sing but found his throat closed. The irony cut deep. Here they stood, celebrating British victory, when British colonial policy had put them in this situation in the first place. When Churchill had abandoned Hong Kong as indefensible. When Empire had decided some lives were expendable in the larger game of war. But it wasn't about Empire. It was about survival. About marking the end of one nightmare even if they didn't know what came next.

Patricia tugged at his sleeve. "Papa, why is everyone crying if we're happy?"

He knelt to his daughter's level, his eyes burning with unshed tears. "Sometimes, sweetheart, we cry when we're very, very happy. When something wonderful happens after we've been sad for a long time."

Chapter 44: Liberation

"Are you happy, Papa?"

Bryn looked at his daughter's face, so thin her eyes seemed huge, and realized he couldn't answer honestly. He wasn't happy. He was relieved, terrified, numb, angry, grateful, and broken all at once. But Patricia needed something simpler than the truth. "I'm happy you're safe," he said. "I'm happy we're together. That's what matters."

Alicia started singing, her voice faint but sincere. Bryn joined her, then Patricia, and finally David. They stood as a family, singing their freedom into the tropical air while Raymond slept peacefully in his mother's arms. This was what they had fought for. Not flags or anthems or Empire's glory. This. The five of them, still breathing, still together.

The Royal Navy medical staff arrived with supplies and expertise. A young doctor wearing the insignia of the Royal Army Medical Corps approached the Williams family during the general assessment. Lieutenant Wellington, his name tag read. His eyes held professional compassion that immediately put Alicia at ease.

"May I examine your baby?" he asked gently, taking in Raymond's tiny form.

Alicia hesitated, that instinctive protectiveness born from three and a half years of guarding her children from any perceived threat. But she handed Raymond over, watching Wellington's every move with hawk-like intensity. The examination was thorough yet gentle. Wellington checked reflexes, listened to Raymond's heart, evaluated his overall condition with practiced efficiency.

"He's small," Wellington said finally, "but stronger than many babies born in these circumstances. You've done remarkably well keeping him alive and thriving."

"I had diphtheria." Alicia's voice was barely audible. "After he was born. I thought I might not survive to see him grow up."

Wellington looked at her with new respect. "You're both here. That's what matters now." He turned to Bryn. "Any immediate health concerns for you, Mr. Williams?"

Bryn shook his head, though he knew he must look as gaunt as everyone else. "I'm as well as can be expected."

The doctor examined Patricia and David next. Both children accepted the examination with quiet patience born from learning early that cooperation was necessary for survival. Wellington's expression grew more grave as he checked them over. "Malnutrition, of course," he noted. "But they're remarkably resilient. Children often are." He looked up at Bryn and Alicia. "We'll be providing supplemental nutrition immediately, but it must be introduced gradually. Too much too quickly after prolonged starvation can be dangerous."

Bryn nodded, remembering the medical training he'd received years ago for his sanitation work. Refeeding syndrome. The body's systems overwhelmed by sudden abundance after learning to function on nothing.

"We understand," he said. "Thank you, Doctor."

Five days after the British arrived, a courier appeared at the camp looking for Bryn Williams specifically. The man wore the khaki uniform of the Colonial Service and carried an official leather document case embossed with the colonial seal.

"Mr. Williams? Mr. Bryn Williams, formerly Deputy Chief Sanitation Officer?"

Bryn's heart quickened. "Yes, that's me."

"I have correspondence for you, sir. From the Hong Kong Government." The courier handed him a thick envelope sealed with red wax. Bryn turned it over in his hands, feeling the weight of official paper, seeing his name written in formal script: *Mr. B. Williams, Stanley Internment Camp.*

Around him, other internees watched with curiosity. Official correspondence meant something important. Possibly life-changing.

"Thank you," Bryn managed.

The courier saluted smartly and departed, leaving Bryn holding the envelope like it might explode. Alicia appeared at his side, Raymond in her arms, her eyes questioning. "What is it?"

They found a quiet corner in what had once been a classroom. Patricia and David played nearby while Bryn carefully broke the seal and extracted the contents. Several sheets of heavy paper, typed with official letterhead.

"GOVERNMENT OF HONG KONG Office of the Colonial Secretary September 1, 1945

Mr. Bryn Williams Stanley Internment Camp Hong Kong

Dear Mr. Williams,

The Hong Kong Government is pleased to extend to you an offer of appointment as Chief Health Inspector within the newly reorganized Public Health Department, to operate under the jurisdiction of the reconstituted Urban Council.

As you may be aware, in the post-war reorganization of colonial administration, the former Sanitary Department is being restructured and modernized. The designation "Sanitation Officer" is being replaced with the title "Health Inspector" to reflect the broader scope of public health responsibilities that will be required in the reconstruction of Hong Kong.

Chapter 44: Liberation

Given your extensive experience and exemplary service record prior to the occupation, and in recognition of the leadership you demonstrated in maintaining sanitary conditions within Stanley Camp during internment, the Government considers you uniquely qualified for this senior position."

Bryn read the words twice, three times, his mind struggling to process what they meant. Chief Health Inspector. Not deputy, but chief. A promotion even after four years of imprisonment.

The letter continued with details about salary and the scope of responsibilities. The Urban Council would oversee municipal services for Hong Kong Island and Kowloon, including water supply, sewage systems, food safety, disease control, and public hygiene. The task was immense. The Japanese occupation had devastated the colony's infrastructure. Cholera, typhoid, and dysentery threatened to sweep through the returning population if immediate action wasn't taken.

"Your expertise in sanitary engineering and public health administration will be crucial to preventing epidemic disease in the coming months. Hong Kong faces challenges unprecedented in its history, and we need men of proven capability and dedication."

Then Bryn reached the paragraph that made his breath catch:

"In recognition of your service and the senior nature of this appointment, the Government is pleased to offer you residence at Number 47 Caine Road in the Mid-Levels. This property, formerly occupied by a senior colonial administrator who did not survive the occupation, has been allocated for your use with immediate effect. The residence includes four bedrooms, servants' quarters, and all modern amenities. It is our understanding that your previous residence on Barker Road was destroyed during the hostilities, and we trust this accommodation will prove suitable for you and your family.

We understand you have family obligations and health considerations following your internment. The Government is prepared to provide immediate housing, medical care for your family, and such resources as may be necessary for your rehabilitation and return to service.

Please indicate your acceptance of this appointment at your earliest convenience. Hong Kong needs you, Mr. Williams.

Yours faithfully,

David MacDougall

Colonial Secretary."

Bryn set down the letter, his hands trembling slightly. Alicia had been reading over his shoulder.

"Chief Health Inspector," she said quietly. "And a house on Caine Road. That's... that's a significant promotion, Bryn."

"Yes."

"Even better than what we had before."

"Yes."

There was something in her voice, a careful neutrality that made him look up sharply. She was staring at the letter, her face unreadable, but he could see the tension in her shoulders, the way she held Raymond just a little tighter against her chest.

"Alicia?" He set the letter down completely. "What is it?"

She was quiet for a long moment. When she finally spoke, her voice was small. "It's a very important job. Very demanding. Hong Kong needs you, they said. The colony needs you."

"Yes, but—"

"Before the war, you worked all the time." The words came out in a rush, like she'd been holding them back. "Early mornings, late nights. Outbreaks on weekends. Emergencies at all hours. I understood. The work was important. But now..." She looked down at Raymond, then over at Patricia and David playing nearby. "I almost died, Bryn. Raymond almost died. We spent four years watching each other starve. Four years of not knowing if we'd survive another day. And now they're offering you the biggest job of your career, and all I can think is..." Her voice cracked. "All I can think is that I just got you back, and I'm afraid I'm going to lose you again. Not to the Japanese this time, but to cholera outbreaks and sewage systems and twelve-hour days."

Bryn felt something tighten in his chest. He'd been so focused on the opportunity, on what he could accomplish, on rebuilding Hong Kong, that he hadn't thought about what Alicia might be feeling. What she might be afraid of. He reached out and took her free hand, waiting until she looked at him. "Listen to me," he said quietly. "I need you to really hear this."

Alicia's eyes were bright with unshed tears.

"You're right," Bryn continued. "Before the war, I let the work consume me. I thought that was what it meant to be good at my job, to be dedicated. I thought serving the colony meant sacrificing everything else." He paused, choosing his words carefully. "But I learned something in Stanley Camp. Something more important than anything I learned about public health or sanitation or disease control."

"What?" she whispered.

"I learned what actually matters." He squeezed her hand. "Every morning in that camp, I woke up and the first thing I did was check on you and the children.

Chapter 44: Liberation

Make sure you were all still breathing. That became my job, Alicia. Not Sanitation Officer. Not health inspector. My job was keeping my family alive. Making sure Patricia and David had something to eat, even if it was just a few grains of rice. Making sure you didn't give up when the fever had you. Making sure Raymond took his first breath and his second and his hundredth."

Alicia's tears spilled over.

"That's still my job," Bryn said firmly. "My first job. My most important job. Yes, I'm going to accept this position, but only if you agree. Yes, I'm going to work hard to rebuild Hong Kong's public health systems. But I'm not going to let it consume me. Not anymore."

"How can you be sure?" Alicia asked. "When the outbreaks happen, when people are dying, how can you just walk away?"

"I'm not going to walk away from people who need help," Bryn said. "But I'm also not going to walk away from you. From the children. From our family." He reached up and brushed away her tears with his thumb. "I spent four years watching you suffer, watching our children go hungry, feeling helpless because I couldn't protect you. I'm not going to waste a single moment of the life we've been given back."

"What does that mean? Practically?" she asked.

Bryn thought about it. "It means I come home for dinner every night unless there's a genuine emergency. It means Sunday is for family, not for paperwork. It means when Patricia wants me to read her a story, I read her a story, even if there are reports waiting on my desk. It means when David wants to show me his stones, I stop and look at his stones." He shifted so he could look at Raymond in Alicia's arms. "It means I'm going to be there when Raymond takes his first steps, when he says his first words. I'm going to teach him to read. I'm going to be the father I didn't have, the father I wished I'd had when I was in the mines."

Alicia was crying harder now, but she was also smiling.

"Before the war, I thought I had to choose," Bryn continued. "Career or family. Success or presence. But Stanley taught me that's a false choice. The work is important, yes. Saving lives is important. But you're not saving anything if you lose your own family in the process. What's the point of preventing disease in the city if I let my own family starve for attention?" He brought her hand to his lips and kissed it. "You are my first priority, Alicia. You and Patricia and David and Raymond. Always. This job will be demanding, yes. There will be long days. But there will also be boundaries. There will be times when I say no, when I say someone else needs to handle it, when I say my family needs me more than the colony does."

Ashes and Dawn

"You mean that?" Alicia asked. "You really mean that?"

"I've never meant anything more in my life." Bryn leaned forward so their foreheads were touching. "I didn't survive four years in hell just to lose you to my own ambition. The work will be there tomorrow. But today, this moment, right now? This is what matters. You. The children. Us."

Alicia closed her eyes, fresh tears streaming down her face. But these were different tears. Relief, hope, gratitude.

Bryn pulled back slightly so he could look directly into her eyes. "But I need to ask you something, and I need you to be completely honest with me."

"What?"

"Do you want me to take this position?" His voice was serious, steady. "Not what you think I want to hear. Not what you think is best for Hong Kong or for our finances or for my career. What do you want? Because if you tell me right now that you need me to say no, that you need me to find something else, something smaller, something that won't demand so much... I'll say no. I'll write to the Colonial Secretary today and decline."

Alicia stared at him. "You would do that? Turn down Chief Health Inspector?"

"Without hesitation." Bryn took both her hands in his. "Alicia, we're partners in this. We always have been, but I didn't always act like it. I made decisions before the war without really asking what you needed. I told myself I was doing it for us, for the family, but I was really doing it for me. For my career. For my sense of importance." He shook his head. "I'm not making that mistake again. This is too important. You spent four years keeping our family alive while I counted rice grains and fixed latrines. You gave birth in a prison camp. You nearly died from diphtheria. You're the one who suffered most, and you're the one who gets to decide if this is what our family needs."

"Bryn..."

"I'm serious, Alicia. If you say no, we'll find another way. I can take a smaller position. I can work as an ordinary health inspector instead of chief. I can find work in the private sector. There are options. But I need to know what you can live with. What you need from me."

Alicia was crying again, but she was also smiling through the tears. She looked down at Raymond in her arms, then over at Patricia and David playing quietly nearby. Then back at Bryn. "You really would turn it down?" she asked. "Just like that?"

"Just like that." Bryn's voice was firm.

She was quiet for a long moment, thinking. Bryn waited, not pushing, letting

Chapter 44: Liberation

her process. "I need to know you mean what you said," Alicia finally answered. "About boundaries. About family first. About being present. If you can truly do that, if you can truly keep those promises..." She took a shaky breath. "Then yes. I think you should take the position."

"You're sure?"

"I'm sure." Her voice grew stronger. "Hong Kong does need you. You're good at this work, Bryn. You understand disease control in ways most people don't. You respect Chinese medicine and traditional knowledge. You can work with people instead of just giving orders. The city needs someone like that right now." She shifted Raymond to one arm so she could cup Bryn's face with her free hand. "And I need to know that I married a man who will keep his word. You've promised me boundaries. You've promised me presence. You've promised me that we come first. If you can keep those promises, then yes. Take the job. Rebuild Hong Kong's health systems. Save lives. But come home to us at the end of the day."

"I will," Bryn said. "I promise you, Alicia. I will."

"Then you have my blessing," she said. "My agreement. My full support. Write to the Colonial Secretary and accept."

Bryn felt relief wash over him, mixed with determination. She had given him her permission, but more than that, she had given him her trust. And he would spend every day proving he deserved it.

"Thank you," he said quietly.

"For what?"

"For believing in me. For trusting me. For being honest about what you need." He kissed her forehead gently. "For being my partner."

"I need to hear this sometimes," she whispered. "I need to know I'm not being selfish for wanting you present. For wanting you here."

"You're not being selfish." Bryn pulled back just enough to look her in the eyes. "You're being wise. You're being the person who kept this family together when everything else fell apart. And I'm going to spend the rest of my life making sure you never doubt that you're my priority."

Raymond stirred in Alicia's arms, making a small sound. Bryn reached over and stroked his son's soft cheek. "All of you," he said. "My whole world."

Alicia leaned into him, and they sat there together, their children playing nearby, the letter from the Colonial Secretary forgotten on the floor. Outside, Hong Kong continued its work of rebuilding. But in this moment, in this small corner of what had been a prison camp, Bryn Williams made a promise more binding than any government contract.

His family first. Always.

"I love you," Alicia said quietly.

"I love you too," Bryn replied. "And I'm going to make sure you never forget it."

They sat in silence for a moment, watching their children play. David was showing Patricia a new stone he'd found, pointing out its interesting features with the seriousness of a geologist. Raymond slept peacefully in Alicia's lap, unaware that his father's decision would determine the course of all their lives.

Bryn thought about Aunt Eileen. His mother's sister, who had taken him in when his father threw him out of the house at fourteen. Who had shown him that there was life beyond the coal mines, that a person could choose their own path rather than accepting the one handed to them by circumstance and class. "You're worth more than what they say you're worth," Aunt Eileen had told him in her small house in Swansea, over tea and fresh bread that had seemed like luxury after the brutality of mining life. "You're smart, Bryn. You're capable. Don't let anyone tell you otherwise. Not your father, not the mine owners, not anyone."

"What are you thinking?" Alicia asked.

"About my Aunt Eileen," Bryn said. "The woman who took me in when my father kicked me out. She always said I should use whatever talents I had to make things better for people who needed help. She believed that work itself had dignity, that using your hands and your mind to solve problems was worth doing even if no one noticed."

"She was wise."

"She was. She saved my life, really. Not just physically, but spiritually. She showed me that I didn't have to be what my father said I was. That I could choose."

The surrender ceremony happened that afternoon. Bryn stood in the crowd of internees, watching as Lieutenant Colonel Tokunaga approached Admiral Harcourt with military precision. The commandant's face showed no emotion as he extended his sword in formal surrender. "I surrender this facility and all personnel under my command to British authority," Tokunaga said in clear English. Admiral Harcourt accepted the sword with equal formality. "The civilian internees are now under British protection. Your cooperation in the transition will be noted."

Bryn's hands clenched into fists at his sides. His fingernails cut crescents into his palms. Snap his neck. Quick. Clean. Justified. The thought came again, unbidden, sharp and vicious as a blade. For one terrible moment, Bryn could see it. Could feel his hands on Tokunaga's throat. Could imagine the satisfaction of violence answered with violence, of making this man understand what he had

Chapter 44: Liberation

done, what he had allowed to happen to innocent people. This man had decided how much rice Raymond would get. Had watched Alicia waste away and done nothing. Had ruled over them like they were livestock, expendable and disposable.

Then Ah-Ming's voice came to him again, calm and certain: "The wheel of karma turns for everyone. Our job is not to punish. Our job is to prevent suffering."

"Bryn." Alicia's voice, soft as prayer. Her thin hand found his arm. "Look at Raymond. Look at our son."

He forced his eyes away from the Japanese officer. Raymond slept in Alicia's arms, his tiny chest rising and falling in the rhythm that had become Bryn's anchor during the darkest days of internment. Not worth it. Not worth what it would cost. Not worth the man he would become. But the rage didn't disappear. It settled into his bones like coal dust, like something permanent and staining. He would carry it forever, this fury at what had been done to his family, to all the families. It would live inside him alongside the love and the hope and the determination to build something better. Some wounds don't heal. They just became part of who you were. But he would not let them define him.

Patricia tugged at his shirt, pulling him back from the darkness. "What will happen to them now, Papa?"

"I don't know, sweetheart." He didn't want to explain war crimes trials or justice to an eight-year-old. Didn't want to discuss whether there was any punishment adequate for what these men had done. Bryn had heard some internees talking about revenge. A few had even suggested killing the guards themselves. But they were in the minority, and as far as Bryn knew, no one had actually acted on those feelings. The desire for violence faded quickly when faced with the reality of what it would cost. The person you would have to become to do it.

The camp began emptying in stages. First the critically ill, then families with young children, then the elderly. The British organized it with military efficiency. The Williams family stayed while others left, waiting their turn. Conditions improved dramatically: more food, better medical care. Bryn spent his days helping organize evacuations. He also borrowed pen and paper from a British officer.

In a quiet moment, Bryn wrote to the Colonial Secretary accepting the position in a simple message. Alicia stood beside him, Raymond in her arms.

"I am honored to accept the position of Chief Health Inspector..."

He finished the letter, signed his name, and sealed it. Tomorrow his new life would officially begin.

Mrs. Pemberton left on a bright September morning, embracing Alicia one last time. "Write to me," she said.

When the Williams family's turn finally came, Bryn felt a strange reluctance. The camp had been their prison for forty-four months, but it had also become their entire world. The boundaries might have been cruel, but they had been clear. The routines might have been tedious, but they were familiar. Leaving meant stepping back into a world that had continued without them. A world that had changed in ways they couldn't yet understand. A world that expected them to simply pick up where they left off, as if four years of hell could be erased with a boat ride and a fresh start.

Patricia sensed his hesitation. "It's okay to be scared, Papa," she said with the wisdom of a child who had seen too much. "Mrs. Wilson says courage means being scared but doing it anyway."

Bryn looked at his eight-year-old daughter and wondered when she had become so wise. When childhood had been stolen and replaced with this premature understanding of fear and survival. "Mrs. Wilson is right," he said. "Are you ready?"

Patricia nodded. David took her hand. And together, the Williams family walked through the gates of Stanley Camp for the last time. Just beyond the gates, Bryn stopped. He couldn't help himself. He turned back to look. The courtyard stretched empty in the morning sun, the same space where they'd stood during roll call, where they'd heard the news of surrender, where two thousand eight hundred people had lived pressed together for forty-four months. The fence that had defined their entire world for so long looked smaller from this side, less imposing, but no less real for what it had represented.

"Will we ever come back here, Papa?" Patricia asked quietly.

Bryn looked at his daughter, then at the camp, then at Alicia holding Raymond. "No, sweetheart. Never. That part of our lives is finished."

"Good," Patricia said with fierce finality. Then she looked up at him. "Can we go now?"

David was already tugging at Bryn's hand, pulling him forward, away from the camp, toward whatever came next. And Bryn let himself be pulled, let his children lead him away from the past and toward the future, one last glance over his shoulder before he turned his back on Stanley Camp forever.

Chapter 45

Reunion

"After the longest night, even the smallest light is a miracle."

Welsh proverb

The truck carrying them rumbled down the winding road away from Stanley Camp, away from four years of captivity, and away from the place that had held them prisoner and somehow kept them alive. Bryn sat beside Alicia in the back, one arm around her shoulders as she cradled Raymond, just one month old, whose tiny face was peaceful in sleep. Patricia, now eight but looking younger from malnutrition, and David, five and a half, knelt on the bench seat with their faces pressed to the canvas opening, watching Stanley disappear into the distance.

Bryn turned to glance back one last time through the gap in the canvas. The camp grew smaller behind them, with the barbed wire fences catching the morning light like cruel jewellery. The buildings where they had endured and survived, where friends had died and babies had been born, where hope had nearly died a thousand times but had never quite gone out, all receded into the distance with each turn of the truck's wheels.

He felt Alicia's body tense beside him as she, too, looked back, her free hand gripping his arm tightly. Her breath caught in a sound that was neither a sob nor relief but something in between. Four years of her life had been spent behind those fences. Four years watching their children grow thin and hollow-eyed. Four years of counting rice grains, rationing water, and making impossible choices. Four years of nearly dying in childbirth, fighting diphtheria with almost no medicine, holding Raymond and wondering if he would survive another day.

"It's over," she whispered, more to herself than to him, as if speaking the words might make them true. "I will never again return here."

Bryn pulled her closer, feeling the sharp angles of her shoulder blade through her worn dress, a reminder of what they had endured. "Yes, never again," he confirmed, his voice rough with emotion he had kept buried for so long that releasing it now felt dangerous, as if opening that dam might drown them both.

Ashes and Dawn

Patricia and David remained silent at the canvas opening, their small faces solemn as they watched the only home they could clearly remember fade behind them. They had entered Stanley Camp as children of four and one. They were leaving as something entirely different—children who had learned about hunger, death, and survival before they learned to read properly, before they understood what childhood was supposed to be.

The camp finally disappeared from sight as the road curved around a hillside. The barbed wire, guard towers, and cramped buildings were gone. Just like that. Four years squeezed into nothing more than a memory, a scar, a story they would carry for the rest of their lives.

Alicia let out a long, shuddering breath and faced forward, away from the past and toward whatever lay ahead. But Bryn saw tears streaming down her face, silent and steady. Not just tears of joy, he understood, but tears for everything they had lost there, for the people who hadn't made it out, for Mrs. Thompson, young Miss Wilson, and all the others whose graves they were leaving behind. Tears for the version of themselves they left behind those fences, people they would never be again.

Bryn pressed his lips to her temple, tasting salt and grief and relief all mixed together. "Against all the odds, we made it out. All of us."

Alicia nodded against his shoulder, holding Raymond even tighter, as if worried he might vanish if she loosened her grip. This baby, who shouldn't have survived, was born into hell and somehow survived it. This miracle, wrapped in a thin cloth, was breathing steadily in her arms.

The road now curved along the coastline, revealing glimpses of the South China Sea through breaks in the vegetation. The water sparkled in the morning sun, indifferent to the suffering that had occurred on its shores, beautiful and eternal and uncaring. Seabirds wheeled overhead, their cries sharp and clear in the humid air, free in ways the Williams family was only beginning to understand they were free again.

As they climbed over the hills and moved toward the city, the destruction became clear. Bryn felt his chest tighten as the scene of devastation unfolded before them. Buildings sat gutted and burned, entire blocks reduced to rubble and twisted metal. The bones of the city lay exposed, raw wounds that would take years to heal.

He recognized this pattern of destruction. Not specifically in Hong Kong, but in the familiar form of power oppressing those beneath it. It differed from the Welsh valleys of his childhood, where coal companies had torn apart mountains and coated everything in black dust, yet the destruction was equally thorough. War machines wrecking cities. The powerful crushed the powerless and called it

Chapter 45: Reunion

progress, necessity, or anything but what it truly was.

Papa, what happened to all the buildings?" David asked, his excitement about the journey fading as the reality of war's aftermath became clear.

Bryn pulled his son closer. "The war happened, son. But it's over now."

The truck slowed as they entered Central, navigating around debris in the streets. Workers were already clearing rubble, their backs bent to the task of rebuilding. Alicia sat up straighter, searching for landmarks among the ruins, her hand tightening on Bryn's arm.

Then she saw it. Or rather, where it had been. "Stop," she whispered. Then louder, her voice breaking: "Stop the truck. Please."

The driver pulled over without question, perhaps understanding that everyone in Hong Kong had ghosts to visit. Alicia stared at a pile of rubble on Queen's Road, her face going pale, all color draining away as recognition hit. "The Golden Phoenix," she said, her voice barely audible. "The dance hall where we met. It's gone."

This was not just Hong Kong being destroyed. It was her Hong Kong, the intimate geography of a life carefully built. The streets where she had walked as a new bride, still amazed that this British official had chosen her despite everything. The shops where she had bought things for their first home together, learning to be a wife and then a mother. All of it was damaged or disappeared; six years of memories reduced to rubble and ash.

Bryn took her hand, the one not holding Raymond, and squeezed gently. "The city will rebuild. Look around you."

Yet amid the devastation, life was indeed returning with stubborn persistence. Chinese vendors had set up makeshift stalls along the sidewalks, selling vegetables and rice from wooden crates. Workers cleared debris with methodical determination, sorting brick from wood, salvaging what could be salvaged. People walked with purpose despite everything, heads up, refusing to surrender to what had been done to them. A woman swept the steps of a damaged shop as if normalcy could be restored through the simple act of cleaning. Children played in the rubble, finding games even in destruction.

The driver called back to them in Cantonese. "Where to, sir?"

Bryn gave him the address of Mary's apartment in Mid-Levels, his pronunciation careful and precise. The truck made its way up the hillside, engine straining on the steep grade, passing more damaged buildings and more signs of the city's long ordeal. When they stopped in front of a narrow building that had somehow survived mostly intact, spared by whatever calculus of chance and trajectory governed bombs, Alicia's hands began to shake.

Bryn knocked on the door of Mary's flat. For a long moment, there was no response, just silence that stretched and stretched until it felt unbearable. Then shuffling footsteps approached from inside, slow and cautious.

The door opened a crack. A woman stood there, thin but alive, her dark hair streaked with gray that had not been there four years ago. She stared at Alicia for one frozen heartbeat that seemed to last forever, her hand flying to her mouth as shock and disbelief warred on her face. "Alicia?" Mary's voice cracked, barely more than a whisper. "*Dios mío...* (My God...) is that really you?" For a moment she just stood there, swaying slightly, as if the sight before her might be a hallucination born of grief and longing. Then she reached out with trembling fingers to touch Alicia's face, testing whether flesh was real or ghost.

"Mary!" Alicia's voice broke completely as recognition and relief flooded through her.

Mary's legs gave way beneath her. She collapsed against the doorframe, and Alicia caught her, and suddenly both sisters were on their knees in the entrance, holding each other, sobbing with a grief and joy so tangled together they could not be separated. Mary's whole body shook with four years of accumulated sorrow finally breaking open.

"*Mi hermana,*" (My sister,) Mary gasped in Spanish, her words tumbling out between sobs. "*Pensé que estabas muerta.*" (I thought you were dead.) "*Cuatro años. Cuatro años pensando que te había perdido para siempre.*" (Four years. Four years thinking I had lost you forever).

"*Estoy aquí,*" (I'm here,) Alicia wept against her sister's shoulder. "I'm here. *Estoy viva.*" (I'm alive). "*Sobrevivimos. Todos sobrevivimos*" (We survived. We all survived).

They clung to each other, rocking back and forth in the doorway, oblivious to everything around them. Mary's hands moved over Alicia's back, arms, and face, as if trying to remember every wound and hollow, every sign of pain written on her sister's body. Alicia could feel how thin Mary had become, could feel her sister's ribs through her dress, along with the trembling that wouldn't stop.

Raymond made a small sound in Alicia's arms, disturbed by the movement and emotion, and Mary pulled back just enough to see the baby. Her eyes went wide with wonder and disbelief mixed together.

"*Un bebé?*" (A baby?) Her voice rose with shock. "*¿Tuviste un bebé?*" (You had a baby)?

Six weeks ago in Stanley Camp. His name is Raymond Brinley Williams."

Mary's face crumpled, her expression twisting with anguish at the thought. "*En ese lugar terrible.*" (In that terrible place). "*Mi Dios, Alicia, en ese lugar del infierno*" (My

Chapter 45: Reunion

God, Alicia, in that place of hell).

"Who is it, Mary?" Another voice from inside the flat, older, trembling with hope and confusion and fear. "*¿Quién es? ¿Quién está en la puerta?*" (Who is it? Who is at the door)?

An elderly woman appeared behind Mary, moving slowly with one hand braced against the wall for support. Lupe Valenzuela looked much older than her years. Her hair was now completely white, and her face was deeply lined with new wrinkles shaped by worry and hardship. Her body was fragile, showing signs of more than just hunger. But when she saw her daughter kneeling in the doorway holding a baby, a spark lit up in her eyes, making her look young again and causing the years to fall away for a brief, precious moment.

"*¿Alicia?*" The word came out as barely more than a breath.

Alicia looked up and the sound that came from her throat was pure anguish and pure joy mixed together in a way that transcended language. "Mama!"

Lupe's knees buckled, all strength leaving her legs. Mary caught her mother with one arm, still holding Alicia with the other, somehow keeping both of them from falling. The old woman's hands reached toward Alicia, shaking violently with emotion and age and the shock of answered prayers.

"*Mi hija. Mi niña. Mi vida.*" (My daughter. My girl. My life). She was speaking Spanish too fast for anyone to follow, prayers and endearments tumbling together in a stream of consciousness. "*Pensé que te había perdido para siempre. Le rogué a Dios cada día. Cada noche. Cuatro años de oraciones.*" (I thought I had lost you forever. I begged God every day. Every night. Four years of prayers).

"*Gracias a Dios*" (Thanks be to God), Lupe kept repeating through her tears like a mantra. "*Gracias a Dios. Gracias a Dio.*" (Thanks be to God. Thanks be to God). " Thank you for bringing her back to me."

Bryn stood back with Patricia and David. He understood the sacredness of this moment, the need for them to have this reunion without interference. Patricia tugged at his hand, her voice small and uncertain, confused by all the emotion swirling around her.

"Papa, who are they?" she asked.

He knelt beside his daughter so he could look her in the eyes, bringing himself to her level. "That's your Aunt Mary. And that's your grandmother, your mama's mother. Your *Abuela.*" (Grandmother).

"From before the war?" Patricia's voice was careful, testing this new information against fragmented memories.

"Yes, sweetheart. Your mama's family. They thought she was dead. They thought we were all dead."

"They thought Mama was dead?" Patricia's voice was quiet, but her eyes held understanding far beyond her eight years, a comprehension of loss that no child should have. "Like we thought they were dead?"

"Yes, exactly like that," Bryn replied.

"But we're all alive." The realization dawned on her face slowly, wonder replacing the careful guardedness she had learned at Stanley Camp, the protective shell she had built around her heart. "We're all alive, Papa. We found them."

David had pressed himself against Bryn's leg, watching the emotional scene with wide, uncertain eyes. At five and a half, he had even fewer memories of his grandmother and aunt than Patricia did, just shadows and impressions from when he was barely two years old.

Finally, Mary managed to pull herself together enough to notice the children standing back uncertainly. She looked up, her face still streaming with tears but somehow smiling at the same time, joy and sorrow written equally on her features. She held out her arms toward them in invitation. "Patricia?" she said tentatively, her voice still shaking with emotion. "*¿Eres tú? ¿Eres mi sobrina?*" (Is that you? Are you my niece?) "Is that really you?"

Patricia nodded and stepped closer, reaching out to gently grasp her aunt's hand. The touch seemed to open something in both of them, and Mary pulled her niece into a tight embrace.

But when Lupe's arms closed around Patricia, she felt it immediately. Felt how light the child was, far too light for an eight-year-old girl. This was not just thinness. This was a body that had been slowly consumed by itself, a child's frame that had eaten its own muscle and fat to survive. Lupe's breath caught in her throat, but she said nothing. Not yet. Not in front of the child. But her eyes met Mary's over Patricia's head, and in that glance passed a shared horror at what these children had endured.

David spotted Lupe across the hallway. He gazed at his grandmother with a look of deep concentration, his small face scrunched up in thought as he searched his memories from when he was barely more than a toddler. His eyes scanned her face, seeking something familiar in her aged features. Then, suddenly, his whole face lit up with recognition, and the memory clicked into place like a key turning in a lock.

"*¡Abuela!*" (Grandmother!) he shouted, using the Spanish word that must have been buried somewhere deep in his mind, preserved through four years of camp life. "*Abuela*, you made me cookies! You made me cookies with sugar on top! And you sang me songs!"

Chapter 45: Reunion

Lupe made a sound that was pure anguish and pure joy mixed together, a cry that came from the deepest part of her soul. She opened her arms and David ran forward without hesitation, crashing into them with the full force of his small body.

She held him tight despite her frailty, her thin arms wrapping around him with surprising strength, rocking him and speaking Spanish too fast for anyone to follow, kissing his hair, his face, his hands with desperate tenderness. But inside, her heart was breaking at what she felt in her arms. "*Mi nieto,*" (My grandson), she sobbed. "*Mi amor. Mi tesoro. Mi corazón.*" (My love. My treasure. My heart). "My grandson. My love. My treasure. *Te recordaste. Te recordaste de tu abuela.*" (You remembered. You remembered your grandmother).

Patricia watched her brother being held and seemed to make a decision born of need and longing. She walked forward with careful deliberation, her movements slow but determined, and tugged on Mary's sleeve. "Aunt Mary? Can you hold me too? Please?"

"*Oh, mi corazón.*" (Oh, my heart). Mary lifted Patricia into her arms with trembling hands, even though the little girl was eight years old and neither of them had the strength they once did.

"We were so hungry, Aunt Mary," Patricia whispered against the fabric of Mary's dress, her voice muffled but clear. "We were so hungry all the time. My tummy hurt every day. Every single day for so long."

Mary's face twisted with pain at the confession, her own tears starting fresh. She held Patricia tighter, one hand stroking the child's hair with infinite tenderness, feeling the fragility of the small skull beneath her palm. "*Lo sé, mi amor. Lo sé.*" (I know, my love. I know.) *Pero estás a salvo ahora.*" (But you're safe now).

Bryn stood back, still holding their few belongings in a canvas sack, watching his family reunite with Alicia's family. His own eyes burned with tears he had not expected, emotions he thought he had buried rising to the surface with surprising force. This was what they had survived for. This moment. This impossible, beautiful moment of finding each other again when so many families had been permanently torn apart.The hallway had become a sacred space, witness to a reunion that transcended ordinary happiness

Alicia finally stepped back after long minutes, wiping her eyes with shaking hands, and seemed to remember Raymond in her arms. The baby had been remarkably quiet during all the commotion, as if sensing the importance of remaining peaceful, but now he was starting to fuss slightly, his small face scrunching up.

"Mama," Alicia said, turning to Lupe with the baby held out like an offering. "Mary. This is Raymond. Your grandson and nephew. Born July 16th in Stanley Camp."

Lupe set David down carefully, whispering a promise that she would hold him again soon, then moved toward Alicia with trembling hands outstretched. When she took Raymond from her daughter's arms, she cradled him with the practiced ease of a woman who had held many babies across many years, but her face showed wonder as if she were holding something precious beyond all measure, a miracle made flesh.

"Born in that terrible place," Lupe whispered, studying Raymond's small face with complete attention, as if memorizing every detail. "Born in darkness and suffering and war. But alive. *Un milagro*." (A miracle). "A miracle. *Un verdadero milagro de Dios*." (A true miracle of God). She kissed Raymond's forehead gently Raymond blinked up at her with solemn dark eyes, alert and aware, as if he understood the significance of this moment even though he was too young to comprehend it.

"He looks like you did when you were born, Alicia," Lupe said softly, her voice filled with memory and love. "The same serious expression. The same way of looking at the world like he's trying to understand it all at once. The same little furrow between his eyebrows."

Mary came closer, still holding Patricia against her hip, to look at her nephew with wonder written on her face. "He's beautiful, Alicia. He's absolutely beautiful. How did you... in that place... how did you keep him alive?"

"I almost didn't," Alicia admitted quietly, her voice heavy with the memory. "I had diphtheria before he was born. High fever. Could barely breathe. I nearly died. There were days when I thought neither of us would survive. Days when I was ready to give up."

Lupe looked up sharply, fresh pain crossing her weathered face as she understood how close she had come to losing her daughter. "Diphtheria? After childbirth? *Oh, mi hija*..." (Oh, my daughter...).

"But I did survive. We both did." Alicia's voice grew stronger with determination and gratitude. "Bryn took care of us when I couldn't care for myself. And the other women in the camp helped.. We all took care of each other's children and shared what little we had. That's how we survived. By refusing to let each other fall."

Lupe turned to look at Bryn properly for the first time, really seeing him as more than just the British official who had married her daughter. She handed Raymond back to Alicia with gentle care, then walked over to Bryn slowly, her steps measured and deliberate. For a moment, Bryn thought she might be angry with him for not protecting her daughter better, for letting her family end up in a camp, for all the suffering they had endured. But instead, Lupe took his face in both her weathered hands with surprising strength and kissed his forehead with

Chapter 45: Reunion

fierce tenderness. "You kept my daughter alive," she said, her voice shaking but determined, her eyes boring into his with intensity. "You kept all of them alive. My grandchildren. You brought them through that hell and brought them back. *Gracias. Gracias, Bryn. Mil gracias.*" (Thank you. Thank you, Bryn. A thousand thank yous).

Bryn found he could not speak past the lump in his throat. He just nodded, his eyes stinging with fresh tears, grateful and humbled by this woman's gratitude for doing what any father and husband would do, what he had been raised to believe a man should do.

"Come in, come in!" Mary finally said after they had stood in the hallway long enough for neighbors to begin openly watching. Her voice was still shaking but stronger now, taking charge with the practical authority of the oldest sister. "All of you! We can't stand in the doorway forever. Come inside. I'll make tea. We have some food. *No mucho, pero algo.*" (Not much, but something). Not much, but we'll share everything we have."

They moved into the flat in a crowd of bodies and emotions and tears that would not stop flowing no matter how hard anyone tried. The space was modest but clean, with sunlight streaming through windows that looked out over the harbor and the damaged city below.

"Sit, sit," Mary insisted, ushering them toward cushions and chairs with nervous energy. "You look exhausted. All of you. You need rest. You need food. *Tienen que comer.*" (You have to eat).

"Tell me everything," Lupe said after they had settled, her voice steadier now even as tears continued to fall silently down her wrinkled cheeks. "Tell me how you survived. Tell me about the camp. Tell me about this precious baby. Tell me everything you can bear to tell."

And so, they talked for hours as the afternoon sun moved across the sky outside the windows, casting shifting light on the walls. The conversation flowed between English and Spanish, filled with tears and occasional laughter, touching on both the terrible and the beautiful. Alicia shared stories about the invasion, those twelve days of fighting that changed everything. She described trying to find shelter as bombs fell and the world they knew was destroyed. She recounted being rounded up with other civilians like cattle and marched to Stanley at gunpoint.

Bryn filled in details about the journey to the camp, about the initial shock of realizing they would be imprisoned for the duration. About the conditions there that grew steadily worse as the years passed, the shrinking rations, the increasing disease, the daily struggle to survive on less and less.

After a while, the conversation turned to Mary and Lupe's own experiences during the occupation. Alicia leaned forward, her expression shifting from grief to concern. "We thought you were in Canada with Greta," she said, confusion clear in her voice. "We thought you had made it out."

The story that emerged over the next hour was one of remarkable courage and kindness, of ordinary people making extraordinary choices at great personal risk. Lupe's voice grew stronger as she told it, as if bearing witness to goodness helped balance the weight of everything terrible they had all endured. "Mr. and Mrs. Chen," she began, her weathered face soft with gratitude and memory. "You remember them, Alicia? They owned the tea shop on Queen's Road, the one with the red lanterns. They had known us since you first came to Hong Kong. She helped us with food and other provisions."

"We must do something to thank them Bryn, once we are settled," Alicia said. Bryn nodded in agreement.

"Mrs. Wong gave us her food ration cards," Lupe added, the catalog of kindness growing. "The seamstress who made your wedding dress, Alicia. Remember how careful she was with every stitch? She said her daughter could share her portion. Mrs. Wong went hungry, truly hungry, so we could eat."

Alicia pressed her hand to her mouth, overwhelmed by the catalog of kindness shown to her family, by the knowledge that strangers had risked everything. "All those people. They could have been killed. Tortured. Their families destroyed. Why would they do that?"

"They were suffering too," Mary said quietly, her voice heavy with the memory of those years. "The Japanese were brutal to everyone, not just to Westerners. Chinese people were rounded up daily, tortured if they were suspected of resistance, executed for black market trading or hiding food or speaking against the occupation or sometimes for no reason at all. But they still chose to help us. They shared what little they had when they themselves had almost nothing."

The words settled over the room like a blessing, a reminder that even in the darkest times, humanity could shine through. Bryn felt something tighten in his chest as he absorbed this story, understanding its significance on multiple levels. These Chinese families had risked everything to save two Mexican women they barely knew, while the British colonial government had left thousands of its own people to starve in camps with inadequate food and medical care. The irony was bitter and profound, a commentary on power and systems and the gap between what governments claimed to value and what they actually protected. But it was not surprising to him. Not really. Not when he thought about it properly, not when he considered his own experiences.

The Chinese families who saved Mary and Lupe understood what Bryn had learned in the coal mines all those years ago, what he had carried with him through everything since. That solidarity was survival. That you took care of your own, and

Chapter 45: Reunion

sometimes your own meant anyone who needed help, anyone who was vulnerable, anyone who was human. It did not matter if you were Welsh or Chinese, Mexican or British, rich or poor. What mattered was that you were human, and humans looked after each other when systems failed, when governments collapsed, when the powerful structures that claimed to protect people revealed themselves as hollow.

"We tried to visit Stanley three times," Lupe said after a pause, her voice breaking with remembered helplessness. "We brought food, medicine, whatever we could gather. But the Japanese guards would not let us near the gates. They threatened us with rifles, screamed at us in Japanese. The third time, they said they would arrest us if we came back. Said they would investigate how two Mexican women had food to spare."

"Every day we prayed," Lupe continued, gripping Patricia tighter in her lap as if she might still lose her. "Every morning and every night. I told God He could take anything from me. My health, my comfort, my sight, my life. Just please keep my daughter safe. Please let her survive this war. Please let me see her face one more time before I die."

As the shadows lengthened and true evening approached, Lupe remembered during a lull in the conversation, her face suddenly brightening. "Oh! I almost forgot in all the excitement. We had a letter last month. From Greta in Canada."

Alicia's head came up sharply, her expression shifting to surprise and hope. "Greta? She made it out?"

"Yes," Mary said, smiling for the first time without tears. "She married a Canadian businessman name Charles Andrews. she met during the war, who someone managed to evade capture and arrange for passage on a private ship through Macao. She's happily settled in Vancouver now. Has a little house with a garden. She's pregnant with her first child. She asks about you in every letter."

"Vancouver," Alicia repeated wonderingly, a small smile breaking through her exhaustion. "She always wanted to see snow. Real snow, not just pictures in magazines." She laughed, a sound both joyful and sad. "At least one of us made it somewhere safe before everything fell apart."

As the evening deepened outside and the light through the windows turned from gold to amber to blue, Bryn cleared his throat, knowing it was time to share the news that would change everything once again. The time had come to reveal what awaited them, to offer what he hoped would be received as a gift rather than an imposition. "We have something to tell you," he said, his voice cutting through the comfortable murmur of conversation. "Something important."

"The government has offered me a position," Bryn continued carefully. "Chief Health Inspector for Hong Kong. They want me to help rebuild the public health system, get the water supply working again, and help manage disease control as refugees return to the city."

Bryn paused, gathering his thoughts, wanting to get this exactly right. He looked at Alicia for encouragement, and she nodded slightly, giving him permission to continue. "The position comes with a house. A large house on Caine Road that belonged to a British official who didn't survive the occupation."

He could see comprehension dawning on their faces, understanding beginning to form about why he was mentioning this. "It's a large house," he continued carefully. "Five bedrooms on the upper floors, plus servants' quarters. Gardens. A view of the harbor. Far more space than the five of us need." He reached over and took Alicia's hand, drawing strength from her touch. "Alicia and I have discussed this at length over the past few days as we prepared to leave camp, and we are in complete agreement." He looked directly at Lupe, then at Mary. "We would like you both to come live with us. Not as guests passing through. As family. For as long as you wish to stay."

Lupe's hand flew to her mouth, her eyes going wide with shock. Mary stared at them with an expression caught between hope and disbelief, as if she had not quite heard correctly.

"We have been apart for four years," Bryn continued, his voice steady and sure despite the emotion threatening to overwhelm him. "Four years of not knowing if we would ever see each other again. Four years of living with uncertainty and fear and grief. Life is too short, and family is too precious, too rare and valuable to waste. We want to be together now. We want the children to grow up knowing their grandmother and their aunt, not just visiting occasionally on holidays but truly knowing you. Living with you. Learning from you. We want to wake up together, eat meals together, face whatever comes next together as a family should."

"All of us under one roof," Alicia added, her voice thick with emotion but determined and clear. "The way families are meant to be. The way we should have been all along if the war hadn't torn us apart. Please say yes."

Lupe looked at Mary with an intensity that spoke of their shared history, a lifetime of communication passing between mother and daughter in a single glance. Years of hardship and survival and love compressed into one wordless exchange that needed no translation. "Are you certain?" Lupe asked after a long moment, her voice trembling with hope and hesitation. "¿*Están seguros?* (Are you sure)?" You have just been freed. You need time to recover, to be together as your own family, to heal. We do not want to intrude on that process. We don't want to be a burden."

"You are not intruding," Bryn said firmly, with absolute conviction. "You are

Chapter 45: Reunion

family. That's what will help us recover most. Having family around us. The children need their grandmother and their aunt. Alicia needs her mother and sister. And honestly..." His voice caught slightly with emotion. "I need family too. Aunt Eileen was the only family I had connection with, and she passed. You are my family by choice and by love. Please say yes."

"Yes," Mary said finally, her voice breaking with emotion even as her face broke into a smile. "*Sí. Sí, nos encantaría*" (Yes. Yes, we would love to). Yes, we would love that more than anything."

Lupe stood carefully, mindful of the sleeping Patricia in her arms, and pulled Alicia into an embrace with her free arm, holding both granddaughter and daughter together. There is nothing we want more than to be with you and our grandchildren. Yes."

"Then it's settled," Bryn said, feeling a weight lift from his shoulders that he had not realized he was carrying. "We'll go see the house together tomorrow morning. All of us. We'll walk through that door as a family."

Mary wiped her eyes and stood with sudden energy, the practical sister taking charge once more. "Then we must have a proper meal to celebrate. *Una cena de familia.*" (A family dinner). I have rice and some vegetables. Not much, but I can make something good."

As Mary and Lupe moved to the small kitchen area, their voices mixing in Spanish and Cantonese as they coordinated the meal, Bryn found himself watching his family with a sense of profound gratitude. Patricia had fallen asleep in the spot where Lupe had been sitting, her face peaceful for the first time in months. David leaned against Alicia, his eyes drooping despite his best efforts to stay awake. Raymond slept, making small, satisfied sounds.

As the meal ended and the dishes were cleared away, the exhaustion that had been held at bay by emotion and excitement finally caught up with all of them. Patricia was already asleep, and David was nodding off where he sat. Raymond had drifted into the deep sleep of the very young, his small face completely peaceful.

"You must all be exhausted," Mary said softly, looking at their faces with concern. "Let me make up places for you to sleep."

The flat had only two small bedrooms, but Mary and Lupe insisted that Bryn and Alicia take one with the baby, while Patricia and David would sleep with their grandmother in the other. Mary would take the sofa in the main room. But before they settled the children for the night, Lupe spoke quietly to Mary. "We should help them wash. The children. They need..." Mary nodded, understanding without words being finished. They heated water on the stove, filled a basin, and brought it to the bedroom with clean cloths and soap. "Let me help you get the children cleaned up for bed," Lupe said gently to Alicia. "You rest with the baby." Alicia was too exhausted to argue. She sank onto the bed with Raymond, watching as her mother and sister began the gentle process of washing Patricia and David.

When both children were clean and dressed in borrowed nightclothes that hung on their thin frames, Lupe and Mary tucked them into bed together in the second bedroom. Patricia curled around David protectively, even in sleep, and David's hand found his sister's, holding tight. Lupe and Mary stood in the doorway for a long moment, looking at the two thin children sleeping peacefully, before retreating to the kitchen where they could talk without being overheard.

"Mother of God," Mary whispered, leaning against the wall. Did you see their bodies?"

"*Los vi*," (I saw them,) Lupe said, her voice shaking."

"How do we..." Mary started, then stopped. "How do we help them recover from that?"

"Slowly," Lupe said, wiping her eyes. "Very slowly. We feed them good food, but not too much at once. We let them rest. We give them safety and love and time. That's all we can do."

Meanwhile, in the other bedroom, Bryn sat on the edge of the bed watching Alicia nurse Raymond. The simple domesticity of it, the normalcy, felt strange after so long. They were in a real room with a real bed. There was food in their stomachs. Their children were safe in the next room. Family surrounded them. And yet Alicia could not stop the tears that fell silently down her cheeks as Raymond nursed.

"What is it?" Bryn asked softly, moving closer.

"I don't know," Alicia said honestly. "Everything. Nothing. I should be happy. I am happy. But I'm also..." She couldn't find the words.

"Overwhelmed," Bryn supplied. "Terrified it will all disappear. Guilty that we made it when so many didn't. Angry at what was taken from us. Grateful to be alive. All of it at once."

"Yes," she breathed. "Exactly that. All of it at once."

She looked down at Raymond nursing peacefully, this baby who had been born into and shared the DNA of a near-death experience that would be there for life. Who would grow up with a full belly and a soft bed and not understand the deep darkness that had almost claimed his life and that of his mother.

"I keep thinking about all the mothers who didn't make it," she said quietly. "All those women who tried so hard to keep their babies alive and couldn't. Why did I? Why did Raymond survive when those babies didn't?"

"I don't know," Bryn said honestly. "I wish I did. I wish there was some reason,

Chapter 45: Reunion

some logic to it. But there isn't. We just... we got lucky. Or God decided we deserved another chance. Or random chance favored us. I don't know."

"And now what?" Alicia asked, her voice small. "Now what do we do with this chance?"

"We live," Bryn said firmly. "We really, truly live. We raise our children. We build a good life. We honor the ones who didn't make it by not wasting a single moment of what we've been given."

Raymond finished nursing and fell asleep, his small face peaceful and content. They laid him in the makeshift bassinet Mary had prepared, watching his chest rise and fall with steady breaths.

"Tomorrow, we see the house," Bryn said. "Tomorrow, we start building our new life."

"Tomorrow," Alicia agreed.

They fell asleep holding hands, the way they had done so many nights in camp when holding hands was all they had, when that simple connection was the only thing that made them feel human.

As the flat settled into the quiet rhythms of sleep and the city outside gradually quieted for the night, seven people who had found each other against all odds rested beneath one roof. Tomorrow would bring new challenges, adjustments, and moments of overwhelming emotion. But tonight, for this one night, they were together, safe, and whole. The reunion they had prayed for was real. The family they had feared was lost forever had been found. And tomorrow, they would begin the journey of learning how to live again.

Chapter 46

Dawn Breaking

"After every long night, the sun returns. This is the promise that keeps us alive."

Welsh proverb

Morning came softly to Hong Kong, light filtering through the windows of Mary's flat with a gentle persistence that seemed to promise something new.

Bryn woke to sensations that felt foreign after four years of camp life. The softness of a real mattress beneath him. The clean smell of laundered sheets. The absence of fear. For a moment, he could not place where he was, and panic started to rise. Then he felt Alicia's warmth beside him, heard Raymond's small sounds from the bassinet, and memory returned. They were free. They were with family. They were safe. He lay still, not wanting to disturb Alicia and Raymond, letting himself feel the simple miracle of waking without dread. No roll call. No guards. No wondering if today would be the day the rations stopped coming entirely. Just morning, and family, and the promise of something new.

The muted sounds of the city filtered through the windows. Workers calling to each other. The rumble of vehicles. The cry of vendors setting up their stalls. Life continuing, rebuilding, refusing to stop. It was beautiful in its ordinary way, this soundtrack of normalcy that they had been denied for so long. Through the thin walls, he could hear Lupe and Mary moving about the kitchen, their voices a comforting murmur in Spanish and Cantonese. The smell of tea brewing reached him, and his stomach responded with an almost painful anticipation. Real tea. Not the weak, bitter substitute they had made from weeds in camp, but actual tea. The children were still asleep. After four years of broken sleep and constant anxiety, after nights spent listening for the sound of guards or air raids or illness, the peace of this morning felt almost unreal. As if someone might burst through the door at any moment and shatter it all.

Alicia stirred beside him, her eyes opening slowly. For a moment, the same confusion crossed her face that Bryn had felt. Then understanding dawned, followed by something that looked like wonder. "We're really here," she whispered, as if speaking too loudly might break the spell. "It wasn't a dream."

"We're really here," Bryn confirmed, reaching out to touch her face gently, reassuring both of them that this was real.

Raymond woke then with a small cry, hungry and ready to start his day with the single-minded focus of the very young. As Alicia settled in to nurse him, Bryn rose and dressed in the clean clothes Mary had left folded on a chair. The fabric felt strange against his skin. Too soft. Too new. His body was so accustomed to rough, threadbare cloth that this gentler touch seemed wrong somehow.

When he emerged from the bedroom, he found Mary and Lupe in the kitchen area, working together with the easy coordination of people who had spent years in close quarters. The small table was set with mismatched cups and plates, but everything was clean and carefully arranged. Steam rose from a pot of congee (rice porridge) on the stove, and the smell made Bryn's mouth water so intensely he had to swallow. "Good morning," Mary said warmly, her smile so different from the tear-stained face of yesterday. The transformation was remarkable. The reunion had lifted some weight from her, made her eyes brighter, her movements more energetic. "We have tea and congee. Not much, but nourishing."

"It smells wonderful," Bryn said honestly. The fragrance of the rice porridge, with its hints of ginger and scallion, was almost overwhelming after years of bland, under seasoned food. His senses felt assaulted by something so simple.

Patricia appeared in the bedroom doorway, rubbing her eyes, her hair standing up in all directions. She looked around the apartment with a sense of wonder, as if making sure that yesterday's reunion hadn't been a dream and that her grandmother and aunt were really here. *"Abuela?"* she said tentatively, testing the word again.

Lupe turned from the stove and held out her arms without hesitation, her face lighting up at the sound of the Spanish word. Patricia ran to her, and Lupe lifted her up despite the girl's size, despite her own age and frailty. But as she held Patricia, she felt again what she had felt yesterday: the shocking lightness, the bones where there should have been flesh. In the morning light, with Patricia's nightgown revealing her thin arms, the evidence of starvation was even more visible. Lupe said nothing, but her eyes met Bryn's over Patricia's head, and he saw the question there. The concern. The barely contained horror at what these children had endured.

David emerged next, more cautious, his eyes finding Mary before his face broke into a shy smile. Mary knelt down to his level, opening her arms, and he walked into her embrace with the trust of a child who remembered love even if he could not fully remember the person offering it.

They gathered around the small table for breakfast, crowded but together. The

Chapter 46: Dawn Breaking

congee that Mary ladled into bowls was simple but perfectly made. The rice had been cooked until it was almost a porridge, thick and comforting, with thin slices of ginger, chopped scallions, and a few precious shreds of chicken mixed in.

When Bryn took his first bite, he had to close his eyes. The flavor was almost painful in its intensity. The ginger sharp and warming. The scallions fresh and bright. The chicken tender and savory. His mouth flooded with saliva, his body responding desperately to real food after years of deprivation.

Alicia emerged from the bedroom with Raymond, and the sight that greeted her made her stop in the doorway. Her family, gathered around a table, eating breakfast together in the warm morning light. Her children with their grandmother and aunt. This ordinary, extraordinary scene that she had thought she would never see again. She sat down with Raymond in her arms, and Mary immediately stood to get her a bowl of congee. When Mary placed it in front of her, Alicia stared at it for a long moment. The steam rising from it. The flecks of green from the scallions. The golden droplets of oil floating on top. She took a bite, and the world tilted. The flavors exploded in her mouth with such force that she had to stop, had to put down her spoon, had to press her hand over her mouth as tears streamed down her face.

"*¿Qué pasa, mija?*" (What's wrong, my daughter?) Lupe asked with immediate concern. "*¿Está mal?*" (Is it bad)?

"No," Alicia managed through her tears. "*Es perfecto.*" (It's perfect). "It's just... I forgot. God, I forgot what food was supposed to taste like. What it could taste like. This is..." She could not find words.

Mary came to her side, placing a gentle hand on her shoulder, understanding without need for explanation. "Eat slowly," she said gently. "Your stomach needs time to adjust. Small bites. Take your time."

They ate slowly, the children's eyes growing wide at flavors they had almost forgotten existed. Patricia ate with the focused concentration she had developed in camp, as if the food might disappear if she did not pay perfect attention to it. David kept looking up at Mary between bites, seeking confirmation that this was real, that no one would take it away. But halfway through the meal, something shifted. Patricia put down her spoon, her hand going to her stomach. Her face paled. "Papa," she said quietly. "My tummy hurts."

Lupe was there immediately, scooping Patricia up despite her own limited strength. "*Está bien, mi amor. Es normal.*" (It's all right, my love. It's normal). "Your belly needs time to learn how to eat good food again. Let's get you some water." The moment passed, but it was a reminder. They were free, yes. They were together, yes. But healing would not be instant. Their bodies carried the marks of what they had survived, and those marks would take time to fade.

After breakfast, they began the process of getting ready to see the house. Mary and Lupe helped the children wash and dress properly, finding clothes that more or less fit from their small reserves. The children submitted to the attention with a patience that seemed far older than their years, accustomed to having every action managed, every moment scheduled.

At precisely ten o'clock, a knock came at the door. James Robertson from the Colonial Office stood there with his clipboard, looking impossibly clean and well-fed to eyes that had seen only starvation for years. His cheeks were full and pink. His clothes were crisp. He radiated health and prosperity in a way that felt almost obscene. "Mr. Williams? I'm here to escort you to your new residence."

The car waiting below was a large multi-passenger black sedan that gleamed in the morning sun. The children stared at it with wide eyes, barely remembering what it was like to ride in such a vehicle. David reached out to touch the polished surface tentatively, as if it might vanish like smoke. The feel of the metal was cool and smooth under his small hand. So different from the rough wood of camp buildings, the rusty barbed wire, the dirt and grime that had surrounded them for years. He pressed his palm flat against it, marveling at the sensation.

"Everyone in?" Jenkins asked with professional cheerfulness, seeming oblivious to the significance of this moment for the family before him.

They crowded into the car, leather seats creaking under their weight. The smell of the interior was overwhelming. Leather and polish and something indefinably clean. Alicia had to resist the urge to open the window, to let in air that did not smell so foreign. As they pulled away from Mary's building, Bryn looked back once at the modest structure that had sheltered his wife's family through four years of occupation. A wave of gratitude washed over him for those walls that had kept them safe, for the Chinese families who had hidden and fed them, for the random mercy that had allowed them to survive when so many had not.

The drive up through Mid-Levels took them past more scenes of destruction mixed with signs of recovery. Workers cleared rubble from the streets, their movements methodical and determined. A shop was opening with fresh produce displayed in wooden crates, the vendor calling out his wares in Cantonese. A group of children played in a vacant lot, their laughter rising above the sounds of reconstruction, proof that life insisted on continuing.

"The city's coming back faster than anyone expected," Robertson commented as he navigated around a work crew. "The Chinese are incredibly resilient. Already rebuilding, already moving forward."

Bryn thought about the Chinese families who had saved Mary and Lupe, who had risked everything out of simple human kindness. Resilient did not begin to cover it. Remarkable. Heroic. Proof that humanity could shine through even the

Chapter 46: Dawn Breaking

darkest times.

Caine Road wound along the hillside in sweeping curves, each turn revealing new views of Victoria Harbour and the city spread below. The morning sun painted everything in shades of gold and blue, the water sparkling with light, the damaged buildings somehow beautiful in the clear morning air. With each curve upward, the view expanded, showing more of the harbor, more of the city, more of the landscape that had witnessed so much suffering and was now bearing witness to recovery.

Patricia pressed her face to the window, watching the city pass by with wide eyes. She had spent four crucial years seeing nothing but the same small area of Stanley Camp, the same buildings, the same wire fence, the same narrow view of sea and sky. Now the world was opening up again, vast and varied and overwhelming.

"Here we are," Robertson announced, pulling up in front of Number 47. "Your new home, Mr. Williams."

For a moment, no one moved. They all simply sat in the car, staring through the windows at the house rising behind its wrought iron fence. The magnitude of what they were being given pressed down on them like a physical weight. After years of having nothing, of owning nothing beyond the clothes on their backs, of living in a space barely large enough for all of them to lie down at once, this seemed impossible.

Three stories of white stucco walls glowing in the morning light like something from a dream. Long verandas wrapping around both the ground and first floors, supported by elegant columns that spoke of money and status. Green shutters flanking tall windows that reflected the morning sun. Red tile roof with generous overhangs designed to weather typhoon seasons. Flowering vines climbing trellises on either side of the entrance, their blooms bright against the white walls. The garden overgrown but promising beauty once tended, once someone had time to care for it again. And beyond it all, the view. Victoria Harbour stretched out below them like a promise, like a future waiting to unfold. The water sparkled in the morning sun. Ships moved across it, bringing supplies, bringing people, bringing life back to this wounded city. The hills of Kowloon rose in the distance across the harbor, holding their own scars, their own stories of survival.

"It's beautiful," Mary breathed from the back seat, her voice filled with wonder and something that might have been disbelief. She had lived through four years of hiding in storage rooms and cramped spaces, of constant fear and near-starvation. This house was like something from another world, another life entirely.

"It's too big," Lupe said practically. "How will we clean such a place? How will we take care of it?"

"You won't have to worry about that, Lupe, servants are being provided for us, and I'll start interviewing them in the next few days," Bryn said firmly.

Robertson pulled keys from his pocket and handed them to Bryn with a small smile. "Welcome home, sir. The house has been provisioned with basic supplies. The Colonial Office wanted to make sure you had everything you need to settle in. There's food in the pantry, linens for the beds, coal for heating water, basic household supplies. Contact your office if you need assistance hiring your servants. If you need anything else, you can reach me at this number." He handed Bryn a card with contact information printed neatly.

"Thank you," Bryn managed, his throat tight with emotion as he took the keys. The metal was cool and solid in his palm, surprisingly heavy. A tangible symbol of security and shelter and a future that extended beyond the next meal, the next roll call, the next day of mere survival.

They climbed out of the car slowly, helping the children down with careful hands, gathering their few belongings. Jenkins drove away with a wave, leaving them standing on the street looking up at what would be their home. The street was quiet at this hour, the other large houses set back behind their own walls and gardens. A few gardeners worked in the distance. A Chinese woman walked past carrying shopping bags, glancing at the family with curiosity before continuing on her way. The normalcy of it all felt strange, disorienting.

"Well," Bryn said after a long moment of silence, his voice not quite steady. "Shall we go in?"

But before anyone could answer, before they could move forward, Bryn found himself rooted to the spot, unable to take that next step. Because standing here, on the threshold of this new life, he could not help but think about those who should have been here but were not. Ah-Min would have had this house running smoothly by now, would have already identified what needed attention, what needed repair. He would have been standing at the door with his quiet dignity, ready to welcome them home with tea already prepared. Mrs. Wu would have had the kitchen organized, would have been planning meals, would have been fussing over the children and insisting they needed to eat more, eat better. Young Mei-Lin would have been delighted by this house, by the children's rooms, by the garden where Patricia and David could play. She would have been unpacking their belongings with careful hands, humming softly while she worked.

But they were gone. All three of them. Killed when the family's house on Barker Road was bombed in those early terrible days of the invasion. He had not been there when they died, but Alicia had.

"Papa?" Patricia's voice broke through his thoughts, small and concerned. "Why are you crying?"

Chapter 46: Dawn Breaking

Bryn had not realized tears were running down his face until his daughter pointed it out. He wiped them away with the back of his hand, but more came to replace them. He knelt down so he was at eye level with Patricia and David, needing them to understand this, needing to speak it aloud before they entered this house and began their new life.

"I'm thinking about Ah-Min and Mrs. Wu and Mei-Lin." Patricia's face grew solemn, that too-old expression settling over her features. She nodded slowly. "Mei-Lin used to braid my hair every morning. She sang me songs in Chinese. Songs about the moon and rabbits."

"Yes, she did," Bryn confirmed, grateful that his daughter carried these memories.

"And Mrs. Wu made special dumplings," David added softly, his own face serious. "On my birthday. She made them shaped like fish."

"She did," Bryn said, his throat tightening at the memory. "She made them especially for you because you loved fish."

"Are they dead, Papa?" Patricia asked directly, with the matter-of-fact tone that children who had lived through Stanley Camp had learned to use when discussing death.

Children who had been through what they had been through did not need to be protected from the concept of death. They had seen too much already, had attended too many makeshift funerals, had watched too many people simply not wake up one morning. Death was not abstract to them. It was real and close and something that happened.

"Yes, sweetheart," Bryn said clearly. "They died when our old house was bombed. They died because they were loyal to our family, because they stayed to protect our home when they could have run to their own families, to safety. They died doing what they thought was right, what they thought was their duty to us." He paused, making sure both children were listening, making sure they understood the importance of what he was about to say.

"I want us to remember them as we start this new life in this beautiful house," he continued. "Remember that we live here in part because of people who gave their lives while serving our family. They deserve to be honored. They deserve to be remembered. We will never forget them."

As they stood there in the morning light, preparing to take these final steps toward their new beginning, the clouds that had been gathering on the horizon suddenly broke apart. Sunlight poured through the gap in a shaft of brilliant gold, illuminating the house, the garden, the harbor beyond with almost supernatural beauty. The light was warm and alive, painting everything with the color of hope renewed, of promises kept, of prayers answered.

"Look," Mary breathed, her voice filled with awe. "The light. The morning light breaking through."

They watched in silence as the light spread across the city below them, touching damaged buildings with gold, making the harbor sparkle like scattered diamonds, painting the ships and hills with colors that seemed too vivid to be real. It felt like a benediction from something larger than themselves, something beyond their understanding. Like the world itself was saying: *"You survived. You made it through the darkness. This light is yours. This dawn is yours."*

Bryn's throat constricted with emotion. Beside him, Alicia was crying, her free hand finding his and gripping tight. Behind them, Lupe and Mary wept quietly, years of accumulated grief and fear finally releasing their hold in the face of this moment of pure grace.

"I keep thinking about all the people who didn't make it," Alicia said softly, her voice thick with survivor's guilt that would probably never fully leave any of them. All the children who died in the camp because their bodies were too weak to fight disease. All the families who were torn apart and never found each other again." Her voice broke. "Why do we get this when they got nothing? What makes us deserve this when they didn't deserve to die?" The question hung in the air, unanswerable because there was no good answer, no satisfactory explanation for why some survived and others did not. No logic to who lived and who died. Just chance and circumstance and the random mercy or cruelty of fate.

"They would want us to live," Bryn said finally, with quiet certainty born from having thought about this question during many sleepless nights in camp. "To really, truly live. Not just survive from day to day, but *live*. To make this chance mean something. To build something good and lasting with the life we've been given back."

Bryn stood up, looking at the house again with new eyes, with clearer vision. At the view beyond it. At the city waiting to be rebuilt. At his family standing beside him in the breaking light of this new day, this new beginning. This is where we start over," he said firmly, his voice carrying conviction and determination and hope all mixed together. "Not by forgetting what happened. We will never forget. We *can't* forget. It's part of us now, part of who we are. But by building something new out of the ruins. By being the family we want to be, not the family circumstances tried to make us. By choosing hope and love and presence every day, even when it would be easier to choose bitterness or fear or isolation."

Bryn continued, looking at each of them in turn. "Tomorrow, we start unpacking our lives, learning out how to live in peace after years of war. Tomorrow, we start learning how to be normal again, whatever that means now.

Chapter 46: Dawn Breaking

We'll have to learn how to sleep without fear of guards. How to eat without rationing every bite. How to trust that tomorrow will come and bring more than just survival."

He paused, his throat tight with emotion. "But right now, in this moment, let us just stand here and look at where we have arrived. Let us remember this feeling. Let us soak it in. Let us remember that despite everything, despite all the odds against us, despite all the reasons we should not have made it, we survived. And we're here. Together. Whole. Free." He looked down at Patricia and David, at their thin faces and too-wise eyes, and felt his heart break and heal at the same time. He looked down at Raymond, the miracle baby. "Let us remember that we made it home."

Raymond stirred in Alicia's arms and opened his eyes, awakened by the sound of his father's voice and the emotion in it. The baby looked around at the assembled faces with that solemn, alert expression that was already so characteristic of him, at the golden light that was filling everything, at the house rising behind them and the harbor spreading below. He did not cry or fuss. He just watched, as if understanding somehow that this was important, that this moment mattered and would be remembered.

"He will remember Stanley Camp although not conscious of it," Alicia said quietly, looking down at her son with fierce love and protectiveness and something that might have been envy for his innocence. "He will grow up knowing this house, this view, this life of relative comfort and safety. He will never know what we went through to get here. One day he will understand the price we paid, the things we saw, the people we lost." Her voice was wistful, tinged with both relief and sadness at this truth.

"We will tell him," Bryn promised with absolute certainty. "When he's old enough, when he can understand, we will tell him everything. We will tell all of them the full story, not just the happy parts. Not to burden them with our trauma, but so they understand. So they know what human beings are capable of, both the terrible and the beautiful. So, they know that suffering does not have to destroy you if you choose not to let it. That love can survive anything if you fight for it. That family is what you hold onto when everything else is taken away. That's the legacy we give them. Not just this house or comfort or opportunity, but the knowledge of what we survived and who we became because of it."

The sun had fully risen now, and the dramatic shaft of light had faded into the general brightness of morning. But the city below them was coming alive. Sounds of commerce and construction and daily life rose up to where they stood. The harbor was busy with boats and ships. Smoke rose from chimneys. Life was asserting itself with stubborn persistence.

Standing there before the closed gate, before the threshold of this new life,

Bryn found himself thinking about the journey that had brought him to this moment.

A lifetime ago, he had been a child in the Welsh coal mines. Covered in black dust so thick it caked in the creases of his skin and under his fingernails. Beaten regularly by an alcoholic father who saw him as nothing more than a source of income, a pair of hands to send into the darkness. Told over and over in words and blows that he was worthless, that he would amount to nothing, that he would die in those mines like every Williams man before him stretching back generations. That boy had been told he had no future, no hope, no way out. That the darkness of the mines would be his whole life and his early grave. That boys like him did not escape, did not rise, did not become anything more than what they were born to be.

But that boy had found courage somewhere deep inside himself, had discovered a spark of defiance that refused to be extinguished. Had stood up to his father that terrible night when he announced he would not go back to the mines. Had walked away with nothing but a canvas bag and his mother's whispered blessing when his father threw him out.

That single act of courage had set him on a path that led here. The journey had not been straight or simple or predictable. He had joined the British Army with Aunt Eileen's encouragement because it was the only escape available to a penniless A Welsh boy with no education and no prospects beyond the mines. Had learned to kill in Egypt, but never was fully committed to the subjugation of the Egyptians by the British Empire. Had learned to question the very empire he served as he watched it crush people who wanted nothing more than to govern themselves, to be free of foreign control.

He had come to Hong Kong and worked his way up through unglamorous public health positions, dealing with sewage and disease and the unsexy work of keeping people alive through clean water and proper sanitation. Had married a Mexican woman when society said she was not quite white enough, when the colonial administration had made him prove her racial acceptability. Had built a comfortable life, perhaps enjoying his colonial privilege a bit too much, perhaps not questioning deeply enough where that comfort came from or what it cost others.

Then the war had come and taken it all away in twelve brutal days. Stripped him down to nothing. Made him a prisoner, a number, a body to be counted and rationed and controlled absolutely. He had watched his children starve slowly, their bodies consuming themselves to survive. Had nearly lost his wife twice, once to illness that should have killed her and once to despair that nearly destroyed her will to live. Had learned what it meant to be truly, completely powerless in the hands of those with absolute power over life and death.

Chapter 46: Dawn Breaking

And now, impossibly, he stood before another chance. Not just at life, not just at survival, but at power. At having influence and resources and the ability to shape things beyond his own small circle. At being able to help or harm, to serve or to dominate, to use power wisely or to abuse it as it had been abused against him.

The boy in that Welsh coal mine would have looked at this house, at this position as Chief Health Inspector, and been disgusted. Would have seen it as joining the enemy, becoming one of the powerful who crushed the powerless, betraying everything he had fought against when he walked away from his father and the mines. But that boy had not held his infant son while wondering if tomorrow would be the day the child died from malnutrition. Had not watched his daughter's personality change as hunger consumed her childhood. Had not counted rice grains and rationed water and made impossible choices about who in the family most needed the extra spoonful of food. Had not learned that the world was infinitely more complex than simply refusing to participate in imperfect systems.

Bryn understood now, standing on this threshold, what his Aunt Eileen had tried to teach him all those years ago when she took him in after his father cast him out. That courage was not just about saying no to what was wrong, not just about walking away from injustice. It was also about saying yes to doing what good you could, even when the situation was not perfect. Even when you were working within systems that were flawed, within structures that were built on inequality.

Because the question was not whether the colonial system was perfect. It was not. It was built on exploitation and racial hierarchy and the fundamental injustice of foreign people ruling over local populations against their will. Bryn understood that now in ways he had not fully grasped before the war, before being powerless himself, before seeing how power could be wielded with such casual cruelty. But he could refuse this position on principle. Could walk away from the colonial government entirely. Keep his hands clean of any association with an imperfect system. Find some other work, something that did not involve accepting power from an empire he had learned to question and criticize.

And who would take his place then? Someone who did not speak Cantonese, who saw Hong Kong's Chinese population as inferior subjects to be managed rather than people to be served. Someone who had never worked alongside Chinese colleagues as equals, who had never learned from Chinese wisdom and knowledge. Someone who would not remember what it felt like to be powerless, to be at the mercy of those who did not see you as fully human.

The question was not whether to accept power. Power existed. Systems existed. The colonial government would rebuild Hong Kong's public health infrastructure with or without him. The question was what kind of person would do that work. And what they would do with that power once they had it.

Bryn knew the answer now, standing in the morning light with his family around him. He would use it to serve. To work *with* Chinese health inspectors and doctors as partners, as equals, as teachers from whom he could learn rather than as subordinates to be ordered about. To remember that the sanitation worker cleaning the streets had as much inherent worth and dignity as any British administrator or colonial governor. To honor the memory of Ah-Min and Mrs. Wu and Mei-Lin by treating every person with the respect and kindness they had shown his family.

He would work within an imperfect system to make it less imperfect. To push it toward justice even when it resisted. To use whatever influence and resources he had to serve rather than to dominate. It was not redemption for the system's sins. It was not even justice for the wrongs that had been done. But it was better than doing nothing. Better than refusing to help because the help came through compromised channels. Better than letting someone who did not care take the position and do active harm.

He was not the angry boy from the coal mines anymore, though that anger still lived in him when he saw injustice or cruelty. Not the idealistic young soldier who thought following orders made you noble and right. Not the comfortable colonial official who had enjoyed his privilege without questioning it deeply enough or working to change the underlying inequalities. Not even the broken prisoner who had counted stones and bugs to stay sane, who had learned to live on almost nothing.

He was all of those people and none of them. A man who understood what it meant to have nothing and to have everything. Who knew both sides of power intimately because he had experienced both. Who had been powerless and was now being offered power. Who had learned through suffering that survival meant choosing carefully, deliberately, consciously what kind of person you became when circumstances tried to break you or corrupt you or turn you into something you did not want to be.

He had a choice now, standing at this gate. He could become like the mine owners who had exploited him as a child. Could become like the colonial administrators who valued some lives over others. Could become like the guards who had wielded their small amount of power in camp with such casual cruelty. Or he could choose differently. Could choose to use power to serve rather than to dominate. Could choose to remember what it felt like to be powerless and make sure he never made others feel that way. Could choose partnership over control, collaboration over command, service over self-interest.

"Bryn?" Alicia's voice called gently, pulling him back from these thoughts. "Are you all right?"

He turned to look at her, at their children, at the family waiting patiently for

Chapter 46: Dawn Breaking

him to unlock this gate and lead them through into their new life.

And something settled in him. Some decision made at a level deeper than conscious thought. Some commitment to the man he wanted to be, the father and husband and public servant he wanted to become, the legacy he wanted to leave. "Yes," he said, "I'm ready."

"Together," Bryn said, offering his hand to Alicia again.

And they walked through. All seven of them. Together. Walking through that open gate toward the house that rose before them in the morning light, toward the door that waited to welcome them home, toward whatever came next.

They walked slowly up the path, the gravel crunching softly beneath their feet. No one rushed. No one hurried. They were savoring this moment, this impossible moment of arriving at a place that would be theirs, that would shelter them, that would become the foundation for whatever life they built from here.

The children pointed at flowers in the overgrown garden, marveling at colors and blooms. Lupe and Mary walked arm in arm, their voices soft as they took in the house, the view, the promise of what lay ahead. Alicia held Raymond close, her other hand tight in Bryn's, as if anchoring herself to this reality, making sure it was real and solid and would not disappear.

As they reached the steps leading up to the front door, Bryn paused and turned to look back one more time.

Behind them, the gate stood open. Beyond it, the street. Beyond that, the city spread out below, damaged but alive, rebuilding itself stone by stone, life by life. The harbor sparkled in the morning sun. Ships moved across the water. The world continued its work of healing and reconstruction. And here they stood. Seven people who had walked through hell and found their way out. Seven people who had lost everything and been given a second chance. Seven people who understood, in ways most people never would, how precious and fragile and beautiful life could be.

"Ready?" Bryn asked one more time, looking at his family gathered around him on these steps.

"Ready," Alicia said, her voice steady now despite the tears on her cheeks.

"Ready," Patricia and David echoed together. Raymond's eyes were open wide.

Bryn fitted the key into the lock of the front door. It turned smoothly. The door swung open, revealing the entrance hall beyond, light streaming through windows, space and possibility waiting to be filled with their lives. He stood on the threshold, one hand on the door, looking at his family.

And standing here on this threshold with his family around him, with the morning sun painting everything in shades of gold and promise, he felt something he had not felt in a very long time. Hope. Real, genuine hope that they could build something good here. That they could heal. That they could become the family they wanted to be. That they could honor the past by living fully in the present, by refusing to waste a single moment of this precious gift of life.

"Come on then," he said, his voice rough with emotion but steady with purpose. "Let's go home."

And together, hands joined, hearts full, eyes bright with tears and hope and gratitude and love, they crossed the threshold. They stepped into the house that would shelter them. Into the life they would build together. Into the future that stretched out before them, unknown and uncertain but no longer terrifying because they would face it together. The door closed softly behind them with a sound like a promise kept, like a prayer answered, like the world itself saying: *Welcome home. You made it. You survived. Now live.*

Outside, the city of Hong Kong continued its work of rebuilding, of healing, of refusing to let destruction have the final word. Ships moved across the harbor. Workers cleared rubble. Vendors called out their wares. Life insisted on continuing.

And inside Number 47 Caine Road, seven people who had survived the unsurvivable began the next chapter of their story. Not the end of their journey, but a new beginning. Not forgetting what they had endured, but choosing to build something beautiful in spite of it. Not pretending the scars did not exist, but learning to live with grace and courage and love despite them.

They had walked through the ashes. They had survived the darkness. And now, together, they would learn to live in the dawn.

The End

Afterword

This story has traced the extraordinary journey of Bryn Williams, from the coal valleys of Wales to war-torn Hong Kong, through captivity, and finally to survival. It is a story of resilience, love, and the human spirit's ability to endure the unimaginable.

When Bryn refused to go back down into those Welsh mines at fourteen, he made a choice that would define the rest of his life. He chose himself over his father's expectations. He chose possibility over certainty. That same stubborn refusal to accept defeat carried him through everything that followed. His journey saw him in the British Army serving in Egypt for seven conflict ridden years, learning how to survive.

He could not have imagined, leaving Egypt that he would find love in Hong Kong with a Mexican woman who had survived her own impossible journey. Their marriage required them to prove Alicia was "white enough" for a British official. It was absurd and it was real, and they did it anyway because love doesn't wait for the world to give permission.

When the Japanese invaded in December 1941, Bryn and his family lost everything in twelve days. The comfortable colonial life, the career, the home. Stanley Camp became their world for nearly four years. They watched their children grow up behind barbed wire, their bodies wasting from hunger, their childhoods stolen.

The birth of Raymond in those final months should not have been possible. Alicia nearly died. The doctors had nothing to work with. But she survived, and he survived, because sometimes the will to live is stronger than circumstances designed to kill.

This is not a story about heroes. Bryn Williams was a man who kept going when stopping would have been easier. He protected his family when protection seemed impossible. He maintained his dignity when everything around him tried to strip it away. He chose, again and again, to build rather than to surrender.

The coal dust that scarred his lungs as a child stayed with him for life. But it never stopped him from breathing, from living, from moving forward. Perhaps that is what resilience really means. Not escaping your past, but refusing to be imprisoned by it.

We all carry scars. We all face our own mines, our own camps, our own wars. What we do with those scars is the choice that matters. Bryn and Alicia Williams chose love over bitterness, hope over despair, and building over breaking.

Their story deserves to be remembered because it reminds us what human beings are capable of enduring, and what makes that endurance worthwhile. Not just survival, but the stubborn insistence on love and connection and dignity even when the world insists such things are pointless.

This is their story. It is also, in its own way, a story about all of people throughout the world who have faced hardship and death, yet somehow managed to survive.

About the Author

Raymond B. Williams is a Canadian author whose work explores the resilience of the human spirit in the face of adversity. His writing blends historical detail with deeply personal storytelling, bringing to life the struggles and triumphs of life.

Ashes and Dawn: Love, Loss and Survival in the Shadow of War is inspired by the true story of his father, Brinley Williams, whose remarkable journey took him from the coal mines of Wales to military service in the British Army in the Middle East and through the crucible of war and captivity in Hong Kong. Through this novel, Raymond Williams seeks to honor not only his father's courage and endurance, but that of his mother and siblings and also the countless untold stories of men and women whose lives were forever shaped by history. The author of this story was himself born in Stanley Camp, as a prisoner of the Japanese in WWII.

Raymond B. Williams has built a forty-year career as an educator, CEO, management consultant, and executive coach. He has published seven nonfiction books and two novels, along with hundreds of articles on leadership, psychology, and human behavior.

He lives in Vancouver, British Columbia, Canada, with his wife Diane, his muse and guiding spirit. They are proud parents of three sons, Travis, Rhett, and Bryn, who continue to inspire his work with their love and encouragement.

www.ingramcontent.com/pod-product-compliance
Lightning Source LLC
Chambersburg PA
CBHW052007070526
44584CB00016B/1655